Controversies in Applied Linguistics

Controversies in Applied Linguistics

edited by
Barbara Seidlhofer

OXFORD
UNIVERSITY PRESS

OXFORD

UNIVERSITY PRESS

Great Clarendon Street, Oxford OX2 6DP

Oxford University Press is a department of the University
of Oxford. It furthers the University's objective of excellence
in research, scholarship, and education by publishing
worldwide in

Oxford New York

Auckland Bangkok Buenos Aires Cape Town Chennai
Dar es Salaam Delhi Hong Kong Istanbul Karachi Kolkata
Kuala Lumpur Madrid Melbourne Mexico City Mumbai Nairobi
São Paulo Shanghai Taipei Tokyo Toronto

Oxford and Oxford English are registered trade marks of
Oxford University Press in the UK and in certain other countries

© Oxford University Press 2003

ISBN 0 19 437444 0

Printed in China

For Sr. Vera Marie de Wolff, O.S.U. – the first person to teach me about the value of controversies, and so much more.

Contents

Acknowledgements

The authors and publisher are grateful to those who have given permission to reproduce the following:

Margie Berns *et al.* for permission to reproduce '(Re)experiencing hegemony: the linguistic imperialism of Robert Phillipson'. *International Journal of Applied Linguistics* 8/2: 271–82; 'Hegemonic discourse revisited'; and 'A Closing Word' by Phillipson and by Berns *et al. International Journal of Applied Linguistics* 9/1: 138–41.

Christopher Brumfit for permission to reproduce 'How applied linguistics is the same as any other science'. *International Journal of Applied Linguistics* 7/1: 86–94.

Ronald Carter for permission to reproduce 'Orders of reality: CANCODE, communication, and culture'. *ELT Journal* 52/1: 43–56; and 'Reply to Guy Cook'. *ELT Journal* 52/1: 64.

Ronald Carter and Michael McCarthy for permission to reproduce 'Correspondence'. *ELT Journal* 50/4: 369–71.

Guy Cook for permission to reproduce 'The uses of reality: a reply to Ronald Carter'. *ELT Journal* 52/1: 57–63.

David Crystal for permission to reproduce 'On trying to be Crystal-clear: a response to Phillipson'. *Applied Linguistics* 21/3: 415–21.

Norman Fairclough for permission to reproduce 'A reply to Henry Widdowson's "Discourse analysis: a critical view"'. *Language and Literature* 5/1: 49–56.

Alan Firth and Johannes Wagner for permission to reproduce 'On discourse, communication, and (some) fundamental concepts in SLA research'. *Modern Language Journal* 81/3: 285–300 and 'SLA property: no trespassing!' *Modern Language Journal* 82/1: 91–4.

Susan Gass for permission to reproduce 'Apples and oranges: or, why apples are not oranges and don't need to be: a Response to Firth and Wagner'. *Modern Language Journal* 82/1: 83–90.

Laura Gavioli and Guy Aston for permission to reproduce 'Enriching reality: language corpora in language pedagogy'. *ELT Journal: 55/3: 238–46.*

Braj Kachru for permission to reproduce 'Liberation linguistics and the Quirk concern'. *English Today* 25: 3–13.

Gabi Kasper for permission to reproduce '"A" stands for acquisition: a response to Firth and Wagner'. *Modern Language Journal* 81/3: 307–12.

Michael Long for permission to reproduce 'Construct validity in SLA research: a response to Firth and Wagner'. *Modern Language Journal* 81/3: 318–23.

Bonny Norton for permission to reproduce 'Social identity, investment, and language learning'. *TESOL Quarterly* 29/1: 9–31; and 'Interpreting data: the role of theory'. *TESOL Quarterly* 30: 337–40.

Robert Phillipson for permission to reproduce 'Linguistic imperialism re-visited – or re-invented. A rejoinder to a review essay'. *International Journal of Applied Linguistics* 9/1: 135–7; and 'Voice in global English: unheard chords in Crystal loud and clear'. *Applied Linguistics* 20/2: 265–76.

Nanda Poulisse for permission to reproduce 'Some words in defense of the pycholinguistic approach: a response to Firth and Wagner'. *Modern Language Journal* 81/3: 324–8.

Steven Price for permission to reproduce 'Comments on Bonny Norton's "Social identity, investment, and language learning"'. *TESOL Quarterly* 30: 331–7.

Luke Prodromou for permission to reproduce 'Correspondence'. *ELT Journal* 50/1: 88–9 and 50/4: 371–3.

Randolph Quirk for permission to reproduce 'Language varieties and standard language'. *English Today* 21: 3–10.

Ben Rampton for permission to reproduce 'Retuning in applied linguistics'. *International Journal of Applied Linguistics* 7/1: 3–25; and 'Problems with an orchestral view of applied linguistics: a reply to Widdowson'. *International Journal of Applied Linguistics* 8/1: 141–6.

Henry Widdowson for permission to reproduce 'Retuning, calling the tune, and paying the piper: a reaction to Rampton'. *International Journal of Applied Linguistics* 8/1: 131–40; 'Positions and oppositions: hedgehogs and foxes'. *International Journal of Applied Linguistics* 8/1: 147–51; 'Discourse analysis: a critical view'. *Language and Literature* 4/3: 157–72; and 'Reply to Fairclough: discourse and interpretation: conjectures and refutations'. *Language and Literature* 5/1: 57–69.

Many people have helped me in various ways in the preparation of this book. First of all, I am grateful to the authors of the controversies themselves for agreeing to have their work reprinted in this rather unorthodox format.

My thanks too to colleagues who have commented on this book at various stages of its development; in particular, Guy Cook, Jennifer Jenkins, Claire Kramsch, and Henry Widdowson. Thanks also to my students at the University of Vienna, whose interest in this kind of controversial exchange first suggested the idea for this book to me.

I have had wonderful support from a number of people at Oxford University Press: Mark Tilley-Watts and Peter Burgess had to grapple with difficult questions of design. Simon Murison-Bowie went through the whole manuscript with his usual care and perception, and admirably dealt with the considerable challenges posed by the complex format of the volume. So did Katharina Breyer.

Above all, my thanks to Cristina Whitecross, who saw the point of this project at once, and had faith in it from start to finish. I very much appreciate the professional and personal support she has provided throughout the process.

Barbara Seidlhofer
Vienna, November 2002

List of texts

Text 12 **Prodromou, L.** 1996. 'Correspondence'. *ELT Journal* 50/4: 371–3.

Controversy 5

Text 13 **Carter, R.** 1998. 'Orders of reality: CANCODE, communication, and culture'. *ELT Journal* 52/1: 43–56.
Text 14 **Cook, G.** 1998. 'The uses of reality: a reply to Ronald Carter'. *ELT Journal* 52/1: 57–63.
Text 15 **Carter, R.** 1998. 'Reply to Guy Cook'. *ELT Journal* 52/1: 64.
Text 16 **Gavioli, L.** and **G. Aston.** 2001. 'Enriching reality: language corpora in language pedagogy'. *ELT Journal* 55/3: 238–46.

Section 3   Critical discourse analysis

Controversy 6

Text 17 **Widdowson, H. G.** 1995. 'Discourse analysis: a critical view'. *Language and Literature* 4/3: 157–72.
Text 18 **Fairclough, N.** 1996. 'A reply to Henry Widdowson's "Discourse analysis: a critical view"'. *Language and Literature* 5/1: 49–56.
Text 19 **Widdowson, H. G.** 1996. 'Reply to Fairclough: Discourse and interpretation: conjectures and refutations'. *Language and Literature* 5/1: 57–69.

Section 4   Second language acquisition

Controversy 7

Text 20 **Firth, A.** and **J. Wagner.** 1997. 'On Discourse, Communication, and (Some) Fundamental Concepts in SLA Research'. *Modern Language Journal* 81/3: 285–300.
Text 21 **Kasper, G.** 1997. '"A" Stands for Acquisition: A Response to Firth and Wagner'. *Modern Language Journal* 81/3: 307–12.
Text 22 **Long, M. H.** 1997. 'Construct Validity in SLA Research: A Response to Firth and Wagner'. *Modern Language Journal* 81/3: 318–23.
Text 23 **Poulisse, N.** 1997. 'Some Words in Defense of the Psycholinguistic Approach: A Response to Firth and Wagner'. *Modern Language Journal* 81/3: 324–28.
Text 24 **Gass, S.** 1998. 'Apples and Oranges: Or, Why Apples Are Not Oranges and Don't Need to Be. A Response to Firth and Wagner'. *Modern Language Journal* 82/1: 83–90.
Text 25 **Firth, A.** and **J. Wagner.** 1998. 'SLA Property: No Trespassing!' *Modern Language Journal* 82/1: 91–4.

Controversy 8

Section 5 The nature of applied linguistics

Controversy 9

Introduction

Critical imagination ... is often the result of culture clash, that is, a clash between ideas, or frameworks of ideas. Such a clash may help us break through the ordinary bounds of our imagination. (Popper 1976: 47, original emphasis)

Why this book?

Why 'controversies'? Some people shy away from 'adversarial exchanges' and think you cannot learn from them. I, however, think you can, and my students tell me they do. So although we sometimes refer to scholars airing their differences in public as an 'unedifying spectacle', I believe, on the contrary, that this form of debate can in fact be edifying. Indeed, the idea for this book occurred to me when I was discussing with my colleagues my observation of how much easier our students find it to get their heads round complex issues, perceive different sides to certain problems, and make up their own minds when they are presented with opposing views rather than (apparent) expert consensus.

My students also tell me that it is initially often hard for them to accept that the 'famous scholars' whose work they study with admiration do not all agree with one another – 'It's a bit like watching your parents having an argument', as one of them put it. Schooled as they are to accept authority rather than challenge it, they tend to be in awe of well-known scholars and find it difficult to let go of the belief that there must be the right answer out there somewhere, and to recognize that uncertainty is part of academic life, at least in the humanities. That is why it seemed appropriate to put together a collection of some documented disagreements in applied linguistics that are known to have started off sustained and productive debates, and generated further arguments (in both senses of the word). This collection also indicates that such controversies do not occur in the isolation in which they are sometimes encountered, but are both numerous and interrelated. In order to ease readers gently into them, they are presented here together with short contextualizing introductions and, importantly, I think, suggestions for how students might not just read but *work with* these controversies.

We think dialogically, there are different voices in us, and thoughts are often in opposition in the same head: pros and cons. In the thinking process it is usual to weigh up different ideas and to resolve differences and contradictions and then come to one's own conclusion. It seems to me that one of the basic processes in education is to encourage people to engage in this kind of mental process. And to this end it can be very stimulating to see this internal process externalized in dialogic interaction, in a way that recalls the Vygotskian notion of the relationship between inner and outer speech.

Who is this book for?

This collection is particularly intended for people in applied linguistics, and perhaps especially in language education, who feel that the topics exemplified here are important for their work, but who do not have the time they would need to read extensively in these areas. For them, the controversies can serve as a kind of shortcut to the most important issues as perceived by the protagonists in these debates. For the same reason, these controversies can be useful for the compilation of reading lists, as well as for pointing out issues to focus on in exam preparation.

The readers I have in mind, then, apart from applied linguists themselves, are typically lecturers and postgraduate students involved in MA or research degree courses, as well as students in English and linguistics departments, very many of which run high-level teacher education courses for future teachers of English.

Many courses with an applied linguistics component around the world already use (some of) the papers included in this book, but until now teachers and students have had to search in libraries to find them, and needless to say, some journals are only available in some of the best-equipped libraries, and thus not accessible to most students worldwide. By bringing together these controversies in one volume, I hope to make them more accessible to teachers and students alike.

What is in this book?

Since, not surprisingly, scholars tend to a) publish their work in places associated with their particular field of research, and b) concentrate on their own views, findings, and interpretations rather than devoting precious space to discussing competing views, it has not been usual publishing practice to bring together, and set off against each other, contrasting views in a number of applied linguistics areas of current relevance. It is thus hoped that this volume fills the gap between what researchers write and what students need, in that it deliberately brings together writings that do not 'naturally' *occur* together (for example, second language acquisition and critical discourse analysis), although they are *taught* together in courses that seek to give an introduction to, or overview of, applied linguistics.

In recent years there have been several issues in applied linguistics which have provoked quite radical disagreement; this has often found expression in published exchanges between scholars in which their respective positions are vigorously asserted and challenged. These exchanges are not only reveal-ing in that the points at issue are made prominent and brought out with particular clarity, but they are appealing, too, in that they represent inter-personal encounters of an intellectual kind. In short, they yield insights about both controversies and protagonists.

All of these exchanges have appeared in journals, even the best-known of which are of limited circulation. As for the specific selection, what I regard to be particularly 'productive' controversies is controversial in itself, and no doubt colleagues in different academic and geographical settings would have made a different selection. So, clearly, I do not claim that those I have chosen will be the most important controversies for everyone. But the point to emphasize here is that the objective of this book is not to provide broad coverage, but to indicate a particular way of dealing with the issues raised in these debates (and so, by implication, with others not included here).

The source papers appear as they were published, and any idiosyncrasies of the original texts have been retained. No attempt has been made to stand-ardize spellings, styles of referencing and similar matters. The papers were chosen according to the following criteria:

- they are published pieces in their entirety, rather than extracts;
- they are written by prominent scholars, and often quoted in the applied linguistics literature;
- they are personal encounters in that the authors make direct reference to each other; and
- they deal with issues which are widely discussed in current applied linguistics.

In addition to dealing with important and topical issues, these papers thus make it clear who the main proponents of the specific issues are, and they bring into sharp relief the main points of contention between them. The fact that publications of this confrontational kind tend to exert a particular fascination on readers opens up educational opportunities in pedagogical settings (university courses in applied linguistics as well as self-study contexts) for the following reasons:

- Because positions in such exchanges need to be set out quite explicitly, they tend to be more accessible than papers which build on a consider-able amount of assumed background knowledge; accordingly, ideas tend to be outlined clearly, and terms defined, and it is spelt out 'who is on which side', which again furthers the accessibility and accultura-tion/initiation into a specific discipline and its discourse.
- There is, by definition, a higher than usual degree of contextualization and historical perspective: of necessity, authors have to refer to who said what first, what the reactions were to this, and who else in the scientific community supports which position.

- 'Personal' controversies help students appreciate that academic debate is not a lifeless affair and that scholars, even the best-known ones, are neither infallible nor dispassionate: they are not just in the business of making well-supported, detached statements, but invest a good deal of personal commitment in their work. Their arguments have an affective edge to them.
- Due to their personal tone, the exchanges are also likely to provoke students to engage with the subject matter in a personal way, asking such questions as: What does all this mean to me? Where do I stand in this dispute? Whose argumentation do I tend to go along with and why? What did I learn from this reading of contrasting views? These are reactions which many teachers in advanced courses find very desirable, but often also quite difficult, to elicit from their students.
- Often (though admittedly not always) these papers provide good models for how to set out one's ideas and opinions, so to a certain extent the suggested source papers can also act as models of how academic discourse in the social sciences is conducted, i.e. as models of the genre 'academic paper'. It is therefore easy to see how the papers can be used in class as objects of analysis with regard to the following conventions and 'tricks of the trade' of academic writing: how is an argument constructed and developed? How are some arguments accepted and others rejected? What is cited as legitimate evidence in support of a certain position, and how? What is put into footnotes/endnotes and why? Which lexical choices are made, for example, of reporting verbs and evaluating items such as adjectives and adverbs? How is hedging effected and which purposes does it serve? How are issues taken up selectively in responses, and others avoided, and how are new ones introduced?

How is this book organized?

The five themes of the controversies appear in separate sections. Each is prefaced by an introduction which briefly sketches out the context of the dispute, and keys readers in to the main points of contention, as 'neutrally' as possible. In addition, comments draw out connections across the controversies, and so indicate relationships among areas of applied linguistic enquiry which have not hitherto been made explicit.

The papers are obviously presented in the chronology of the developing debate itself; where there is more than one controversy, these are also arranged chronologically. At the end of each section there is a list of annotated bibliographical references for further reading, so that readers can refer the controversy to a fuller context of work in the area, and to any further developments in recent publications (including further controversies).

Ways of working with this book

In applied linguistics especially, most people know more in one or two fields than in the others, though to varying degrees they will have had contact with all of the areas exemplified. Hence there can be no such thing as a best selection of papers for a volume such as this one, let alone a general recommendation as to how it might be used in the most productive way.

What I want therefore to emphasize is that for the introductions to the five sections, I have limited my own contribution to what I hope will be a maximally helpful contextualization for relative novices in the area in question. However, since the main objective is to stimulate critical engagement with the issues discussed, I feel that some readers, at least, will benefit from a number of quite specific but open questions that might help them focus on particular points of content and presentation. These study questions are included at the end of this volume, and can be applied variously and selectively at the discretion of different readers (or teachers). The fact that they can all, in principle, be asked about each component of this book (including my own introductions!) ensures that they cannot selectively favour some views over others.

At all events, it is hoped that the reader's own engagement with the controversial issues in these pages will reveal with particular force just how diverse, dynamic, and intellectually stimulating the field of applied linguistics can be.

Further reading

It may seem strange to have suggestions for further reading provided in the introduction to a book. However, since the question of whether controversies can be conducive to a deeper understanding of relevant issues is itself controversial, it is not surprising to find that this question has given rise to a (fairly compact) controversy in its own right which readers might like to seek out: Kramsch (1995a) – Byrnes (1995) – Bernhardt (1995) – Kramsch (1995b).

While primarily addressing questions concerning foreign language education in the United States of America, the arguments themselves will be recognized by all applied linguists working in institutional contexts. In the first paragraph of her stimulus paper, Kramsch says:

> I am not sure that 'achieving consensus' is the proper phrase for what we
> should be doing in foreign language education. Consensus can sometimes be the
> death of intellectual enquiry; it can be a major obstacle to educational change.
> Furthermore, I do not share the opinion that intellectual and systemic differences
> are undesirable 'obstacles' to the articulation we seek between the different
> sectors of the educational system. Rather, they might be viewed as opportunities
> for an ongoing dialogue that respects differences instead of trying to erase them.
> (Kramsch 1995a: 6)

The gist of Kramsch's conclusion is that exploring differences is more important than achieving consensus, and articulating questions is more important than agreeing on answers. Such a view could serve as a motto for the present volume.

Readers interested in the discoursal strategies writers employ when they engage in what Eija Ventola terms 'Alignment and Bashing' might like to consult Ventola (1998).

And finally, readers might like to supplement the controversies collected in this volume by consulting mainstream journals that have regular sections dedicated to this kind of adversarial exchange. These include 'Forum' in *Applied Linguistics* (Oxford University Press), 'Notes and Discussion' in *Language and Literature* (Sage Publications), 'Debate' in the *International Journal of Applied Linguistics* (Blackwell Publishers), 'Point and counterpoint' in the *ELT Journal* (Oxford University Press), 'Comments and Reply' in *World Englishes* (Blackwell Publishers), 'The Forum' in *TESOL Quarterly* (Teachers of English to Speakers of Other Languages, Inc.) and 'Lingua Franca' in the journal *Lingua* (Elsevier Science).

References

Bernhardt, E. 1995. 'Response to Claire Kramsch'. *ADFL Bulletin* 26/3 (Spring 1995): 15–17.

Byrnes, H. 1995. 'Response to Claire Kramsch'. *ADFL Bulletin* 26/3 (Spring 1995): 13–15.

Kramsch, C. 1995a. 'Embracing conflict versus achieving consensus in foreign language education'. *ADFL Bulletin* 26/3 (Spring 1995): 6–12.

Kramsch, C. 1995b. 'Reply to Heidi Byrnes and Elizabeth B. Bernhardt'. *ADFL Bulletin* 26/3 (Spring 1995): 17.

Popper, K. 1976. *Unended Quest. An Intellectual Autobiography*. London: Fontana/Collins.

Ventola, E. 1998. 'Interpersonal choices in academic work' in A. Sánchez-Macarro and R. Carter (eds.). *Linguistic Choice across Genres*. Amsterdam: John Benjamins Publishing Company.

Section 1
The global spread of English

One of the liveliest current debates, and also one of particular relevance to language education, revolves around the accelerating global spread of English, and the urgent socio-economic, ideological, and ecological issues raised as a consequence of this spread. The source papers in this volume take up questions of standard language and indigenized varieties and then home in on the ongoing debate about linguistic imperialism and the hegemony of English.

The global spread of English is not only an issue for teachers and learners of English. The unprecedented spread of one language and the extent of its use as a global lingua franca in many walks of life raises as many questions and concerns as does economic and cultural globalization. A fact which must certainly not be overlooked is that talk about 'the global spread of English' does not mean that having access to English in order to gain access to knowledge is a commodity available to all who desire it, nor that English as an international means of communication is welcome wherever it is available – far from it. It is precisely because this topic, understandably, provokes strong feelings that it seems particularly important to understand the underlying issues.

McKay (2002: 20) identifies three main problem areas:

> The main negative effects of the spread of English involve the threat to existing languages, the influence on cultural identity, and the association of the language with an economic elite.

The papers brought together in this section variously address these issues as well as several others. And it may well be that for readers who have become more sensitive to the discourses of power in world politics since 11 September 2001, many of these issues have taken on increased significance and urgency, and indeed may appear in a new light. Clearly, the unprecedented spread of English also has unprecedented cultural and political implications, for which Pennycook (1994: 36) uses the term 'worldliness'. This he takes

> to refer to the material existence of English in the world, its spread around the world, its worldly character as a result of being so widely used in the world, and its position not only as reflective but also as constitutive of worldly affairs.

Since the controversies collected in this book are arranged chronologically in each section, we start here with an exchange between two prominent scholars who could be called 'archetypical proponents' of the contrasting attitudes they represent: Randolph Quirk, 'champion of Standard (native) English', and Braj B. Kachru, 'champion of non-native Englishes'. Quirk founded the Survey of English Usage, and drew on the descriptions of educated British English which this database yielded for the two celebrated grammars of English (Quirk *et al.* 1972; Quirk *et al.* 1985) that his name has become inextricably connected with. Kachru, a native of Kashmir, India, as a professor of linguistics and comparative literature at the University of Illinois, USA, pioneered the description of the developmental processes and manifestations of non-native Englishes.

Given the focal areas of concern of these two scholars, the description of the standard language for one and the advocacy of the 'legitimacy' of non-native varieties for the other, it is not surprising that debates between them go back quite a way. A famous example is the exchange between Quirk and Kachru in a volume published on the occasion of the fiftieth anniversary of the British Council. Entitled *English in the World: Teaching and Learning the Language and Literatures* (Quirk and Widdowson 1985), this also provides the backdrop to the papers below, and is referred to repeatedly. In his 1985 paper 'The English language in a global context', Quirk made the following much-quoted statements about standard English, which foreshadow his paper in this collection:

> I believe that the fashion of undermining belief in standard English has wrought educational damage in the ENL countries, though I am ready to concede that there may well have been compensating educational gains in the wider tolerance for an enjoyment of the extraordinary variety of English around us in any of these countries. But then just such an airy contempt for standards started to be exported to EFL and ESL countries, and for this I can find no such mitigating compensation. The relatively narrow range of purposes for which the non-native needs to use English (even in ESL countries) is arguably well catered for by a single monochrome standard form that looks as good on paper as it sounds in speech. There are only the most dubious advantages in exposing the learner to a great variety of usage, no part of which he will have time to master properly, little of which he will be called upon to exercise, all of which is embedded in a controversial sociolinguistic matrix he cannot be expected to understand.
> (Quirk 1985: 6)

It will be interesting to see whether this statement is in keeping with what Quirk says in 1990. Kachru's 1985 paper was entitled 'Standards, codification and sociolinguistic realism: the English language in the outer circle', and again it foreshadows the exchange below in that it focuses on standards – but notice the plural. The last noun phrase of Kachru's title, 'the outer circle', may require a brief gloss for those not familiar with the term, and Kachru gives just such an explanation in his 1985 paper:

> The initial questions about the universalization of English are: What is the major stratification of use due to the internationalization of English? And, what are the

characteristics of such stratification? The spread of English may be viewed in terms of three concentric circles representing the types of spread, the patterns of acquisition and the functional domains in which English is used across cultures and languages. I have tentatively labelled these: the inner circle, the outer circle … , and the expanding circle. In terms of the users, the inner circle refers to the traditional bases of English. … Numerically, the outer circle forms a large speech community with great diversity and distinct characteristics. The major features of this circle are that (a) English is only one of two or more codes in the linguistics repertoire of such bilinguals or multilinguals, and (b) English has acquired an important status in the language policies of most of such multilingual nations. … The third circle, termed the expanding circle, brings to English yet another dimension. Understanding the function of English in this circle requires a recognition of the fact that English is an international language, and that it has already won the race in this respect with linguistic rivals such as French, Russian and Esperanto, to name just two natural languages and one artificial language. The geographical regions characterized as the expanding circle do not necessarily have a history of colonization by the users of the inner circle. … This circle is currently expanding rapidly and has resulted in numerous performance (or EFL) varieties. … The outer and the expanding circle cannot be viewed as clearly demarcated from each other; they have several shared characteristics, and the status of English in the language policies of such countries changes from time to time. What is an ESL region at one time may become an EFL region at another time or vice versa.
(Kachru 1985: 12ff.)

In summary, then, and simplifying somewhat, we can say that English is a first language in the Inner Circle, an additional language in the Outer Circle, and a foreign language in the Expanding Circle. Below, we thus have an exchange between a scholar from the Inner Circle and a scholar from the Outer Circle. Indeed, Quirk uses a topical debate about the teaching of English in an Inner Circle country, Britain, as the starting point for a defence of teaching Standard English across all three of Kachru's circles. A point quite crucial to his argument is his claim that there are not any institutionalized non-native varieties (p. 5), and this of course is a statement that Kachru cannot let pass unchallenged.

Text 1

Randolph Quirk

Language varieties and standard language

A few months ago, the Department of Education and Science in London published a very important document on the teaching of English. On the teaching of English, that is to say, in Britain (Kingman, 1988). I would like to invite you to consider to what extent – if any – this report has relevance for the teaching of English *outside* Britain: specifically, in countries such as Japan and Germany, Senegal and India – countries where English is not a native language.

But first a word on the report in its own British context. Why did our Secretary of State, Mr Kenneth Baker, decide to set up a distinguished committee of inquiry on this subject? And distinguished it most certainly was: fifteen men and women comprising eminent writers like Antonia Byatt, P.J. Kavanagh, journalists like Keith Waterhouse, linguists like Henry Widdowson and Gillian Brown; educators like Brian Cox; and there was the broadcaster Robert Robinson, the Oxford professor of poetry Peter Levi, the research industrialist Charles Suckling, the whole committee presided over by the mathematician Sir John Kingman. They were brought together from their diverse fields because the Secretary of State and many others in Britain have been dissatisfied with the teaching of English in British schools: dissatisfied with *what* is taught, *how* it is taught, and *the results* of the teaching as they show in the capabilities of school leavers.

Varieties of English

The conclusions of the Kingman Committee strike most people as wholly sensible. It is the duty of British schools, says the report, 'to enable children to acquire Standard English, which is their right' (p. 14) – a statement which may seem so obvious and unsurprising that the only *surprise* is why it needs to be stated.

The very first page of the report explains: the committee found that teachers were distracted by the belief that children's capacity to use English effectively 'can and should be fostered only by exposure to varieties of the English language'. It is not of course that the committee deny the interest and importance of the variation within English – still less that such variation exists. They would agree, I am sure, that our ability to vary our language according to our social and regional backgrounds, our professional careers, and indeed our creative urges as individuals, is at the very heart of the gift that human language bestows. And this has been made clear in the first report of the follow-up working party chaired by Brian Cox (Cox, 1988). No, what they are saying is that the interest in varieties of English has got out of hand and has started blinding both teachers and taught to the central linguistic structure from which the varieties might be seen as varying.

This may well be true, but I think there is a more serious issue that I would like to address, and that is the profusion and (I believe) *con*fusion of *types* of linguistic variety that are freely referred to in educational, linguistic, sociolinguistic, and literary critical discussion. Let me give some recent examples where the word *English* is preceded by an adjective or noun to designate a specific 'variety':

American English
Legal English
Working-class English
Computer English
BBC English
Black English
South Asian English
Queensland Kanaka English
Liturgical English
Ashkenazic English

Scientific English
Chicago English
Chicano English

Some of these you'll have come across, others you may not, but it will take only a moment's reflection to convince you that – whether familiar or not – these varieties are on desperately different taxonomic bases. For example, *legal English* refers to a style that may be used equally (and perhaps indistinguishably) in American English and British English. *Ashkenazic English* is a term which has been used to characterize the usage of Ashkenzai Jews in the United States, but whether it holds for Ashkenazim living in Britain or Australia or indeed Israel, I don't know.

When Braj Kachru (1982) talks about *South Asian English*, he is referring to audible similarities in the way Indians, Pakistanis, Bangladeshis and Sri Lankans speak English; but when E. G. Bokamba (1982) refers to *African English*, he seems not to be claiming linguistic similarities but only the common ground that the work so labelled was written in Africa by black Africans. Fernando Peñalosa (1980) applies the term *Chicano English* to the English used by those of Mexican Spanish origin in the U.S.A. and he contrasts it with *Anglo English* – not presumably a synonym for *American English* since it would doubtless exclude both the English of black Americans and perhaps equally the *Anglo-English* of Britain. When Dell Hymes (1981) uses *Indian English*, it refers to the English not of India as Kachru uses it but to the English of Amerindians of whatever group in North America: Cherokees in Oklahoma, Hopis in Arizona, Navahos in Utah, and it is not clear to me whether the designation seeks to capture linguistic features held in common by such dispersed fragments of different groups from among the pre-European inhabitants.

In the preface to her recent study, *Norms of Language* (1987), Renate Bartsch says 'I have written this book in ... the German variety of English' (of which my wife, herself a German and a professor of linguistics in Hamburg, was previously unaware, but which Professor Bartsch says is 'a version of one of the many varieties of the supervariety International English'). Let me try to find a path through this maze of varieties and super-varieties by attempting a taxonomy (see panel 1).

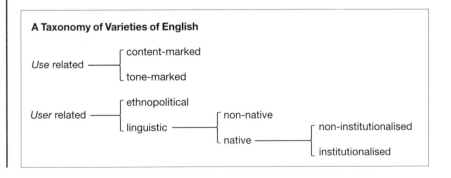

A Taxonomy of Varieties of English

Use related ── content-marked / tone-marked

User related ── ethnopolitical / linguistic ── non-native / native ── non-institutionalised / institutionalised

Use-related and user-related varieties

The first distinction we need to make is between those varieties that are *use*-related and those that are *user*-related. The former concerns varieties that an individual assumes along with a relevant role: and a given individual may have a mastery of several such varieties. A woman who is a lawyer must express herself in *legal English* in drafting an agreement, in *tennis English* when she confesses that her friend beat her 'in straight sets'; she may write articles for the Sunday Times in *literary English*, and her word-processor makes her feel the need to master a little *computer English*.

From such *use*-related varieties, we distinguish *user*-related varieties, where in general an individual is tied to one only: Americans, for example, express themselves only in *American English*, the British only in *British English* – and they know that they sound phony if they try to switch between varieties. But two lawyers corresponding on a case across the Atlantic both switch into *legal English*, however much each colours his or her legal English with the user-related American or British variety of the language.

Within the user-related varieties, however, we must distinguish between varieties identified on ethnopolitical grounds and those identified on linguistic grounds. Only thus can I make sense of Bokamba's *African English* or Peñalosa's *Anglo English* or Dell Hymes's sense of *Indian English* (all of which seem to be concerned with ethnopolitical statements – in contrast with Kachru's sense of *Indian English* which plainly has a linguistic basis).

This is an important distinction and it is one that should be confronted by those who speak about *Taiwanese English* and *Hong Kong English*, for example, since on linguistic grounds there are similarities that relate not to the political labels *Hong Kong* and *Taiwanese* but to the Chinese that is spoken in both areas. The distinction also reveals the ambiguity in the term *Chinese English* itself: English as used in the People's Republic *or* features of English influenced by a Chinese L1 (whether in China, Taiwan, Singapore, or Malaysia). One must seek analogous clarification about the variety called *Black English*: if it covers all the blacks in North America, any linguistic basis becomes rather broad; and if it is extended to include the English of blacks in Britain, a linguistic basis becomes almost incredible – especially since the term *Black* is assumed not only by Britons of Afro-Caribbean origin but equally by many who are of Pakistani and Indian origin as well.

Keeping to the linguistic branch from this node, we face another distinction: that between non-native varieties of English and native varieties, the former including long-recognised types like *Indian English* (in Kachru's sense), *Nigerian English*, *East African English*, and presumably 'the German variety of English' in which Renate Bartsch says she wrote *Norms of Language*. Just as presumably, they include what I called ten years ago the *performance varieties* (cf. Quirk, 1981) by means of which one can sometimes recognise the ethnic background of a person by his or her English: *Russian English, French English, Japanese English*. The problem with varieties in this branch is that they are inherently unstable, ranged along a qualitative cline, with each speaker seeking to move to a point where the varietal characteristics reach vanishing point, and where thus, ironically, each variety is best manifest in those who by commonsense measures speak it worst. (cf. Quirk, 1988)

The other branch from this node is the native varieties – *American English, Australian English, British English, New Zealand English, South African English, New England English, Yorkshire English*, and so on. And within these we make our final distinction: between *non-institutionalised* varieties and those varieties that are *institutionalised* in the sense of being fully described and with defined standards observed by the institutions of state. Of the latter, there are two: *American English* and *British English*; and there are one or two others with standards rather informally established, notably *Australian English*. But most native varieties are not institutionalised and while sharing a notable stability as compared with non-native varieties, they resemble these to a slight extent in being on a socioeconomic cline, such that the features marking an individual as being a speaker of Yorkshire English or New York English tend to disappear the higher up the socioeconomic scale he or she happens to be.

Native and non-native

Now, of all the distinctions I've made, the one that seems to be of the greatest importance educationally and linguistically is that between native and non-native: it is the distinction that is probably also the most controversial. Indeed, I have made it the more controversial by implicitly excluding from the non-native branch a node which permits the *institutionalised-non-institutionalised* distinction to apply to them. I exclude the possibility only because I am not aware of there being any institutionalised non-native varieties, a point to which I shall return later.

Let me just refer, however, to some recent psycholinguistic work by René Coppieters (1987) which strikingly underscores the *native/non-native* distinction. Coppieters worked with a group of about twenty native speakers of French and with a similar-sized group of non-native speakers – all of whom with a high level of performance, all of them resident in France for at least five years and using French as their working language. Indeed the mean residence level was 17 years and many of the group were believed by French people to be native speakers.

Yet in a range of interesting and sophisticated elicitation tests, the success rate of the non-natives fell not merely *below* but *outside* the range of native success to a statistically significant degree (p<.005) (see panel 2). For example, in judging and exploring the semantics of paired sentences involving the imperfect tense and

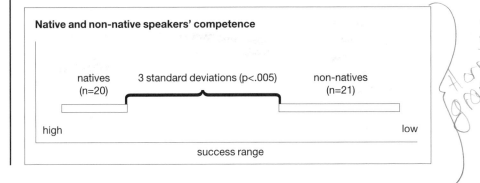

Native and non-native speakers' competence

the passé composé, what we may call the 'failure' rate of the natives was 2%, that of the non-natives 41.5%. For example:

Il a soupçonné quelque chose, j'en suis sûr.
Il soupçonnait quelque chose, j'en suis sûr.

The difference in the sets of scores was reflected in the comments by the non-natives. Though they always managed to understand and make themselves understood fairly well through the linguistic and situational context, they said repeatedly that they had developed no intuitions about the distinction between the imperfect and the passé composé: and two who said just this had worked in important professional positions in France for 15 and 21 years respectively. It would be interesting to see similar controlled experiments for English with such pairs as 'The spacecraft is now 1000 km from [±the] earth', 'She [±has] lived there for three years.'

The implications for foreign language teaching are clear: the need for native teacher support and the need for non-native teachers to be in constant touch with the native language. And since the research suggests that natives have radically different internalisations, the implications for attempting the institutionalisation of non-native varieties of any language are too obvious for me to mention.

Standard English

Instead, let me return to the broader issue of language varieties as it concerned the Kingman Committee, since they saw this as bound up with uncertain attitudes to *standards*, noting that some teachers of English believed 'that any notion of correct or incorrect use of language is an affront to personal liberty'.

It would take me too far from the subject of this lecture to examine why so many teachers should have turned away from concentrating on Standard English, from criticising a student's poor usage as incorrect, and should have preferred to explore the variety of language that students bring to their classrooms from very different social and regional backgrounds. Suffice it to say that the reasons have been idealistic, humanitarian, democratic and highly reputable, reasons which honourably motivated student teachers. And why not, indeed? If recent history has given us a 'liberation theology', why not also a 'liberation linguistics'?

The trouble, as the Kingman Committee sees it, is that such an educational fashion went too far, grossly undervaluing the baby of Standard English while *over*valuing the undoubtedly important bathwater of regional, social and ethnic varieties: giving the impression that any kind of English was as good as any other, and that in denying this, nothing less was at stake than 'personal liberty' itself. By contrast, the Kingman Report sees such an educational ethos as trapping students in their present social and ethnic sectors and as creating a barrier to their educational progress, their career prospects, their social and geographical mobility. Command of Standard English, says the Report, so far from inhibiting personal freedom, 'is more likely to increase the freedom of the individual than diminish it' (Kingman, 1988, p. 3).

English in non-English-speaking countries

Let me now turn from the fairly parochial issue of teaching English in Britain to the teaching of English in non-English speaking countries – where overwhelmingly greater numbers of students are involved. Most of the Kingman Report should surely have no bearing upon *them*. Since students in the Soviet Union or Japan bring little English of their own to the classroom, there can be no question of the teacher performing his or her task by merely exposing them to the 'varieties of English language' around them. They come to learn a totally unfamiliar language, so there can be no question of the teacher rejecting the 'notion of correct or incorrect' use of English. And all the students know perfectly well that, as Kingman says, their command of Standard English is likely to increase their freedom and their career prospects. So of course they – teachers and taught alike – accept the basic conclusion that it is the institution's duty to teach Standard English. ⟶ British English

At any rate, that is what one would *expect* to be the position with teaching English as a foreign language, and it is the position that is assumed by most foreign ministries of education and by most foreign students – and their parents.

But the contrast between teaching English to English boys and girls in Leeds and teaching English to Japanese boys and girls in Kobe is not as neat and absolute as I have made it seem. Some schools in London and New York, for instance, have so many pupils from a non-English speaking background that the techniques and approaches of teaching English as a foreign language have to be adopted – in precisely the same schools and often by the same teachers as those where the ideals of what I've called 'liberation linguistics' are still enthusiastically served up, however much they are just stale leftovers from the 1960s.

Let me give you a New York example. A well-respected educationist wrote an article a year or so ago on the teaching of English to the many thousands of New York children who come from Spanish-speaking homes (Goldstein, 1987). These children, she said, identify far more with the black children in the streets around them than with white children, and for that reason the English they should be taught is not Standard English but what she calls Black English. This is the English that will help them to relate to their peers outside the classroom; and after all, she pointed out, a sentence like 'I don't have none' shows 'a correct use of Black English negation' (p. 432). ⟶ what about the streets? ⟶ succeeding past

Now, that article was published in one of the best known international journals, read by teachers of English not only in the United States but in Italy, Greece, China, and Japan – by the most professionally-minded, in fact, of English language teachers throughout the world. The context in which the article was *written* of course is clear enough, but what about attempts to adapt its message in the very different contexts in which it is *read*?

We must not forget that many Japanese teachers, Malaysian teachers, Indian teachers have done postgraduate training in Britain and the United States, eager to absorb what they felt were the latest ideas in English teaching. Where better, after all, to get the latest ideas on this than in the leading English-speaking countries? The interest in 'varieties of English language', called in question on the first page of the Kingman Report, has in fact been widely stimulated, as we know from university theses being written in a whole host of countries: with titles like *Malaysian English, Filipino English, Hong Kong English, Nigerian English, Indian English*.

The countries last mentioned here, of course, are chiefly those where English has had an *internal* role over a long period for historical reasons. English was indeed the language used by men like Gandhi and Nehru in the movement to liberate India from the British raj and it is not surprising that 'liberation linguistics' should have a very special place in relation to such countries. Put at its simplest, the argument is this: many Indians speak English; one can often guess that a person is Indian from the way he or she speaks English; India is a free and independent country as Britain is or as America is. Therefore, just as there is an *American English* (as recorded, for example, in the Webster Collegiate Dictionary), and a *British English* (as recorded, for example, in the Concise Oxford), so there is an *Indian English* on precisely the same equal footing (and of course a *Nigerian English*, a *Ghanaian English*, a *Singaporean English*, a *Filipino English*, etc., etc.).

No one would quarrel with any of this provided there was agreement within each such country that it was *true*, or even that there was a determined policy to *make* it true. So far as I can see, neither of these conditions obtains, and most of those with authority in education and the media in these countries tend to protest that the so-called national variety of English is an attempt to justify inability to acquire what they persist in seeing as 'real' English.

A colleague of mine who this year spent some time working in Kenya told me in a letter: 'There is heated debate here as to whether there is such a thing as 'East African English' or whether the local variety is just the result of the increasing failure of the education system.' In his book on English in Nigeria, O. Kujore (1985) says that although earlier observers have talked freely of *Standard Nigerian English*, the fact is 'that any such standard is, at best, in process of evolution'. Similar doubts about Filipino English have recently been expressed in *English Today* (16, 1988) and they confirm my own observations in Manila. It is reported that, not long before her death, Mrs Indira Gandhi returned rather angry from an international conference – angry because she had been unable to understand the English used there by a fellow-Indian delegate. She demanded that her Ministry of Education do something about standards of English.

Within India itself, the status of *Indian English* is the more difficult to establish in that, among the few organisations using the term officially, the Indian Academy of Literature applies it in a purely ethnopolitical sense to literary work in English written by ethnic Indians.

No one should underestimate the problem of teaching English in such countries as India and Nigeria, where the English of the teachers themselves inevitably bears the stamp of locally acquired deviation from the standard language ('You are knowing my father, isn't it?') The temptation is great to accept the situation and even to justify it in euphemistically sociolinguistic terms.

A few months ago, discussing these matters in the Philippines, I heard a British educational consultant who had worked for a year or so in Manila tell Filipino teachers that there was no reason for them to correct the English of their students if it seemed comprehensible to other Filipinos. Whether the listening teachers felt relieved or insulted I don't know, but of one thing I was sure: the advice was bad. Filipinos, like Indians, Nigerians, Malaysians, are learning English not just to speak with their own country folk but to link themselves with the wider English-using community throughout the world. It is neither liberal nor liberating to permit learners to settle for lower standards than the best, and it is a travesty of liberalism to tolerate low standards which will lock the least fortunate into the least rewarding careers.

Half-baked quackery

When we turn from the special problems of countries like India and the Philippines to countries like Spain and Japan which have little or no legacy of localised English on the streets, in offices, or in markets, we would surely expect to find no such conflicts about teaching Standard English. And so it is for the most part, no doubt. But not entirely. Ill-considered reflexes of liberation linguistics and a preoccupation with what the Kingman Report calls 'exposure to varieties of English language' intrude even here. And this in two respects.

First, the buoyant demand for native-speaking English teachers means that one occasionally finds, in Tokyo or Madrid, young men and women teaching English with only a minimal teacher training, indeed with little specialised education: they're employed because, through accident of birth in Leeds or Los Angeles, they are native speakers of English. Not merely may their own English be far from standard but they may have little respect for it and may well have absorbed (at second or third hand) the linguistic ethos that is simplified into the tenet that any English is as good as any other.

Sysha!

One such young Englishman approached me after a lecture I'd given in Madrid a few months ago. Why, he asked, had I distinguished between the nouns *message* and *information* as countable and uncountable? His students often wrote phrases like *several informations* and since he understood what was meant, how could they be wrong? In some wonderment that I was actually talking to a British teacher of English, I gently explained about Standard English being the norm by which we taught and made judgments. He flatly disagreed and went on to claim that he could not bring himself to correct a Spanish pupil for using a form that had currency in an English dialect – *any* English dialect. 'She catched a cold' is as good as 'She caught a cold', he ended triumphantly and strode away.

not in my German class

Let's hope that such half-baked quackery is rare because the *other* respect in which 'exposure to varieties' is ill-used is not all that rare, I fear. This is where academic linguists from Britain or America, sometimes with little experience of foreign language teaching, are invited to advise on teaching English abroad. If by training or personal interest they share the language ethos that the Kingman Report criticises, their advice – merely a bit controversial in its original British or American educational context – is likely to be flagrantly misleading when exported with minimal adaptation to, say, Japan. Indeed, it can even happen with consultants who have years of hands-on ELT experience.

An example. A year or so ago, the Japan Association of Language Teachers invited a British educationist to address their annual convention. I learned about this from a worried Japanese official who drew my attention to the text of this British expert's address published in Tokyo. It warned teachers not to make 'overly hasty judgments about the language performance of learners', and particular emphasis was given by the expert to the following statement: 'Language behaviour which at first sight appears to be flawed may in fact be a manifestation of a new – though as yet unrecognised – variety of English.' (Coleman, 1987, p. 13). I was also asked about the *Four Seasons Composition Book* (Pereira & O'Reilly, 1988) in which Japanese students are told that 'if you can make yourself understood … that is good enough' since their attempts constitute 'a respectable variety of English'.

oy vey!

conversational vs. business

The implications of this, if hard-working Japanese teachers took such advice seriously, are quite horrendous. Students, 'liberally' permitted to think their 'new variety' of English was acceptable, would be defenceless before the harsher but more realistic judgment of those with authority to employ or promote them. They have in effect been denied the command of Standard English which, to quote the Kingman Report yet again, 'is more likely to increase the freedom of the individual than diminish it' (p. 3).

Standard English alive and well

Certainly, if I were a foreign student paying good money in Tokyo or Madrid to be taught English, I would feel cheated by such a tolerant pluralism. My goal would be to acquire English precisely because of its power as an instrument of international communication. I would be annoyed at the equivocation over English since it seemed to be unparalleled in the teaching of French, German, Russian, or Chinese.

I would be particularly annoyed at irrelevant emphasis on the different varieties of English when I came to realise they mattered so little to native speakers of English – to those who effortlessly read the novels of Saul Bellow, Iris Murdoch, and Patrick White, perceiving no linguistic frontier to match the passports (American, British and Australian) of these writers. And when I came to realise that the best grammars and dictionaries similarly related to a Standard English that was freely current throughout the world.

Indeed, the widespread approval of the Kingman Report confirms that the mass of ordinary native-English speakers have never lost their respect for Standard English, and it needs to be understood abroad too (cf. Hao, 1988; Yashiro, 1988) that Standard English is alive and well, its existence and its value alike clearly recognised. This needs to be understood in foreign capitals, by education ministries, and media authorities: and understood too by those from the U.K. and the U.S.A. who teach English abroad.

Of course, it is not easy to eradicate once-fashionable educational theories, but the effort is worthwhile for those of us who believe that the world needs an international language and that English is the best candidate at present on offer. Moreover, the need to make the effort is something for which we must bear a certain responsibility – and in which we have a certain interest.

References

Bartsch, R. (1987). *Norms of language: Theoretical and practical aspects.* London: Longman.

Bokamba, E. G. (1982). The Africanization of English. In B. B. Kachru (Ed.), *The other tongue: English across cultures* (pp. 77–98). Urbana, IL: University of Illinois Press.

Coleman, H. (1987). Is the 'false beginner' a false concept? *The Language Teacher, 11* (14), 11–17.

Coppieters, R. (1987). Competence differences between native and near-native speakers. *Language, 63,* 544–573.

Cox, B. (Chairman). (1988). *English for ages 5 to 11.* London: National Curriculum Council.

Goldstein, L. M. (1987). Standard English: The only target for nonnative speakers of English? *TESOL Quarterly, 21*, 417–436.

Hao, K. (1988). The view from China. *English Today, 13*, 50–52.

Hymes, D. (1981). [Foreword]. In C. A. Ferguson & S. B. Heath (Eds.), *Language in the USA*. London: Cambridge University Press.

Kachru, B. B. (Ed.). (1982). *The other tongue: English across cultures*. Urbana, IL: University of Illinois Press.

Kachru, B. B. (1983). *The Indianization of English: The English language in India*. New York: Oxford University Press.

Kingman, J. (Chairman). (1988). *Report of the committee of inquiry into the teaching of English language* [The Kingman Report]. London: Her Majesty's Stationery Office.

Kujore, O. (1985). *English usage: Some notable Nigerian variations*. Ibadan: Evans.

Peñalosa, F. (1980). *Chicano sociolinguistics*. Cambridge, MA: Newbury House.

Pereira, J., & O'Reilly, E. (1988). *Four seasons composition book*. Kyoto: City Press.

Quirk, R. (1981). International communication and the concept of nuclear English. In L. E. Smith (Ed.), *English for cross-cultural communication* (pp. 151–165). London: Macmillan.

Quirk, R. (1988). The question of standards in the international use of English. In P. H. Lowenberg (Ed.), *Language spread and language policy*. Washington, DC: Georgetown University Press.

Yashiro, K. (1988). Sociolinguistic considerations for teaching English as an international language in Japan. *The Language Teacher, 12*(4), 14–16.

Text 2

Braj B. Kachru

Liberation linguistics and the Quirk Concern

In his two recent papers, Sir Randolph Quirk, former President of the prestigious British Academy, and the founder of the Survey of English Usage, has expressed several concerns about the current paradigms used for describing various issues related to the diffusion of English worldwide (see Quirk 1988 and 1989/90); he has particularly addressed the question of standard and variation.

These concerns were first expressed by Quirk in a somewhat different tone in 1985 at the 50th Anniversary Celebration meeting of the British Council in London (Quirk 1985).[1] I believe that the vital concerns expressed by him, though specifically addressed to the global spread of English, are not peculiar to English. In the literature we see that more or less identical concerns have been expressed with reference to other languages of wider communication: this includes languages restricted to a specific country (e.g. Hindi in India) or those which cut across national boundaries (e.g. Swahili in East Africa, Bahasa Malaysia in South East Asia, and French in Francophone countries).[2] The Quirk concerns are, then, worth considering whether one is concerned with the language policy of a specific nation or with language policies and attitudes which cut across languages and cultures.

The case of English is important to language policy makers for other reasons, too. The global functions of English bring to the forefront a number of variables which, I believe, have generally eluded language policy makers. These variables are rarely mentioned in the literature on language diffusion, language use, language shift and language maintenance.[3] I am particularly thinking of 'unplanned' or 'invisible' policies as opposed to 'planned' or 'visible' policies.[4] The concerns discussed here go much beyond specific issues, since Quirk has thrown his net very far and wide, covering a wide range of attitudes and issues: it is not possible to disentangle all the issues here.

In ideological terms, the main thrust of Quirk's recent paper (1989/90) is to express deep dissatisfaction with what he terms *liberation linguistics*. In Quirk's paper, there is a presupposition that liberation linguistics has an underlying ideological motivation, an articulated philosophical and political position. He says 'English was indeed the language used by men like Gandhi and Nehru in the movement to liberate India from the British raj and it is not surprising that 'liberation linguistics' should have a very special place in relation to such countries.'

Quirk does not use any ideological terms for *his* concerns; that does not, however, mean that his position cannot be related to an ideological position. After all, it is rare that there is a position without an ideological backdrop. It seems to me that Quirk's position is not much different from what in another context has been termed *deficit linguistics*. This concept has so far primarily been used in the context of language learners with inadequate competence in using the vocabulary, grammar, and phonology of a language (e.g., Williams 1970; see also Phillipson and Skutnabb-Kangas 1986). It has also been used for 'deficit' in organization of discourse and style strategies, and inadequate competence in manipulation of codes (e.g., Bernstein 1964 and later). During the past two or three decades a considerable body of literature has developed on this topic – both pro and con. A well-argued case against the deficit position, specifically with reference to Black English, is presented in Labov 1972. The Quirk concerns, of course, go beyond Black English and have global implications on research and the teaching of English.

The Quirk concerns

The concerns Quirk expresses are an attack on the positions which linguists (or, should I say sociolinguists?) have taken about the spread of English, its functions and its multinorms;[5] in other words, on the recognition of pluricentricity and multi-identities of English. These concerns encompass a medley of issues, six of which I shall discuss here.

The first concern is that the recognition of a range of variation for English is a linguistic manifestation of underlying ideological positions. In Quirk's view, 'liberation theology' has led to the demand 'why not also a "liberation linguistics"?' Quirk believes that the result of this ideological underpinning is that 'the interest of varieties of English has got out of hand and has started blinding both teachers and taught to the central language structure from which varieties might be seen as varying'.

The second is that there is a '*con*fusion of types of linguistic variety that are freely referred to in educational, linguistic, sociolinguistic and literary critical discussion' (his emphasis).

The third is that the use of the term 'institutionalized variety' with the non-native varieties of English is inappropriate. He says, 'I am not aware of there being any institutionalized non-native varieties'. He provides supporting evidence for his position from a native and non-native speakers' competence test for French (Coppieters 1987). On the basis of which he concludes that there is

> ... the need for non-native teachers to be in constant touch with the native language. And since the research suggests that *the natives have radically different internalizations*, the implications for attempting the institutionalization of non-native varieties of any language are too obvious for me to mention (emphasis added).

One might mention here, as an aside, that this position is diametrically opposed to the position expressed in Quirk et al (1972:26), and again in Quirk et al (1985:27–28) where it is stated that in the case of English such [institutionalized] varieties

> ... are so widespread in a community and of such long standing that they may be thought stable and adequate enough to be institutionalized and hence to be regarded as varieties of English in their own right rather than stages on the way to a more native-like English.

The reference here is to the speech fellowships of English in South Asia, West Africa and Southeast Asia.

And now, coming back to Coppieters's test for French, Quirk comes to the conclusion that non-native teachers should be in 'constant touch' with the native language. Additionally he is concerned about the 'implications for attempting the institutionalization of non-native varieties of any language'.

However, there are problems in accepting the conclusions. The solution of 'constant touch with the native language' does not apply to the institutionalized varieties for more than one reason: first, the practical reason that it is simply not possible for a teacher to be in *constant* touch with the *native* language given the number of teachers involved, the lack of resources and overwhelming *non-native* input; second, the functional reason; that the users of institutionalized varieties are expected to conform to local norms and speech strategies since English is used for interaction primarily in intranational contexts. And, the last reason takes us to the psycholinguistic question of 'internalization'. The natives may have 'radically different internalizations' about their L1 but that point is not vital for a rejection of institutionalization. In fact, the arguments for recognizing institutionalization are that non-native users of English have internalizations which are linked to their own multilinguistic, sociolinguistic and sociocultural contexts. It is, in fact, precisely for this reason that a paradigm shift is desirable for understanding and describing the linguistic innovations and creativity in such varieties (see Kachru 1986a, and Paul Christophersen's comment on Quirk and the Coppieters paper in *ET23*, pp. 61–63).

Quirk also seems to believe that institutionalization is a conscious process which is *attempted* with definite ends in mind – political ends not excluded. I am not so sure of that: institutionalization is a product of linguistic, cultural and sociolinguistic processes over a period of time. Attitudinally, one may not recognize these processes and their linguistic realizations, but that does not mean they do not exist.

The fourth concern is that there is a recognition of variation within a non-native variety. He is concerned about the 'disclaimer of homogeneity' and 'uniform competence' (1988:235) in such varieties of English. To Quirk, recognition of variation within a variety is thus confusing and unacceptable.[6]

The fifth concern is that there is a widely recognized and justified sociolinguistic and pedagogical distinction between ESL and EFL. Quirk ignores this distinction partly because, as he says, '... I doubt its validity and frequently fail to understand its meaning' (1988:236). However, in Quirk 1985, he recognizes the validity of this distinction and explains the difference of this 'terminological triad' succinctly: the EFL users '... live in countries requiring English for what we may broadly call "external purposes" ...' (p. 1); the ESL countries are those 'where English is in widespread use for what we may broadly call "internal" purposes as well' (p. 2); and the ENL countries are '... where English is a native language' (p. 2).[7]

And the last concern is that there is recognition of the 'desirability of non-native norms' (1988:237). To illustrate his argument, Quirk says that 'Tok Pisin is displaying gross internal instability and is being rejected in favor of an external model of English by those with power and influence' (1988:237).

These six concerns do not exhaust Quirk's list of manifestations of 'liberation linguistics', but they do capture his main arguments. In articulating his concerns, Quirk is not presenting an alternate model for describing and understanding the diffusion, functions and planning of multilingual's linguistic behavior with reference to English. However, the arguments present do contribute toward developing a framework for deficit linguistics. What precisely does Quirk's 'deficit linguistics' entail? I believe that it entails the following six important assumptions:

1 Rejection of the underlying linguistic motivations for the range of variation, and suggesting that such variational models are motivated by an urge for linguistic emancipation or 'liberation linguistics'.
2 Rejection of the sociolinguistic, cultural, and stylistic motivations for innovations and their institutionalization.
3 Rejection of the institutionalization of language (in this case, specifically English) if used as a second language.
4 Rejection of the cline of varieties within a non-native variety.
5 Rejection of the endocentric norms for English in the Outer Circle.
6 Rejection of the distinction between the users of what I have termed 'the Outer Circle' (ESL) of English (Kachru 1985), and 'the Expanding Circle' (EFL), Quirk settles for a dichotomy between native speakers vs. non-native (L2) speakers.

A historical context for Quirk's concern

The concerns which Quirk has articulated in his usual elegant style are of course not new. They have been expressed at various periods not only about English, but about Sanskrit, Greek, Latin, Spanish, Hindi, and so on. In addition, the deficit models have been used both in L1 and L2 situations.

Just over two decades ago, Prator (1968), a distinguished American teacher and teacher trainer, took more or less an identical position as that of Quirk. However, there was a difference; in Prator's view the 'heresy in TESL' was being committed by cousins on the other side of the Atlantic. It was Britain preaching 'liberation linguistics' (see Kachru 1986b). There is, as Graeme Kennedy (1985:7) says, referring to Quirk's 1985 paper, 'a delicious irony' in that 'Professor Quirk's paper reflects, in many respects, the position Prator advocated …'. Kennedy continues 'however, since the orthodoxy has changed, it might be argued that Professor Quirk articulates a new British heresy. You simply cannot win.'

Kennedy sees the question of standards as 'fundamentally an attitudinal and especially an aesthetic one' (p. 7). Crystal commenting on the same paper (1985:9–10), brings to the discussion another important dimension when he says, 'what concerns me, however, is the way in which all discussion of standards ceases very quickly to be a linguistic discussion, and becomes instead an issue of social identity and I miss this perspective in his paper.' Here Crystal has put his finger on a vital sociolinguistic point.

Myths vs. multilingual realities

The Quirk concerns are, of course, motivated by a venerable scholar's life-long desire for maintenance of what he considers 'standards' for international English and the world's need for a functionally successful international language. And there is no disagreement that English is 'the best candidate at present on offer' (Quirk 1989/90). One indeed shares this concern. However, it seems to me that in expressing this concern, he has not only thrown out the bath water, but with it the baby of many sociolinguistic realities. And to me, recognition of the sociolinguistic realities does not imply 'an active encouragement of the anti-standard ethos' (Quirk 1985:3), nor does it imply 'to cock a snook at fashionably infashionable elitism by implying (or even stating) that any variety of language is "good", as "correct" as any other variety' (Quirk 1985:5).

Quirk seems to perceive the spread of English primarily from the perspective of monolingual societies, and from uncomplicated language policy contexts. The concerns he expresses are far from the realities of multilingual societies, and negate the linguistic, sociolinguistic, educational and pragmatic realities of such societies. I shall briefly discuss some of these realities here.

1. *Linguistic realities.* The linguistic realities provide a complex network of various types of convergence; these are more powerful in moulding linguistic behavior than are outsiders' attitudes towards such modulated linguistic behavior (cf. Hock 1986, 498–512; Lehiste 1988). The basic criteria for marking pragmatic success is in terms of functional effectiveness with other members of the interactional network. This is particularly true of languages of wider communication or contact languages (e.g., the *bazaar* varieties).

2. *Sociolinguistic realities.* Sociolinguistic realities bring us closer to the functional context of language, attitudes, and identities. In Quirk's denial model sociolinguistic realities have no place. In institutionalized non-native varieties of English (and I know Quirk now rejects this concept) this context is particularly relevant as has already been demonstrated in a number of studies (e.g., see Kachru 1986b for references).

3. *Educational realities.* The educational realities open up a can of worms with a multitude of problems: classroom resources, equipment, teacher training, teaching materials and so on.

An additional point to be considered here is the input which a learner of English receives in acquiring the language. The input for acquisition, the model to be followed and the speech strategies to be used are provided by the peer group, the teachers and the media. And, there is an additional attitudinal aspect to it: the expectation of the interlocutors in an interactional context.

The recognition of institutionalization of a language in language policies is only partly an attitudinal matter. To a large extent it is a matter of the recognition of the linguistic processes, history and acculturation of the language in a region, and functional allocation of a variety. All these aspects must be viewed in their totality. When the Indian Constitution considers English as an 'associate' official language, there is a message in it. When Chinua Achebe considers English as part of Africa's linguistic repertoire, this statement is indicative of a social, cultural, and linguistic reality. The claim that Indian English should be considered an *Indian* language (cf. Kachru 1989) on its functional basis is a recognition of several sociolinguistic realities. These realities must be taken into consideration while discussing the language policies in these countries.

Chinua Achebe's perspective, or Raja Rao's positive identity with English are, of course, valuable from one perspective. However, equally valuable, if not more so, is the position of those Africans and Asians who are denigrating English, foreseeing its doom. To them, its immense functional power, its social prestige, and its 'spell' on the people are suspect. Ngugi (1981:5) is concerned that 'African countries, as colonies and even today as neo-colonies, came to be defined and to define themselves in terms of the languages of Europe: English-speaking, French-speaking or Portuguese-speaking African countries.' To him the 'biggest weapon' is 'the cultural bomb', and

> 'the effect of a cultural bomb is to annihilate a people's belief in their names, in their languages, in their environment, in their heritage of struggle, in their unity, in their capacities and ultimately in themselves ... It makes them want to identify with that which is furthest removed from themselves; for instance, with other peoples' languages, rather than their own' (1981:3).

Then, there is the voice of Pattanayak (1985:400) from another continent who says that

> 'English language in India has fostered western orientation and reduced the self-confidence of its users. Its dominant use in education has created a system which has bypassed the majority; in administration it has denied the majority participation in the socioeconomic reconstruction of the country and has made justice unjusticiable [sic]. Its use in the mass media threatens to homogenize cultures, obliterate languages and reduce people into a mass.'

The recognition of the realities of multilingual societies means relating policies concerning world Englishes to the complex matrix of identities and uses. Let me briefly outline here what I have said about this point in an earlier paper (Kachru 1987). The institutionalization and continuously expanding functions of English in the Outer Circle depend on several factors which demand demythologizing the traditional English canon. The 'invisible' and not often articulated factors are, for example: (1) The Outer Circle users' emotional attachment to English. The result is that the *our* code vs. *their* code dichotomy, as suggested by Quirk, becomes very blurred. This attachment is evident in response to questions asked to creative writers in English who write exclusively in English or in English and their 'mother tongues'.[8] (2) The function of English as part of code extension in the verbal repertoire of a multilingual. It is not only a question of code alternation in the sense of switching between codes but also in 'mixing' of codes (e.g., English and Indian languages). (3) Recognition of English as a nativized and acculturated code which has required local non-Judeo-Christian identities. (4) Recognition of English as a contact code for *intra*national function, the *inter*national functions being marginal.

World Englishes and language policies

What lessons does the spread of English have for our understanding of approaches to language policies and their formulation? There are several lessons which help us in sharpening our conceptualization and formulation of language policies.

1. *Pressure groups and change.* The first is the close relationship between the various pressure groups and their influence on changes in the policies. The parameters of language policies are only partially in the hands of the planners. The spread of English during the post-colonial period provides several case studies: India, Malaysia, Indonesia, Bangladesh. In all these countries the recommendations of the planners had to be changed to meet the real political demands or to project an ideological image (e.g., that of Islamization in Bangladesh, and the calming of Muslim fundamentalist groups in Malaysia).

2. *Unplanned parameters.* The second is the power of *unplanned* language planning, as opposed to that of planned (*visible*) language planning. Visible language planning refers to the organized efforts to formulate language policies by recognized agencies. On the other hand, unplanned language 'planning' is the efforts of generally unorganized, nongovernmental agencies for acquiring and using a language. This point is well illustrated in Pakir (1988) and Y. Kachru (1989). In fact, the invisible language policies are often contrary to the policies espoused by the state or other organized agencies. And such invisible pulls seem to be more powerful than the visible ones. Who are the initiators of invisible language policies? The studies on, for example, Singapore and Malaysia show that invisible language planning is determined to an extent by the attitude of parents toward a language, the role of the media, the role of the peers, and the societal pressures. What we notice, then, is the conflict between the *slogan* concerning the language policies and the *action* in actual execution of the policies; there is abundant cross-cultural evidence to support this point (see Kachru 1986b).

The other dimension of invisible language policies involves the role of creative writers in moulding language policy. I am not aware of this aspect being seriously considered in the literature on this topic. Two examples related to the use of English come to mind: one from Southeast Asia and another from South Asia. In Singapore the stated language policy is a non-recognition of what has been termed the *basilect*. However, as Pakir (1988) shows, this variety plays an important role in the verbal repertoire of Singaporeans. That this variety is a viable medium for literary creativity is demonstrated in the poems of, for example, Arthur Yap, and in fiction by Catherine Lim and others (see Kachru 1987). The result is that in spite of the language policy makers' open rejection of this variety, the basilect variety continues to function as a valuable linguistic tool in the verbal repertoire of Singaporeans.

In two South Asian countries, Pakistan and Sri Lanka, it is the efforts of literary writers in addition to other invisible planners that keeps English a candidate in their language policies. Hashmi (1989:8) considers Pakistani literature in English 'as a national literature' which is responsive 'to the society in which it is created, and to the sensitivities that the society engenders.' In Sri Lanka, English came back in a somewhat 'unplanned' way since 'the monolingual Sinhalese and Tamil had ... no means of communication with members of other communities' (Wijesinha 1988:1). And in India, as in other regions of the Outer Circle, as Narasimhaiah argues (nd:14) it was '... a different racial and national genius and different social realities' which 'called for departures from the normal English syntax, different intonational contours and made it inevitable for Indian writers to assimilate them into their own speech rhythms' (see also Kachru 1986a).

Invisible strategies are used not only when it comes to an imposed colonial language, as in the case of English: the same strategies are adopted in multilingual societies as a reaction – in favor or against – other languages of wider communication. Consider India's case again: In the Hindi belt of India (*madhya desa*), the speakers of what were considered the dialects of Hindi are establishing the rights of their own languages. The cases in point are that of Maithili in the state of Bihar and Rajasthani in the state of Rajasthan. The main reasons for this vibrantly articulated trend are;

1   to establish an *identity* within a larger speech community,
2   to mark *ingroupness* to obtain and retain power in a democratic society,
3   to establish a *pressure group* for economic and other advantages, and
4   to assert *cultural separateness* in literary and other traditions.

In South Asia and Southeast Asia, to consider just two regions, we have cases of numerous strategies used to frustrate the organized language policies. But that is not all. There are also cases of invisible language planners frustrating the unrealistic language policies: again one thinks of Singapore or Bangladesh. In Bangladesh, when it formed a part of Pakistan, the Pakistani policy of language imposition was repeatedly rejected and in the process several people were killed during the language riots. February 24 is annually observed as Language Martyr's day in Bangladesh. These are important cases of language and identity which result in significant human sacrifice and suffering. The question of identity with language equally applies to English, too. It is in this sense that English has multi-cultural identities.

The Quirk concerns and language policies

One might ask in what sense the Quirk concerns are relevant to the theoretical, sociolinguistic and pragmatic issues related to language planning? The 1988 and 1989/90 papers of Sir Randolph Quirk are thought-provoking in more than one way. One most important contribution of the papers is that they provoke us to ask some serious questions about language policies and attitudes, which are not generally asked in the literature on the topic. Consider, for example, the following four questions.

The first is of a theoretical nature: Can language policies be formulated and implemented in a theoretical vacuum (whether one is talking of a theory of sociolinguistics or contact linguistics)?

The second is related to attitudes and identities: Can attitudes and identities be separated while discussing language policies, standardization and the norm?

The third question takes us to the politics of language policies: What role, if any, is played by political leaders in imparting language policies, whether visible or invisible? The visible aspect of it is illustrated by the Islamization and Arabization (e.g., Bangladesh), or Hindu fundamentalism and Sanskritization (e.g., India). The invisible aspect of it is the concern for native-like standards or about falling standards of English expressed by political leaders as mentioned by Quirk (Indira Gandhi of India and Lee Kuan Yew of Singapore).

The fourth question takes us to the age old topic in second-language acquisition: What, if any, are the strategies which influential and powerful native-speakers use to control the direction of English, its innovations and its acculturation?

In the three papers mentioned earlier, Quirk has not answered any of these questions: that he has raised some very provocative questions is, of course, in itself a contribution to an intense debate. These questions are closely related to contact linguistics, sociolinguistics, pragmatics and literary creativity. These areas are vital for our understanding of language acquisition, use and creativity in human language.

It seems to me that any language policy divorced from 'a renewal of connection' (to use a Firthian term) with these theoretical areas is not going to be insightful. One can not develop a language policy merely on attitudes. Attitudes may indeed be important exponents of an underlying motive for language policies as, for example, was the 'Imperial Model' discussed by Quirk. But mere attitude cannot provide a sound base for developing a policy. In my view, Sir Randolph Quirk has presented a serious theoretical dilemma to us by suggesting that the spread of English and its resultant linguistic, sociolinguistic and literary consequences be seen purely from an attitudinal perspective. I believe that language history is not on his side.

It seems to me that there are several fallacies in conceptualizing world Englishes in the Outer Circle: these are primarily of four types: theoretical, methodological, linguistic and attitudinal. I have discussed these in detail in Kachru 1987 [1989].

In Quirk's arguments one notices a subtle rejection of the *deviational, contextual, variationist,* and *interactional* approaches for the understanding and description of the implications of the spread of English. While supporting the deficit approach, Quirk does not identify in any of his three papers the methods one might use in controlling codification around the world: I have discussed elsewhere (1985) four types of codification traditionally used for implementation of language policies. These are:

1. *Authoritative or mandated codification.* This includes policies generally adopted by the academies. A good example of this is the French Academy established in 1635. As is well-known, there were two attempts to set-up such academies for English: the first in England in 1712, and the second in the USA in 1780. And both failed. Perhaps history has a lesson for us.

2. *Sociological or attitudinal codification.* This is reflected in social or attitudinal preference of certain varieties. Abercrombie (1951:14) has called it the 'accent bar'. However, this bar does not apply to 'accent' only but it often extended to other levels too: grammatical, lexical, discoursal and stylistic.

3. *Educational codification.* This refers to codification determined by the dictionaries, the media, teacher's attitudes and so on.

4. *Psychological codification.* A good example of this is the psychological constraints put on the ritualistic use of Sanskrit. The *correct* use was a precondition for *effective* use of the language and incorrect use could result in the wrath of gods.

In the case of English there is essentially no authoritative codification, unless, of course, we grant authoritative sanction to various dictionaries and language manuals; the codification for English is primarily sociological, educational and indeed attitudinal. It seems to me that the deficit approach fails not only for the reason that it is based on several fallacies, it also fails for the reason that it is based on, at least, four false assumptions about the users and uses of English.

The first assumption is that in the Outer and Expanding circles (that is, Quirk's ESL and EFL countries), English is essentially learnt to interact with the native speakers of the language. This, of course, is only partially true. The reality is that in its localized varieties, English has become the main vehicle for interaction among its non-native users, with distinct linguistic and cultural backgrounds – Indians interacting with Nigerians, Japanese, Sri Lankans, Germans with Singaporeans, and so on. The culture-bound localized strategies of, for example, politeness, persuasion, and phatic communion transcreated in English are more effective and culturally significant than are the 'native' strategies for interaction.

The second assumption is that English is essentially learnt as a tool to understand and teach the American or British cultural values, or what is generally termed the Judeo-Christian traditions. This again is true only in a marginal sense. In culturally and linguistically pluralistic regions of the Outer Circle, English is an important tool to impart local traditions and cultural values. A large number of localized linguistic innovations and their diffusion is related to local cultural and sociopolitical contexts.

The third assumption is that the international non-native varieties of English are essentially 'interlanguages' striving to achieve 'native-like' character.[9] This position has been taken by, among others, Selinker (1972). In reality the situation is, as Quirk et al observed in 1972 and again in 1985, that such institutionalized varieties are 'varieties of English in their own right rather than stages on the way to more native-like English.' This is a sociolinguistically correct position (see Sridhar and Sridhar 1986; see also Lowenberg and Sridhar eds. 1985).

The fourth assumption is that the native speakers of English as teachers, academic administrators and material developers are seriously involved in the global teaching of English in policy formulation and in determining the channels for the spread of language. In reality that is again only partially true.

In proposing language policies for English in the global context, the situation is indeed complex, and there are no easy answers. There is thus a need for a 'paradigm shift' as has been proposed in several recent studies. The paradigm shift entails reconsidering the traditional sacred cows of English which does not necessarily mean as Quirk suggests (1985:3), 'the active encouragement of anti-standard ethos'. The list of such sacred cows is long; I do not propose to list all of them here. But let me mention just three theoretical constructs which linguists and language teachers have considered sacred. I'm not sure that these are still sacred for English. I am thinking of concepts such as the 'speech community' of English, 'ideal speaker-hearer' of English and the 'native speaker of English.[10]

In the context of world Englishes, what we actually see is that diversification is a marker of various types of sociolinguistic 'messages'. Let me briefly mention some of these here from an earlier study on this topic (Kachru 1987). First, English as an exponent of distance from the Inner Circle – it may be social, cultural, and ideological distance. Second, English as a marker of 'creativity potential'. This aspect is clearly evident in the innovations used in creative writing of Ahmad Ali, Mulk Raj Anand, Raja Rao, Salman Rushdie, Ngugi wa Thiongo and Amos Tutuola. Third, English as a marker of the 'Caliban Syndrome', a linguistic response to what Ngugi has called the 'cultural bomb' effect of the colonial powers. There is no doubt that the 'linguistic bomb' is somewhat diffused by giving it a local identity and a new name.

The earlier diffusion of English, as Quirk rightly suggests, followed the Imperial model of language spread. However, that historical fact has changed with later sociolinguistic realities, acculturation and diversification of the language. A rejection of this reality implies codification as a means of linguistic control. And that is a very 'loaded weapon'. This linguistic control is exercised in three ways: by the use of channels of codification and the control of these channels; by the attitude toward linguistic innovations, and their diffusion by those who are not part of such speech fellowships; and by the suggestion of dichotomies which are sociolinguistically and pragmatically not meaningful. Let us not forget that this subtle linguistic control provides immense power to those who have the power and can *define*. One can not, therefore, ignore the warning of Tromel-Plotz (1981:76) that 'only the powerful can define others and can make their definitions stick. By having their definitions accepted they appropriate more power.'

And making these definitions stick is not power in an abstract sense only. There is more to it in economic terms: a recent report says, 'the worldwide market for EFL training is worth a massive £6.25 billion a year according to a new report from the Economic Intelligence Unit' (*EFL Gazette*, March 1989). The economics of determining and proposing language policies has never been so vital before. What effect 'liberation linguistics' may have in marketing English is just being studied.

There is no doubt that the current debate on the 'liberation model' vs. 'deficit model', particularly with reference to English, is presenting numerous theoretical and pragmatic challenges to language policy makers. We have so far tackled issues of standardization and corpus planning in local and regional terms, except in the case of survival registers where international codification has been proposed (e.g., SEASPEAK). However, world Englishes raise questions about international standardization with new parameters: *us* vs. *them*. This, in my view, is an unprecedented challenge to language policy makers. It takes us across languages and cultures, practically on every continent. The Quirk concern clearly articulates the dilemma, but, as Crystal has rightly pointed out (1985:9–10), completely misses the perspective of 'social identity'; the issues have been divorced from sociolinguistic and pragmatic contexts.

Conclusion

To conclude, let me share with you a true story narrated to me by a former Ambassador of India to the USA.[11] The story is a touching one, about a young American scholar who spent several years in a village in Bihar State in Eastern India.

At the time of his departure to the USA, the village council (*panchayat*) gave him an Indian style farewell. During the ceremony, one member of the village council, in his own dialect, requested the village headman to ask the young American guest if there are water buffaloes in his country, the USA. The puzzled young American replied 'No'. This response completely surprised, and somewhat shocked, the villager, and he innocently remarked that if the chief guest's country has no water buffaloes, it must be a poor country! And lo and behold, before the farewell ceremony concluded, the young American scholar was presented with two healthy water buffaloes and the head of the village council was profusely apologizing for giving him just two buffaloes. But he reassured the puzzled young American with folded hands (an Indian gesture of respect) that he should rest assured: in course of time, after reaching the USA, these two healthy buffaloes would multiply and make his native America prosperous.

And thereby hangs a linguistic tale; in this well meaning story there is a message for all of us who have suggestions for determining policies about English around the world. What is actually 'deficit linguistics' in one context may be a matter of 'difference' which is based on vital sociolinguistic realities of identity, creativity and linguistic and cultural contact in another context. The questions are: can sociolinguistic realities be negated? And, can international codification be applied to a language which has over 700 million users across the globe? If the answer to the second question is 'yes', it is vital to have a pragmatically viable proposal for such codification. We have yet to see such a proposal.

Notes

1   Quirk and Widdowson eds. 1985 contains the main papers presented at the conference and the discussion.
2   For Hindi see Sridhar 1988, for other languages see e.g., Coulmas ed. 1988.
3   See e.g., Kachru 1988 and Phillipson and Skutnabb-Kangas 1986.
4   See e.g., Pakir 1988, Kachru, Y. 1989.
5   This includes, e.g., Ayo Bamgbose, John R. Firth, M. A. K. Halliday, Larry E. Smith, Peter Strevens, Edwin Thumboo. My position in this connection is presented in papers published since 1962. A number of these are in Kachru 1983, 1986b, and Kachru ed. 1982.
6   For a detailed discussion of the functional reasons of variation see Kachru 1986b.
7   For a sociolinguistically and pragmatically motivated discussion of this triad see Kachru 1985.
8   See e.g., Lal 1965.
9   For questions concerning this position see studies in Sridhar and Lowenberg eds. 1985.
10 For a detailed discussion see Kachru 1988. See also Paikeday 1985.
11 K.R. Narayanan told me this story in 1983. It has also been published in his book *India and America: Essays in Understanding* (1984; Washington DC: The Information Service of the Embassy of India, p. x).

References

Abercrombie, David. 1951. 'R. P. and Local Accent.' *The Listener*, 6 Sep 1952. [Reprinted in D. Abercrombie, *Studies in Phonetics and Linguistics*, London: Oxford University Press.]

Bernstein, Basil. 1964. 'Elaborated and Restricted Codes: Their Social Origins and Some Consequences.' *American Anthropologist* 66:55–69.

Coppieters, R. 1987. 'Competence Differences Between Native and Near-Native Speakers.' *Language*, 63, 544–573.

Coulmas, Florian. (ed.) 1988. *With Forked Tongues: What are National Languages Good For?* Ann Arbor, MI: Karoma.

Crystal, David. 1985. Comment. In Quirk and Widdowson ed. 1985.

Hashmi, A. 1989. 'Prologomena to the Study of Pakistani English and Pakistani Literature in English.' Paper presented at the International Conference on English in South Asia, Islamabad, January 4–9, 1989.

Hock, Hans Henrich. 1986. *Principles of Historical Linguistics*. The Hague: Mouton de Gruyter.

Kachru, Braj B. 1983. *The Indianization of English: the English Language in India*. Delhi: Oxford University Press.

Kachru, Braj B. 1985. 'Standards, Codification and Sociolinguistic Realism: The English Language in the Outer Circle.' In *English in the World*. Edited by Randolph Quirk and H. G. Widdowson. Cambridge: Cambridge University Press.

Kachru, Braj B. 1986a. 'The Bilingual Creativity: Discoursal and Stylistic Strategies in Contact Literatures in English.' In *Discourse Across Cultures: Strategies in World Englishes*. Edited by Larry E. Smith. London: Prentice-Hall.

Kachru, Braj B. 1986b. *The Alchemy of English: the Spread, Functions and Models of Non-native Englishes*. Oxford: Pergamon Press.

Kachru, Braj B. 1987. 'The Past and Prejudice: Toward de-Mythologizing the English Canon.' *Linguistic Topics: Papers in Honor of M. A. K. Halliday*, edited by R. Steel and T. Threadgold. Amsterdam and Philadelphia. J. Benjamin.

Kachru, Braj B. 1988. 'The Spread of English and Sacred Linguistic Cows.' In Lowenberg ed. 1988.

Kachru, Braj B. 1989. 'Indian English.' *Seminar*. July 1989.

Kachru, Braj B. ed. 1982. *The Other Tongue: English Across Cultures*. Urbana, IL: University of Illinois Press.

Kachru, Yamuna. 1989. 'Modernization of Indian Languages: English in Unplanned Corpus Planning.' Paper presented at the 1989 Mid-America Linguistics Conference, University of North Iowa, October 6–7, 1989.

Kennedy, Graeme. 1985. Comment. In Quirk and Widdowson eds. 1985.

Labov, William 1972. *Language in the Inner City: Studies in the Black English Vernacular*. Philadelphia: University of Pennsylvania Press.

Lal, P. 1965. *Modern Indian Poetry in English: an Anthology and a Credo*. Calcutta: Writers Workshop.

Lehiste, Ille. 1988. *Lectures on Language Contact*. Cambridge, MA: MIT Press.

Lowenberg, Peter, ed. 1988. *Language Spread and Language Policy: Issues Implications and Case Studies. (GURT 1987)* Washington DC: Georgetown University Press.

Lowenberg, Peter and S. N. Sridhar eds. 1985. *World Englishes and Second Language Acquisition Research*. Special Issue of *World Englishes*, 5.1.

Narashimhaiah, C. D. nd. 'Indian Writing in English: A Reply to Dom Mornes.' In *Indian Literature in English: Contemporary assessments*, edited by C. N. Narashimhaiah and C. N. Srinath. Bangalore: Wiley Eastern (P) Ltd. (A Dhvanyaloka Publication)

Ngugi, wa Thiongo. 1981. *Decolonizing the Mind: The Politics of Language in African Literature*. London: James Currey. 1981.

Paikeday, T.M. 1985. *The Native Speaker is Dead!* Toronto: Paikeday Publishing.

Pakir, Ann. 1988. 'Education and Invisible Language Planning: the Case of English in Singapore.' Paper Presented at the 1988 Regional Seminar on Language Planning in Multilingual Settings: The Role of English. National University of Singapore, Singapore, 6–8 September 1988.

Pattanayak, D. P. 1985. 'Diversity in Communication and Languages; Predicament of a Multilingual State: India, a Case Study.' In *Language of Inequality* edited by N. Wolfson and J. Manes. The Hague: Mouton.

Phillipson, Robert and Tove Skutnabb-Kangas. 1986. *Linguicism Rules in Education*. Part I. Denmark: Roskilde University Centre, Institute VI.

Prator, Clifford. 1989. 'The British Heresy in TESL.' In J. A. Fishman, C. A. Ferguson, and J. D. Gupta eds. *Language Problems in Developing Nations*. New York: John Wiley.

Quirk, Randolph. 1985. 'The English Language in a Global Context.' In R. Quirk and H. G. Widdowson eds. 1985, pp. 1–6.

Quirk, Randolph 1988. 'The Question of Standards in the International Use of English.' In Peter Lowenberg ed. 1988, pp. 229–241.

Quirk, Randolph 1989/1990. 'Language Varieties and Standard Language.' *JALT Journal* 11.1., pp. 14–25; *English Today 21*, Jan 90.

Quirk, Randolph and Henry Widdowson eds. 1985. *English in the World: Teaching and Learning of Language and Literature*. Cambridge: Cambridge University Press.

Quirk, Randolph, S. Greenbaum, G. Lecch and J. Svartvik. 1972. *A Grammar of Contemporary English*. London: Longman.

Quirk, Randolph, S. Greenhaum, G. Leech and J. Svartvik. 1985. *A Comprehensive Grammar of the English Language*. London: Longman.

Selinker, Larry. 1972. 'Interlanguage.' *International Review of Applied Linguistics*. 10. pp. 209–231.

Sridhar, K. K. and S. N. Sridhar 1986. 'Bridging the Paradigm Gap: Second Language Acquisition Theory and Indigenized Varieties of English.' *World Englishes*. 5.1, 3–14.

Sridhar, S. N. 1988. 'Language Variation, Attitudes, and Rivalry: The Spread of Hindi in India.' In Lowenberg ed. 1988.

Tromel-Plotz, Senta. 1981. 'Languages of Oppression.' Review Article. *Journal of Pragmatics*. 5, 67–80.

Wijesinha, R. ed. 1988. *An Anthology of Contemporary Sri Lankan Poetry in English*. Colombo: The British Council, Sri Lanka.

Williams F. 1970. *Language and Poverty*. Chicago: Markham.

The number of issues raised by these two scholars is of course considerable, and different readers will vary in the significance they attribute to one or the other point raised or challenged. It cannot be the purpose of the editor's commentary here to enumerate these issues or to highlight those that seem to her to be particularly important – indeed, to do this would be to run counter to the objective of encouraging readers to get a better grasp of what they themselves make of this controversy. However, at the end of this section, there are some pointers to further readings (and sometimes even further controversies) that pursue some of the aspects addressed in the above papers in more detail.

The next controversy revolves around the notion of 'linguistic imperialism', and starts with an account of how Robert Phillipson's book (which bears that title) was read at an American university by the participants in a graduate seminar led by Margie Berns. So, while this exchange also looks at the issues surrounding the global spread of English, this time mainly from the point of view of its political implications, the focus of attention here is on the *mode* of argumentation rather than the issues themselves – although, of course, content and form are inevitably interrelated.

The papers that follow hardly need any introduction as the background is set out very clearly in the first one. In fact, this controversy seems particularly well suited for the present volume as it explicitly puts up-front the very process of critical evaluation and discussion which this book seeks to encourage.

Phillipson's *Linguistic Imperialism* has been so influential and is referred to so frequently that most readers will probably be familiar with it. For those who are not, Berns *et al.* provide a thumbnail sketch of the book (pp. 35–6) so that it is possible to follow the arguments without having read it. Obviously, it is hoped that the controversy which follows below will make more people want to read the book, and join in the critical discussion that Phillipson and his quite numerous critics have been conducting over the years.

Text 3

Margie Berns, Jeanelle Barrett, Chak Chan, Yoshiki Chikuma, Patricia Friedrich, Olga-Maria Hadjidimos, Jill Harney, Kristi Hislope, David Johnson, Suzanne Kimball, Yvonne Low, Tracey McHenry, Vivienne Palaiologos, Marnie Petray, Rebecca Shapiro and Ana Ramirez Shook
Purdue University

Review Essay
(Re)experiencing hegemony: the linguistic imperialism of Robert Phillipson

Reading Robert Phillipson's Linguistic Imperialism *in a graduate seminar in World Englishes at Purdue University prompted intense discussion and debate not only of the issues of language dominance and spread that the author raised, but also of the rhetorical style and strategies that he chose to present a story of linguistic oppression. This article documents the reactions of seminar participants to how Phillipson presented his argument and their conclusion that the rhetorical choices he made seriously affected their ability to find his story convincing. In particular, participants – representing English language speakers in Brazil, Greece, Hong Kong, Japan, Singapore, and the USA – identified problems with the author's claims and credibility, style and tone, and terminology and coverage. They also discovered that this book, which they expected to be a narrative of hegemony, was instead an illustration of the use of narrative as a hegemonic tool.*

> In Britain and Europe we are taught that anyone who thinks he has a monopoly of the truth is probably a charlatan, and we will find bits of the truth in different places, and part of our training is to make syntheses which we develop as we go along.
> Peter Strevens (cited in Phillipson, p. 269)

The notion of English as a tool of linguistic and cultural domination has gained attention in English language studies in part due to the work of Robert Phillipson. In *Linguistic Imperialism* (1992), a book-length treatment of this subject, Phillipson claims to explore 'the contemporary phenomenon of English as a world language … and analyze how the language became so dominant and why' (p. 1). His primary concern is language policy and planning in so-called Third World countries, especially in Africa, and ways in which so-called First World countries have influenced educational development and English learning there through foreign policy.

For these reasons, *Linguistic Imperialism* was on the reading list for a graduate seminar in World Englishes in which we[1] participated during the fall semester of 1996 at Purdue University. As language teachers and researchers, we were eager to learn about 'the ideology transmitted with, in, and through the English language, and the role of language specialists in the cultural export of English' (p. 1). We anticipated that the perspective and focus of this former British Council employee and an activist in support work for Namibia's SWAPO would complement views with which we had already become familiar in other readings, e.g. *The Other Tongue* (Kachru [ed.] 1992). We devoted three weeks of the course to reading, reaction, and discussion, and in that time found much to discuss and debate with respect to Phillipson's account and analysis of English and English language teaching (ELT) world-wide. Spirited, often passionate dialogue was the norm as we argued for or against points he was attempting to make or tried to clarify our own positions on the issues he presented. Our interactions with Phillipson through the text and each other were enriched and vitalized by the diversity of our linguistic, cultural, and educational backgrounds as well as our aspirations and academic interests. We were students of language pedagogy, linguistics, literature, and cultural criticism working toward Master's and Doctorate degrees; we held or aspired to academic positions in higher education, private language schools, or primary and secondary schools in our home countries or abroad; we were from rural and urban environments in Brazil, Greece, Hong Kong, Japan, and Singapore as well as diverse linguistic and cultural regions of the USA: Alaska, Arkansas, Kentucky, Michigan, New Jersey, Oklahoma, Texas, and Washington.

As would be expected in a seminar, we spent a lot of time seeking to understand and interpret Phillipson's account of linguistic imperialism and trying to find meaningful connections to existing knowledge and to our interests in English language teaching. We also spent considerable time on the way Phillipson told his story to us, his readers, as we soon became distracted by the narrative structure and rhetorical strategies he employed. After closer scrutiny, we came to realize these aspects were contributing to his failure to completely persuade us of the validity of his claims or his credibility as narrator.

This was the impetus for the following review essay, which is an account of difficulties found with Phillipson's rhetorical style and of insights gained into the discourse of linguistic hegemony. We believe it is important to document this experience and present it in a public forum because the author has achieved prominence as an authority on the subject of linguistic imperialism and because the book addresses issues of critical importance to teachers and scholars of English in the global context. Since published critiques of *Linguistic Imperialism* (e.g. Bisong 1995; Davies 1996; Holborrow 1993) have focused on content more than form we saw a place for our views. In doing so, we seek to take our discussion beyond the seminar room into a larger forum and contribute to ongoing dialogue on the social and cultural roles of English around the world and the roles and responsibilities of language teaching specialists in its spread.

Overview of *Linguistic Imperialism*

To provide the context of our discussion for readers who may be unfamiliar with the book, we begin with an overview. The 365 pages of *Linguistic Imperialism* are divided into ten chapters, a bibliography, and an index. Chapter 1 lays out the ideological and theoretical foundations with definitions of such terms as *core*, or *centre*, and *periphery countries* (compare Kachru's [1992] *inner, outer,* and *expanding circles*) and the theories of language and power which guide the exploration in subsequent chapters. Phillipson provides background on his 25 years of involvement in English language teaching with the British Council in Africa and western and south-east Europe and identifies his primary motivation for writing the book as 'the belief that language pedagogy, the scientific study of language learning and language teaching, has been isolated from the social sciences too long' (p. 2). Additional contextual information is provided in chapter 2 with a history of the spread and role of English in such countries as Japan, where English is an international link language, and Nigeria, where English has a colonial heritage and serves intra-national purposes. In this chapter he also explains that this book examines only the linguistic imperialism of Great Britain and the United States, not the promotion, for example, of Russian in the former Soviet Union and Eastern Europe. Chapters 3 and 4 deal extensively with the theory of power underpinning the book and the notions *linguistic imperialism* and *linguicism*. The former occurs when 'the dominance of English is asserted and maintained by the establishment and continuous reconstitution of structural and cultural inequalities between English and other languages' (p. 47). The latter is 'a set of practices and beliefs which represent an attempt by those involved in language matters to give signification to a complex segment of reality, which itself meshes with political, ideological and other factors' (p. 56). The theoretical foundations of these concepts are described and linked to cultural imperialism in such fields as science, the media, and education. In addition, Phillipson reviews previous work relevant to English linguistic imperialism, particularly that of Ronald Wardhaugh, whose 'liberalistic approach' (p. 99) and 'parliamentary theory of knowledge' (p. 102) he rejects, and Louis-Jean Calvet, whose Marxist views, rhetorical strategies, and military themes he embraces.

With the background and framework described, chapters 5 and 6 begin the analysis. Phillipson turns to past and present colonial language practices, as well as policies and activities of Britain and the USA in promoting English world-wide. The analysis continues in chapters 7 and 8 with the focus on English language teaching. He examines in particular Britain's role in educational practices in Third World contexts, seven tenets of language teaching which he claims guide these practices, and the role of both research on English language teaching and foreign aid directed at education. In chapters 9 and 10 the author shifts to an investigation of various arguments used to promote English and how they relate to a theory of power. The case of an official language for Namibia, a country in which Phillipson has been politically active on behalf of SWAPO, illustrates this relationship. The final chapter provides a summary and identifies areas for further research and study with respect to English language teaching and linguistic imperialism.

Seminar reactions

The effect of Phillipson's style and the stages in our reactions are summarized in the comments of a classmate from Hong Kong, who keenly identified with the conditions the book described. In class she gave moving accounts of the influence of British colonizers and their imposition of English in her home country. She earnestly wanted us to appreciate how right Phillipson was and for us to understand Hong Kong's plight as a colony. At first, she became frustrated with the rest of us for focusing on how he was delivering his message rather than attending to the content. Eventually, upon reading further into the book, she too became disappointed with Phillipson's failure to reach us. In a reaction paper, she developed the following analogy to express her feelings:

> You have a case and a lawyer with the background and experience to handle it. Although the trial begins well, you eventually come to feel hopeless and helpless as you watch your lawyer lose the case because of over-confidence, a style of argument that offends everyone in the courtroom, violation of courtroom procedures, and lack of convincing and relevant evidence. To make matters worse, not only do you lose this session in court, but you have no second chance, no right to appeal. The verdict has been delivered and the case closed.

We found this analogy apt for a variety of reasons and organized our reactions around them under these categories: rhetorical choices in authorial voice, authority and audience; solutions to problems described and directions for change; and the nature of hegemony. Throughout we have chosen to speak both as individuals and as a seminar so that multiple and multi-dimensional voices can be heard in response to Phillipson's solitary and one-dimensional voice.

Authorial voice, authority and audience

The story of English language teaching and its role in contributing 'constructively to greater linguistic and social equality' and how 'a critical ELT [could] be committed, theoretically and practically, to combating linguicism' (p. 319) certainly warrant extensive and critical discussion. However, from the very first chapter these issues did not command our attention. Instead, Phillipson's rhetoric and ethos dominated class discussions and reaction papers. These initial discussions and responses touched on matters of claims and credibility, style and tone, and terminology and coverage.

Numerous questions concerned his rhetorical style, which some of us characterized as 'aggressive' or, more colloquially, as 'in your face'. We spent considerable time sorting through our negative reactions and trying to understand why even those among us most likely to be in sympathy with his position were offended by his tone and as a result distracted from the story he wanted to tell. Why, the 'closet radicals' among us asked, when reading this cultural critique, a topic of keen interest to us, did we not feel the strong sense of agreement Phillipson expected, but instead had a reaction more like repulsion followed by a grudging sense of agreement?

We found some assertions and terminology potentially puzzling, even insulting, if not simply misleading. One instance was reference to Scandinavia as a 'country' (pp. 17, 25, 317). Those of us from Brazil and Greece, in particular, found *Third World* outdated as well as pejorative. Similarly curious was reference to communicative language teaching as a 'bandwagon' (p. 14), a poor descriptor in our view of an approach to language teaching (and not just of English) which has proven effective in developing learners' ability to interpret, express and negotiate meaning – their own meanings – for nearly three decades in diverse contexts around the world. We were also uncomfortable with the characterization of periphery countries, i.e. those who generally attempt to follow the linguistic norms of the core English-speaking countries, as 'dominated poor ones' (p. 17). As our Japanese classmate pointed out, Japan, with its gross national product second only to the United States, can hardly be considered poor or dominated.

Reliance on opinion, innuendo, and generalization rather than substantiated claims and details also proved troublesome. It seemed to us that the author was more concerned with imposing his views, which we were to accept on faith and not on the basis of evidence that would allow us to draw our own conclusions. For instance, when identities of sources were not given, we were left to guess who or what they might be, e.g.: 'Academic apologists for the spread of English estimate …' (p. 30); 'This proposal is put forward in the pages of a scientific journal …' (pp. 30–1); '… language specialists disconnect culture from structure' (p. 59); and 'one ELT expert in Southern Africa' whose words are cited from a private conversation (p. 239). Passing remarks and comments similarly begged elaboration or explanation, for example: 'many Danes would be alarmed to hear' that English is the second mother tongue of Danes' (p. 9); 'the USA … left Unesco precisely because it could no longer impose its will on that organization' (p. 9); 'The advance of English, whether in Britain, North America, South Africa, Australia or New Zealand has invariably been at the expense of other languages'

(p. 17); ELT professional discourse '*disconnects* culture from structure by limiting its focus to technical matters' (emphasis original, p. 48), and 'Formal education in Africa and Asia in its present form tends to impede economic growth …' (p. 239). Phillipson also claims that 'ELT has not been seen in a wider educational perspective' (p. 251). While he is not explicit on this point, we assume he is speaking of Great Britain, since we know from our own experience this is not the case for the United States.

In Phillipson's discussion of Ronald Wardhaugh's (1987) book, *Languages in Competition: Dominance, Diversity and Decline*, he describes this study as 'mainly anchored in the sociology of language, even if he [Wardhaugh] is a linguist' (p. 101). We were uncertain about the inference we were to draw from 'even if'. Was Phillipson making a statement here about the domain of linguistics and its relation to sociolinguistics? Or about the credentials required to write about the sociology of language, which we were to infer Wardhaugh lacked, and as a consequence he could not be considered qualified to study the same phenomena that Phillipson was investigating?

When evidence for claims was offered, it often struck us as incomplete or misleading. For example, on p. 290 Phillipson tabulates results from a language planning study done by the United Nations Institute for Namibia (UNIN). Unfortunately, the meaning of the table is obscured by missing information. He uses a plus/minus system to code variables, but we are not told what the plus or minus signifies. This omission was curious at a point where Phillipson was attempting to provide 'a more objective measure' than that used in the UNIN report. From our backgrounds in research design we know that statistics can be powerful evidence in making a case when used appropriately. Phillipson, in a description of multilingualism on p. 21, used statistics both as percentages and raw numbers to show the increase in the use of languages other than English in the US:

> In the 1960 census, 11 per cent of Americans declared that a language other than English was their mother tongue (Fishman 1972: 109). Since then, there have been large numbers of Asian and Latin American immigrants. According to the 1980 census, more than 23 million Americans spoke languages other than English in their homes … (King and Vallejo 1986).

However, if accurate, these figures represent a decrease, not an increase in mother tongues since 23 million is just 10% of the 1980 population of 227,726,000.

One of Phillipson's major, if not primary, objectives was exposing the English language and ELT specialists as sources of socio-economic underdevelopment in the so-called Third World. Yet this cause–effect relationship was not transparent to us in spite of our willingness to be introspective about our responsibilities as language teachers. On p. 23 he accused the English language of playing an important role in bringing about the underdeveloped economy and inefficient educational systems in former British colonies. Phillipson seemed to be asserting here that the language and the privilege its speakers enjoy are the sole cause of such socio-economic complications. But this is not necessarily so, since other mitigating factors surely could contribute to a country's weak economic structure or 'backwardness'. This reasoning struck us as fair neither to the language itself, which is incapable of the agency and intentionality implied, nor to the people involved in its spread, the users of English whose internationality is presumed. In either case, making an accusation against English is not the same as offering an argument. It is merely an accusation, nothing more, and as such only diminishes the importance of the issue at hand and ultimately performs a disservice to those whose cause is championed.

By the time we read the last two chapters of *Linguistic Imperialism*, a number of us were losing patience and feeling increasingly hostile toward what we saw as Phillipson's condescending and patronizing attitude toward his readers. This response intensified in chapter 9, 'Arguments in linguistic imperialist discourse', which a few of us considered one of the more convincing chapters. In it Phillipson presents the opposition's views and refutes them, a move we had been expecting much earlier. We were curious about his choice to reverse the more familiar sequence of refutation followed by argumentation, especially since several of us felt that doing so denied us information and perspectives that would have allowed for more informed reading of previous chapters. In chapter 10, the final chapter, Phillipson poses the question: 'Are there periphery-English countries where an increased use of English has been accompanied by less exploitation, more democratization, and prosperity?' (p. 314). At this point, many of us felt particularly manipulated and used; by delaying acknowledgment of this possibility to the very end he had withheld an important consideration from us. If any credibility or authority remained, it was considerably eroded at this point.

Whatever his motives were for what we perceived as a serious lack of awareness of audience or respect for appropriate rhetorical strategies, it would appear that Phillipson was not as consistently cognizant of his own politics as he presumed to be of ours. While he wrote under the guise of theoretical criticism of ELT, he was also ascribing guilt to ELT practitioners. It seems he failed to consider that ELT was his audience, and that since it was an academic one as well, we would therefore be savvy to his confrontational style and language and could deflect this with our own evidence to the obverse. Furthermore, he seemed to assume that we were unaware of the rhetorical tactics used in other radical causes. That we were indeed aware made it especially distressing for many of us to see the similarity of Phillipson's rhetorical strategies of overgeneralizations and unsubstantiated claims to those he philosophically opposes. For example, 'English Only' proponents in the USA in their zeal to deny linguistic rights to language minorities, and to 'enshrine English' (p. 21), as Phillipson characterizes it, present only their side of the issue and play on people's fears and prejudices rather than rely on rational arguments and presentation of both sides of a highly complex and politically charged issue.

Voices from the periphery

To capture differences between the role of English in the countries with which he is concerned, Phillipson uses the label *centre* to characterize the oppressor countries, Great Britain and the USA, and *periphery* to characterize the oppressed countries he is speaking on behalf of, e.g. Namibia or Brazil. We were fortunate that the seminar had representatives from both groups and that those among us from the periphery were willing to share first-hand experiences with the observations of the alleged linguistic hegemony of English in their home countries. We found it enlightening to get views *from representatives of the margins*, rather than simply have Phillipson tell us *about the margins*. The significance for us of hearing these voices, found lacking in Phillipson's presentation, was expressed in a reaction paper:

> These perspectives highlighted the value of such immediate sources in countering the natural human tendency to look at the world from one's own experience and allowed us to reflect on the effects of ELT beyond the limits of personal experience and one's own language, whether on the political right or left.

These voices, then, added depth to the arguments Phillipson presented, both those he refuted and promoted. Of particular value to us was a classmate's account of the role of English in Singapore, her home country. For Phillipson, the situation she describes and represents would be a classic case of hegemony: the colonized, the oppressed – in this case Singaporeans – in accepting the learning and use of English are victims of hegemony from English. This account is excerpted from a reaction paper written mid-way through our reading of *Linguistic Imperialism*:

> English in Singapore has fulfilled a number of conflicting roles simultaneously. This is the language that has helped the growth of solidarity between the 'natives', which has reduced our sense of the foreignness of the foreign power.
> It is natural to think that one would be instinctively resistant to a foreign power which has taken control of one's country and implements a whole new language. However, given the present status of English as an international language and the privileges that attach to it, I feel that former British colonies are fortunate to a certain extent, for, if it had not been for colonization, they might never have achieved the proficiency and competence in the language they now have. The spread of English might not have been so dominant and the development of indigenized varieties, such as Singaporean English, might not have come about at all. I don't think we can deny that it is the colonial linguistic inheritance of English that accounts for much of the phenomenon of World Englishes today.

While this story may fit Phillipson's model of linguistic imperialism and provide evidence of Singapore's *false consciousness*, her narrative did not end here. Later, after this Singaporean related her views to the rest of us, a classmate from Hong Kong asked whether Singaporeans feel proud to be proficient in English. Her written response suggested not only a pragmatic approach to the sociolinguistic reality of English in Singapore, but also a perspective on resolving problems associated with the spread of English.

> I was asked if Singaporeans feel 'proud' to be proficient in the English language. Although it was definitely unpleasant to be colonized by another country, I have to say that the British in one way or another paved the way for the development of Singapore and have educated us in English and have enabled us to benefit from all its advantages as its standing as a global language. However, we have not by any means lost our cultural heritage. Multilingualism is prevalent and we are rich in the use of different languages and dialects, which we speak and use whenever the situation calls for it, depending, for example, upon the listener and context.

> One thing I would like to clarify is that we do not view and value the language in a mercenary sense – we have gone way beyond that. We study and use the language because it has developed into a language of our own that is used comfortably among ourselves – as my family and I do at home – a language we are able to identify and call our own. We are definitely not boastful or conceited in our proficiency in English. In fact, being part of a multilingual community, we feel most comfortable code-switching to another language if it makes the person we are speaking with more at ease.

A means of interpreting this perspective came from another periphery voice. Also speaking in pragmatic terms about the role of English and means of dealing with the reality of its global dominance and spread, a class member from Brazil introduced to our discussions the issue of personal choice, which was not part of Phillipson's narrative. This perspective is important here, we believe, because it represents a different kind of periphery country, one that was not colonized by the British or the United States. Thus it is an illustration of why periphery countries cannot be considered in monolithic terms.

> We live in a world we did not personally choose to be the way it is. Nevertheless, most of us try to make the most of the situations we face in life. Something similar can be said about language and the situation created in the former colonies. Even though the introduction of English was not a personal choice of individuals there, it happened. However, repeating and recounting the event and its consequences will not make the problem go away. Nor will criticizing those individuals who choose to incorporate English into their linguistic repertoire, be it an inner, outer, or expanding circle variety. Might this choice not be a way for them to cope in the best way they can with a situation they did not choose in the first place? For example, one could argue that those learning English or parents who insist upon their children learning English do so as a means of empowering themselves and their children and of widening their range of communication possibilities and thus learning to interact with various networks. Are they necessarily denying their own origins and cultures by doing so? Is it possible that they are making their cultures stronger by learning to negotiate in an international language? The issue of personal choice can be taken a step further when considering the dichotomy of the dominated and the dominating. Do we have to accept one of these roles? Where do we fit if we, as individuals, prefer to think of ourselves as educators who choose to empower others by helping them further their knowledge, develop their abilities and make their own choices?

Solutions and directions for change

The critical analysis of a problem does not necessarily have to be accompanied by a solution. Often problematizing the situation is sufficient for the writer-observer's goal to be met; the readers' consciousness is raised and they themselves are moved to act to improve conditions. And this we believe was a goal of *Linguistic Imperialism* since Phillipson makes reference to the possibility of change at the end of chapter 3: 'The existence of *alternatives* to the prevailing hegemony provides openings both for influencing the dominant order and for challenging it' (emphasis original, p. 76). However, he offered no plan of action, an omission which left us unclear about the changes he would advocate. Without such a plan, how could his goal to inspire activism in us be met? For example, he argued that even though ELT is believed to be non-political, it inevitably lent itself to the achievements of political goals in developing countries. Was he suggesting a total withdrawal from ELT activities in these countries? If so, what new model would he propose to take its place? Similarly, the English language teaching specialists among us were uncertain about how to refer to ourselves after reading chapter 7, 'Creating a profession: the structure and tenets of ELT', where Phillipson questions notions of professionalism as they relate to the practices of ELT and compares these practices to indoctrination. We concluded that in order to be politically correct and enlightened, we were not to consider ourselves language teaching *professionals* because of the negative connotations Phillipson assigns this term. Yet, because he provided no alternatives, we were uncertain just how we were to identify ourselves.

Even if we agreed with his discussion of hegemony and linguistic imperialism, we were still students and teachers of applied linguistics and as such would have welcomed, first, an acknowledgment of the history of the roles of centre and periphery in the production and perpetuation of linguistic imperialism and, second, a directive for making change and progress, a prescription for a solution that would be amenable to both groups. This more productive position would have addressed the key question that begged for an answer: how do we – both groups – break free of the hegemony that Phillipson asserts we help to create and further? Or was Phillipson, by not providing a model, implying that we were to wait for a Paulo Freire to speak for the subordinate group and show the way? Sincere change needs to be effected by the group making the policy, but as Freire (1970) says, there must first be dialogue between oppressor and oppressed. However, we did recognize that, if Phillipson had proposed a solution, he would have written himself out of a job, since with increased independence and a voice for themselves, periphery countries would no longer need him to speak on their behalf.

Narrative as a hegemonic tool

Edward Said (1979) has argued that the dominant group needs the subordinate one to gird its feelings of superiority. At the same time, those who claim some membership in the dominant group do not always blindly perpetuate hegemonic practices, as there are hierarchies within the hegemony, and membership in one stratum does not presuppose membership in them all. This point was illustrated when one of us, speaking from personal experience, observed how being a woman and a Jew in the patriarchal and Christian society of the USA can make one sensitive to inequality and aware that one cannot be allowed to speak for the majority. This observation resonated with all of us – whether from the border region of Mexico and Texas or a periphery country, whether male or female, or of middle class urban or working class rural background – and deepened our understanding of the nature of hegemony.

Ultimately, we learned that hegemony can occur on a smaller scale, as when the reader of a book begins to believe what the writer believes, or when the reader internalizes what the writer proposes even though such acceptance of the writer's ideas and beliefs may not objectively be in the reader's best interest. Our reading of *Linguistic Imperialism* is such a case. While Phillipson was concerned with exposing the hegemonic agenda of ELT professionals and representatives of American and other center-country aid agencies, we grew increasingly aware of *his* hegemonic agenda. Phillipson has argued that ELT is political in that it has had an agenda all along. Not only did his rhetoric parallel this position, it represented his argument. He wanted us to see several features of ELT: that it has been a dominating force within periphery country cultures; that ELT specialists have used the English language and its culture as a force to eliminate other languages and cultures; and, finally, that we as ELT specialists – from either the center or periphery – have been personally and collectively responsible for the success of the ELT project. For us, the process of reading his argument resulted in conflict and confusion while we experienced a range of reactions from mild amusement to disappointment to extreme offense. For eight chapters we were carried along on a narrative that relentlessly drove Phillipson's point home. Then came the last two chapters which struck us as so anticlimactic, as if they were an afterthought, that we were not quite sure how to interpret them and their relation to the previous chapters. The outcome was that we resigned ourselves to acceptance of his complacent regard for the English language and where it stands today: on the verge of becoming a world language.

Throughout the book we felt that Phillipson was seeking to impose his agenda and to dominate us through the imperialism of the printed word. By being told what we should believe rather than being allowed the experience of discovery and then understanding, we grew to resent his paternalism and as a result felt colonized in a sense by his authorial imperialism. Therein lies the textual analogy that Phillipson either deliberately or inadvertently created to represent linguistic imperialism and its aftermath. We say *deliberately* because the power structure he outlined followed the narrative structure of *Linguistic Imperialism*, and *inadvertently* because it could be pure chance that the structure and rhetorical strategies of the book so intensely gave us the flavor of what a dominated culture might feel when it becomes the victim of oppression.

Conclusion

Phillipson's book is about his engagement in social and political activism and his commitment to championing increased sensitivity to the language policy and planning dilemmas created in multilingual settings by the dominance of one language or language variety. We applauded this activist stance and found refreshing the idealism and fervor he brought to solving problems of language and identity. We also shared his outrage and sense of injustice at the linguistic condition that can prevail where English has been imposed by force, and at the oppression and loss of autonomy perpetrated by purveyors of English.

However, our approval and empathy were significantly tempered by our response to his style, which struck us as inappropriate. We did not seem to be the intended audience; yet we felt strongly that his story and its implications and ramifications were indeed relevant to us – language researchers and teachers from around the world – and that we must indeed be the audience he wanted to reach since we had the most to learn from his story. Yet we were not reached. Phillipson intended to write a narrative of hegemony, but he produced a hegemonic narrative instead. As a result, we were not converted, only provoked (and not in the way he probably intended), and he lost us as an audience. But this was his loss alone; we only gained from reading this book. By writing as he did, Phillipson served as a lightning rod which sparked valuable discussion in which we could articulate assumptions and work out conflicts which would not have arisen otherwise. *Linguistic Imperialism* gave us something to react against and a means for strengthening our own perspectives as we resisted Phillipson's. And in this process of intellectual exploration and development, we came to value even more the need to hear and consider multiple voices and multiple views. For it is through all of our stories, we believe, that Phillipson's goal of a more profound understanding of English as a world language and of the role of language specialists in its learning can be attained.

Notes

1   Margie Berns led the seminar in which the other authors were enrolled. All authors thank their partners, friends, and each other for feedback, commentary and encouragement on the concept and content of the project. Special thanks to the members of the Women's Writing Group and to Tony Silva, all of Purdue, for thoughtful and thought-provoking critiques of the manuscript throughout its development.

References

Bisong, J. (1995) Language choice and cultural imperialism: a Nigerian perspective. *ELT Journal* 49.2: 122–32.

Davies, A. (1996) Ironising the myth of linguicism: review article. *Journal of Multilingual and Multicultural Development* 17.6: 485–96.

Freire, P. (1970) *Pedagogy of the oppressed.* New York: Continuum.

Holborrow, M. (1993) Review of the book *Linguistic Imperialism. ELT Journal* 47.4: 358–60.

Kachru, B. (1992) The second diaspora of English. In T. W. Machan & C. T. Scott (eds.) *English in its social contexts.* New York: Oxford University Press. 230–52.

— (ed.) (1992) *The other tongue: English across cultures.* Urbana, IL: University of Illinois Press.

Phillipson, R. (1992) *Linguistic imperialism.* Oxford University Press.

Said, E. (1979) *Orientalism.* New York: Vintage.

Wardhaugh, R. (1987) *Languages in competition: dominance, diversity and decline.* Oxford: Blackwell.

Text 4

Robert Phillipson
University of Roskilde, Denmark

Linguistic imperialism re-visited – or re-invented. A rejoinder to a review essay

It is a semiotic axiom that reception of a product is not determined by the sender of the message. Information on how a book is received, understood, and interpreted is thus helpful and healthy for any author to receive. But scholarly

they interpreted so badly, maybe you weren't clear enough in the first place

dialogue can only generate light as well as heat if there is a fair measure of consensus about the code and the object of the communication. I cannot dispute the validity of the feelings that my book is reported as having aroused in contributors to the review essay by Berns et al. (1998). What I can question is the misrepresentation of what my book states, and how it is portrayed in the report from this graduate class. The essay contains a clutch of factual errors and claims that can easily be ascertained if the original work is consulted each time a page reference is given. More fundamentally, the review is:

biased, in that clearly my book asks uncomfortable questions of those whose business is promoting the learning of English, but to blame the messenger and the packaging of the message is an easy form of escape from the issues raised in the book;

Are they not free to defend themselves?

theoretically inconsistent, in that although the experience of reading the work has triggered a great deal of reflection, key concepts are misapplied when I am accused of authorial imperialism; since my views form part of scholarly dialogue, I have no structural power, hegemonic or imperialist, to dictate how others should respond to the work;

internally inconsistent, in that I am simultaneously charged with being patronising while being accused of not providing solutions to the dilemmas the graduate students find themselves in;

unfair, when accusing me of speaking on behalf of people in the periphery, and failing to point out that my own understanding of the complexity of English world-wide has been profoundly influenced by scholars from the periphery;

perverse, in that claims are attributed to me that are the opposite of what I state in the book (e.g. treating periphery countries in a monolithic way, ELT as the sole cause of socio-economic underdevelopment, ...);

selective, for instance a Singapore participant's observations on English in Singapore are cited but not that I explore the topic in the book in a far from simplistic way (pp. 314–7);

one-sided, in that critiques of my work are quoted but not my responses to these (Phillipson 1996, 1997).

I too

So all in all I must admit that I am not too disturbed by a review led by Margie Berns, granted that reviews by eminent scholars have called the book 'a benchmark' (Fishman), 'brilliant' (Tollefson), and 'required reading for all concerned with the development and implementation of language policy' (Spolsky). I have been told by some ESL teachers that it has changed their lives, individual scholars from several Asian countries have offered to translate it, and it has been interestingly followed up in a range of post-communist and post-colonial contexts.

blah blah blah

I would, however, be the first to agree that the book is far from being, and never claims to be, the last word on linguistic imperialism but represents an initial step on a long tortuous journey, with many competing narratives and interpretations. For those interested in exploring the validity of the conceptual framework of linguistic imperialism and the empirical reality of linguistic imperialism in different parts of the world, see Fishman, Conrad & Rubal-Lopez (eds., 1996), my review of this (1999a), and Ricento (1999). Interested scholars are welcome to consult my home page, which lists all my publications, or to contact me on e-mail for a complete list of reviews of the book.
http://www.babel.ruc.dk/~robert/

approved reviews!

References

Berns, Margie et al. (15 named graduate students at Purdue University) (1998)
(Re)experiencing hegemony: the linguistic imperialism of Robert Phillipson.
Review essay. *International Journal of Applied Linguistics* 8.2: 271–82.
Fishman, J., Conrad, A. W. & Rubal-Lopez, A. (eds.) (1996) *Post-imperial English:
status change in former British and American colonies, 1940–1990.* Berlin &
New York: Mouton de Gruyter. (*Contributions to the Sociology of Language* 72.)
Phillipson, R. (1992) *Linguistic imperialism.* Oxford University Press.
—— (1996) Linguistic imperialism – African perspectives. *English Language
Teaching Journal* 50.2: 160–7.
—— (1997) Realities and myths of linguistic imperialism. *Journal of Multilingual
and Multicultural Development* 18.3: 238–47.
—— (1998) Globalizing English: are linguistic human rights an alternative to
linguistic imperialism? *Language Sciences* 20.1: 101–12.
—— (1999a) Review of Fishman, Conrad & Rubal-Lopez (eds.) (1996) *Post-
imperial English. Language.*
—— (1999b) Going beyond diagnoses of linguistic imperialism. In Ricento (ed.)
Ideology, politics and language policies.
Ricento, Tom (ed.) (1999) *Ideology, politics and language policies.* Amsterdam:
John Benjamins.

Text 5

Margie Berns, Jeanelle Barrett, Chak Chan, Yoshiki Chikuma,
Patricia Friedrich, Olga-Maria Hadjidimos, Jill Harney,
Kristi Hislope, David Johnson, Suzanne Kimball, Yvonne Low,
Tracey McHenry, Vivienne Palaiologos, Marnie Petray,
Rebecca Shapiro, and Ana Ramirez Shook
Purdue University

Hegemonic discourse revisited

*It is necessary to trust in the oppressed and in their ability to reason. Whoever
lacks this trust will fail to initiate (or will abandon) dialogue, reflection, and
communication, and will fall into using slogans, communiqués, monologues, and
instructions.*
Paulo Freire (1970: 53)

In our review essay we raise several questions and issues regarding the content,
style, and tone of Robert Phillipson's book. Specific examples with page numbers
and citations are provided to illustrate and support such claims and concerns as
vagueness in identifying sources to support assertions (p. 275), mixing of
percentages and raw numbers in the presentation of statistical data (p. 276), or
employment of particular rhetorical strategies (p. 277). In his rejoinder, rather
than address such issues or answer our questions, Professor Phillipson responds
with name-calling, applying the labels *unfair, perverse, selective, one-sided,
biased, theoretically inconsistent,* and *internally inconsistent.* The following
addresses each of these attributions and shows that the theoretical, professional,

and epistemological issues associated with each are considerably more complex and consequential than his facile treatment of them implies.

Professor Phillipson says it is 'unfair' to fail to mention that scholars from the periphery have profoundly influenced him when he is 'accused' in the review of speaking on behalf of people in the periphery. The question of periphery scholars' influence on his understanding, however deep, is not at issue in our review. What is of concern is the value and necessity of hearing actual voices and views from the periphery (p. 277) that provide rich perspectives on and insights into the complexity of English worldwide.

According to Professor Phillipson we are 'perverse' for attributing claims to him which, he says, are the opposite of what is stated in the book. However, without evidence or precise references to particular passages in his book, we cannot address this concern. If mistakes have been made in attribution, we regret them.

The terms 'selective' and 'one-sided' are used to identify alleged omissions of relevant information. 'Selective' is our failure to cite the passage in his book that explores the topic of English in Singapore (pp. 314–7) when in our review the Singaporean's own account of English in her country is cited (p. 278). It is not our intention to suggest that he did not explore the topic in the book or that he did so in other than 'a far from simplistic way'. Rather, our purpose is to balance an outsider's narrative with insiders' first-hand accounts of life with English on the periphery – experiences as legitimate as any exploration undertaken by an outsider.

Professor Phillipson claims it is 'one-sided' to leave out citations of his responses to the critiques of his work that are cited in the review, namely, Bisong (1995), Davies (1996), and Holborrow (1993) (p. 272). The relevance for including his reactions to other critics is unclear, as the scope of our essay is restricted to his book and does not extend to his responses of others' reviews. Our citation of previously published book reviews, a practice consistent with scholarly writing, is to distinguish our focus and approach from those taken by other scholars.

With regard to the question of selectivity, Professor Phillipson decontextualizes what Joshua Fishman and Bernard Spolsky have said about his book when he cites them as scholars who have praised his work. Fishman does call the book a 'benchmark', and Spolsky identifies it as 'required reading'. However, the larger context of these selected quotations shows that they had much more to say which is not so positive. Fishman writes:

> The analysis of a worldwide data-set is probably most in need of such methodological checks because, in addition to the danger of self-confirming hypotheses, no one researcher can fully digest all of the data needed (quite a bit more being needed than the rather limited interviews and documents Phillipson analyzes) in order to come to solid conclusions … . His book will obviously become a benchmark, argument-presenting rather than conclusion-clinching though it be, both for those who agree with his premises and methods as well as for those who think social sciences and serious social commentary or exposé should differ in their approaches to evidence and to proof. (1993: 400)

And while Spolsky does close his review by saying the book is 'required reading', earlier he states that 'the broadness of coverage and the selectivity of citation to support the polemic detract from the confidence one has in his general arguments, which require much more hard evidence' (1995: 233). Such qualified praise of

Professor Phillipson's book echoes concerns raised in our review and complements other matters we address, especially the central issues of right to language choice, periphery representation, and authorial responsibility.

In using the label 'biased', Professor Phillipson asserts that we escape dealing with an unpleasant message by blaming the messenger and 'the packaging'. He cites the (unattributed) semiotic axiom that the sender of the message does not determine reception of a product. Thus, for him, the messenger is separate from the message, rhetorical and linguistic choices are neutral, and it is possible to simply report the news without making news. Regardless of whether or not he firmly holds to this epistemologically naïve position, his suggestion that by focusing on 'the packaging' we took an 'easy form of escape' from the issues in his book is unfounded. While the review's stated purpose is 'an account of difficulties found with Phillipson's rhetorical style and of insights gained into the discourse of linguistic hegemony' (p. 272), it also documents ways in which the complex issues associated with English in the world were grappled with, as in the following:

> We ... found much to discuss and debate with respect to Phillipson's account and analysis of English and English language teaching (ELT) world-wide. Spirited, often passionate dialogue was the norm as we argued for or against points he was attempting to make or tried to clarify our own positions on the issues he presented ... we spent a lot of time seeking to understand and interpret Phillipson's account of linguistic imperialism and trying to find meaningful connections to existing knowledge and to our interests in English language teaching. (p. 272)

Subsequent pages report the Hong Konger's strong identification with the conditions the book described (p. 274), the Singaporean's response to the significance English has for her (p. 278), and the Brazilian's perspective on the role of personal choice in the spread of English (p. 279).

When he is charged with authorial imperialism, Professor Phillipson responds that 'key concepts are misapplied' and we are 'theoretically inconsistent'. He explains that, since his 'views form part of scholarly dialogue', he has 'no power, either structural, hegemonic or imperialist, to dictate how others should respond'. This position is curious for two reasons. First, if he has no power, how is it that his book 1) was published by an international publisher of the stature of Oxford University Press; 2) has been so widely reviewed; and, 3) as he points out, has changed people's lives? Second, if scholars have no structural authority or authorial power, why, in his declaration that he is 'not too disturbed' by our review, does he find it necessary to invoke the names of 'eminent' scholars and cite their praise of his book? We can only infer that scholars, accomplished ones in particular, do have positions of power within structures that enable and influence scholarship and its dissemination.

Professor Phillipson says it is 'internally inconsistent' to simultaneously charge him with being patronizing and to accuse him of not offering solutions and directions for change. In the review (pp. 279–80), we ask for proposals, plans of action, and alternative models of ELT, directives and solutions that the reader can consider as solutions for change. Offering of ideas and strategies, which is constructive, is quite different from telling readers – either explicitly or implicitly – what to believe, which is condescending. This is noted in our discussion of his use of narrative as a hegemonic tool:

Throughout the book we felt that Phillipson was seeking to impose his agenda and to dominate us through the imperialism of the printed word. By being told what we should believe rather than being allowed the experience of discovery and then understanding, we grew to resent his paternalism and as a result felt colonized in a sense by his authorial imperialism. (p. 281)

Professor Phillipson's book has enjoyed considerable success and has influenced English as a Second Language studies as well as individual lives. As stated in the review, we too

gained from reading this book. By writing as he did, Phillipson served as a lightning rod which sparked valuable discussion in which we could articulate assumptions and work out conflicts which would not have arisen otherwise. (p. 281–2)

His response to our essay has provided another opportunity for negotiation of meaning through interaction with message, messenger, and medium. Professor Phillipson states in his rejoinder that 'scholarly dialogue can only generate light as well as heat if there is a fair measure of consensus about the code and the object of the communication'. If this is so, then failure to address concerns and questions raised in a critical review, refusal to provide evidence for claims, and assuming a position of superiority over those who seek dialogue make such consensus difficult, if not impossible. By choosing to package his message in a discourse that is unceasingly hegemonic, Professor Phillipson ignores issues and questions raised in the review. Consequently, we still wait for answers to major concerns – both theoretical and empirical.

References

Bisong, J. (1995) Language choice and cultural imperialism: a Nigerian perspective. *ELT Journal* 49.2: 122–32.

Davies, A. (1996) Ironising the myth of linguicism: review article. *Journal of Multilingual and Multicultural Development* 17.6: 485–96.

Fishman, J. (1993) Review of *Linguistic imperialism. Modern Language Journal* 77: 399–400.

Freire, P. (1970) *Pedagogy of the oppressed.* New York: Continuum.

Holborrow, M. (1993) Review of the book *Linguistic imperialism. ELT Journal* 47.4: 358–60.

Phillipson, R. (1992) *Linguistic imperialism.* Oxford University Press.

Spolsky, B. (1995) Review of *Linguistic imperialism. Journal of Pragmatics* 23. 227–33.

Text 6

Robert Phillipson

A closing word

My rejoinder did not go into detail with specific points made in the review by Berns et al. but suggested that there were many factual errors and false claims that could easily be ascertained if my book is consulted each time Berns et al. refer to particular pages. This still holds. Doing this would be more productive than accusing me of failing to answer questions. What I can exemplify here is the way in which mis-readings of my text (now my rejoinder as well as the book) are used as a prop for attributions which are pure fantasy.

My rejoinder distinguishes between the messenger, the packaging of the message, and issues. This observation leads Berns et al. to falsely ascribe to me a scholarly position in which 'rhetorical and linguistic choices are neutral' and related charges. This is a curious attribution when clearly much of the book has to do with applied linguists needing to critically examine concepts and the professional traditions and tenets that we have adopted, often in a rather unconscious way. Not surprisingly this is noticed by acute readers such as Joshua Fishman (in the review already referred to), who praises the book for 'fostering the auto-critical sensitivities of the English teaching profession and of sociolinguistics as a whole'. Berns et al. repeatedly use the rhetorical strategy of erecting an inventive and invented platform upon which to make further denunciations and unwarranted generalisations. Accusing me of epistemological naivety, authorial power, and hegemony does not make the attributions any less false.

Hopefully readers will choose to spend more time on the book itself than this puzzling but frustrating debate.

Margie Berns *et al.*
A closing word

We along with Professor Phillipson hope that readers will become familiar with his book as well as with our critique and draw their own conclusions.

It will be apparent that many of the concepts and terms discussed in the above papers relate to the first controversy, such as Kachru's inner, outer, and expanding circles. Other ideas and arguments mentioned in passing here take centre stage in the next exchange, notably Phillipson's insistence that the social sciences ought to figure much more prominently in discussions of English as a global language, as well as in the study of language learning and teaching.

While Berns *et al.* is an account of how the participants in a graduate seminar reacted to *Linguistic Imperialism,* and so puts Robert Phillipson in the role of an author whose work is scrutinized, the tables are turned in this next controversy, in which Phillipson is a reviewer, and the book reviewed is David Crystal's *English as a Global Language.* As the editors of *Applied Linguistics* explain,

When the review was published it had already appeared in a similar but shorter version in the *European English Messenger* (EEM), the publication of ESSE, the European Society for the Study of English. Since then there has been a reply by Crystal and a further response by Phillipson in the *EEM.*

It is not the general policy of *Applied Linguistics* to republish material that has already appeared in any form elsewhere, but in the circumstances we feel that it is appropriate to publish a reply by Crystal.
(*Applied Linguistics* 21/3, 2000: 415)

Since it is hoped that readers of this book will by now have got into the (irre-sistible) habit of reading closely and critically, they might wonder what the logical relationship is between the two paragraphs quoted above: if it is 'not the general policy of *Applied Linguistics* to republish material that has already appeared in any form elsewhere', then why, one might ask, was Phillipson's review republished in an extended form, and why is the explanation about the prior publication of the papers by both authors only given as a preliminary remark introducing Crystal's reply, rather than Phillipson's review in the previous volume of *Applied Linguistics*? This is by no means a rhetorical question – the answer is not known to the present writer. But it is the sort of question which inevitably poses itself once one has switched into the sceptical reading mode this volume seeks to encourage.

Another such question concerns the terminology editors use for the categories of contributions that journals publish. *Applied Linguistics* has two main kinds, articles and reviews. Phillipson's paper is called a 'review article' – a term usually employed for a review of several books on a similar subject, for example, '(new) books on pronunciation teaching'. In this case, however, Phillipson takes Crystal's book as a starting point for a discussion of issues which he argues are dealt with either inadequately or not at all (but should have been). In his response, Crystal quotes 'a truth recently reiterated by Alberto Manguel':

> a reviewer is a reader once removed, guiding the reader, not through the book, but through the reviewer's reading of that book (Manguel 1999: 217).

Here, then, is Phillipson guiding us through his reading of Crystal's book, and then Crystal guiding us through his reading of Phillipson's review, followed by Phillipson guiding us through his reading of Crystal's reading:

Text 7

Robert Phillipson

**Voice in Global English:
Unheard Chords in Crystal Loud and Clear**

David Crystal: *English as a Global Language*. Cambridge University Press 1997

> The story of English throughout the period is one of rapid expansion and
> diversification, with innovation after innovation coming to use the language as
> a primary or sole means of expression. It is not possible to identify cause or
> effect. So many developments were taking place at the same time that we can
> only point to the emergence, by the end of the nineteenth century, of a climate
> of largely unspoken opinion which had made English the natural choice for
> progress (p. 75).

At the end of the twentieth century David Crystal sees English as symbiotically linked to 'progress'. The questions that he explores in this slim volume are of momentous importance. The fates of the world's citizens are increasingly decided on in English, so there is every reason to explore whether there are links of cause and effect between global English and the processes and structures that it is involved in. Crystal's book ignores the fact that global (and local) inequalities are increasing, and that the 'innovations' of the global system are having catastrophic ecological and cultural effects. He sees no causal relationship between the globalization of English and the demise of other languages, which are apparently not 'the natural choice for progress'. To write the story of 'English as a global language' in the form of a book for the general public, Crystal has had to address fundamental and challenging issues of approach and validity in relating value judgements and ideological preferences to types of data and permissible generalizations. English is now so ubiquitous, interlocking with social phenomena and with other languages in so many diverse ways, that there are serious methodological and ethical problems in selecting, packaging, explaining and interpreting the topic.

Crystal is an eminent scholar and popularizer, several of whose earlier books I admire. This book is intended, according to the cover blurb, for 'anyone of any nationality concerned with English: teachers, students, language professionals, politicians, general readers and anyone with a love of the language'. A global audience indeed. This involves the author in needing to face at least two daunting challenges: how to remain scholarly in unravelling the interconnections between English and the multiple purposes it serves in what Crystal regards as a political minefield, and how a British view can present itself as universally relevant and appropriate. In my view the book fails on both scores, and granted Crystal's reputation, influence, and substantial rhetorical skills, needs very careful scrutiny.

The book is structured around three basic questions: what makes a world language, why is English the leading candidate, and will it continue to hold that position? There is an introductory general chapter, followed by a historical run-through of the establishment of English worldwide, a chapter on 'the cultural foundation', with sub-sections entitled political developments, access to knowledge, and 'taken for granted'; a chapter on 'the cultural legacy' with sub-sections on international relations, the media, travel, safety, education, and communications, and a concluding section, 'the right place at the right time'; and a final chapter called 'the future of global English', with sub-sections on the rejection of English, new Englishes, fragmentation of the language, and the uniqueness of global English. In fact nearly half of this chapter is devoted to the current debate in the US about English Only legislation, implying that Crystal's understanding is that the internal affairs of the present-day US are central to the future of 'global' English. This seems to be endorsing what George Bernard Shaw presciently wrote in 1912, 'what has been happening in my lifetime is the Americanization of the world' (cited in Holroyd 1997: 660).

Crystal claims that the book is without 'any political agenda'. He stakes out this defensive position since he does not wish to be identified with the protagonists of US English, who first commissioned a work from him on global English. But surely even the wish to be apolitical involves political choices, not least in relation to choice of scientific disciplines that can clarify his questions, their procedures and epistemological roots. While he draws on information from a wide variety of sources, his loyalty is to linguistics (e.g. p. 113), which is of little avail when studying colonialism, globalization, cultural hegemony, education, and the media, and even when defining multilingualism, official, national and minority languages. Lack of any grounding in the social sciences is a major weakness of the work.

'History'

The area that Crystal does attempt to draw on is 'history', but I doubt whether many historians would be impressed. In the sections referred to as 'America' (oops, he does not mean the two continents, but the USA – this terminology is not merely a slip, his synecdoche reflects a hegemonic preference), 'Canada', and 'The Caribbean' (pp. 26–35), there is no reference to the First Nations, the indigenous peoples and their languages, except when he notes that the 'explorers' encountered 'conflict with the native people'. The continent is presented as though there were no languages before Europeans took over. Amerindian languages do not warrant a mention.

When presenting the story of the dominance of English in the main 'English-speaking' countries, he writes:

> No special mention is made of English in any of the documents which are significant for the history of Britain, and English has never been formally declared the official language of that country. Nor was English singled out for mention when the Constitution of the United States was being written. Rulings are needed to regulate conflict. If there is no conflict, there is no need for rulings. (p. 75)

How can anyone suggest that language issues have been free of conflict in Ireland, Scotland and Wales, or the USA? Or that documents confirming the dominance of English were never written (Crystal himself refers to Macaulay's celebrated minute on language in India, which set the tone for the entire colonial education adventure), laws enacted, and policies implemented? There is a huge literature on these issues, British (e.g. Crowley 1991, 1996) and North American (e.g. Heath and Mandabach 1983, Crawford 1992, Hernández-Chávez 1994).

The description of South Africa (pp. 38–41) manages not to refer to apartheid or to name any African languages. The Indians that were brought over as indentured labour from 1860, and who had few rights, linguistic or other, prior to 1991, are described as having 'arrived'. 'White government' is a careless reference to Afrikaners in power (white South Africans of non-Boer origins were not in political power after 1947). The reference to 'South African politicians in recent years' is to Afrikaners, hence excludes Nelson Mandela (whose Afrikaans was learned late in life). This invisibilization of blacks (in parallel with that of the indigenous groups in the Americas) is well, let us say, a trifle eurocentric and scarcely appropriate for someone wishing to address a 'global' audience. 'National' identity would also need more careful handling, so as to distinguish a Zulu or Xhosa 'nation' from a South African one.

Overall what is missing is any presentation of the way multilingualism has been managed in South Africa throughout this century. There is only passing reference to the exciting efforts currently under way to implement a multilingual policy as a key feature of the new dispensation, and on which there is a copious scientific literature (e.g. Heugh *et al.* 1995; Barkhuizen and Gough 1996; McLean and McCormick 1996; Webb 1996) as well as the key language policy document, the LANGTAG Report (1996). There is a fascinating unresolved tension in contemporary South Africa between the thrust of English and official multilingualism. South African policy-makers are also well aware of the way English serves the interests of elites rather than the entire population in most of its neighbouring countries, for instance in Namibia (Pütz 1995), which Crystal inexplicably omits to cover, along with Botswana and Lesotho, in the section on 'former colonial Africa'.

This might be because Namibia was never technically a British colony, but probably has more to do with Crystal's attempt to pack the 'historical context' of English of a large number of countries into very limited space. This leads to bald and selective coverage: Cameroon is described as highly multilingual, Nigeria with its 400+ languages not so. Ghana was 'the first Commonwealth country to achieve independence'. What about India, Pakistan, Ceylon, Burma, not to mention the dominions? (Some of the formulations, and inexactitudes, are lifted verbatim from Crystal's *Cambridge Encyclopedia of the English Language*, CUP 1995.) There is no reference to the many African scholars who have pleaded for the upgrading of African languages and denounced 'aid' that strengthens European languages.

Fundamentally Crystal's story of globalizing English is eurocentric and triumphalist, despite his protestations to the contrary. Military conquest is identified in Crystal's general introduction as an essential phase in global conquest (p. 7), but his narrative avoids any upsetting talk of bloodshed, let alone that what colonizers saw as triumph involved capitulation and domination for others. Thus he refers soothingly to a 'successful British expedition against the Ashanti to protect trading interests'. The struggle for Kenya's freedom from colonial rule involved a spot of 'unrest (the Mau Mau rebellion)'. In describing the transfer of power in Zimbabwe, white Rhodesia's Unilateral Declaration of Independence is mentioned, but not its illegality, nor anything as messy as a war of liberation. One can only hope that history writing for British schools has progressed beyond this eurocentric one-sidedness. Couldn't decolonizing the mind (Ngũgĩ's book is quoted 114–5) be a task as much for Europeans as Africans?

Language and global relations

Crystal rightly notes in his introductory chapter that military success paves the way for a relationship in which economic matters are paramount. He even once refers to 'economic imperialism' (p. 74), but distances himself from such an unpalatable term by putting it in inverted commas. Nor does he reflect on whether economic and linguistic under-development might be inter-related, such that, for instance, the parlous state of publishing in most postcolonial states is connected to market forces that benefit British publishers, in an unequal relationship that is skewed in favour of the strong.

Crystal does not assess whether linguistic imperialism, however it is defined, has ever existed, or might still do so, which is puzzling, granted that theory-building, description and analysis of linguistic dominance are flourishing (e.g. Tollefson 1991; Phillipson 1992a; Dasgupta 1993; Dendrinos 1993; Pennycook 1994; Mühlhäusler 1996; Fishman *et al.* 1996; Kachru 1997), reflecting a variety of approaches and interpretations.

Crystal does not explore the unpleasant fact that most former colonies are now undemocratic, even if (or perhaps partly because?) they have maintained English as the official language, and the majority of the population in post-colonial states are governed in a language that they do not understand, and live in abject conditions. He does little to explain why the linguistic hierarchies imposed in the colonial age largely still remain in place. The uncomfortable and tragic fact is that the present world order clearly serves the interests of some – the West and the elites who collaborate with them – better than others. Without appropriate language policies the global system would not function.

A recent study of British foreign policy since 1945 begins by stating: 'It appears to be a widely held assumption that Britain (and indeed the Western states as a whole) promotes certain grand principles – peace, democracy, human rights and economic development in the Third World – as natural corollaries to the basic political and economic priorities that guide its foreign policy' (Curtis 1995: 1). Curtis's book documents in great detail how false this view is, and how the media have uncritically promoted this deceptive vision. His concluding chapter states:

> One basic fact – of perhaps unparalleled importance – has permeated a number of studies and is well understood: the mass poverty and destitution that exist in much of the Third World are direct products of the structure of the international system. Moreover, an elementary truth is that the world's powerful states have pursued policies with regard to the Third World which knowingly promote poverty. (Curtis 1995: 236)

Crystal's apparent assumption that English is exclusively for the good in North–South relations seems to prevent him from probing into just how the position of English has been achieved and from attempting to assess the significance of the various factors that figure in his narrative. He writes blithely that during the twentieth century the world presence of English 'was maintained and promoted, almost single-handedly, through the economic supremacy of the new American superpower' (p. 8). Single-handedly? What about World Bank policies? Development 'aid'? Post-colonial education? The publishing business (not least the Cambridge and Oxford University Presses, Longman *et al.*) that makes English Language Teaching (selectively reported on, p. 103) a multi-billion pound global business? British academics have drawn considerable profit (in several senses) from the patronage of the British Council and publishers (trips globally to lecture, donations of books, etc.). There are ethical problems in all such activities (Kaplan 1995; Hamelink 1997; Swales 1997, Tomaševski 1997). Applied linguistics involves addressing serious ethical questions (see, for instance, the thematic number on this topic of *Issues in Applied Linguistics* 4/2: 1993).

Many ethical issues are directly related to 'world' English, its conceptualization, forms and functions. For instance, the post-communist world has been exposed to a great deal of scientific and linguistic contact with western interests in recent years, in a fundamentally asymmetrical relationship between scholars in east and west. The implications are becoming increasingly clear to those at the consuming end of global English. The distinguished Hungarian linguist Miklós Kontra reports (personal communication, 17 December 1997):

> I am increasingly coming to the conviction that the international language English not only opens gates but closes them too. It closes the gates of

information flow in all cases where what does get translated into English is partial, inadequate, uninformed, etc. And there are an embarrassingly large number of such cases even within such a field as sociolinguistics.

Kontra has also drawn to my attention a lively debate in Hungary on 'Colonisation or partnership? Eastern Europe and western social sciences' – see the special issue of *replika*, 1996, which is concerned with issues of scientific agenda-setting and funding, of national scholarship and global – meaning largely American – interventions and pressures.

What I am basically suggesting is that Crystal's book contains a narrative with selective exemplification, much of the data being, as one would expect, factually correct (with surprising errors, see also below), but that his own agenda has a free run, granted that the apparatus of scholarly documentation has been avoided, ostensibly since this is a popularizing book. There are therefore very considerable types of information that are simply excluded, namely those that do not fit into the world-view underpinning his narrative.

Language in education

Crystal's admission that there are other views is reflected in quotations from Gandhi and Ngũgĩ 'rejecting' English (114–5), however the implications of this position are buried in comments on the expense of bilingualism. He does not name counter-examples, such as Scandinavian competence in English being compatible with all affairs being conducted in local languages. Nor reflect on the cultural distance between the world of English and education for cultural continuity or subsistence farming needs in Africa. Ngũgĩ has in fact nothing against the English language as such. What he objects to are the purposes to which it is put in Kenya and global capitalism (Ngũgĩ 1993). Critical intellectuals in countries like Kenya end up in prison (without charge or trial) and exile, their voices unheeded by decision-makers locally and globally.

Language in education policy is a clear instance of where Crystal writes as though he is unaware of the relevant literature. In his attempt to present both sides of the US official English story, he goes through the political and socio-economic arguments for and against, but when he gets to the educational issues, he abandons this structure, noting that 'it is too complex an area to be given summary treatment in the present book' (p. 127). The same could be said for Crystal's entire enterprise: he has unjustifiably over-simplified the complexity and reality of global English. In relation to educational language policy, I can think of a dozen scholars who would be able to summarize the issues concisely, for instance the contributors from Belgium, California, Australia, Austria, Canada, Spain, Estonia, Russia, India and New York to Tove Skutnabb-Kangas's book *Multilingualism for All* (1995). Closer to Crystal's Welsh home, there are distinguished scholars (see Baker 1993), but none, significantly but not surprisingly, from England. Few if any scholars in bilingual education or foreign language pedagogy would endorse without qualification the belief that 'the earlier the better' is the key solution to second or foreign language learning (p. 15), since there is massive scientific evidence to the contrary, and looking at a single factor such as age is educationally unsound.

The English Only movement has spawned a substantial literature, so that the idea that arguments for what is 'a bad cure for an imaginary disease' (Nunberg 1997: 44) can be loyally and neutrally presented as though they are equally valid seems to me to be a denial of scholarly responsibility. The intellectual community in the United States, including the most prestigious professional associations working with language, is massively against English Only. One would not suspect this from reading Crystal's book.

The assumption that experts from countries such as the UK or the US, deeply monolingual and with a very patchy record of foreign language learning, can contribute to policy on education and language matters in multilingual societies is completely counter-intuitive. However this is one of the 'triumphs' of the English Language Teaching business. Though the ideologies and practices of this paradigm are increasingly being questioned by critical intellectuals in North and South, linguistic hierarchies reminiscent of the colonial period, and master-minded by the type of linguistics and applied linguistics department that Crystal used to work for, still underpin much World Bank and IMF education policy, which currently sets the tone for 'aid' alongside notoriously anti-social, poverty-inducing structural adjustment policies:

> the World Bank's real position ... encourages the consolidation of the imperial languages in Africa ... the World Bank does not seem to regard the linguistic Africanisation of the whole of primary education and beyond as an effort that is worth its consideration. Its publication on strategies for stabilising and revitalising universities, for example makes absolutely no mention of the place of language at this tertiary level of African education. (Mazrui 1997: 39)

A set of agenda-setting World Bank reports on basic education in eastern African countries barely refers to local languages (see Phillipson 1992b). The ensuing educational 'aid' reflects the belief that only European languages are suited to the task of developing African economies and minds, the falsity of which many African scholars have shown, Ansre, Bamgbose, Kashoki, Mateene, Ngũgĩ (references in Phillipson 1992a). Even the World Bank is currently reassessing its policies, since educational results are poor when mother tongues are neglected (Dutcher 1997).

Language rights

Another area that Crystal's book might have drawn inspiration from is language rights (see Skutnabb-Kangas and Phillipson 1994, and the thematic issues of the *International Journal of the Sociology of Language* 127: 1997 and of *Language Sciences* 20/1: 1998). Language rights are occasionally mentioned but the nature of the rights is not explored. On the contrary, Crystal notes that as soon as minorities achieve rights, the majority needs to have their rights affirmed, whereas the guiding principle of human rights law is that it is the oppressed that need protection. On the other hand language policy analysis might need to assess the antagonism of dominant groups to minorities (as in the US and much of the western world) when devising schemes for the management of multilingual societies, including the ensuring of rights for speakers of minority languages in the face of dominant group intolerance (Grin 1994).

When it comes to voluntary associations of states such as the European Union, the issue of language rights in such fora as the European Parliament and the EU Commission in Brussels is central to all communicative activities (Labrie 1993). Crystal's description (pp. 81–2) correctly reflects the fact that English is expanding in EU use, but not what the implications are for all the relevant languages, or for a supra-national entity that is supposed to build on principles of democracy, pluralism, and equality between the member states, including their languages.

A close reading of his text reveals a surprising clutch of basic errors.

- Crystal refers to nations each having the right to use their 'own language', where what he is referring to is the right of citizens of each member state to use the language that was accorded rights when the state joined the EU. For instance the Irish opted for English, the Irish language being a treaty language but not an official or working language. In several member states there are several major national groups; in Belgium, Finland and Spain there is more than one official language. Members of the Welsh or Basque nations would not get far in Brussels in their languages.
- The number of member states was not 11 but rose to 15, and the number of official languages to 11, when Austria, Finland and Sweden acceded to the EU in 1995.
- Crystal uses inappropriate terminology when he refers to 'translation' and 'translators' when what he is describing is interpreters providing interpretation services at meetings.
- The parenthetic suggestion is thrown in that some countries might be 'asked' to give up their languages, a risk that English-speakers presumably regard as not one that they might incur. Crystal's loose formulation is that 'countries' could be asked to give up their 'official status', when what he is presumably referring to is languages. While the de facto hierarchy of working languages means that member states implicitly accept that some working languages are more equal than others, it is quite another matter to propose limitations on official languages, since these are the dominant language of member states, and EU law takes precedence over national law in member states: any limitation on the translation of EU written documents (for instance if all Italians could only read them in English or French) is juridically unthinkable and totally unacceptable in a democracy.
- The European Bureau for Lesser Used Languages (an important-sounding body) is spuriously referred to as an authority on demographic data for linguistic competence whereas in fact the Bureau deals exclusively with non-official languages, i.e. Friesian, Welsh, Catalan, etc. Data on the use and learning of the official languages of the EU is in fact collected by other EU bodies with such predictable names as Eurostat and Eurobarometer.

More fundamentally the weakness of Crystal's description is that practicalities are referred to rather than the more important issues of linguistic equality or language rights. And, predictably, it just so happens that Crystal cites English as the solution to the practical problems. Crystal mentions the way 'relay' interpretation operates (described in Dollerup 1996), but he is evidently not familiar with the scholarly literature in which other policy options have been considered (see Ammon 1996;

Schlossmacher 1996; Quell 1997). The existing studies relate to which languages are used most frequently at meetings, which are used as the initial drafting language of documents, what principles guide EU language policy, what Members of the European Parliament and civil servants working for the EU feel would be an appropriate solution to some of the practical problems of administering a cumbersome interpretation and translation system (a possible reduction of the number of oral working languages, polyglot competence), and more utopian solutions such as using Esperanto as a relay language.

How is it that English happens to be 'in the right place at the right time'?

Crystal interprets his narrative as showing that English was 'in the right place at the right time', rather than as an expression of structural and material power and particular interests. This trivializes the issue and is in fact in conflict with the analytical underpinning he begins the book with, where he admits that what is decisive for the expansion of a language is power of various kinds. I can cite a couple more examples of how his data lead him to endorse the expansion of English rather than the cause of global multilingualism.

- There is a tendency to draw on anecdotes (the Secretary-General of the Commonwealth said …) rather than the relevant scholarship.
- No geolinguistic data is provided on the maps that occupy a relatively large amount of space.
- Coca-colonization is exoticized through quoting an Italian form of the word (p. 86), as though it does not exist in English. The New Shorter Oxford English Dictionary (1993 edition) glosses it as the spread of American culture as represented by Coca-Cola, and dates it as mid-twentieth century. The term Macdonaldization is now more common in scholarly circles (e.g. Hamelink 1994).
- While it is correct that use of English in higher education is expanding in western Europe, it is false to suggest that it is becoming the 'normal medium of education' in countries such as the Netherlands (p. 102), or for that matter any other EU country. It is also a fallacy to assume that it is preferable to teach advanced courses in the natural sciences in English if the textbooks in use happen to be American. This is a recipe for diglossia and accelerating the marginalization of languages that have hitherto been used in all domains (see Phillipson and Skutnabb-Kangas forthcoming).
- The loss of the world's linguistic resources is trivialized as being a matter of 'anxieties' about a single world language, instead of issues of linguicide being explored along with the links between bio-diversity and linguistic diversity (see, e.g., UNESCO's World Commission on Culture and Development 1995; Maffi *et al.*: in press).

My fundamental fear is that this book could easily be misused by monolingual English-speakers, and is unlikely to promote the cause of global linguistic diversity. Nothing that I have written means that I am blind to the fact that English can open many doors (its alchemy, in Braj Kachru's memorable phrase) but we do know how and why it does so, and what the implications are for other languages, to a far greater extent than Crystal demonstrates.

Crystal's celebration of the growth of English fits squarely into what the Japanese scholar, Yukio Tsuda, terms the Diffusion of English Paradigm, an uncritical endorsement of capitalism, its science and technology, a modernization ideology, monolingualism as a norm, ideological globalization and internationalization, transnationalization, the Americanization and homogenization of world culture, linguistic, cultural and media imperialism (Tsuda 1994). Tsuda's alternative is an Ecology of Language Paradigm, the key features of which are a human rights perspective, equality in communication, multilingualism, the maintenance of languages and cultures, the protection of national sovereignties, and the promotion of foreign language education (for elaboration see Phillipson and Skutnabb-Kangas 1996).

There are still significant limitations to work in this area (see, for instance, Manfred Görlach's insightful review of Fishman, Conrad, and Rubal-Lopez's book, 1997), but the flow of books is persistent and gathering force. One that I can warmly recommend, exploring many of the same themes as Crystal, is David Graddol's *The future of English?* (1997), commissioned by the British Council. It is a very astute, sober and scientifically informed book on global English and what factors will influence its fate. My analysis of Crystal's book has tried to concentrate on its scholarly shortcomings rather than any assumed differences between his ideology and mine. He and I may well agree that what is needed in the field of global English is to clarify the nature of scholarship that can support those struggling for the maintenance of our fragile global language ecology.

Note

I am very grateful for responses to a first draft of the review to David Graddol, François Grin, Martin Kayman, Miklós Kontra, Alastair Pennycook, Bent Preisler, Tove Skutnabb-Kangas, and a very insightful reviewer for the journal. The usual disclaimers apply.

References

Ammon, U. 1996. 'The European Union (EU – formerly European Community): Status change of English during the last 50 years' in J. A. Fishman, A. W. Conrad and A. Rubal-Lopez (eds.). 241–67.

Baker, C. 1993. *Foundations of Bilingual Education and Bilingualism*. Clevedon: Multilingual Matters.

Barkhuizen, G. P. and D. Gough. 1996. 'Language curriculum development in South Africa: What place for English?' *TESOL Quarterly* 30/3: 453–72.

Cobarrubias, J. and J. A. Fishman. (eds.). 1983. *Progress in Language Planning: International Perspectives*. Berlin: Mouton de Gruyter.

Crawford, J. (ed.). 1992. *Language Loyalties. A Source Book on the Official English Controversy*. Chicago and London: Chicago University Press.

Crowley, T. 1991. *Proper English? Readings in Language, History and Cultural Identity*. London: Routledge.

Crowley, T. 1996. *Language in History: Theories and Texts*. London: Routledge.

Curtis, M. 1995. *The Ambiguities of Power. British Foreign Policy since 1945*. London: Zed Books.

Dasgupta, P. 1993. *The Otherness of English: India's Auntie Tongue Syndrome.* Delhi and London: Sage.

Dendrinos, B. 1992. *The EFL Textbook and Ideology.* Athens: Grivas.

Dutcher, N. (with the collaboration of G. Richard Tucker (1997 – undated)). *The Use of First and Second Languages in Education: A Review of International Experience.* Pacific Islands Discussion Paper Series, 1. East Asia and Pacific Region, Country Department III. Washington, DC: The World Bank.

Fishman, J. A., A. W. Conrad, and A. Rubal-Lopez. (eds.). 1996. *Post-Imperial English: Status Change in Former British and American Colonies, 1940–1990.* Berlin and New York: Mouton de Gruyter.

Görlach, M. 1997. 'Review of Fishman, Conrad, and Rubal-Lopez 1996.' *Sociolinguistica* 11: 215–18.

Graddol, D. 1997. *The Future of English?* London: The British Council.

Grin, F. 1994. 'Combining immigrant and autochthonous language rights: A territorial approach to multilingualism' in T. Skutnabb-Kangas and R. Phillipson (eds.). 31–48.

Hamelink, C. 1994. *Trends in World Communication: On Disempowerment and Self-empowerment.* Penang: Southbound, and Third World Network.

Hamelink, C. (ed.). 1997. *Ethics and Development: On Making Moral Choices in Development Cooperation.* Kampen: Kok.

Heath, S. B. and F. Mandabach. 1983. 'Language status decisions and the law in the United States' in J. Cobarrubias and J. A. Fishman (eds.). 87–106.

Hernández-Chávez, E. 1994. 'Language policy in the United States: A history of cultural genocide' in T. Skutnabb-Kangas and R. Phillipson (eds.). 141–58.

Heugh, K., A. Siegrühn and P. Plüddemann. (eds.). 1995. *Multilingual Education for South Africa.* Johannesburg: Heinemann.

Holroyd, M. 1997. *Bernard Shaw. The One-volume Definitive Edition.* London: Chatto and Windus.

Kachru, B. B. 1997. 'World Englishes and English-using communities.' *Annual Review of Applied Linguistics* 17: 66–87.

Kaplan, R. B. 1995. 'Iceberg tips and first steps: A call to action.' *TESOL Matters* 5/2: 16.

Labrie, N. 1993. *La construction linguistique de la Communauté européenne.* Paris: Henri Champion.

LANGTAG Report. 1996. 'Towards a national language plan for South Africa. Final Report of the Language Plan Task Group (LANGTAG), presented to the Minister of Arts, Culture, Science and Technology, 8 August 1995.' (chair Neville Alexander). Pretoria.

Maffi, L., T. Skutnabb-Kangas, and J. Andrianarivo, in press. 'Language diversity' in Darrell Posey and Graham Dutfield (eds.): *Cultural and Spiritual Values of Biodiversity.* New York: United Nations Environmental Programme and Cambridge: Cambridge University Press.

Mazrui, A. 1997. 'The World Bank, the language question and the future of African education.' *Race and Class* 38/3: 35–48.

McLean, D. and K. McCormick. 1996. 'English in South Africa 1940–1996' in J. A. Fishman, A. W. Conrad, and A. Rubal-Lopez, 303–38.

Mühlhäusler, P. 1996. *Linguistic Ecology: Language Change and Linguistic Imperialism in the Pacific Region.* London: Routledge.

Ngũgĩ wa, T. 1993. *Moving the Centre. The Struggle for Cultural Freedoms.* London: James Currey, Nairobi: EAEP/Portsmouth, NH: Heinemann.

Nunberg, G. 1997. 'Lingo-jingo, English only and the new nativism.' *The American Prospect*, July–August 1997: 40–7.

Parakrama, A. 1995. *De-hegemonizing Language Standards: Learning from (Post) Colonial Englishes about 'English'.* Basingstoke: Macmillan.

Pennycook, A. 1994. *The Cultural Politics of English as an International Language.* Harlow: Longman.

Phillipson, R. 1992a. *Linguistic Imperialism.* Oxford: Oxford University Press.

Phillipson, R. 1992b. 'Review of Casmir M. Rubagumya (ed.), "Language in education in Africa: a Tanzanian perspective".' *Applied Linguistics* 13/4: 432–4.

Phillipson, R. 1998. 'Globalizing English: Are linguistic human rights an alternative to linguistic imperialism?' *Language Sciences*, 20/1: 111–12.

Phillipson, R., and T. Skutnabb-Kangas. 1996. 'English only worldwide or language ecology?' *TESOL Quarterly* 30/3: 429–52.

Phillipson, R., and T. Skutnabb-Kangas, forthcoming. 'Englishization as one dimension of globalization.' *AILA Review* 13, special number on English in the world, David Graddol and Ulrike Meinhoff (eds).

Pütz, M. (ed.). 1995. *Discrimination through Language in Africa? Perspectives on the Namibian Experience.* Berlin: Mouton de Gruyter.

Quell, C. 1997. 'Language choice in multilingual institutions: A case study at the European Commission with particular reference to the role of English, French and German as working languages.' *Multilingua* 16/1: 57–76.

Schlossmacher, M. 1996. *Die Amtssprachen in den Organen der Europäischen Gemeinschaft.* Peter Lang, Frankfurt am Main.

Skutnabb-Kangas, T. (ed.). 1995. *Multilingualism for All.* Amsterdam: Swets and Zeitlinger.

Skutnabb-Kangas, T. and R. Phillipson. (eds.). 1994. *Linguistic Human Rights: Overcoming Linguistic Discrimination.* Berlin: Mouton de Gruyter (pbk., 1995).

Swales, J. 1997. 'English as Tyrannosaurus Rex.' *World Englishes* 16/3, 373–82.

Tollefson, J. 1991. *Planning Language, Planning Inequality.* Harlow: Longman.

Tomaševski, K. 1997. *Between Sanctions and Elections. Aid Donors and Their Human Rights Performance.* London: Pinter.

Tsuda, Y. 1994. 'The diffusion of English: Its impact on culture and communication.' *Keio Communication Review* 16: 49–61.

Webb, V. 1996. 'Language planning and politics in South Africa.' *International Journal of the Sociology of Language* 118: 139–62.

World Commission on Culture and Development. 1995. *Our Creative Diversity.* Paris: UNESCO.

Text 8

David Crystal
University of Wales, Bangor

On trying to be crystal-clear: a Response to Phillipson

Applied Linguistics published a review article by Robert Phillipson on David Crystal's book *English as a Global Language* in issue 20/2. Here follows a rejoinder by David Crystal.

When the review was published it had already appeared in a similar but shorter version in the *European English Messenger (EEM)*, the publication of ESSE, the European Society for the Study of English. Since then there has been a reply by Crystal and a further response by Phillipson in the *EEM*.

It is not the general policy of *Applied Linguistics* to republish material that has already appeared in any form elsewhere, but in the circumstances we feel that it is appropriate to publish a reply by Crystal.

Any further contribution related to the matters raised in Phillipson's review and Crystal's reply should be submitted for publication in the article section of this journal.

It is an axiom of contemporary linguistics that language events should always be seen in context. This applies to books as well as to the reviews they receive. And in accepting the editors' kind invitation to respond to the review by Phillipson (1999a) of *English as a Global Language (EGL)*, I must begin by doing some contextualizing – some discourse analysis, even – for it is not otherwise possible to make sense of it. Only by careful reanalysis of the quotations used, and of the context in which they appear, can one identify the hidden agenda which motivates a review of this kind. I hope the exercise will be useful to readers, who will undoubtedly encounter the ideology involved from time to time, and who may be wondering how best to deal with it.

What mindset has Phillipson brought to the task? Here are two illuminating extracts from towards the end of the review. 'The assumption that experts from countries such as the UK or the US, deeply monolingual and with a very patchy record of foreign language learning, can contribute to policy on education and language matters in multilingual societies is completely counter-intuitive' (p. 271). And next: 'linguistic hierarchies reminiscent of the colonial period, and master-minded by the type of linguistics and applied linguistics department that Crystal used to work for, still underpin much World Bank and IMF policy' (p. 271). You might like to read these quotations again – yes, you from any linguistics or applied linguistics department anywhere – he is talking about you, not just me. Simply by being professionally involved in linguistics you are, it seems, imperialist and triumphalist, and if you are from a department in Britain or the USA, your inherent monolingualism makes you incapable of saying or doing anything useful in relation to multilingualism. Ignore the fact that hundreds of linguists from monolingual countries have spent years working with minority and multilingual situations, are fluent in more than one language, and are worried sick at the moment by the endangered language situation in the world today. Ignore the vast amount of work that has gone on within sociolinguistics. None of that can help. Linguists are misguided, incapable, conspiratorial people, with a colonialist political agenda.

Phillipson complains about me: 'his loyalty is to linguistics' (p. 266) (ignore his reference to my page 113, where there is no mention of this issue). He's absolutely right – but the kind of linguistics he is thinking of isn't anything like the world I know. Apparently if you're a linguist, so says this review, your work is valueless when you come to study globalization, education, or the media. Eat your hearts out, educational linguists, anthropological linguists, sociolinguists, clinical linguists, critical linguists, and others. You're all wasting your time. Personally, I think it is an insult to 30 years of sociolinguistic research to suggest that linguists have nothing to say about 'multilingualism, official, national and minority languages' (p. 266). In fact, where would such topics be today without sociolinguistics? 'Lack of any grounding in the social sciences is a major weakness of the work' (*EGL*, that is) (p. 266). But to me, linguistics is a social science.

Let me begin by doing some basic discourse analysis to show how an ideologically fuelled selection of information works in a review of this kind. The account of *EGL's* content is a good example. Phillipson's summary is in terms of chapters. Why? Because that suits his argument. If you look towards the beginning of his review (p. 266), you will find the briefest of remarks about each chapter, with the whole summary taking up 20 lines in all; and of this 20, he devotes 10 to an account of ch 5. He states that 'nearly half of this chapter' is on US English, 'implying that Crystal's understanding is that the internal affairs of the present-day US are central to the future of "global" English'. It sounds impressive – half a chapter devoted to this topic. That sounds like real evidence of a right-wing plot lurking somewhere around.

But when we summarize the book in terms of pages, a very different picture emerges. Excluding the preface and further reading, *EGL* takes up 140 pages. Ch. 1 (pp. 1–24) asks why there is a global language; Ch. 2 (pp. 24–63) outlines the historical context; Chs 3 and 4 (pp. 64–112) present the cultural context; and Ch. 5 (pp 113–40) discusses the future. Note that only 27 pages – just over an eighth of the book – are devoted to Ch. 5. And only just over 11 of these are devoted to the official English issue in the USA. It is plain that the US English issue is not a major topic for me. Nor, indeed, is the book chiefly about the future of English – an emphasis, which distinguishes Graddol (1998) from mine. The bulk of my book is elsewhere.

I put those pages about US English in, incidentally, because I had had an opportunity to learn a great deal about the official English movement while I was writing the book, and I had not found a summary of the arguments for and against it anywhere in my reading. Most people outside the USA are not aware of what has been going on there. References to the US situation are often wrong, and usually oversimplified. Phillipson is no exception. He says, 'the intellectual community in the United States … is massively against English Only' and 'one would not suspect this' (p. 271) from reading *EGL*. There are two points here. First, my exposition was chiefly about US English, not 'English Only': there are important differences between the various US protectionist movements – but it is important not to oversimplify what is a very complex situation. Second, I don't know what Phillipson means by 'the intellectual community in the United States', but I would have thought that my extensive quotation in *EGL* from the Linguistic Society of America's official statement on the matter, and some associated proposals, would do to represent that perspective. But I was forgetting. They're linguists, of course. They don't count.

The content summary of the book is just one example of the way Phillipson's political views have led him to misrepresent *EGL*. But the whole review is like this. Phillipson begins with politics, quoting my observation that the book has been written 'without any political agenda' (p. 266). Out of context, it does sound silly, and this then allows him to impute political naivety: 'even the wish to be apolitical involves political choices' (p. 266). But the context of my remark, in the preface, was the competing agendas of the two positions outlined there. My observation refers to the fact that I was not adopting either of those agendas. It is well-known that there are two senses of the word 'political' in English, one referring to a general concern for the state and its citizens, and the other for the partisan world of party politics (compare *OED political*, senses 1 vs. 4). Phillipson has blurred those meanings: I say I am not taking sides (sense 4); Phillipson tries to get you to believe that I am saying my book is outside politics (sense 1).

Phillipson then moves on to history. Here's how he tries to justify his claim that my historical account is unimpressive. First, he notices that I head a section in my 'historical context' chapter (Ch. 2) 'America'. 'Oops', he says, Crystal 'does not mean the two continents, but the USA – his synecdoche reflects a hegemonic preference' (p. 266). Well oops to you too, Phillipson. I chose that title for one reason only: the fact that the section begins with pre-US events, in 1584, and continues with pre-independence issues for two of its four pages. To have used the heading 'USA' – now that would have been a real cause for criticism. But has Phillipson told you in his review that my American section is so wide-ranging? Look very hard before you answer.

Second, he quotes my observation (in relation to the specifically US situation) that 'Rulings are needed to regulate conflict. If there is no conflict there is no need for rulings' (p. 267). He then adds that this must 'suggest that language issues have been free of conflict in Ireland, Scotland, Wales, or the USA'. (In an earlier version of his review (Phillipson 1998), he has 'USA' turn up as 'North America'. Oops again?) How he reads in that implication is beyond me, as on the very next page I refer to the conflicts which have given rise to official language issues in Ireland, Wales, Quebec, and New Zealand. But what you need to notice is that the contested proposition is *his* implication, not mine. This proposition then becomes the theme of the rest of the relevant paragraph in his review. So when he concludes, 'there is a huge literature on these issues' (p. 267), the position which warrants this imputation of ignorance is not one which is actually represented in my book.

He also picks on my South Africa section, in Ch. 2. This doesn't satisfy him either, because I don't use the word *apartheid* (p. 267). On the other hand, such phrases as 'political divisions', 'authority and repression', and the like are very much in evidence in that part of *EGL*. Plainly apartheid is being referred to, in spirit if not in name. The criticism turns out to be trivial. Similarly, he complains that I do not give the names of any African languages. True enough – but what is the force of that observation? Is he saying that when I say 'The 1993 Constitution names eleven languages' I should have listed them all by name? A criticism of 'poor history' needs more than this.

Several parts of the review compete for the prize of 'selective quotation of the year'. He complains that I don't describe past language policies in South Africa and have 'invisibilized' the blacks (p. 267) – a typical piece of polemic, which quickly becomes nonsensical as you read the relevant pages. For there you will find such phrases as 'spoken by the black population', '[used] by increasing numbers of the (70 per cent majority) black population', 'a series of government surveys among black parents', and so on. The word 'black' turns up repeatedly. Why would anyone not see this? Only if they don't want to see it.

Or again, 'There is no reference to the many African scholars who have pleaded for the upgrading of African languages and denounced "aid" that strengthens European languages' (p. 268). Yet in the next paragraph he acknowledges that I have referred to Ngugi, and if he had wanted to he could have mentioned my references to Chinua Achebe and others. Chapter 5 in fact begins by referring to the rejection of English. Why would a reviewer not want to draw the reader's attention to this?

And when I do say something about South Africa that Phillipson wants to see – referring to the country's new multilingual policy, and the position of English in the new political situation – this is dismissed as a 'passing reference' (p. 267). So let's try another piece of elementary discourse analysis here. The section on South Africa is 80 lines long. What would you expect a 'passing reference' to be – 3 or 4 lines max? I begin my comments on these matters with the remark 'There is thus a linguistic side to the political divisions which have marked South African society in recent decades' – and developing the point from there to the end of the section takes 35 lines. Why call something 'passing', when it plainly isn't, or say there is no description of past language policies when there plainly is?

Another thing about political mindsets is that they tend to be obsessed with certain words and phrases, and if they are not present, the content they represent is deemed to be absent. Their owners look for the letter, and not for the spirit. So, Phillipson objects to the way my narrative 'avoids any upsetting talk of bloodshed ... capitulation ... domination ...' (p. 268). Evidently my use of such words as 'slavery', 'stealing our talents and geniuses' and 'humiliating experiences' (pp. 114–15) doesn't count as being part of the language of domination. Or again, Phillipson reduces my deeply felt concerns about dying languages to a word, picking 'anxieties' out of context, and allowing that to represent my position (p. 274). He might have selected other words I use – 'urgency' or 'tragedy' (p. 18), for instance – but that of course wouldn't have suited his purpose.

Where Phillipson recognizes that I do refer to other views, such as Gandhi's and Ngugi's, he says I have 'buried' their remarks 'in comments on the expense of bilingualism' (p. 270). If you look at the relevant quotations in *EGL*, you will find that they are spread over two pages, in a section prominently headed 'The rejection of English' (p. 114), and that the reference to the cost of bilingualism occurs in a single sentence over a page later. This does not sound like 'buried'. Moreover, the sentence on bilingualism is immediately preceded by one in which I applaud 'the promotion of bilingual or multilingual policies'. Phillipson doesn't draw your attention to that.

'Buried' is just one of several loaded terms scattered throughout this review. Here are a couple more examples. He says that 'some of the formulations ... are lifted verbatim' from my *Cambridge Encyclopedia of the English Language* (p. 268). Note the shiftiness implicit in the term 'lifted'. However, the reliance on *CEEL* is something I've already drawn the reader's attention to in my Preface. Or again, 'Crystal ... writes blithely' (p. 269) that I overstate the role of America in my account of the growth of global English. Note the weasel word, suggestive of an uncritical carelessness. I stand by my phrasing – I said 'almost single-handedly' – and the book certainly doesn't ignore the British Council and ELT, for example (see pp. 103–4). But I remain convinced that, without America, English would not be a global language now; and that only America could have put English in this position. It may be a debatable view, but it certainly isn't a blithe one.

Here are some other Phillipson imaginings. '[Crystal] sees no causal relationship between the globalization of English and the demise of other languages' (p. 265). Phillipson ignores my section on language death, in which I deplore such demise. I call it 'an intellectual and social tragedy' (p. 17). That's pretty strong, wouldn't you say? I say quite clearly that we need a general perspective on language dominance and loss. Big languages have been killing off little languages throughout history. Today, thanks to decades of work in sociolinguistics, we stand a chance of becoming aware of what the issues are and doing something about it. But, from a modern perspective, the 'bad guys' have been the languages of all the major expansionist nations – and I include Russian, Chinese, and many languages of Africa alongside such cases as English, Spanish, Portuguese, and French. I agree that as English becomes more global, there are increasing risks for some other languages, but the view that there is a 'causal relationship between the globalization of English and the demise of other languages' is the kind of gross oversimplification that I want nothing to do with. English as the cause of the death of languages in Australia? Certainly. In Brazil? I don't think so.

Or again, Phillipson notices that I refer to 'economic imperialism', but because I put it in quotes he sees me as finding it 'unpalatable' and wanting to 'distance' myself from it (p. 268). What I find unpalatable, in fact, is Phillipson's naive historicism, in which the past is interpreted through the mores of the present. The reason why I use quotes should, once again, be obvious from the context, where I am describing a historical sequence of events, and the quotes symbolize the novelty of the concept at the time.

Or again, 'Crystal notes that as soon as minorities achieve rights, the majority needs to have their rights affirmed' (p. 272) – as if I was recommending this to be a desirable procedure. In fact, I am simply stating what has so often happened: 'In such cases, the dominant power would sometimes take measures to preserve it … by giving it special recognition' (p. 76). Of course 'the guiding principle of human rights law is that it is the oppressed that need protection' (p. 272). *EGL* never suggests otherwise. Indeed I make several suggestions in that direction. 'It is good to see' the endangered languages protection movements, I say at one point (p. 18), and then: 'movements for language rights … have played an important part …'. A little later: 'Languages of identity need to be maintained' (p. 22). Phillipson doesn't quote these sentiments, of course. They would militate against the stereotype he is attempting to create.

'Fundamentally', Phillipson says, 'Crystal's story of globalizing English is eurocentric and triumphalist, despite his protestations to the contrary' (p. 268). It is difficult to know what to say, when someone hides behind pompous language in order to call you a liar. Younger, better-built, and more explosive linguists would probably go and punch him on the nose. Older, flabbier, and mild-mannered ones have to be content with simply restating their position. I am not triumphalist about English. Never have been. Never will be. Anyone who has read my work on language would know that. This is the point about context again: authors need to be taken as wholes. Phillipson purports to admire my earlier books, but anyone who has actually done me the honour of reading my views over the years knows how much I value languages, and celebrate them in all their forms. I have spoken and written on behalf of minority languages for years.

I have had an active interest in the position of my other language, Welsh. I could list my successes (and failures) in promoting Welsh in my corner of Wales, I was even once – I offer this point to Phillipson, no charge – called anti-English. So when I said, clearly and quietly, in my Preface, that I have tried to write a book which is not triumphalist, I meant it. When I talk about 'the unpalatable face of linguistic triumphalism' (p. 13), I meant it. I know that there are those around who cannot see a sentence such as 'English is a world language' without condemning it as triumphalist, so I took the trouble to spell out my position clearly. At the time I thought I was overdoing it. Now I realize that maybe I didn't stress the point enough.

It is difficult to avoid the impression that Phillipson wishes I had written some other kind of book, in which his own views should have figured more largely. At one point, he thinks *EGL* should be a book on minority languages, in which the European Union situation would be fully explicated (pp. 272–3). At another, he wants it to be about the American indigenous peoples and their languages (p. 266). At another, he seems to want it to be about language dominance in general: *EGL*, he says, 'ignores the fact that global (and local) inequalities are increasing, and that the "innovations" of the global system are having catastrophic ecological and cultural effects' (p. 266). I found that point especially ironic, because just after I had finished writing *EGL* I began work on various projects to do with endangered languages (see Crystal, 2000). Perhaps my awareness of these impending projects kept me from including more on the endangered languages issue in *EGL*. If it did, the imbalance has now been made good.

I can understand Phillipson wanting the position he espouses in his own book to be given greater prominence in mine. He'll be pleased to see that I added a reference to it, and a few others, when the Press gave me the opportunity to make some minor changes for the paperback edition (Phillipson 1998). But that's as far as I would want to go. When I read *Linguistic Imperialism*, I was unimpressed by the curious hotchpotch of political innuendo which it manifested. I was unconvinced by the 'great plot' scenario painted there. Whatever truth there might be in the view that there is a correlation between linguistic and political hierarchy, I felt that the case was blown by its overstatement. There was nothing to be gained by attempting to restate or counter that kind of polemic, I thought. There are real issues of pain and tragedy caused by language policies around the world, but they are not helped by the one-sided, black-and-white picture which Phillipson presents. I think I can see – I certainly try to see – both sides of the coin. Phillipson does not even try. And along with all polemicists he condemns any attempt at a balanced statement, using the classic language of their trade to do so. All polemicists say of their opponents that they have been 'selective', that they use 'biased and ideologically loaded claims', that they 'trivialize' the issues. They fail to see the ideological mote in their own eye. They fail to detect subtlety. Phillipson, for example, has totally missed the conventional irony implicit in my use of the phrase '[English being] in the right place at the right time' (p. 273). When someone says this, they are typically reflecting on the unexpected and often undeserved good fortune of the recipient. If I say, when John turns up at the bar just as I'm offering to buy a round of drinks, 'John's always in the right place at the right time', I am not praising him, nor being triumphalist about him. The usage is ironic. Rather than trivializing the issue, the phrase adds a depth to it, which Phillipson has completely missed.

Phillipson concludes: 'My analysis of Crystal's book has tried to concentrate on its scholarly shortcomings rather than any assumed differences between his ideology and mine' (p. 274). Well, he has tried and failed. The review is a mass of ideology, innuendo, and misrepresentation. My favourite is 'Crystal's apparent assumption that English is exclusively for the good' (p. 269), though a close second is the 'daunting challenge' I am supposed to have set myself, in writing this book, namely 'how a British view can present itself as universally relevant and appropriate' (p. 265). The review, in short, is little more than a pastiche, in which a selection of pages (about a fifth, I estimate) have been used to represent the book as a whole. And then, after all the selective quotation, Phillipson says it is me who is excluding types of information 'that do not fit into the world-view underpinning his narrative'! (p. 271). It is me who is supposed to have 'unjustifiably over-simplified the complexity and reality of global English'! (p. 271). This kind of thing does not help me, nor the audience interested in world English issues.

Did I get anything useful from this review at all? By hunting behind the verbal smokescreen ('inconsistency and errors') I did actually get something out of his remarks on Africa. I described Cameroon as multilingual, but not Nigeria (I certainly should have done that – in my other writing Nigeria is my main example of West African multilingualism). Also, when I said 'Ghana was the first Commonwealth country to achieve independence, in 1960', I meant 'in Africa', and it was silly not to have made that clear. Also, I didn't include separate sections on Namibia, Botswana, and Lesotho, and it would have been good to do so. This is the sort of helpful comment one likes to see in a review, as it can genuinely improve the quality of a work. If only there were more points like that in Phillipson's review. But most of the important linguistic issues which I do raise in *EGL* he passes over in silence. Is the possible emergence of a World Standard Spoken English a plausible scenario? Is a global language such a unique event? Is there really a research advantage to those who have English as a first language (let us hear the views of those whose English is fluent)? Are there other factors which have fostered the growth of global English in addition to the ones I list? Have I overestimated any of the ones I do list? Phillipson pays no attention to Chapters 3 and 4, which are (in my view) the core of the book, taking up a third of its pages. I hope the debate in *AL*, if it grows, will concentrate on such substantive issues.

In his penultimate paragraph, Phillipson affirms the validity of a two-paradigm view of the world, as labelled (by Tsuda): a 'diffusion of English paradigm' and an 'ecology of language paradigm'. Phillipson puts me 'squarely' within the former. Unpalatable as it is to be made to think in this two-term way, I would place myself just as 'squarely' within the latter, citing various publications as evidence (including Crystal 2000). But I do not share Phillipson's black-and-white view of life. I see the issues as more dynamic, interactive, and multi-faceted. Phillipson's review demonstrates a truth recently reiterated by Alberto Manguel: 'a reviewer is a reader once removed, guiding the reader, not through the book, but through the reviewer's reading of that book' (Manguel 1999: 217). Phillipson has seen in my book only what his ideology lets him see, and when he has not found what he expected to be there, he has read in meanings to suit. Other reviewers, I am happy to say, have seen things differently. To take an example, chosen because it addresses Phillipson's basic accusation that *EGL* is 'triumphalist', one reviewer – reading the same book – observes that 'the tone is not triumphalist' (Maley 1999). Another concludes that 'Crystal deplores the triumphalism in English articles about the spread of English' (Rogaly 1997). A third, having suggested the scenario that English is so far ahead of other languages that English speakers can relax, says: 'Actually, Crystal does not want us to relax, and urges against triumphalism. He warns of the resentment, envy, anger of the non-English mother-tongue speakers who feel disadvantaged. Or who, worse still, feel their mother tongue or identity threatened' (Hanson 1997). I agree with that, and rest my case.

References

Crystal, D. 2000. *Language Death.* Cambridge: Cambridge University Press.
Graddol, D. 1997. *The Future of English?* London: The British Council.
Hanson, J. 1997. 'The mother of all tongues.' *Times Higher Education Supplement*, 11 July.
Maley, A. 1999. 'Review of *English as a Global Language.*' *English Language Teaching Journal* 53/2.
Manguel, A. 1999. 'The irresolutions of Cynthia Ozick' in Alberto Manguel, *Into the Looking-Glass Wood*. London: Bloomsbury. 214–24.
Phillipson, R. 1998. 'Global English.' *The European English Messenger*, 7/2, 53–6.
Phillipson, R. 1999a. 'Voice in Global English: unheard chords in Crystal loud and clear.' *Applied Linguistics* 20/2: 265–76.
Phillipson, R. 1999b. 'Rejoinder.' *The European English Messenger*, 8/1: 65–6.
Rogaly, J. 1997. 'Awkward in arias – fluent in everything else.' *Financial Times Week-End Section* 24 May: 2.

Text 9

Robert Phillipson

A closing word

Edward Said, in his 1993 Reith lectures (published as *Representations of the Intellectual*, Penguin, 1994) describes the role of the intellectual as: 'to raise embarrassing questions, to confront orthodoxy and dogma (rather than to produce them), to be someone who cannot easily be co-opted by governments or corporations ... someone whose whole being is staked on a critical sense, a sense of being unwilling to accept easy formulas, or ready-made clichés, or the smooth, ever-so-accommodating confirmations of what the powerful or conventional have to say, and what they do' (pp. 9, 17). The global linguistic ecology would benefit if all academics could live up to this ideal.

Scholarly dialogue would benefit if there was more openness and willingness to explore alternative perceptions and readings. Crystal's response indicates that in the 'political minefield' (his term) of English as a global language, he is convinced that his paradigm can safely navigate the hazards, whereas my alternative paradigm is valueless and interfering. His defensive concentration on the man rather than the ball and an agenda that he fabricates for me reveals little effort to address the substance of my critique or probe into his own ideological or epistemological position. It is more comforting for him to attack my assumed motives, concede a few scholarly peccadilloes, and explain away or misrepresent other valid objections, rather than address more fundamental issues of bias and perspective.

His imprudently frank comments on my book *Linguistic Imperialism* clearly indicate that he did not come to my review with an open mind, quite the opposite. Crystal saw no reason to 'restate or counter' the position that I am assumed to represent. This arrogance ignores the substantial efforts of many scholars in many parts of the world to link English to processes of structural power, globalisation and linguistic hierarchies. Crystal's response provides fascinating insight into the workings of the mind of those who are promoting the cause of English worldwide (a primary purpose of the British Council, on whose august board Crystal now sits). If I really was adrift in my analysis of contemporary global English, it is unlikely that my book would have already been reprinted three times, that people from China, Japan and Korea have offered to translate it, and that some people have told me the book changed their lives. To portray me as a misguided irrelevance cushions Crystal from acknowledging that there are many who are attempting to navigate in and chart this particular minefield.

What comes through Crystal-clearly in his response is that he has chosen to spin webs of discourse in the garb of a folk tale narrative, with appropriately patronising discourse markers for the reader, and a villain that he creates to allow his interpretive fantasy free rein. This is escapism masquerading as discourse analysis, so as to channel the aggression he admits to feeling. One is tempted to conclude that big shots like Crystal (Said's 'powerful or conventional') regard themselves as above criticism. As I know that many people, in many parts of the world, share my view of the imperfections of the book, his personalised diatribe more than ever convinced me that his book should not go unchallenged. A longer version of my review is in press with the publishers of *Applied Linguistics* (20/2): 288–299, after going through the standard peer review processes. It contains many more examples of where Crystal has cut scholarly corners.

Book reviews are a significant means for our scholarly community to dialogue and remain dynamic. Reading reviews of one's own books is often an uncomfortable experience. In the course of the 1990s I have reviewed books for *Applied Linguistics, Language in Society, International Journal of the Sociology of Language, Language, Sociolinguistica*, and *World Englishes* (for details see my home page <http://babel.ruc.dk/~robert/>). On no occasion have I had cause to be as critical as in the case of Crystal's book. For dialogue to be possible however, both parties have to contribute constructively. If I failed, at least so far as the author was concerned, it was not for want of trying.

A final remark about this controversy. Crystal says in several places that he is employing some ('basic', 'elementary') discourse analysis to counter what Phillipson has said about his book, and indeed this is also what Berns *et al.* are doing in their contribution. This procedure aims to get at the way something is expressed and to make it an object of reflection, and this of course is precisely what the study questions at the end of this book are intended for. It is hoped that the questions readers are invited to address, probably selectively, after reading each exchange will help sharpen perceptions, and articulate with precision the reasons why some arguments seem more or less convincing than others – in short, to achieve a better understanding of our own reading of these papers. Section 3 of this volume, which focuses on critical discourse analysis, may of course spark off many more ideas as to how a critical or 'resistant' reading of texts might be achieved.

Further reading

As will already have become apparent from the references in the articles included here, the literature relevant for a critical reflection about the global spread of English is vast and so cannot all be mentioned here. However, a selection of what might be considered the most prominent contributions to the discussion appear in the suggestions for further reading below.

Crystal (1997); McArthur (1998); Graddol (1997): These three texts describe and document, in considerable detail, the spread of English as an international means of communication. Crystal's and McArthur's books are more focused on the history of the globalization of English, whereas Graddol, as the title of his book suggests, is more interested in making projections for the future based on the present situation.

Kachru (1986) [1991]; Kachru (1992): These are two key works about the spread and diversification of English and the separate social identity of different varieties or versions of the language. It was Kachru who first put these issues on the academic agenda and these two books have been used as points of reference for most subsequent discussion about the role and status of Englishes in the world.

A key paper in this area stressing the importance of codification of non-native varieties is Bgambose (1998).

See also Smith and Forman (1997), a collection of conference papers which focus close attention on a range of issues and implications arising from the diversity of Englishes in the world.

Bex and Watts (1999): This is a collection of papers about the nature and role of standard English and the educational and socio-political implications of its privileged status in comparison with other varieties of the language (reviewed by Alan Davies in *Applied Linguistics* 22/2 (2001): 273–82).

See also the controversy between Trudgill and Stein and Quirk on the relationship between Standard English and dialectal varieties, particularly in relation to first language education: Trudgill (1995) – Stein and Quirk (1995) – Trudgill (1996).

For descriptive rather than argumentative work, see Trudgill and Hannah (1995).

The whole issue of language variation, of which the spread of English is only one example, if a particularly striking one, is of course very complex and has long been a major preoccupation for sociolinguists and grammarians. See, for example, Quirk (1995); Trudgill (2002); Lowenberg (1988).

Pennycook (1994); Phillipson (1992); Skutnabb-Kangas (2000): All these three books concern themselves essentially with questions of ideology and the extent to which the spread of English as an international means of communication serves to sustain the privilege and power of its native speakers, and diminishes the vitality of other, smaller languages.

Brutt-Griffler (2002): this is a thorough and dispassionate enquiry into the issues, contending that English owes its existence as a world language not to imperialism alone but also to the struggle against imperialism. It gives detailed documentation of the development of English during the post-colonial era, and emphasizes the need for second language acquisition researchers to investigate the use of English in bilingual speech communities.

See also Fishman, Conrad, and Rubal-Lopez (1996).

House (2002); Jenkins (2000); Seidlhofer (2001): The central concern of these authors is how the spread of English has led to its functioning as a lingua franca among speakers of other languages. They discuss the distinctive features in the phonology, lexicogrammar, and pragmatics of English as a lingua franca and the pedagogical implications their findings might have.

Widdowson (1994); Canagarajah (1999); Gnutzmann (1999); McKay (2002): The central concern in these texts is with what implications the changed role and status of English as an international language have for the teaching of that language. Questions discussed include what model of the language should serve as a goal for learning, how the cultural identity of learners is affected, and how socio-political issues enter into the way the language is defined as a school subject. All of the authors show, in their different ways, how concepts of English as an international language lead us to question comfortable and well-established assumptions about English-language pedagogy.

And finally, for those with an appetite for further controversies in this area: Bisong (1995)—Phillipson (1996). This is a debate arising out of Phillipson (1992), with Bisong, writing from the point of view of an outer-circle English speaker, challenging Phillipson's arguments about the imposition of English, and Phillipson replying.

Widdowson (1997)—Brutt-Griffler (1998): Here Brutt-Griffler questions Widdowson's characterization of English as an international language as essentially the use of English for specific purposes, and argues that this effectively reduces the status of non-native varieties.

References

Bgamboṣe, A. 1998. 'Torn between the norms: innovations in world Englishes'. *World Englishes* 17/1: 1–14.
Bex, T. and R. J. Watts (eds.). 1999. *Standard English: The Widening Debate*. London: Routledge.

Bisong, J. 1995. 'Language choice and cultural imperialism: a Nigerian perspective'. *ELT Journal* 49/2: 122–32.

Brutt-Griffler, J. 1998. 'Conceptual questions in English as a world language'. *World Englishes* 17/3: 381–92.

Brutt-Griffler, J. 2002. *World English. A Study of Its Development.* Clevedon: Multilingual Matters.

Canagarajah, S. 1999. *Resisting Linguistic Imperialism in English Teaching.* Oxford: Oxford University Press.

Crystal, D. 1997. *English as a Global Language.* Cambridge: Cambridge University Press.

Fishman, J. A., A. W. Conrad, and A. Rubal-Lopez (eds.). 1996. *Post–Imperial English: Status Change in Former British and American Colonies, 1940–1990.* Berlin and New York: Mouton de Gruyter.

Gnutzmann, C. (ed.). 1999. *Teaching and Learning English as a Global Language.* Tübingen: Stauffenburg.

Graddol, D. 1997. *The Future of English?* London: British Council.

House, J. 2002. 'Developing pragmatic competence in English as a lingua franca' in Knapp and Meierkord.

Jenkins, J. 2000. *The Phonology of English as an International Language.* Oxford: Oxford University Press.

Kachru, B. 1985. 'Standards, codification, and sociolinguistic realism: the English language in the outer circle' in Quirk and Widdowson.

Kachru, B. 1986 [1991]. *The Alchemy of English: The Spread, Functions and Models of Non-native Englishes.* Oxford: Pergamon. [Reprinted: University of Illinois Press, Urbana, Il.]

Kachru, B. (ed.). 1992. *The Other Tongue.* 2nd edition. Urbana and Chicago: University of Illinois Press.

Knapp, K. and C. Meierkord (eds.). 2002. *Lingua Franca Communication.* Frankfurt: Peter Lang.

Lowenberg, P. (ed.). 1988. *Language Spread and Language Policy: Issues, Implications, and Case Studies. (Georgetown University Round Table on Languages and Linguistics 1987).* Washington: Georgetown University Press.

Manguel, A. 1999. 'The irresolution of Cynthia Ozick' in A. Manguel. *Into the Looking-Glass Wood.* London: Bloomsbury.

McArthur, T. 1998. *The English Languages.* Cambridge: Cambridge University Press.

McKay, S. 2002. *Teaching English as an International Language: Rethinking Goals and Approaches.* Oxford: Oxford University Press.

Pennycook, A. 1994. *The Cultural Politics of English as an International Language.* London: Longman.

Phillipson, R. 1992. *Linguistic Imperialism.* Oxford: Oxford University Press.

Phillipson, R. 1996. 'Linguistic imperialism: African perspectives'. *ELT Journal* 50/2: 160–7.

Quirk, R. 1985. 'The English language in a global context' in Quirk and Widdowson.

Quirk, R. 1995. *Grammatical and Lexical Variance in English.* London: Longman.

Quirk, R., S. Greenbaum, G. Leech, and J. Svartvik. 1972. *A Grammar of Contemporary English.* London and New York: Longman.

Quirk, R., S. Greenbaum, G. Leech, and J. Svartvik. 1985. *A Comprehensive Grammar of English*. London and New York: Longman.

Quirk, R. and H. G. Widdowson (eds.). 1985. *English in the World: Teaching and Learning the Language and Literatures*. Cambridge: Cambridge University Press.

Seidlhofer, B. 2001. 'Closing a conceptual gap: the case for a description of English as a lingua franca'. *International Journal of Applied Linguistics* 11/2: 133–58.

Skutnabb-Kangas, T. 2000. *Linguistic Genocide in Education – or Worldwide Diversity and Human Rights?* Mahwah, NJ and London, UK: Lawrence Erlbaum Associates.

Smith, L. and M. Forman (eds.). 1997. *World Englishes 2000*. Honolulu, Hawai'i: College of Languages, Linguistics and Literature and the East-West Center.

Stein, G. and R. Quirk. 1995. 'Standard English'. *The European English Messenger* IV/2: 62–3.

Trudgill, P. 1995. 'Dialect and Dialects in the New Europe'. *The European English Messenger* IV/1: 44–6.

Trudgill, P. 1996. 'Standard English and the National Curriculum'. *The European English Messenger* V/1: 63–5.

Trudgill, P. 2002. *Language Variation and Change*. Edinburgh: Edinburgh University Press.

Trudgill, P. and J. Hannah (eds.). 1995. *International English: a Guide to Varieties of Standard English*. 3rd edition. London: Arnold.

Widdowson, H. G. 1994. 'The ownership of English'. *TESOL Quarterly* 28/2: 377–89.

Widdowson, H. G. 1997. 'EIL, ESL, EFL: global issues and local interests'. *World Englishes* 16/1: 135–46.

Section 2
Corpus linguistics and language teaching

Topic 1 in this book, the global spread of English, is an issue that most people – even those not professionally concerned with language – would agree is highly controversial. This is not at all the case with the second topic in the book, the relationship between corpus linguistics and language teaching. Indeed, one of the interesting things about it is precisely that at first sight, even among linguists and language teachers themselves, this relationship seems straightforward and unproblematic. It turns out, however, that probing into this relationship leads to reflections not only about the nature of language description and language teaching, but also about perceptions of the relative professional standing and competence of these two groups.

To quote a recent example, Michael Stubbs (2001) is a linguist who, in his response to Widdowson (2000) (another controversy, indeed!) regards the questions Widdowson raises about direct applications of corpus data to language teaching as 'much ado about nothing' and 'a non-issue':

> ... see in particular Sinclair's (1991) response to Widdowson (1991), which makes clear that there is often much ado about nothing. Sinclair (1991) 'wholly endorses' (p. 491) Widdowson's view of the rights of pedagogy to determine its own affairs, and comments that
>
>> Corpus linguistics ... has no direct bearing on the way languages may be presented in a pedagogical context. ... Corpus linguistics makes no demands on the methodology of language teaching. It is not geared to serving any particular method, and the current software is quite neutral (Sinclair 1991: 489–99).
>
> These conciliatory remarks show that some criticism is over a non-issue. Sinclair does then make a fundamental point (p. 490) about data: 'many spokespeople in language education are nervous about new evidence, about having to say new and different things about a language'.
> (Stubbs 2001: 170, n.1)

Judging from this extract, there would indeed seem to be agreement about 'the rights of pedagogy to determine its own affairs' between linguists and applied linguists. However, statements Sinclair makes elsewhere are difficult to reconcile with his 'conciliatory remarks' quoted by Stubbs, namely that 'corpus linguistics has no direct bearing on the way languages may be presented in a pedagogical context'. For instance, Sinclair (1997) offers a set of precepts, and he says explicitly that they are 'precepts for language teachers', for instance: 'Present real examples only' (Sinclair 1997: 30ff.).

For the realm of pedagogy, then, Sinclair's insistence that 'real examples only' should be presented is translated into guiding principles in books for teachers, as in Willis's *The Lexical Syllabus*:

> Contrived simplification of language in the preparation of materials will always be faulty, since it is generated without the guide and support of a communicative context. Only by accepting the discipline of using authentic language are we likely to come anywhere near presenting the learner with a sample of language which is typical of real English.
> (Willis 1990: 127)

Others would argue that communicative contexts are not confined to native-speaker language use but can be created in the classroom itself. However, the combination of the prestige which corpus linguistics is enjoying, quite deservedly, in the area of linguistic description with the undiminishing popularity of concepts and slogans such as 'authenticity', 'real language' and 'native-speaker discourse' seems to have resulted in a kind of natural alliance between linguistic description and pedagogic prescription. This can make it difficult for dissenting voices to make themselves heard and to explain why things are not all that straightforward. It may be why, at first sight, this topic looks like a non-issue. However, the papers that follow suggest otherwise. They represent an invitation to think through some of the most fundamental questions all language teachers and applied linguists are involved in, whether they confront them explicitly or not. As Aston (2001b: 3) emphasizes, it is now 'technically and economically feasible for many language teachers and learners to use corpora if they so desire. This change of climate makes it all the more important that the roles of corpora in language teaching and learning should be discussed and evaluated'.

For everybody concerned with the teaching and learning of modern languages, and English in particular, corpus linguistics clearly represents a challenge to traditional ideas. It impinges on our professional lives in a major way, in the shape of corpus-based, or at least corpus-referenced, dictionaries, grammars, as well as syllabuses and materials designed with reference to frequency lists and collocational analyses. In many (though by no means the majority of) language classrooms computers are available, so that in principle it is possible for teachers and learners to explore corpora together and even to compile their own, tailor-made ones for specific purposes. Easy-to-use concordancing tools can be employed for what has been termed 'data-driven learning' (cf. Johns and King 1991). There has even been a call to 'cut out the middle man' (Johns 1994: 297), i.e. the teacher, by giving learners direct access to corpus data.

The major reorientation that corpus linguistics has brought for language description is generally welcomed as an important development from discovery procedures which rely on elicitation and/or native-speaker intuition. What is far less clear is what exactly the availability of new descriptions of a language means for the teaching of it. Obviously, the way language is actually used and the regularities of that use as revealed in corpus descriptions must be an important consideration in language teaching. After all, it has always been assumed that what learners should eventually achieve in proficiency is normal language, and since corpus descriptions provide new information about these norms hitherto not available, they clearly are relevant to the setting of goals for language courses. But it is also obvious that new findings cannot go directly into syllabuses and teaching materials without any pedagogical treatment: the very existence of classrooms, syllabuses, and teaching materials makes some pedagogic agency a logical necessity. In this respect it is interesting to look back at the classic *Fundamental Concepts of Language Teaching* (1983), where in a chapter entitled 'Linguistic theory and language teaching: reassessment and current status' H. H. Stern describes the following development during the 1970s:

> ... a shift was taking place from 'applying' linguistics directly to treating linguistics as a resource to be drawn on for the benefit of pedagogy with complete independence of mind.
> (Stern 1983: 174)

However, what Stern described with approval as an achievement of an earlier era still seems to be far from universally accepted by either teachers or linguists. There is, then, plenty of scope for negotiation and dialogue between corpus linguistics and language teaching, and this is essentially what the papers in this section are all about.

The issue they take up is one broached over a decade ago by Widdowson concerning the relationship between what linguists describe and what language teachers need to 'prescribe' as appropriate for learning (Widdowson 1991).[1] Widdowson argues that even if there is reason to suppose that corpus descriptions capture the reality of the language from the users' point of view (itself a contentious claim) it does not follow that they meet the conditions of pedagogic effectiveness. It might be helpful to quote a paragraph or two from this paper, since they provide a framework of reference for the exchange that follows:

> Language teaching cannot simply be based on descriptive facts, whether these are facts of attested frequency of usage which emerge from text analysis or facts of psychological reality in the minds of users such as conceptual elicitation might reveal.

---

[1] The plan for the current volume originally included the widely-quoted controversy between Widdowson (1991) and Sinclair (1991) precisely because it brings out the issues involved with particular clarity. Unfortunately, permission to republish Sinclair's paper could not be obtained and so this exchange could not be printed here.

These are 'factors' to be considered, of course, but not facts to be uncritically incorporated into prescriptions. Their relevance is not self-evident. It has to be established
by reference to pedagogic criteria. This is because, obviously enough, our business in
language teaching is not with the members of language user communities but with the
members of language learner communities. They too develop cognitive representations of lexis and grammar, prototype words and sentences which they may or may
not make manifest in actual performance, and which constitute the interim competence of their interlanguage. To the extent that second language acquisition research
has indicated the nature of such representations, it too provides us with factors to consider. But again, factors to consider, not facts to conform to. For even if we were
confident that we knew what the mental grammars and lexicons of learners (some
learners at least) were like, pedagogy would not, as a matter of fact, be bound by
them. They would provide a point of reference, but only *one* point of reference. There
are others to be taken note of as well in plotting a course of instruction. To be effective,
such a course might well lead the learners in directions very different from those they
would be naturally disposed to follow. One might argue indeed, that if it did not, there
would hardly be any point in plotting a course in the first place.

Language prescriptions for the inducement of learning cannot be based on a
database. They cannot be modelled on the description of externalised language,
the frequency profiles of text analysis. Such analysis provides us with facts, hitherto unknown, or ignored, but they do not of themselves carry any guarantee of
pedagogic relevance. The pioneers of corpus analysis, though their techniques
were crude, unaided by technology, showed a subtlety of perception in this regard
not always evident in their successors. ... pedagogic prescription specifies a succession of prototypes, preliminary versions of the language, each as a basis for later
improved models. In this way, learners are guided through the stages of induced
interlanguage by a process of gradual approximation to the norms of the language
user community. For learners the language is not real or authentic until they have
learned to realize and authenticate it. This process of authentication through interim versions of the language has to be guided by reference to other factors as well
as those of frequency and range of actual use, as was recognized by the pedagogic
pioneers in text analysis that I referred to earlier. ... Such factors have to do with
usefulness rather than use. Thus words and structures might be identified as
'pedagogically' core or nuclear, and preferred as a prototype at a particular
learning stage because of their coverage or their generative value, because they are
catalysts which activate the learning process, whatever their status might be in
respect to their actual occurrence in contexts of use.
(op. cit.: 20ff.)

There are, then, Widdowson argues, two sides to be taken into account in
equal measure in language teaching, as its name indicates – and neither the
'language' nor the 'teaching' side can have a monopoly on determining what
goes on in classrooms:

This does not, to be sure, deny the relevance of the facts revealed by the corpus
description of usage, or the elicitation of user knowledge. They do indeed reveal
facts, particularly about collocation and formulaic associations of syntax and
lexis, which are not otherwise accessible. But they represent the goal toward which

the learners have to be directed, and these facts need to be incorporated into pedagogic prototypes at appropriate stages. It would be as much a mistake to uncritically dismiss these facts as it would be to uncritically accept them. The point is that
their relevance and appropriacy to the learning process are matters of empirical
pedagogic enquiry ....

   The prescription of language for such contexts of instruction can, and should
be, informed by the description of language in contexts of use, but not be determined by it. And the cognitive representations, the prototypes, as interim interlanguage versions which activate learning are not the same as those which figure as
established features of knowledge in the minds of language users. For prescription
has its own conditions of adequacy to meet, and it is the business of language
pedagogy, and nobody else's business, to propose what these conditions might be.
(op. cit.: 22, 23)

But, as Widdowson indicates, questions about the pedagogic relevance of
descriptive findings go back to much earlier work in text analysis, and it is
important to put these questions into their wider historical context. Although
the analysis of actually occurring text has become a major development in linguistic description in recent years and has entered the linguistic mainstream
because of the available technology, this kind of analysis does not only date
from the arrival of the computer. In the 1930s and 1940s an enormous
amount of work was done, laboriously because manually, on word frequencies in actual use (for example, Palmer 1933; Swenson and West 1934; Palmer
and Hornby 1937; Palmer 1938), resulting eventually in such landmark publications as West's *General Service List* (1953). What is of particular interest
to note here is that this work was initiated by people concerned with language
teaching, particularly English-language teaching – the linguist and the teacher
were one and the same person. That is to say, the work was pedagogically
motivated (as indeed was the work of Gougenheim *et al.* 1956). The findings
were therefore also interpreted from a pedagogic point of view by the very
people who conducted the linguistic-descriptive research (notably Harold E.
Palmer, Michael West, and A. S. Hornby: see Howatt 1984: Chapters 16–18).
This meant that descriptive facts such as frequency, range, and collocation
were considered in close conjunction with pedagogic criteria such as teacha-
bility, learnability in classroom contexts, coverage value, and so on.
Interestingly, Mackey discusses possible conflicts among these criteria and
how they might be pedagogically resolved, thus anticipating a number of
issues raised in the papers below (cf. Mackey 1965: 188–90).

   It will be relatively easy to recognize these fundamental issues in the
papers which follow, even though in some cases different terms are employed
by different authors. What makes these papers particularly accessible is that
they also relate teachers' and learners' experiences and observations and
offer examples from language-teaching materials.

   The first exchange below is actually cast in the form of letters and thus
particularly personal and lively: a (public) correspondence conducted

between two prominent British corpus linguists, Ron Carter and Michael McCarthy of Nottingham University, and Luke Prodromou, an English-language teacher resident in Thessaloniki, Greece (and subsequently a research student at Nottingham). As Prodromou indicates, his letter initiating the exchange was prompted by an *ELT Journal* article by Carter and McCarthy in the year preceding the correspondence.

Text 10

Luke Prodromou

Correspondence

From Luke Prodromou

The title of McCarthy and Carter's article on the grammar of spoken English: 'Spoken grammar: what is it and how can we teach it?' (49/3) captures very well the strengths and the weaknesses of the authors' argument. The title reflects the tension between applied linguistics research, on the one hand, and pedagogic issues on the other. In this response to the article I would like to address the question of how the insights of research are transferred to the classroom, and what the specific proposals made by McCarthy and Carter might imply for the cultural content of classroom materials. In particular, what does the grammar of informal spoken English mean for the non-native speaker of English, and what is the pedagogic relevance of this particular variety of English in the context of English as an international language?

Undoubtedly, the description of informal spoken English is full of fascinating insights for both the teacher and anyone interested in the English language, and McCarthy and Carter are right to recommend that anyone wishing to teach this particular variety of English should take into account the actual features of the language as revealed in the Nottingham corpus and not some putative language based on written English. Having said that, I feel McCarthy and Carter make a number of assumptions about what we teach and how we teach which have worrying cultural and pedagogic implications.

Assumption 1

The main thrust of their argument is that samples of informal spoken English are a more appropriate basis for classroom materials than the 'spoken' English found in textbooks. The English often found in textbooks is indeed 'unnatural' compared to the informal British English found in the corpus, but the question EFL teachers (as opposed to ESL teachers) round the world may be asking is how 'unnatural' is textbook English when compared to less informal varieties of English, spoken not only by British native speakers but also by the more than 300 million speakers of English as a second language and the 100 million or so speakers of English as a foreign language? The 'unnaturalness' factor also needs to be seen in the light of English as a means of communication not as addressed to native speakers but as a lingua franca between one non-native speaker and another. Before making decisions about classroom materials and methods, as McCarthy and Carter do, one would also like to know whether American or Australian informal speech manifests the same linguistic features as British informal English.

McCarthy and Carter's reference to informal British English as 'real' English recalls the campaign for 'authentic' materials which accompanied the rise of communicative language teaching in the 1970s and 1980s. This movement culminated in a whole range of textbooks containing pedagogically irrelevant and demotivating materials drawn from native-speaker contexts such as railway timetables, advertisements, letters to British newspapers, and endless consumer leaflets which had little to offer EFL students and did little to meet their communicative needs. To assume that what is 'real' is also interesting and useful is a fallacy. What is 'real' and interesting (whether spoken or written language) to the native speaker as a member of a particular speech community may be utterly boring to the non-native speaker. Indeed, the meaning of such 'real' samples of language may be difficult to recover if you are not a member of the particular linguistic and cultural community which gave rise to these samples of language in the first place. This brings me to the second assumption made by McCarthy and Carter.

Assumption 2

The authors suggest language awareness activities as a means of exploiting informal British English in the classroom. It is clear that though they place the emphasis on receptive understanding they also see the material leading to improved production of language by students. To what extent are non-native speakers able to learn informal British English? My feeling as a bilingual/bicultural speaker of English is that informal British English is a variety of English intimately tied up with the culture of the interlocutors, either on a local personal level or on a more general cultural level. In other words, you cannot speak like the British in an informal context if you do not share their interpersonal cultural assumptions and experiences – in short if you do not assume at least some of the defining features of a British identity. If you cannot draw on the often implicit and highly elusive cultural resources of native speakers you cannot, to put it bluntly, 'speak like them'. This point is clearer if we add to McCarthy and Carter's lexical and syntactic description a phonological dimension: if a non-native speaker attempts to speak informal British English without the stress, rhythm, tone of voice, and intonation of a native speaker he or she will produce a variety of non-native English that sounds as odd, if not odder, than 'English modelled on an almost exclusively written version of the language' (McCarthy and Carter 1995: 207).

As an awareness-raising activity, looking at informal British English is no more valuable than looking at other culturally-loaded language, such as advertisements, headlines, or railway timetables. Indeed, most non-native speakers are more likely to encounter these more 'writerly' varieties than the informal 'genres' arising from the Nottingham spoken corpus.

Assumption 3

To what extent are non-native speakers able to teach informal British English? In my experience, most non-native speaking teachers would probably find it very difficult, without the requisite linguistic and cultural background, to cope with the samples quoted by McCarthy and Carter, compared to a whole range of less informal varieties which are more accessible and recoverable outside their original context. I hope I am not underestimating my colleagues, but I feel the pedagogic outcome of the linguistic proposals made by McCarthy and Carter would be to reinforce the professional supremacy of the native speaker. Getting students to use the past continuous and tag questions in neutral 'writerly' ways is difficult enough for most teachers without the extra challenge of past continuous and tails as used by British native speakers when they are on their cultural home ground. The 'expertise' of the native speaker will be clearly superior when it comes to teaching varieties of English which are often domestic and so subtly intuitive and culturally embedded (see Rampton 1990; Phillipson 1992).

Like previous models of language learning this century, McCarthy and Carter's model assumes that a significant number of learners of English around the world are investing considerable time, money, and resources in order to speak to native speakers and be spoken to by native speakers. Indeed, this is one possible reason for learning English, especially among learners planning to study in the UK or spend two weeks in the summer there on holiday. The rest of the world, I suspect, mostly needs English as a lingua franca for interpersonal and professional contact between non-native speakers of the language.

In conclusion, as a teacher I welcome the challenge and the insights of work from applied linguists like McCarthy and Carter. However, I would query the instant transferability of research in general to the pedagogic domain before a process of mediation takes place in order to ascertain and meet learners' and teachers' needs and wants. The two domains of research and classroom practice must work together for the benefit of the learner. This is a time-consuming process which hopefully will explore the issues involved: linguistic, pedagogic, and cultural. It is also a two-way process.

References

Phillipson, R. 1992. 'ELT: the native-speaker's burden?' *ELT Journal* 46/1: 12–18.
Rampton, M. B. H. 1990. 'Displacing the native speaker: expertise, affiliation, and inheritance', *ELT Journal* 44/2: 87–101.

Text 11

Ronald Carter, Michael McCarthy

Correspondence

In his letter to *ELT Journal* (Volume 50/1) Luke Prodromou challenges several assumptions in our paper 'Spoken grammar: what is it and how can we teach it?' (Volume 49/3). We are admirers of Luke Prodromou and even though we disagree with him in places, we have always found his writings on ELT provocative and stimulating. Our aim in this brief reply is to acknowledge the importance of the issues he raises and to attempt to take a little further a debate which all concerned believe to be of considerable importance to ELT. Central to this debate is the role of corpus-based description of the English language. We do not believe corpus-based studies of English will go away. They will grow steadily and, as the COBUILD project has already done, will force us to revise long-cherished understandings about the English language. In particular, we consider that descriptions of spoken English, which have so far only rarely entered standard grammars and dictionaries, will continue to present challenges to teachers of English at all levels and in all contexts. We know that Luke Prodromou is not directly advocating this position, but it would be an unfortunate consequence of his position if teachers felt they could comfortably dismiss findings which simply do not fit what we know or do already.

We would also ask if it is not patronizing to learners to decide in advance that they need not have access to certain kinds of English because it probably does not meet their requirements. Is this not also a restriction in learner choice? And, even though we know or should know that native speakers do not own the language, does it not ignore a psychological reality in that all of us as language learners and teachers are intrigued by real discourse and by what native speakers do with it?

We know from our own knowledge of our first language that in most textbook discourse we are getting something which is concocted for us, and may therefore rightly resent being disempowered by teachers or materials writers who, on apparently laudable ideological grounds, appear to know better. Information or knowledge about language should never be held back; the task is to make it available, without artificial restrictions, in ways which most answer learners' needs.

The charges against our ideological and cultural assumptions are well made; indeed, we agree with Luke Prodromou that informal spoken English carries a subtext of cultural assumptions, and that native speaker teachers may feel more comfortable with such intimate and interpersonal uses of English, including its intonation. But one counter argument might be that, if findings such as those outlined in our paper are not absorbed into classroom and teacher development materials, then the 'power' of the native speaker may never be properly challenged. (Incidentally, we think it may also be naive to assume that any version of international English is not embedded in all kinds of cultural, value-laden inflections.) The real challenge is surely to provide descriptions and to develop materials which serve the needs of teachers in all situations, whether they be native or non-native, so that they can decide how best to make such hitherto unrecorded aspects of English more widely accessible. Teachers may, of course, decide *not* to make use of such material, but it is important that they should know why they decide to withhold what they decide to withhold from their learners.

Our view is that a process of description of spoken grammar, and the development of appropriate pedagogies of presentation, will create more *choices* for learners. It is important that we recognize that there is more to language than 'neutral' information transfer, and that learners also need to be able to choose to express the kinds of affect, attitude, evaluation, and interpersonality which are a marked feature of spoken language. These features are more likely to be located at the more informal ends of the spoken–written continuum, and we can learn much, therefore, from comparison between formal and informal grammars and from helping learners develop a feel for such differences. And we hope soon to be in a position to demonstrate some of the features which are common to formal and informal grammars in other international Englishes.

We are currently exploring the possibilities of different methods of classroom presentation of different genres of spoken grammar, and will remain alert to Luke

Prodromou's observations. At present, methods include a mainly language awareness, consciousness-raising approach directed to helping learners notice some of the different lexical and grammatical choices available to them in different contexts. For example, different levels of formality in service encounters, different styles of interview and discussion, audience-sensitive telephone calls, informal narratives and anecdotes, language in use in joint tasks, and so on. Among the pedagogic issues we are exploring are: the extent to which authentic data can be modified (so that key spoken forms can be highlighted); tasks involving comparison of real and concocted data; role play involving exposure to raw data, and so on. Our main pedagogic effort is to find the best ways of moving from awareness to appropriate use.

In this regard we applaud Luke Prodromou's appeal for a new paradigm for applied linguistics in which those who are primarily either descriptive linguists, or materials developers, or classroom teachers work more closely together, asking questions about the how as well as about the what. Trialling and improving such material requires the kind of collaborative approach outlined by Luke Prodromou, and we are the first to concede that things should not be wholly entrusted to those whose primary job is to do the descriptive language research. But we reiterate that not to engage with such material and data runs the risk of disempowering teachers and learners and of seriously restricting their choices as users of both written and spoken English.

So far the debate has focused on spoken *grammar*. Our research is also opening up faultlines in the description of continua between spoken and written *vocabularies* of English, revealing some imbalances in existing descriptions, and clearly demonstrating the different expressive choices available to native speakers. It would be regrettable if some teachers, however culturally sensitive they are, were to choose too rigidly which choices learners should have.

Note

The descriptive and pedagogic research described here is being mainly undertaken in the English Studies Department of Nottingham University. The CANCODE project, as it is called, is a joint enterprise between Nottingham University and Cambridge University Press (CANCODE stands for 'Cambridge and Nottingham Corpus for the Description of English'). All data collected are the property of Cambridge University Press. Future plans include an extension of the corpus to include parallel data from other world Englishes, and we greatly welcome the opportunity to explore different varieties of English in the context of different discourse communities afforded by this extension and by the many other corpora of international Englishes which are becoming available.

Text 12

Luke Prodromou

Correspondence

As I was going through some plays by Arthur Miller and Harold Pinter with an advanced student of mine she asked me whether she should use the following 'authentic' English expressions when talking to native-speakers: 'bottoms up', 'between the devil and the deep blue sea', 'feeling chuffed', 'ba**ing away', and 'bo***cks'. She asked if native-speakers used language like this, and I replied 'In some cases, yes'. I added that I thought she should avoid using them, however, because they were taboo words, or restricted to British or American English, or because, not having a native-speaker accent, some of the expressions might sound odd when she spoke them. However, she wanted very much to speak real English, and so a few days later she tried out some of the idioms on me. She came up with 'your bottom is up' and 'I am chaffed'. I suggested she stick to 'Cheers' and 'Very pleased' instead.

This story illustrates my concern over when and how we should introduce students of English as a Foreign Language (as opposed to a Second Language) to real and authentic English. The use of words like 'real' and 'authentic' by Ron Carter and Michael McCarthy in their letter above therefore begs a lot of questions. It would seem difficult to resist the tide of words laden with positive associations that Carter and McCarthy mobilize in their response to my argument that the 'real' spoken English they describe in their work is only one, albeit fascinating, variety of modern English, which if introduced on a large scale into most EFL classrooms would disable not only the learner but the non-native teacher, too (see Widdowson, 'Authenticity and autonomy' (Volume 50/1)). How can one not agree with them that it is a bad thing to restrict learner choice? How can one object to anything that is authentic and real as opposed to concocted? Who wants to be inauthentic or – even worse – unreal? As a teacher or course designer, one would feel most illiberal and undemocratic withholding information and knowledge from the learner. Methodologically, 'awareness raising' and 'consciousness raising' are key words in any progressive teacher's repertoire. However, apart from their feel-good quality, what do 'choice', 'real', 'authentic', and 'knowledge' mean in this particular context, i.e. the teaching of English as an international language in a wide variety of sociocultural situations? After all, Coca-Cola also claims to be 'the real thing'.

Consider this syllogism:

1 Informal British English is real and authentic because it is the product of people communicating in the here and now;
2 The forms – lexical, grammatical and discoursal – which give authentic utterances their 'here and nowness' are determined by contextual features such as who the interlocutors are, where they are, their relationship, the purpose of the communication, their previous knowledge, their shared assumptoms, the micro-culture of the situation, and the broader macro-culture of the society they have been immersed in all their lives.
3 One vital dimension of the here and now of authentic spoken discourse is the phonology that accompanies it, which of course has important semantic and discourse functions.
4 These contextual features in the here and now, taken as an integrated whole, are what shape the linguistic choices the speakers make, and give natural discourse its vitality and meaning.
5 What happens when I take this natural discourse out of its original context and transplant into another context, another time and place, for example, by

putting it into a textbook for the consumption of learners of English as a Foreign Language? Is it still authentic, real, and natural? When you displace authentic discourse in time and place and strip it of the contextual features that gave it life in the first place, does it not lose its 'here and nowness', and therefore its authenticity? Even if in its original context it had some sound and fury, does it not become a shadow of its former self, signifying far less than it did?

6 Conclusion: such displaced discourse may not be concocted but it can hardly be presented to students as real and authentic, at least *for them*.

The most reliable way to test what I have just written is to take extracts from the Nottingham corpus and give them to a non-native speaker to read aloud.

One also wonders whether informal British English is perhaps a variety of the language which most students are unlikely to encounter for extensive periods, let alone have to produce, simply because they do not belong to the micro or macro-culture of the British native-speaker.

To argue that presenting such displaced language to students is to give them the choices they are entitled to is simplistic. Given the time and constraints under which most students learn and most teachers teach we cannot take a free market approach to syllabus design, an approach which says: make language freely available and let the student choose the language they want. This is what Carter and McCarthy suggest. However, courses have to be designed, with the students' involvement, according to perceived needs and objectives and, given the time and resources available, a selection has to be made from the infinite possibilities of modern English. This is why I may decide to 'withhold' (as Carter and McCarthy put it) from my teenage student real and authentic extracts from the *Wall Street Journal* on leading industrials, gilts, conventionals and quiet builders.

These extracts may be real and natural English to the members of the Wall Street discourse community, but to the rest of the world they are worse than concocted textbook English. Authenticity is in the eyes of the participants: it is inseparable from context – take context away and you have, potentially, concocted a most frustrating and meaning-less encounter with language. I may choose not to make such varieties of English an integral part of my syllabus simply because they are extremely context and culture-bound as well as being inappropriate to the needs and interests of my learners.

Pedagogically speaking, the question of lexical and grammatical forms is only one way in which we engage students and motivate them to learn a foreign language: content is another, and Carter and McCarthy ignore the risk that undiluted authentic material often runs, of being utterly boring to anyone not involved in the original interaction. What are the extracts in the corpora *about*, and will they engage my students? This is a question teachers are entitled to ask about any potential syllabus items.

Again, on the pedagogic level, the mind of this teacher boggles at the thought of any but very advanced students engaging in the kind of linguistic awareness-raising activities outlined by Carter and McCarthy in their original article and in their letter. The revised methodological proposals in their letter now include role play involving exposure to raw data, which confirms that they see EFL/ESL students responding to and producing Pinteresque utterances like these from the Nottingham corpus:

— D'you want a biscuit
— Erm
— Biscuit
— Er yeah
— (pause)
— All right
— Yeah
— (pause)
— Didn't know you used boiling water
— Pardon
— Didn't know you used boiling water
— Don't have to but it's ... they reckon it's erm
— (pause)
— Tony was saying they should have the heating on by about Wednesday.

The question is this: is the choice we are faced with really between this kind of English and 'concocted' language, as Carter and McCarthy say? My feeling is that there is a place for both undoctored authentic material and for specially written or adapted material depending on the level, age, and needs of the learners in a particular time and place. The kind of authentic English we *do* choose to draw on need not be as culturally loaded as informal British English – there are less culturally marked varieties as one moves towards the more formal, or standard, end of the spectrum and towards varieties of English used by native and non-native speakers in local and international contexts. Carter and McCarthy refer repeatedly to English, spoken language, and spoken grammar as if these were single, homogeneous entities: whatever happened to world Englishes? In sum, I feel much of what corpora of British informal English are throwing up should be considered carefully by all teachers of EFL and especially ESL; to anyone interested in language the study of such discourse is an endless source of fascination and increased awareness of how language works. Some of the less culture-bound insights of corpora of informal British English will be absorbed into the mainstream of lexis and grammar of English as an international language, which as Carter and McCarthy say, also needs to be explored through corpora. Textbook writers, like myself, even when they write 'concocted' materials for particular levels of students, will henceforth be obliged to take into account and incorporate some of the more common core features revealed by the Nottingham corpus. Carter and McCarthy may be interested to know that as an author I have already begun to incorporate some of their insights into textbook materials. As one variety of English amongst others, informal British English may well form part of the exposure we would like our students to have to the many facets of English as an international language. In this sense, the dialogue initiated by the work of Carter and McCarthy is challenging, and of enormous benefit to all of us involved in ELT. One merely wishes there were less haste in moving from the laboratory to the classroom.

Luke Prodromou,
Thessaloniki, Greece

Moving on chronologically, one of the above authors also features in the next exchange: in a (then newly introduced) section of the *ELT Journal* called 'Point and Counterpoint', Ron Carter's paper prompts a response by Guy Cook, an applied linguist now at Reading University, and well-known for his work on discourse analysis, literature, and language play. His remarks on Willis and Lewis will probably make readers want to consult the works cited by these authors directly. What might also be interesting to watch out for is whether any differences in Carter's stance can be discerned in comparison with what he said in response to Prodromou two years earlier, and also which arguments are reiterated that were put forward by Widdowson (1991) in the paper quoted from above.

This controversy is concluded in a particularly constructive way by a paper by Gavioli and Aston, published much later but in the same journal. This article revisits some of the issues considered by Carter and Cook, examines Carter's examples with reference to actual corpus evidence, puts the issues into wider perspective, and extends the discussion to the potential of corpora as tools in the hands of learners.

Text 13

Ronald Carter

Orders of reality: CANCODE, communication, and culture

This article is concerned with the topic of language awareness in relation to spoken texts and their cultural contexts. The topic has become more relevant in recent years, as we have witnessed the development of more and more corpora of spoken English; more exciting developments in the work of COBUILD; the growth of the British National Corpus, with its spoken components; and the development of CANCODE by the author and Michael McCarthy at Nottingham University, with the support of Cambridge University Press. The data in this paper are drawn from everyday situations of language use collected for CANCODE and developed with an eye to their potential relevance for ELT.

Real English

The CANCODE[1] data is, of course, real data. Now 'real' is a word I'd like to dwell on for a moment because it is widely used at present in our cultures, particularly in our ELT culture. For example:

　　Real ale
　　Get real!
　　Enjoy that real country taste of Crackerbarrel cheese
　　You're out of touch with reality
　　Real English
　　Coca Cola … The Real Thing

The word 'real' invariably carries positive associations. People believe they want or are told to want or, indeed, *actually* want what is real, authentic, and natural in preference to what is unreal, inauthentic, and unnatural.

Three questions

Three significant concerns have emerged in the course of our research at
Nottingham University. First, there are many features of real, naturally-
occurring, spoken standard English grammar which are not recorded in the
standard grammars of the English language. The major standard grammars are,
of course, based largely on the written language and on examples drawn from
single-sentence, sometimes concocted, written examples.[2] This raises the first
question: in the light of new evidence, should we make any changes to the
grammar we teach? Second, all the data collected so far have been collected in
specific cultural contexts, almost all involving native speakers of English.
CANCODE is soon to be extended to include several other international varieties
of English, but at present all the examples illustrate standard British spoken
English and aspects of British English cultures. This raises the second question:
do we want the native speaker as our model, particularly if it means that we
have to take the native speaker's culture as well? Third, is there an automatic
transfer from natural, real, corpus-based spoken English to the textbooks and
pedagogies used for the teaching of English as a second or foreign language? In
other words, and this raises the fourth question: in the light of all this new
information, should we modify our teaching materials or not?

What can real spoken English reveal?

There is a focus in CANCODE on interpersonal communication in a range of
social contexts and, wherever possible, differences and distinctions are drawn
between the kinds of language used in those contexts. By providing many
examples of English used in informal contexts, comparisons can be made
which are of potential use to language teachers and learners, since they
illustrate how speakers make different choices according to the situation they
are in.

The key theoretical and practical concerns are not with general sociological
categories but with specific language choices: which forms of language do we
choose for which purposes, and which interpersonal choices do we make
according to whom we are interacting with? The key issue for materials writers
and teachers, therefore, is whether we can generate and teach materials which
help learners to choose and interact appropriately, particularly along a
continuum from written to spoken discourse.

Here are some examples of what CANCODE shows us about choices in the
spoken language:

Three-part exchanges

Question and answer sequences in many real conversations are never simply
questions and answers because they are accompanied by a follow-up move in
which, in the third part, the questioner offers some kind of comment on or even
evaluation of the answer:

A: What part of London are you staying in?
B: In Hyde Park.
A: Oh, are you? That's a nice district.

A: What time is it?
B: A quarter past six.
A: Is it? I thought it was later.
(CANCODE)

The third part in such exchanges is regularly filled by what Lewis (1993) would call 'lexical chunks', that is, fixed or routinized phrases such as 'Really?', 'That's interesting', 'That's nice', 'I thought so', or 'I guessed as much'. Indeed, it is worth noting that the absence of a follow-up comment can make a question and answer sequence rather cold and impersonal. It is worth scrutinizing English language coursebooks to check whether there are more three-part than two-part exchanges. Our research at Nottingham University suggests that in some ELT materials and English language coursebooks, at least, two-part exchanges may be more common. (For further discussion see McCarthy and Carter 1994, Chapter 5; Tsui 1994.) However, in materials based on real English, such as the Collins *Cobuild English Course* (Willis and Willis 1988), we note that three-part exchanges are more common. Clearly there are issues here of a tension between truth to the language and pedagogic judgement. Or it may just be that you don't know these things about the spoken language until you collect real data.

Vague language

We are overwhelmed in our data by examples of what Channell (1994) has termed 'vague language'. Several English language coursebooks do not exhibit many examples of vague language, even though it is always pragmatically highly significant, and nearly always enables polite and non-threatening interaction. For example:

See you *around* six

Q: What time are we meeting?
A: Oh, seven-thirty *or thereabouts*.

There were *about* twenty *or so* people at the dinner.
(CANCODE)

In the case of time and number reference, vague language is non-authoritarian and puts speakers on an immediately casual and equal footing with their interlocutors. Comparison with utterances marked by their precision (e.g. 'See you at seven-twenty') reveals how much more formal and directive they are (see also Carter 1987).

Ellipsis

Ellipsis is one of the most frequent grammatical features found in our data, and its pervasive and endemic character is in inverse proportion to the sparse treatment it receives in many traditional grammars and course materials. (More detailed description is given in McCarthy and Carter 1995). Preliminary exploration of data from other varieties of informal, spoken, international English reveals that ellipsis is also pervasive in these varieties.

Realities and coursebooks

In the examples below, real conversational data collected in a hairdressing salon (Example 1) is contrasted with an invented dialogue in a similar situation (Example 2), taken from a widely used and internationally renowned coursebook.[3]

Example 1
[In the hair salon]
A: Do you want to come over here?
B: Right, thanks (3 secs) thank you
A: Tea or coffee?
B: Can I have a tea, please?
A: Do you want any sugar?
B: Er, no milk or sugar, just black thanks
C: Right.
B: I hate it when your hair just gets so, you know a bit long
    [C: Yeah] and it's just straggly.
C: Right.
B: It just gets to that in-between stage
    [C: Yeah] doesn't it where you think oh I just can't stand it any more (2 secs)
    I think when it's shorter it tends to, you notice it growing more anyway
    [C: Mm] you know it tends to grow all of a sudden ...
(CANCODE)

Example 2
[At the hairdresser's]
Jane: ... Oh, yes, my husband's wonderful!
Sally: Really? Is he?
Jane: Yes, he's big, strong, and handsome!
Sally: Well, my husband isn't very big, or very strong ... but he's very intelligent.
Jane: Intelligent?
Sally: Yes, he can speak six languages.
Jane: Can he? Which languages can he speak?
Sally: He can speak French, Spanish, Italian, German, Arabic and Japanese.
Jane: Oh! ... My husband's very athletic.
Sally: Athletic?
Jane: Yes, he can swim, ski, play football, cricket and rugby ...
Sally: Can he cook?
Jane: Pardon?
Sally: Can your husband cook? My husband can't play sports ... but he's an excellent cook.
Jane: Is he?
Sally: Yes, and he can sew, and iron ... he's a very good husband.
Jane: Really? Is he English?
(Hartley and Viney, *Streamline English Departures*, Unit 14) (1978)

The real data in Example 1 contains features familiar to anyone who has scrutinized real English spoken discourse: a preponderance of discourse markers ('right' as an acknowledgement); ellipsis; the use of hedges (particularly the adverb 'just'); vague language ('you know', 'that in-between stage'); supposedly ungrammatical forms ('a tea'); as well as the use of 'tend to' to describe habitual or regular actions and events. ('Tend to' is one of the most frequent verbs in the CANCODE data, but while several of the standard grammars recognize its semi-modal status, they give more attention to the more central modals, and do not differentiate the verb's provenance in spoken compared to written discourse.)

Example 2 works well pedagogically. One of the main points of the exchange is to teach the modal verb 'can', and this point of presentation overrides other features of the situation. There is thus a further pedagogic reality to be noted: that in some successful coursebooks, rather than the dialogue taking precedence over the linguistic features to be learnt, the language teaching points take precedence over the reality of the dialogue. Many materials writers and teachers would say that in most circumstances such design features are inevitable. In other words, we should look at how much practice is given in this material, particularly in the posing and answering of questions, and in the use of the modal *can*, as well as at how much vocabulary is introduced and practised. In this respect, compare it to the real hair salon data, where the exchanges are natural but not lexically rich – as is common in informal conversations, the same words tend to be recycled, and the topics are seldom noted for their interesting content. In many classrooms, straggly hair which grows too quickly may have a limited topic life.

There are a number of general observations which can be made about the nature of interpersonal interaction in Example 1 which marks it off as naturally-occurring discourse. For example, speakers interrupt each other and speak at the same time. There are longish pauses, back-channelling, and the use of contentless utterances such as 'yeah', and 'Mm' which indicate that contact is being maintained, and serve to oil the wheels of the conversation; utterances are incomplete or are completed by the other speaker; and the conversation drifts along without any marked direction. By contrast, the language of some coursebooks represents a 'can do' society, in which interaction is generally smooth and problem-free, the speakers co-operate with each other politely, the conversation is neat, tidy, and predictable, utterances are almost as complete as sentences, no-one interrupts anyone else or speaks at the same time as anyone else, and the questions and answers are sequenced rather in the manner of a quiz show or court-room interrogation.

The two texts therefore represent different orders of reality. The scripted text is *unreal* English, which is unlikely to be reproduced in actual contexts of use but is easier to comprehend, and more real pedagogically; the unscripted text is *real* English, but more difficult to comprehend and to produce, and therefore likely to be considered less real pedagogically. It is worth scrutinizing the spoken materials we use in our teaching in the light of these poles of reality.

Here are two more samples of the corpus data, both taken from service encounters of the kind which are regularly reproduced in teaching materials.

Example 3
[In the post office]
A: Right, send that first class, please.
B: That one wants to go first class, right we'll see if it is, it's not 41, it's a 60, I thought it would be, I'd be in the … 60 pence … there we are.

A: Lovely, thank you.
B: Okay, 70 80 whoops 90 100.
A: Thanks very much.
B: Thank you
(CANCODE)

Example 4
[In the post office]
A: Can I have a second class stamp, please.
B: You can … there we are.
A: Thank you.
B: And one penny.
A: That's for me to spend is it?
B: That's right.
A: I bought a new book of ten first class when I was in town today and
I've left them at home in me shopping bag.
B: Have you?
A: And I've got one left.
B: Oh dear.
A: Bye.
B: Bye.
(CANCODE)

These data are interesting, in particular, for the number of exchanges which are interpersonal rather than simply transactional and informative. Examples 3 and 4, for instance, illustrate the extent to which the exchanges are three-part rather than two-part exchanges, and with a third part which is markedly interactive and affective in some way, sometimes to the point of inserting personal anecdotes, discourse markers, or non-propositional language ('whoops'). Notice again how the spoken grammar breaks the rules of textbook grammar ('Right, send that first class please'), in that real spoken standard English not infrequently combines politeness markers and imperatives. Or 'That one wants to go first class', when a modal verb is used ungrammatically (but, in spoken standard British English, perfectly normally) with a non-animate subject such as a parcel.

In Example 5, also a service encounter, the situation is markedly different:

Example 5
[In a fish and chip shop]
A: Can I have chips, beans, and a sausage?
B: Chips, beans, and a sausage.
A: Yeah.
B: Wrapped up?
A: Open, please.
(CANCODE)

In terms of speaking cultures, the data illustrate some of the possible dangers of real speech, which is often messy and untidy, and embedded deeply in cultural understandings of various kinds to the point where individual words and choices of grammatical form can be of considerable cultural significance. Notice here, for example, how the word 'open' becomes contextually constructed into an antonym of 'wrapped up', and carries a specific cultural meaning of food being served in paper so that it can be eaten immediately, even perhaps while walking home. How far should such allusions be removed, and how relevant is it to learn to make cultural observations of the kind that fish and chip shops in Britain are just as likely, if not more, to sell sausages, burgers, and curry with chips as they are to sell fish and chips?

The language of the fish and chip shop is mainly transactional and, in fact, anything more interactive and interpersonal would be out of place because there are normally long queues of hungry customers in the shop. We should note in this respect how appropriate the ellipsis is, and how in such circumstances the full forms would be unnecessarily elaborated and even long-winded. However, some coursebook exchanges employ full forms, on the perfectly realistic pedagogic premise that you cannot ellipt utterances until you know and have first practised the full forms from which the reductions are made. Having said that, ellipsis is not particularly pervasive, even in intermediate to more advanced coursebooks, and learners are rarely presented with opportunities to understand which choices of which alternative forms are appropriate for which communicative purposes.

Speaking cultures

One common feature of the CANCODE data is the large number of formulaic, fixed phrases that are used in spoken discourse. The findings again endorse the view expressed in Lewis (1993) that the language is made up of lexical chunks, and that language teaching and learning should give more systematic attention to such high profile features of the language. Many of the most fixed of fixed expressions are, of course, quite culture-bound. And learners who are taught to read and see through such language can learn quite a bit about the cultures in which the language is embedded.

For example, what can we learn about English culture from the following idioms and fixed phrases, all of which involve some reference to foreign, in this case mainly European, nations?

Dutch courage
to go Dutch
double-Dutch
Dutch cap
If that's true, then I'm a Dutchman
Dutch auction

It's all Greek to me
Beware of Greeks bearing gifts

French leave
French letter
French kiss
French lessons

Here we learn several useful and widely used phrases, but we can also learn something about British insularity, and that distrust of foreigners to the point where the British can be interpreted as believing almost all of them to be either unintelligible, untrustworthy, or 'unreal'. The phrases also reveal attitudes towards other languages than English, such as a feeling of linguistic superiority, and the suspicion that foreigners engage in sexual practices we dare not even mention, except by giving them a foreign name.

Other examples could, of course, be enumerated. One major issue here is the extent to which such cultural particulars are removed from data developed for purposes of classroom teaching and learning. It is argued below that such particulars can and should be retained in materials, provided a discovery-based language awareness component is used simultaneously to develop sensitivity to language and to enhance cultural understanding. Such skills are a not inessential component of 'seeing through', i.e. reading and learning how to interpret all cultural features and products, whether that culture be constructed with a small or a large 'c'. (See Brown 1990, Carter 1995, Carter and Nash 1990, Kramsch 1993.)

Conclusions

What conclusions can be drawn from the discussion so far?

1   On the one hand, we have real English which, as far as classroom treatment is concerned, can be unrealistic; and on the other hand, we have unreal textbook English which, as far as classroom treatment is concerned, is frequently handled in pedagogically viable and realistic ways.
2   Much spoken English is impregnated with cultural values. On the one hand, it is patronizing of teachers, coursebook writers, and materials designers to say to learners that we know what you should have and will therefore remove and neutralize all but the most accessible cultural reference. Is this realistic, when learners seem to want to know what real English is, and are generally fascinated by the culturally-embedded use of language of native speakers? Above all, learners know from their L1 experience when they are in the presence of concocted and culturally-disinfected dialogues.

On the other hand, we might want to argue that roughly 80 per cent of all spoken interaction in English is between non-native speakers, for example between a Turkish secretary and a Japanese supplier. For most learners, therefore, interactions with native speakers will be rare. It is surely unrealistic, and at the same time an imposition, to expect learners to acquire naturalistic, real, native-speaker English when they simply don't need it (Prodromou 1990, Rampton 1990, Phillipson 1992).
3   Those who argue that non-native speakers do not need exposure to real English assume that language learners only need to learn to transact, and have no real need to interact in the target language. On the other hand, it can be argued that, more often than is realized, language users at all levels also need to build relationships, express attitudes and affect, evaluate and comment, and make the propositional content of a message more person-oriented.
4   There are thus issues of power and empowerment at stake here. On the one hand, real English advantages and empowers the native-speaker teacher, but disempowers the non-native speaker teacher. It is yet another version of cultural and linguistic hegemony. On the other hand, it would be clearly disempowering, and once again patronizing to teachers and learners, to say that we can ignore a lot of these informal and interactive meanings, because one outcome would be to deprive the learner of pedagogic, linguistic, and cultural choices. Which strategy and ideology is the more disempowering?

Correctness and variable rules

It is, of course, misleading to suggest to learners of English that grammar is simply a matter of choices. Grammatical rules exist; they have been extensively codified, and form the core of the structure of (both spoken and written) language. Rules exist, for example, that prescribe that in Standard British English a plural subject has to be followed by a plural form of the verb, and that it is simply and unequivocally *incorrect* for us to write or say, therefore, that 'the buildings is very high'. Within a central core, choices are not possible.

As we have seen, however, there are areas of meaning which are selected within the grammar. Within the domain of spoken grammar we have also seen that it may be more accurate to speak in terms of variable rather than absolute rules for certain choices.

My own position is simply to say that teachers and learners can always choose *not* to teach and learn those areas of language where rules are more probabilistic than determinate, but that they have no choice at all if such options are not made available. Learners should not be patronized by being told that they do not need to bother with all this real English. They should not be disempowered, and syllabuses should not be deliberately impoverished. Also, learning a language should, in part at least, involve developing something of a 'feel' for that language. The folk-linguistic term 'feel' has been around for many years in language teaching, but it has remained a largely unanalysed concept. Learners who concentrate on the more rule-bound and referential domains are unlikely to develop the kind of sensitivity, personal response, and affect which probably underlies 'feel', and which goes some way to helping them discover, understand, and begin to internalize the expressive as well as the referential resources of a language.

Corpora of real, naturally-occurring English are not going to go away, and will become increasingly sophisticated and accessible. What are some possible solutions to these dichotomies? What might then be on our agenda as far as pedagogies for speaking Englishes and speaking cultures are concerned?

Pedagogies for speaking Englishes and speaking cultures

Language awareness

Recent research in the field of second language acquisition and development (Fotos 1994; Ellis 1991) has pointed to some advantages in procedures which raise learners' consciousness of particular grammatical forms. In spite of numerous pedagogic advantages, communicative teaching has not encouraged in students habits of observation, noticing, or conscious exploration of grammatical forms and function. In the case of the examples here such procedures may be especially appropriate, since we are attempting to introduce understanding of tendencies, variable rules, and choices according to context and interpersonal relations.

Thus, learners need to be made more aware of the differences in the use of different forms by exploring different Englishes in different contexts. Coursebooks might focus on particular learning priorities but also ensure that some opportunities are built in for students to learn to observe differences between coursebook and real English, preferably by focusing on passages with more or less the same content: for example, two dialogues in a hairdresser's shop or in a post office. We can all see, I am sure, a number of interesting ways in which modern communicative methodologies such as gap-filling, information gap, rewriting, and role play could help to enhance language awareness of the different grammatical choices, the different Englishes involved. Recent publications by McCarthy (1991), Nunan (1993), Bolitho and Tomlinson (1994), Brazil (1995), Woods (1995), and Van Lier (1995), in particular, offer a number of interesting possibilities, especially if the primary concern is with the development of reception and comprehension skills.

Text modification and modelling

Example 6 is a further illustration of the issues involved. It is a sample of data from CANCODE selected to illustrate tails in use. A is telling B what route he took in his car to get to B's house. Both A and B engage in a kind of phatic exchange, commenting on and reinforcing each other's remarks on the journey in a friendly, informal, and suitably interactive, interpersonal style. Repeated tails ('nice it was' and 'nice run that') figure prominently in the exchange:

Example 6
A: And I came over Mistham by the reservoirs, nice it was.
B: Oh, by Mistham, over the top, nice run.
A: Colours are pleasant, aren't they?
B: Yeah.
A: Nice run, that.
(CANCODE)

One conclusion reached so far in the preparation of discourse grammar materials is that a middle ground between authentic and concocted data might be occupied which involves modelling data on authentic patterns. (See also McCarthy and Carter 1994: 197–8.) Here is an example of a possible re-modelling of the data above:

A: And I came over by the village of Mistham. It was nice it was.
B: Oh, you came over the top by Mistham. That's a nice journey.
A: The colours are pleasant, aren't they?
B: Yes.
A: It was a nice journey that.

The attempt here by the materials developer is to achieve clarity, tidiness, and organization for purposes of learning, but at the same time to ensure that the dialogue is structured more authentically and naturalistically by modelling on real corpus-based English. It remains to be seen whether this is a weak compromise or a viable strategy. It could be argued that modelling data involves tampering with it to an extent that produces distortion; for example, if in the above data ellipsis is removed and difficult lexis and reference tidied up, then distortion may be introduced. Ellipsis may be a natural syntactic partner for tails structures (we do not yet know enough about such phenomena), and should therefore be retained. Similarly, tails and ellipsis may in turn sit more naturally alongside informal lexis such as 'run' (rather than 'journey'). At present research and materials development are continuing on the basis that text modification and modelling are viable strategies.

One interesting research possibility which may emerge from this process is a description of acceptable degrees of approximation to spoken English norms on the part of second and foreign language learners of English at different levels of development.

I have already reported that preliminary research indicates that ellipsis is a resource for expressivity and for contextually-sensitive informality in a number of Englishes as well as in British English. Which forms of ellipsis and in which combinations with other forms might be learnt by learners at which levels, and what would constitute acceptable use in the process of developing more complete control of the relevant forms? I comment below on a research paradigm for applied linguistics which may help us begin to develop such research.

Use of literary/drama dialogues

As far as teaching spoken Englishes is concerned, literary dialogues, either dialogues in contemporary novels or modern plays, can be very effectively exploited for purposes of developing more authentically-based speaking and listening skills. If we look at the dialogue from Harold Pinter's *The Birthday Party* (Example 7), we can see that, as with most contemporary playwrights, Pinter writes naturalistic dialogue, but it is dialogue which does not include the usual interruptions, hesitations, false starts, or speaking at the same time which characterize real spoken English. Such a practice makes such dialogue highly suitable for classroom exploitation. Witness the excellent literary materials, which make much use of dialogue (Tomlinson 1994, Maley 1993, Maley and Duff 1990). Such books bring text modification and language awareness closer together. At the same time, literary dialogues usually involve some kind of problem to which the dialogue is either directly or, as is often the case with Pinter, indirectly addressed. (For example, in this dialogue Stanley has to try to resolve how and why McCann, a relative stranger, appears to know so much more than he does about his, Stanley's birthday.) Such dialogues can be used to help learners to develop skills of interpretation, reading between the lines, and problem-solving of the kind which can be of use in interpersonal interaction – a point made extensively in recent writings on the value of stylistics in the teaching of language and literature, (Widdowson 1983, 1992; Carter and Long 1991; and Cook 1993, who discusses dialogic types in literary and advertising discourse). And we should not forget how problem-free and co-operative some coursebook dialogues are.

Example 7

McCann *is sitting at the table tearing a sheet of newspaper into five equal strips. It is evening. After a few moments* **Stanley** *enters from the left. He stops upon seeing* **McCann**, *and watches him. He then walks towards the kitchen, stops, and speaks.*

Stanley.   Evening.
McCann.   Evening.
Chuckles are heard from outside the back door, which is open.
Stanley.   Very warm tonight. *(He turns towards the back door, and back.)*
                 Someone out there? …
McCann.   I don't think we've met.

Stanley.	No, we haven't.
McCann.	My name's McCann.
Stanley.	Staying here long?
McCann.	Not long. What's your name?
Stanley.	Webber.
McCann.	I'm glad to meet you, sir. (*He offers his hand.* **Stanley** *takes it, and* **McCann** *holds the grip*) Many happy returns of the day. (**Stanley** *withdraws his hand. They face each other.*) Were you going out?
Stanley.	Yes.
McCann.	On your birthday?
Stanley.	Yes. Why not?
McCann.	But they're holding a party here for you tonight.
Stanley.	Oh really? That's unfortunate.
McCann.	Ah no. It's very nice. (*Voices from outside the back door*)
Stanley.	I'm sorry. I'm not in the mood for a party tonight.
McCann.	Oh, is that so? I'm sorry.

(Harold Pinter, *The Birthday Party*, Act Two: 37–8)

Living in the real world: paradigms for applied linguistic research and development

The findings described in this paper are the findings and observations of linguists whose aim is to extend descriptions of the spoken English language, with particular reference to ELT. One established paradigm in this enterprise is for researchers to describe the language, and then to pass over the findings to practitioners in order that they can seek appropriate applications. The dangers inherent in such a paradigm are that the process is monologic, that linguists pursue their own agenda in isolation from the practical problems of teaching and learning, and that there is a mismatch between theory and practice which can result in potentially valuable insights being dismissed by teachers, teacher trainers, and materials designers, because they do not accord with existing orders of reality, and may therefore be perceived to be threatening.

Even though our research team at Nottingham University is exploring pedagogies and extending the varieties of spoken English which form its database, and is involved in textbook development, the same dangers are none the less inherent. Researchers do not own the teaching learning process any more than native speakers own the language.

If applied linguistics research in general, and in particular cases, is not to forfeit any real claim to being applied linguistics, then, as Prodromou (1996) argues, a new, more dialogic paradigm needs to be developed in which linguist, materials developer, and teacher work together to set an agenda and jointly to trial and review the pedagogic potential of new descriptive findings. Promising beginnings such as the Materials Development Association (MATSDA) have been made,[4] but if some of the issues raised in this article are to be properly pursued, this paradigm, or something like it, will need to be made a reality. In the meantime, we should continue to think about the best ways of 'getting real' about speaking Englishes.

Acknowledgement

The author and publisher are grateful to Faber and Faber Ltd and Grove Atlantic Incorporated for their kind permission to reproduce an extract from *The Birthday Party* by Harold Pinter © Harold Pinter 1959, 1960, 1965.

This article is based on an opening plenary lecture delivered at the 30th IATEFL conference at the University of Keele, April, 1996, with the title 'Speaking Englishes, Speaking Cultures'. The spoken style of the presentation is in part retained in this version, which has been revised in the light of comments received, especially at an IATEFL panel discussion held at the conference. Thanks are due for their comments to the audience and to co-panellists Felicity O'Dell, John Sinclair, and Michael Lewis, in particular. I have also learnt much from correspondence with Luke Prodromou, published in *ELT Journal* 50/1 and 50/4. I am also grateful to Michael McCarthy, co-director of the CANCODE project for his continuing insights, advice, and guidance. An earlier version of the first part of the paper was delivered at the British Council ELT Conference in Milan 1995. This article relates to other work I have done on language awareness in relation to written texts and their cultural contexts, which was the subject of a plenary lecture at IATEFL in 1991, and published as Carter (1993).

Notes

1 The corpus referred to is based at the Department of English Studies at the University of Nottingham and at Cambridge University Press as part of the Cambridge International Corpus. The working corpus from which examples can be drawn will soon total five million words, though the main aim is to construct a qualitative corpus and not simply a large quantitative corpus. (For further discussion of corpus design, see Carter and McCarthy 1995, McCarthy and Carter 1995, Hudson, Carter, and McCarthy 1996.) CANCODE stands for 'Cambridge and Nottingham Corpus of Discourse in English'. All data collected is the property of Cambridge University Press. Plans are already laid to extend the corpus to include a wider variety of international Englishes produced in different discourse communities, and to compare non-British spoken Englishes with the kinds of British English data reported on in this article.

2 An exception is the revised edition of *Practical English Usage* (1995) by Michael Swan, which contains a very thorough treatment of more spoken and informal grammatical forms such as ellipsis.

3 There is no intention here to criticise the authors of *Streamline English*, who would have not have had systematic access to any 'real' data and who, in any case, produced a pedagogically innovative and internationally successful coursebook which is still widely in use today.

4 MATSDA was founded by Brian Tomlinson of the Faculty of Humanities, University of Luton, 75 Castle Street, Luton, Beds LU1 3AJ, UK, from whom further information may be obtained. A first publication bringing together work by descriptive linguists, materials developers, and classroom practitioners is Tomlinson 1997.

References

Brazil, D. 1995. *A Grammar of Speech*. Oxford: Oxford University Press.

Bolitho, R. and B. Tomlinson. 1994. *Discover English*. 2nd edn. London: Heinemann.

Brown, G. 1990. 'Cultural values: the interpretation of discourse'. *ELT Journal* 44/1: 11–17.

Carter, R. A. 1987. *Vocabulary: Applied Linguistic Perspectives*. London: Routledge.

Carter, R. A. 1993. 'Language awareness for language teachers' in M. Hoey (ed.). *Discourse and Description*. London: Collins.

Carter, R. A. 1995. *Keywords in Language and Literacy*. London: Routledge.

Carter, R. A. and M. Long. 1991. *Teaching Literature*. Harlow: Longman.

Carter, R. A. and M. J. McCarthy. 1995. 'Grammar and the spoken language'. *Applied Linguistics* 16/2: 141–58.

Carter, R. A. and W. Nash. 1990. *Seeing Through Language: A Guide to Styles of English Writing*. Oxford: Blackwell.

Channell, J. 1994. *Vague Language*. Oxford: Oxford University Press.

Cook, G. 1993. *The Discourse of Advertising*. London: Routledge.

Ellis, R. 1991. 'Grammaticality judgements and second language acquisition'. *Studies in Second Language Acquisition* 13: 161–86.

Fotos, S. 1994. 'Intergrating grammar instruction and communicative language use through grammar consciousness-raising tasks'. *TESOL Quarterly* 28/2: 333–51.

Hudson, J., R. A. Carter, and M. J. McCarthy. 1996. 'Spoken English corpus design'. Mimeo, Department of English Studies, University of Nottingham.

Kramsch, C. 1993. *Context and Culture in Language Teaching*. Oxford: Oxford University Press.

Lewis, M. 1993. *The Lexical Approach*. Hove: Language Teaching Publications.

Maley, A. 1993. *Short and Sweet Volume 1*. Harmondsworth: Penguin.

Maley, A. and A. Duff. 1990. *Literature*. Oxford: Oxford University Press.

McCarthy, M. J. 1991. *Discourse Analysis for Language Teachers*. Cambridge: Cambridge University Press.

McCarthy, M. J. and R. A. Carter. 1994. *Language as Discourse: Perspectives for Language Teaching*. Harlow: Longman.

McCarthy, M. J. and R. A. Carter. 1995. 'Spoken grammar: what is it and how do we teach it?' *ELT Journal* 49/3: 207–18.

Nunan, D. 1993. *Introducing Discourse Analysis*. Harmondsworth: Penguin.

Phillipson, R. 1992. *Linguistic Imperialism*. Oxford: Oxford University Press.

Prodromou, L. 1990. 'English as cultural action' in R. Rossner and R. Bolitho (eds.). *Currents of Change in English Language Teaching*. Oxford: Oxford University Press.

Prodromou, L. 1996. Correspondence. *ELT Journal* 50/1: 88–9.

Rampton, M. B. 1990. 'Displacing the native speaker: expertise, affiliation, and inheritance'. *ELT Journal* 44/2: 97–106. Republished in T. Hedge and N. Whitney. 1996. *Power, Pedagogy, and Practice*. Oxford: Oxford University Press.

Swan, M. 1995. (revised edn.). *Practical English Usage*. Oxford: Oxford University Press.

Tomlinson, B. 1994. *Openings*. Harmondsworth: Penguin.
Tomlinson, B. (ed.). 1997. *Materials Development in L2 Teaching*. Cambridge: Cambridge University Press.
Tsui, A. 1994. *English Conversation*. Oxford: Oxford University Press.
Van Lier, L. 1995. *Introducing Language Awareness*. Harmondsworth: Penguin.
Widdowson, H. G. 1983. 'Talking Shop'. *ELT Journal* 37/1: 30–6.
Widdowson, H. G. 1992. *Practical Stylistics*. Oxford: Oxford University Press.
Willis, J. and D. Willis. 1988. *Collins Cobuild English Course*. London: Collins.
Woods, E. 1995. *Introducing Grammar*. Harmondsworth: Penguin.

The author

Ronald Carter is Professor of Modern English Language in the Department of English Studies, University of Nottingham, and is co-director with Michael McCarthy of the CANCODE project. Professor Carter has published widely in the fields of language teaching, applied linguistics, and literary studies. Recent publications include *Exploring Spoken English* (Cambridge University Press 1997), *Investigating English Discourse: Language, Literacy and Literature* (Routledge 1997), *Keywords in Language and Literacy* (Routledge 1995), and (with Michael McCarthy) *Language as Discourse: Perspectives for Language Teaching* (Longman 1994).

Text 14

Guy Cook

The uses of reality: a reply to Ronald Carter

Introduction

Computerized language corpora have inspired some of the most important insights in recent linguistics. They have shown us, for example, that actual language use is less a matter of combining abstract grammar rules with individual lexical items, and more a matter of collocation; that there are grammatically possible utterances which do not occur, and others which occur with disproportionate frequency; that in systematic descriptions of occurrences, grammar and lexis cannot be as easily separated as they have been traditionally, either in pedagogy or in linguistics. Ronald Carter is right to find such insights 'exciting', and his own work with Michael McCarthy on the CANCODE corpus, has added to them. As his article illustrates very well, the grammatical constructions we find in actual conversations are not always accounted for in traditional grammars.

Clearly all these findings are important, and they do have implications for language teaching. The problem is, however, that some corpus linguists (e.g. Sinclair 1991, Stubbs 1996) overreach themselves. They talk as though the entire study of language can be replaced by the study of their collections, and as though all important insights will emerge only from automatic searches of their data and nowhere else. Clearly such solutions to the study of complex human phenomena exert a good deal of seductive power. If the traditional concern of linguistics – language in all its cultural and psychological complexity – could be replaced by a neat computer bank of data, life would be much simpler.

Yet the leap from linguistics to pedagogy is – as Carter realizes – far from straightforward. He is not one of the extremists, and his paper is, for that reason, a worthwhile and interesting contribution to language teaching. He proceeds cautiously, providing some interesting 'real' data, and pointing out significant differences between actual and textbook English. He does not say one should replace the other. In his view, materials should be influenced by, but not slaves to, corpus findings. (In this he seems to agree with the view of Summers and Rundell (1995) that pedagogic materials should be 'corpus based not corpus bound', and to disagree with the COBUILD slogan that they should be 'corpus driven' (Stubbs 1997).) This is eminently reasonable, though for that very reason not particularly radical. My problem with what Carter says is that he seems a little hesitant – or perhaps unwilling – to say where he stands. Does he reject the fundamentalist views of those linguists and language teaching theorists for whom corpus findings are the only source of truth?

My first aim in this reply is to pursue some of the shortcomings of corpus-driven approaches which I think Carter avoids confronting. I shall also consider some of the more extreme applications of corpus findings to language teaching. My argument is that there is an important difference between the hard and soft line approaches, that the former, by appearing to offer yet another easy 'scientific' solution, can do immense damage, and that we all, including Carter, would do well to consider more precisely whether we think corpus findings merely add a new dimension to earlier approaches, or replace them.

Uses and abuses of corpora

A number of false conclusions can be reached about corpora. It is often assumed, for example, that as a description of language behaviour, they are the only valid source of facts about language; the same as a description of language in the mind; provide a goal and a route for language learning. There is much in computerized corpus analysis to make us reconsider received ideas about the learning, representation, and use of language. But where pedagogy is concerned, corpus statistics say nothing about immeasurable but crucial factors such as students' and teachers' attitudes and expectations, the personal relationships between them, their own wishes, or the diversity of traditions from which they come. Consequently computer corpora – while impressive and interesting records of certain aspects of language use – can never be more than a *contribution* to our understanding of effective language teaching.

Corpus as fact

Even as a record of 'facts' computer corpora are incomplete. They contain information about production but not about reception. They say nothing about how many people have read or heard a text or utterance, or how many times.[1] Thus a memo hastily skimmed by one person and consigned to the wastepaper basket counts equally with a tabloid headline read by millions, or with a text, such as a prayer or poem, which is not only often repeated but also deeply valued. Occurrence, distribution, and importance, in other words, are not the same. This applies to whole texts, but also to shorter units. Some phrases pass unnoticed precisely because of their frequency, others strike and stay in the mind, though they may occur only once. And because different individuals notice different things, such saliency can never be included in a corpus. The same is true of a whole host of aspects of language use: metaphors, speech acts such as apologies or compliments, interactive events such as interruption or awkward uses, levels of formality. They are not 'facts' but matters of varying perception. It is a truism to observe that there is no straightforward correlation between the words people use, the intentions they had in them, and the interpretations which other people put upon them. If this were not so, there would be no disputes over the meaning of what people say.

Corpus as record

Corpora are records of language behaviour. The patterns which emerge in that behaviour do not necessarily and directly tell us how people organize and classify language in their own minds[2] and for their own use, or how language is best systematized for teaching. Linguists' analyses of these data are not necessarily users' analyses, or those which are most useful to teachers and learners. They are just one kind of fact. The ways in which grammarians and pedagogues have organized their material – in grammars, syllabuses, and dictionaries – are also facts about language. So are people's emotional beliefs that one type of language use is better than another. We should not promote some kinds of facts at the expense of others.

Corpora are only partial authorities. The cumulative language experience of an individual, though less amenable to systematic access, remains far larger and richer. Even a three hundred million word corpus is equivalent to only around three thousand books, or perhaps the language experience of a teenager. This is why our intuition (in effect our random and incomplete access to our total experience of the language) can still tell us facts about the language which can not be evidenced by a corpus (Widdowson 1990). For example, the canonical forms of sayings and proverbs occur very rarely in corpora, though they are obviously well known by people (Aston 1995). Such omissions, however, are not merely a quantitative issue; they cannot be remedied simply by making corpora larger and larger. They are inevitable in an approach which accepts only one of the three sources of fact about language: observation; and ignores or villainizes two others: introspection and elicitation. For there are aspects of language which are known but not used. Corpus linguists are fond of observing that the commonest uses of words are not the same as their standard definitions. 'I bet' for example, is more rarely used in the sense of 'wager', and most often in the sense of 'suppose' (Sinclair 1987: xvi). But this unsurprising observation does not at all invalidate the view that 'wager' is a central prototypical meaning for many speakers to which more colloquial uses are attached. (And indeed, the 'wager' meaning is still given as the first meaning of 'bet' in the Cobuild dictionary.)

Description and prescription

But let us assume for the sake of argument that corpora are accurate records of language behaviour, that they *do* catalogue and reveal all the important 'facts' about the language. The question then arises as to whose language behaviour is accurately recorded – and the question takes on a particularly sinister significance when the corpora in question start being used not as data for descriptive linguistics, but as sources of prescription for TESOL. For the answer to the question is (as Carter seems painfully aware) that corpora are primarily records of native speakers' language behaviour. 'Real' language in effect means native-speaker English, and the only language excluded from this category (apart from the invented examples of linguists and textbook writers) is that used to and by language learners. To his credit, Carter confronts this issue, and intends to remedy it. But the proposed addition of 'a wider variety of international Englishes' (see Note 2, page 54) will not solve the problem. This will only add other standard Englishes as spoken by their own native speakers.

And then a second question arises to which Carter explicitly refers, but does not answer. Why should the attested language use of a native-speaker community be a model for learners of English as an international language? If a certain collocation occurs frequently among British or American English speakers, must it also be used by the Japanese or the Mexicans? This is where we encounter an easy slippage from description to prescription, in effect making the former into the latter. The English which is used by one or more native-speaker communities, it is implied, ought to be the English learned for international communication.

The ready-made lexical phrases which corpora reveal to be so frequent in native speaker use are moreover – as Carter readily recognizes – very often culturally specific and loaded. In deploying such units, the foreign speaker is very likely to produce corpus-attested but contextually inappropriate language. (This is why attempts to teach set phrases are likely to be as tragicomically disastrous in lexical syllabuses as they were in functional ones.) Carter's own example of repeated tails ('nice it was', 'nice run that') may well be frequent in data, but successful deployment by a foreign learner could easily go wrong. In the terms of Hymes's (1972) four parameters of communicative competence, corpus-driven language teaching always risks stressing what is actually done at the expense of what is appropriate in a particular context.

Pedagogical issues

In an extensively quoted, and in itself excellent, essay by Pawley and Syder (1983) on native-like selection and fluency, corpus-based language teaching finds a source of inspiration, providing a potential link between the facts of language behaviour and a theory of how language is acquired and processed in the mind. Here is the claim that mature native speakers (for this is whom the essay is explicitly about) have 'hundreds of thousands' of institutionalized lexicalized or semi-lexicalized units in memory. Though many of these units can be analysed grammatically, the likelihood is, so the argument goes, that they are often produced and understood holistically. Native speakers acquire, represent, and process language in lexicalized chunks as well as grammar rules and single words.

Yet it by no means follows that foreign learners must do the same. They may not want to study language in this way; they may live within culturally diverse pedagogic traditions not compatible with this approach; they may not aspire to or need native-like English; they may not have as much time available as native-speaker children; above all, as adults with conscious learning strategies available to them, they can choose. And why should they not choose to continue viewing the language as grammar structures and slot-filling words? This may not lead to native-like English, but it may lead to communicative and expressive English. It may be learnt more quickly. And it will avoid the tedious rote learning of mundane phrases, or the bewildering refusal to teach grammar, which are the inevitable consequences of an overemphasis on 'lexical chunks'.

Yet even if appearing native-like were accepted as the goal of language learning, it would still not follow that frequency and desirability are the same. There is a hidden irony in the dogma that frequent native-like collocations are the best model to imitate. It is that even *within* the native-speaker community it is often the infrequent word or expression which is most powerful and most communicatively effective, and therefore most sought after. This is also why foreigners' speech is often expressive and striking. Both for native and non-native speakers there is an alternative goal to seeking the most usual, the most frequent or, in short, the most clichéd expression. It is the goal of rich, varied, and original language. Among native speakers it is unusual language which is valued. Should non-native speakers be treated differently?

This leads to the important point that not all types of language are equally valued, either by native speakers or foreign learners. Something is not a good model simply because it occurs frequently. A good deal of actual language use is inarticulate, impoverished, and inexpressive.[3] Inevitably, because one cannot teach everything, part of the job of teachers and course designers is to select the language use which they wish their students to emulate. Many foreign language students have strong feelings about this too. They do not want to learn just any English because it occurs in a corpus, and it is patronising to overrule them. In advocating selection and modelling of corpus data, in the use of literary rather than transcribed dialogues, and in his recognition that one of the topics in his authentic data ('straggly hair') may have a limited topic life in many classrooms, Carter seems to agree.

To be corpus driven, in short, deprives everyone (native and non-native speaker alike) of the opportunity for choice and to make their own impact on the language. Corpora are inevitably records of what has happened rather than what is happening. They present us with a *fait accompli*, a fixed product rather than an open process.

Means and ends

So corpora do not necessarily provide a goal for language learners. Yet even if they did, it would not follow that the best route to this goal is to present real language use, and to try to persuade them to emulate it straight away. Here there is a certain oddity in the corpus argument. Of course expert-speaker use of the language, and the rules which generate it, is usually more complex than that of language learners. If it were not, there would be nothing to learn. Hardly surprisingly, the description of English which emerges from corpus analysis (taking into account as it does the way in which linguistic items and structures vary across genres, social groups, and linguistic contexts) is dauntingly complex and particular. But this description cannot be presented to students all at once. The issue still remains how to simplify and stage the language presented to learners, and to simplify the rules used to explain it, in a way which will enable them to come gradually closer to native speaker use (if that is their goal). Surely the point of grammars and textbooks is that they select, idealize, and simplify the language to make it more accessible? Indeed, this seems to be Carter's view too.

For language teachers the issue remains as to what the principles for selection, idealization, and simplification should be. Here there is already a wealth of long-standing ideas (dating back at least to the work of Palmer (1921) and West (1926) concerning the relationship between the frequency with which an item occurs and the point at which it should be taught – ideas of which many corpus linguists, in their haste to advertise themselves as promulgating a totally new approach to language, seem unaware. For example, an item may be frequent but limited in range, or infrequent but useful in a wide range of contexts. Or it may be infrequent but very useful, or appropriate for some pedagogic reason. These are factors beyond mere description. Unlike many corpus linguists, Carter does show himself aware of such considerations in his conclusions. But that leaves me wondering whether his approach is such a break from tradition as he suggests.

The hard line

This brings me from Carter's views – moderate, sensible, and informed – to the more extreme, but unfortunately associated, views of language teaching based on corpus linguistics. Here is the belief that what is perceived as a linguistic revolution necessarily constitutes a pedagogic one. Very often writers are carried away by a single insight into *language*, taking it illogically to be sufficient to change *language teaching*. Thus Willis (1990) elevates frequency counts to the guiding principle for his lexical syllabus. Lewis (1993) considers the high occurrence of lexical chunks as a cue to decree (in a diatribe characterized by bombastic assertion rather than reasoned argument) that language teaching has changed forever, to be replaced by 'the way forward' (p. 196), with an ominously authoritarian definite article: his own lexical approach. 'Abstract, absolute knowledge of a system has had its day', and people who think otherwise 'are wrong' (p. 74); 'woolly mindedness in this matter leads to bad practice which has negative long term effects' (p. 167).

Such approaches are firmly in the tradition of using linguistics theory to dictate to language teaching practice. Their gross over-generalization and over-confidence are potentially damaging to good teaching practice. They invoke corpus linguistics as an unassailable authority, side-step all serious engagement in debate, and cannot take on board the kind of reservations expressed by Carter. Such corpus-driven pedagogy is a vain attempt to resuscitate a patriarchal attitude to ELT, invoking the latest linguistics theory to intimidate teachers into believing that all previous practice, all their own and their students' intuitions, all the culturally various pedagogic traditions in which they work and study, are, as Lewis would put it, 'wrong'.

Conclusion

I have contrasted throughout this reply what I see as the soft and the hard line views of the relevance of corpus findings to language teaching. In the one, we have the voice of moderation urging a limited application – 'modelling' as Carter calls it – which by virtue of its very reasonableness does not amount to anything very radical. In the other, we have the stronger view: evangelical, authoritarian, and dismissive of tradition, assuming that a little of the latest linguistics theory is all that is needed to change the course of language teaching. I believe that if Carter were to follow his arguments through to their conclusion, he too would explicitly reject, as I do, the more extreme versions both of corpus linguistics and of corpus-driven language teaching. But it is by no means clear whether he does so.

Notes

1 This point has been made by corpus linguists themselves (Francis 1979, Stubbs 1996:11) but the point is not adequately taken on board, either in corpus construction or analysis.
2 Stubbs (1996: 21) tells us that the 'deep patterning' revealed by corpus analysis is 'beyond human observation and memory'.
3 This issue is clouded by snobbish and chauvinistic claims that a particular national or sociolect is better than another. But this is not a necessary component of the notion that certain usages – literary, written, or simply eloquent and elegant ones – are more desirable models than others.

References

Aston, G. 1995. 'Corpora in language pedagogy: matching theory and practice' in G. Cook and B. Seidlhofer (eds.). *Principle and Practice in Applied Linguistics*. Oxford: Oxford University Press.

Francis, W. N. 1979. 'Problems of assembling and computerising large corpora' in H. Bergenholtz and B. Schader (eds.). *Empirische Textwissenschaft*. Berlin: Scriptor.

Hymes, D. 1972. 'On communicative competence' in J.B. Pride and J. Holmes (eds.). *Sociolinguistics*. Harmondsworth: Penguin.

Lewis, M. 1993. *The Lexical Approach*. Hove: Language Teaching Publications.

Palmer, H. E. 1921. *The Principles of Language Study*. London: Harrap (Republished by Oxford University Press, 1964, edited by R. Mackin).

Pawley, A. and F. Syder. 1983. 'Two puzzles for linguistic theory: nativelike selection and nativelike fluency' in J. Richards and J. Schmidt (eds). *Language and Communication*. London: Longman.

Sinclair, J. *et al.* 1987. *Collins Cobuild English Language Dictionary*. London: Collins.

Sinclair, J. M. 1991. *Corpus, Concordance, Collocation*. Oxford: Oxford University Press.

Stubbs, M. 1996. *Text and Corpus Analysis*. Oxford: Blackwell.

Stubbs, M. 1997. Review of *Using Corpora for Language Research*. *Applied Linguistics* 18/2: 240–3.

Summers, D. and M. Rundell (eds.). 1995. *Longman Dictionary of Contemporary English*. London: Longman.

West, M. P. 1926. *Learning to Read a Foreign Language*. New York: Longmans, Green.

Widdowson, H. G. 1990. 'Discourses of enquiry and conditions of relevance' in J. E. Alatis (ed). *Linguistics, Language Teaching and Language Acquisition*. Washington DC: Georgetown University Press.

Willis, D. 1990. *The Lexical Syllabus*. London: Collins.

The author

Guy Cook is a Reader and Head of Languages in Education at the London University Institute of Education. He has worked as a school teacher in Egypt, Italy, and the UK, and as a lecturer at the University of Moscow and the University of Leeds. His publications include *The Discourse of Advertising* (Routledge 1992), *Discourse and Literature* (Oxford University Press 1994), and (with B. Seidlhofer) *Principle and Practice in Applied Linguistics* (Oxford University Press 1995) He is currently working on a new book entitled *Language Play, Language Learning* (Oxford University Press, forthcoming).

Text 15

Ronald Carter
University of Nottingham

Reply to Guy Cook

Guy Cook's generous, well-tempered, and sharply probing response to my article is much appreciated. And he is right to recognize that I and my close colleague Michael McCarthy have been in the teaching profession too long to believe that new approaches to language description can or even should revolutionize language teaching. It is clear that Guy Cook and I agree upon much.

I certainly do reject extreme forms of corpus-driven language teaching, but I do believe that we need to encourage more not less corpus-based language description, particularly of Englishes in international contexts of use. Otherwise there is the danger, which Guy seems not to confront, that we might too readily continue to assume that we always know what learners want, and that we can easily avoid the inverted élitism which relies too unquestioningly on Southern British middle-class English, on introspection and intuition, and on letting 'Japanese communicate with Mexicans' in their quaint 'expressive' English. Guy Cook is not alone in sidestepping the question of where learners are to get their models of English from, which models they might actually want, and how any such model is to be described. And do the unspeakable and tortuously dotty structures used in SLA grammaticality judgements show the way forward? I think not. But corpus work forces such questions upon the profession.

Guy Cook is undoubtedly right to say that language description is not the same as language teaching, but the profession can only benefit from better descriptions. I doubt whether Palmer and Blandford (1924), in their early work on spoken pegagogical grammar, would have shrunk away from the chance of looking at several million words of real speech using concordance software and a pentium processor. In this connection, 'tails' (see Carter and McCarthy 1997) may well be new to language teachers, but they are not new to the English language; they may well be universal in international Englishes (which is why we need more, not fewer, corpora); and they are not more likely to 'easily go wrong' than interrogatives or the present continuous. Revolutions in language teaching usually lead to counter-revolutions (and not a lot of progress). The best corpus-based language teaching represents an evolution which, I predict, will be seen to be radical only after several years have passed.

References

Carter, R. A. and M. J. McCarthy. 1997. *Exploring Spoken English*. Cambridge: Cambridge University Press.
Palmer, H. E. and F. G. Blandford. 1924. *A Grammar of Spoken English*. (3rd edn., revised and rewritten by R. Kingdon). Cambridge: Heffer.

Note

I am grateful to my colleague Michael McCarthy for discussion of points raised in these papers.

Text 16

Laura Gavioli and Guy Aston

Enriching reality: language corpora in language pedagogy

In recent years there has been considerable discussion of how far ELT syllabuses and materials should be 'corpus-driven' in order to better reflect linguistic reality. In this paper we argue that this debate has tended to overlook the potential of corpora as tools in the hands of learners, for whom they can provide a wide range of opportunities to observe and participate in real discourse for themselves.

Introduction

Ever since the *Cobuild* project started producing corpus-based dictionaries, grammars, and materials for ELT, applied linguists have been divided between those who have seen the findings and methods of corpus linguistics as providing new ways forward in language teaching, and those who have warned against over-enthusiasm. In a debate in *ELT Journal* 52/1 (1998), Ron Carter and Guy Cook focused on two of the main terms of this argument. First, they asked how far the analysis of corpora provides descriptions of the workings of 'real English'; second, they asked whether such English is what foreign learners need. In this paper, we begin by summarizing our own position on these issues, and then go on to argue that the terms of this debate should be redefined in relation to learners' needs to experience language as 'real' for themselves.

Can corpora capture reality?

The largest corpora of English are still smaller than the average adult user's experience of the language, and very different in their composition (most notably in the ratio of speech to writing). Nonetheless, they provide evidence about linguistic performance which can undoubtedly be helpful in deciding what we should teach.

First, they can be used to test claims based purely on intuition. For instance, Carter (1998: 43) proposes that the word 'real' 'invariably carries positive associations', as in 'Real ale', 'Get real!', 'Real English', 'that real country taste', etc. But if we look up 'real' in the 100-million word British National Corpus (BNC),[1] the picture is rather different. We find that the most frequent lexical items to collocate with 'real' are 'world(s)', 'life/lives', 'term(s)', and 'problem(s)'. Can we really say that 'the real world', 'real life', 'in real terms', or, most strikingly, 'a real problem', have positive associations? The corpus evidence makes it clear that the linguistic 'fact' Carter proposes is over-generalized, and suggests that we might want to reformulate it somewhat for teaching purposes.

Second, corpora can help clarify our motives for teaching particular features. Carter discusses a number of spoken formulae which carry 'cultural' content, including expressions referring to other nations: 'Dutch courage', 'to go Dutch', 'double-Dutch', 'Dutch cap', 'Dutch auction', 'then I'm a Dutchman', etc. He goes on to claim:

> Here we learn several useful and widely used phrases, but we can also learn something about British insularity, and that distrust of foreigners to the point where the British can be interpreted as believing almost all of them to be either unintelligible, untrustworthy, or 'unreal'.
> (Carter 1998: 49)

Judging from publicly-available corpora of speech, however, these expressions are far from 'widely used'. In the spoken component of the BNC (10 million words), 'go Dutch' and 'double-Dutch' each occur twice, 'I'm a Dutchman' once, while 'Dutch cap', 'Dutch courage', and 'Dutch auction' are not found at all.[2] A similarly-sized British speech component of the Bank of English[3] presents an even more desolate picture: there are four instances of 'double-Dutch', and that is all. Given these very low frequencies, these items would only seem worth teaching if we have other good reasons for doing so. In the passage cited, Carter actually suggests two such reasons: 'double-Dutch', 'go Dutch', and indeed, 'Dutch cap', could all be useful expressions for a learner wishing to avoid social embarrassment in Britain; and the study of British insularity, as revealed through linguistic references to foreign nationals and nations, could constitute a stimulating activity which could increase learners' awareness of cultural issues.

The inclusion in syllabuses of language which is very rare in large corpora thus calls for justification, and the same is equally true for the exclusion of language which is common. As we saw with 'real', corpora can remind us of frequent uses which might otherwise tend to be ignored. Thus McCarthy and Carter (1995) notice the frequency in speech of the semi-modal 'tend to' (it occurs almost as often as 'ought' in the BNC spoken component). Although this verb has traditionally received little attention in teaching, it arguably provides learners with a valid alternative to frequency adverbs such as 'usually' and 'often'. A more problematic case noted by the same authors is that of structures with 'tails' (as in 'That's enough, *don't you think?*'), which are rarely found among the prototypical patterns presented by textbooks. While their frequency in conversation suggests they should be included in syllabuses, other considerations may argue against this, at any rate from the perspective of spoken production. Their use being highly context-dependent, they seem difficult to teach and harder to master than other markers of affect with similar functions. The point is that while corpora do not tell us what we should teach, they can help us make better-informed decisions, and oblige us to motivate those decisions more carefully.

Can corpora provide valid models for learners?

Most existing corpora are collections of spoken and/or written texts produced by native speakers. Both Cook (1998) and Carter (1998) ask whether learners in fact need to imitate native-speaker behaviour, and whether, in consequence, corpus data are relevant to them as models – a doubt, incidentally, which relates not only to corpora, but to 'authentic' materials in general. There is, however, no reason to assume that the materials we present to learners should constitute models for imitation (were this the case, it would be difficult to imagine a role for literature, advertising, or other 'creative' genres in the language classroom), and it would be wrong to expect corpus data to do so either. When linguists abstract generalized patterns from corpora, and interpret the data as exemplifying them, these patterns are rarely immediately apparent. Sinclair, who attempted to include only actual corpus instances as examples in the *Cobuild* dictionary (Sinclair 1995), reports how difficult it was to find instances which reflected 'typical' usage in every respect (Sinclair and Kirby 1990: 114–15). The *Cobuild* team was, moreover, only looking for single sentences exemplifying a limited range of features. The chances of finding a complete corpus text which consistently shows typical usage is minimal, so if we want to propose a model of conversation at the hairdresser's, we will almost certainly do better to use an invented dialogue than a corpus extract – though we may want to compare it with corpus extracts before proposing it to students.

It is precisely because they do not simply offer models to imitate, however, that corpus data seems valuable for learners. As Leech and Candlin (1986: xiv–xvi) observed well over a decade ago, data from corpora has to be interpreted subjectively. Their reality, from this point of view, is a characteristic not just of the data, but above all of the interpretative process. For learners, the reality of corpus data would seem principally to lie in the extent to which they can interpret them to create models of their own.

From real texts to real discourse

In one of his most widely-quoted distinctions, Widdowson (1978) contrasts *genuineness* (a quality of texts) and *authenticity* (a quality of discourse interpretation). Viewed in these terms, corpora of naturally-occurring texts provide samples of genuine language, since they are produced by speakers and writers with real communicative goals. The reproduction of such samples in pedagogic contexts does not, however, guarantee them authenticity as discourse, which depends on their context of reception. In their discussion, both Carter (1998) and Cook (1998) seem to treat reality as an inherent characteristic of materials, i.e. as a matter of genuineness of the text. But if – as communicative language teaching has traditionally held – learning is primarily a product of discourse authenticity, the question is not whether corpora represent reality, but rather whether their use can create conditions that will enable learners to engage in real discourse, authenticating it on their terms – and whether this engagement can lead to language learning.

Widdowson (1998) claims that learners will often be unable to authenticate real texts, since they do not belong to the community for which those texts are designed, and are therefore unqualified to participate in the discourse process.

This, however, overlooks the fact that there is an alternative way of authenticating discourse, by adopting the role of an observer (Aston 1988). While the participant interacts with the text as an intended recipient, the observer views this interaction from the outside, adopting a critical, analytic perspective. Observer as well as participant roles can allow learning: observation allows strategies of interaction to be noticed, while participation allows such strategies to be tested.

Corpora clearly allow many opportunities to authenticate discourse through observation. As already noted, unlike the examples provided by textbooks and dictionaries, the samples of language provided by corpus data do not immediately illustrate particular linguistic patterns. A concordance does not make sense in itself: sense has to be attributed to it by the reader, who must infer patterns which will as far as possible account for the data. In other words, a concordance can be viewed as a text that provokes 'a pragmatic reaction' in the observer (Widdowson 1998: 713). As we shall see in the following examples, this pragmatic reaction can also constitute a focus for discourse participation, thereby allowing learners to alternate and integrate these two roles.

Learners using corpora

EXAMPLE I

A learner whose essay contained the sentence 'Students should avail themselves of the resources of the school to develop their computing skills' received the comment from his teacher that this use of 'avail' was odd. In the *Cobuild* dictionary (Sinclair 1995), he found that 'avail oneself of' was a formal use: was the inappropriacy of his sentence simply due to its over-formality? He turned to look for corpus evidence in a one million-word collection of newspaper articles (*MicroConcord Corpus A*: Murison-Bowie 1993). Searching for the pattern *avail**, he found 122 occurrences, one of 'to no avail', 13 of 'availability', and 108 of 'available'. Skimming these citations, he considered rewriting his sentence as 'Students at the school should profit from the resources available to develop their computing skills.' This seemed to match a common pattern in the data, but it did not seem to express exactly what he had wanted to say.

He then looked at the two-million word *BNC Sampler*.[4] Here he finally found an instance of the reflexive verb ('They wanted to avail themselves of the opportunity for the imposition of bail conditions'), as well as 5 of 'to no avail', 39 of 'availability/ies', and 382 of 'available'. Sorting the latter, he noticed 114 occurrences of 'made available'. Examining these prompted him to rewrite his sentence as 'School resources should be made available to students to develop their computing skills', which he said captured what he had wanted to say better than his initial proposal.

This learner's interaction with these corpora took place at various levels. First, he posed such questions as 'What's wrong with this form?', and 'What's wrong with the dictionary description?' Examining concordances as an observer, he noticed various more frequent patterns, which he then tried to adapt to the context of his own discourse. While the patterns he noticed initially did not meet his requirements, further data allowed him to come up with a model which he could apply to solve his problem as a discourse participant writing a text. The search also helped him in his role as a critical observer of the dictionary description. He found that *avail* was not very frequent, that it was mainly used in the phrase 'to no avail', and that the one occurrence of the reflexive verb 'avail oneself' was, as the dictionary suggested, rather formal.

This interaction engaged the learner both as a discourse observer (the critical analyst of the corpus and dictionary data) and as a participant (the writer of the essay), who in both those roles exploited his 'pragmatic reaction' to the concordance data. He did not simply look for a model to imitate, which he could cut and paste, but rather for patterns that he could adapt to fit his own text. He thus constructed a model from the data which he could also authenticate in his own discourse – something he had not been able to do with the dictionary.

EXAMPLE 2
Insofar as they provoke 'pragmatic reactions', corpus data also provide learners with motivations for participating in discourse through spoken interaction. Different learners will often notice different things in concordances, and draw different conclusions. By comparing their analyses, they may arrive at interpretations which are more comprehensive, or more generalizable. Where concordance lines are selected at random, rather than ad hoc to exemplify a specific interpretation, such discussion can be open-ended, leaving learners free to negotiate their findings. For instance, in a group looking at concordances of '*food*' and its Italian equivalent *cibo*, some learners observed that *food* occurred much more frequently than *cibo* (186 vs. 20 times per million words); others that *cibo* often referred to animal rather than human foodstuffs; and others that *cibo* frequently collocated with negatively-connotated expressions, as in *mancanza di cibo* ('lack of food') and *il cibo scarseggia* ('food is short'). Discussing these findings, the group concluded that *food* has a larger spectrum of meanings than *cibo*, the two words only being equivalent in a few cases ('food rationing', 'food shortages'), and that other words were needed to translate expressions like 'Chinese food', 'food chain', and 'food industry' into Italian ('*cucina* cinese', 'catena *alimentare*', and 'industria *alimentare*'). They thus came to jointly hypothesize a difference in the meanings of the two words: a negative, more restricted meaning for *cibo*, and a neutral, more general one for *food* – a contrast they judged useful both from a language learning and from a translation perspective.

Seen more generally, discussing their findings may also raise learners' awareness of broader lexical, grammatical, and textual issues (one interesting aspect of grammar highlighted by the *food/cibo* example was the non-correspondence of noun + noun pairings in English and in Italian). Contemporary ELT has dedicated more attention to the development of tasks and activities where learners can use the language than to enhancing their awareness of its formal properties, and consciousness-raising work has predominantly focused on processes of communication and of learning. Discussing corpus data enables learners to develop their own descriptive frameworks, and to question and critique those of teachers, textbooks, and reference materials (as where the search for *avail* helped reinterpret the dictionary's account). This may help them view such descriptions in less prescriptive terms, and to interact with them more critically in establishing their own views of language reality.

EXAMPLE 3

Corpora consist of texts, and as well as the formal characteristics of those texts, their meanings may also attract attention. Anyone who has consulted concordances will have experienced the pragmatic reaction of curiosity at particular citations, wondering where they come from and what their source texts are about. Where the corpus is consulted directly on the computer, you can indulge such curiosity by reading the text from which the citation comes, shifting your role from that of an observer to that of a participant in the reading process: Widdowson's caveat that genuine texts may exclude learners from discourse participation is made less problematic by the large number of texts available, amongst which learners can choose examples which they find it possible to authenticate in reading. For instance, we touched earlier on the use of expressions with *Dutch*. A search for 'double Dutch'/'double-Dutch'/'doubledutch' in the full BNC (spoken and written texts) elicits the following concordance:

I: Looked likely to be unplaced in	**Double Dutch's** race at Ascot, but finished powerfully
ls, who cut the second favourite,	**Double Dutch**, from 7–1 to 6–1 and Royal Square froɪ
it could be the fact that I backed	**Double Dutch** at 10–1 as a saver simply because I thi
and, imported NZ Ch. Javictreva	**Double Dutch** from the UK. She was bred by Noreen
ɪlts take over skipping ropes and	**double-dutch**, 1920s style, fills the screen. There is a c
ere entered there. Most of it was	**double-dutch** to me but I could make out the names
tions might have been written in	**double Dutch.**| William turned from the maddening
t, diplomacy . . . Hotel-keeping's	**double Dutch** to me at the moment — but I catch on t
ɪnd he did. | ENGLISH EXPERTS'	**DOUBLE DUTCH** . . . || In the past week any number

Here we not only discover that this expression is rare, but also that it is the name of a racehorse. The interested user can find out quite a lot about horse racing from the first four citations, and considerably more by reading the texts from which they come. To readers of the *ELT Journal*, however, the final citation in this concordance may be of greater interest, so let us turn to its source:

ENGLISH EXPERTS' DOUBLE DUTCH . . .

In the past week any number of interested parties have been granted the 30 second television sound bite in order to voice an opinion or two about the way English should be taught in our schools.

It is disturbing to think any of them are in a position of influence in the education field since to a man they seem only capable of talking in cliché-riddled sentences or civil service speak. [...]
Daily Mirror

Here we – or the advanced learner – can discover other things than just the use of 'double Dutch', with its clearly negative connotations. The extract makes it clear that this text is criticizing English language experts for their own poor command of the language. At the same time, however, it illustrates how English popular newspapers employ ridicule, portraying themselves (and their readers) as paragons of plain English and common sense. If so inclined, the user can search the corpus for other similar texts (perhaps by looking for the phrase 'It is X to think'), in the hunt for other uses and objects of this strategy of cultural derision. The extract also includes several other expressions which may be unfamiliar ('any number of', 'interested parties', 'sound bite', 'an opinion or two', 'to a man', 'cliché-riddled', 'civil service speak'), and the user may find it interesting to search the corpus for other instances of these. Bernardini (2000) shows how a large mixed corpus like the BNC can provide a vast terrain for self-directed exploration: with initial guidance, learners can investigate one linguistic or encyclopedic curiosity after another, focusing on a variety of texts and features from a point of view of meaning or of form.

Searching for meanings as well as forms again allows learners to alternate the roles of discourse observers and participants as they interact with corpus data. The task of exploring the corpus can also provide the basis for participating in further discourse. Pairs of learners can investigate a text together, different learners can investigate different texts and report and discuss their findings, and so on. Some of our students who worked with concordances of *food*, for instance, came across the phrase 'food for thought', and investigated the text from which it came; they then told other students of their discoveries, and subsequently tried to use this expression in their own writing. The teacher can assist these processes by suggesting and illustrating possible activities, encouraging learners to switch backwards and forwards between observer and participant perspectives.

Implications

While corpora have traditionally been viewed as resources for teachers and materials designers, we also see them as resources for learners to use directly, inside and outside the classroom. As well as allowing teachers to make better-informed choices, they also allow learners to problematize language, to explore texts, and to authenticate discourse independently and collectively, adding to the reality of the corpus the reality of their own experience of it. In between these two extremes, various degrees of mediation are, of course, possible. For instance, corpus texts and concordances for analysis by learners can be selected and pre-edited by the teacher (as proposed in Tribble and Jones 1990) or, indeed, by the materials designer (e.g. Goodale 1995). This may help learners pass gradually from 'easy' concordances where recurrent patterns are evident, to those which call for more complex categorization and interpretation. Corpora themselves can be graded, starting with small collections of texts of a similar type and then passing to larger and more heterogeneous ones, so that learners move from sources of data which are more limited and manageable to others which are richer and more varied. In these ways it seems possible to progressively develop learners' autonomy, so that they become able to select and interact with appropriate data independently (Gavioli 1997).

We believe that encouraging the use of corpora by learners, and rendering that use effective, depends upon three main requisites. First of all, learners need access to corpora. They need to be able to compare data from different sources, and to discuss language use in relation to different types of text, topic, and genre. Corpora of spoken language, written language, specialized language, particular geographical and social varieties – including 'lingua franca' English – may all prove useful, as well as large mixed corpora such as the Bank of English and the British National Corpus. Though small specialized corpora may occasionally be created by teachers (or indeed, by learners), larger corpora will have to be provided by publishers, and in this respect it is unfortunate that many of the corpora developed for research are not yet publicly available. Secondly, more user-friendly software to interrogate corpora is required. In our experience, the most suitable concordancer for everyday classroom use is still *MicroConcord* (Scott and Johns 1993); more recent programs present a forbidding range of complex options which can easily confuse the learner. Thirdly, more research is needed into the design of corpus-based activities, and into their selection and grading. What is it worthwhile to look at in concordances, for whom, and from what corpora? How can corpus-based activities best be integrated with 'normal' language teaching, at different levels of proficiency? How can learners (and teachers) best be trained to profit from these resources? While Carter (1998: 64) claims that the evolution represented by the best corpus-based language teaching still needs some time before becoming evident, we believe that there are already fairly clear lines along which work should proceed. Involving learners in corpus use may help to clarify these directions significantly, as well as helping to enrich the reality of the language for them.

Notes

1 Concordances of up to 50 lines from the British National Corpus can be obtained free of charge from the BNC server at the British Library. A fuller service is available to annual subscribers. See *http://info.ox.ac.uk/bnc* for details.
2 Interestingly, the one occurrence of 'I'm a Dutchman' in the BNC is 'To use an old-fashioned London phrase, I'm a Dutchman', providing further evidence that this expression may be rare.
3 Part of the Bank of English can be accessed through CobuildDirect. See *http://titania.cobuild.collins.co.uk/form.html* for details.
4 The BNC Sampler CD-ROM can also be purchased from Oxford University Computing Services. See *http://info.ox.ac.uk/bnc* for details.

References

Aston, G. 1988. *Learning Comity: An Approach to the Description and Pedagogy of Interactional Speech*. Bologna: Cooperativa Libraria Universitaria Editrice.
Bernardini, S. 2000. 'Systematizing serendipity: proposals for large-corpora concordancing with language learners' in L. Burnard and T. McEnery (eds.). *Rethinking Pedagogy from a Corpus Perspective*. Bern: Peter Lang.
Carter, R. 1998. 'Orders of reality: CANCODE, communication and culture', and 'Reply to Guy Cook'. *ELT Journal* 52/1: 43–56; 64.
Cook, C. 1998. 'The uses of reality: a reply to Ronald Carter'. *ELT Journal* 52/1: 57–63.
Gavioli, L. 1997. 'Exploring texts through the concordancer: guiding the learner' in A. Wichmann, S. Fligelstone, T. McEnery, and G. Knowles (eds.). *Teaching and Language Corpora*. London: Longman.
Goodale, M. 1995. *Concordance Samplers 2: Phrasal Verbs*. London: Collins COBUILD.

Leech, G. N. and C. N. Candlin. 1986. 'Introduction', in G. Leech and
   C. N. Candlin (eds.). *Computers in English Language Teaching and Research*.
   London: Longman.
McCarthy, M. and R. Carter. 1995. 'Spoken grammar: what is it and how can we
   teach it?' *ELT Journal* 49/3: 207–18.
Murison-Bowie, S. (ed.). 1993. *MicroConcord Corpus A*. Oxford: Oxford
   University Press.
Scott, M. and T. Johns. 1993. *MicroConcord*. Oxford: Oxford University Press.
Sinclair, J. M. (ed.). 1995. *Collins COBUILD English Dictionary*. 2nd edn.
   London: Collins.
Sinclair, J. M. and D. Kirby. 1990. 'Progress in English computational
   lexicography', in J. Foley (ed.). 1996. *J. M. Sinclair on Lexis and
   Lexicography*. Singapore: UniPress.
Tribble, C. and G. Jones. 1990. *Concordances in the Classroom*. London:
   Longman.
Widdowson, H. G. 1978. *Teaching Language as Communication*. Oxford:
   Oxford University Press.
Widdowson, H. G. 1998. 'Context, community and authentic language'. *TESOL
   Quarterly* 32/4: 705–16.

The authors

Laura Gavioli and Guy Aston teach English language and linguistics in
universities in Italy, at Modena and Bologna respectively. Both belong to a
research group investigating the uses of corpora, small and large, in language and
translation teaching. Their publications in this area include papers in *Teaching
and Language Corpora* (Longman), *Rethinking Language Pedagogy from a
Corpus Perspective* (Peter Lang), and *Learning with Corpora* (CLUEB/
Athelstan). Guy Aston is also co-author (with L. Burnard) of *The BNC
Handbook: Exploring the British National Corpus with SARA* (Edinburgh
University Press).
Email: gavioli@sslmit.unibo.it; guy@sslmit.unibo.it

Further reading

The purpose of the following suggestions for further reading is to point readers to publications with the same focus as that of this whole controversy, i.e. the relationship between corpus linguistics and language teaching (and not, for instance, corpus linguistics as such).

Aston (2001a) provides a helpful and wide-ranging discussion of the roles of corpora in language and translation teaching, and all papers are illustrated with practical examples from English, French, or Italian as a foreign language. Aston's introductory 39-page chapter, 'Learning with corpora: an overview' is the most informative and balanced way into the subject available anywhere. According to the editor's preface (in reference to points made in 'one of the earliest discussions of corpora in language teaching', namely Kennedy 1992, itself well worth seeking out), the papers in this collection show how:

- corpora can provide teachers and learners with information about the language and the culture which can complement and integrate that available from other sources, such as textbooks, teachers, and reference materials. This can effectively increase their competence and awareness, as well as developing their ability to evaluate information from other sources more critically
- corpora have a wide range of potential pedagogic uses, many of them very different from those of descriptive linguistics
- work with corpora need not simply focus on linguistic 'facts', but can be fully compatible with a focus on the learner and on the learning process, from a meaning- as well as from a form-focussed perspective.
(Aston 2001b: 3ff.)

Similar concerns are addressed in the publications which came out (and hopefully will continue to come out) of a series of bi-annual conferences specifically dedicated to exploring the relationship between corpus linguistics and language teaching, the Teaching and Language Corpora conferences (TALC for short). These include the following volumes, which deal with principles of pedagogical corpus applications as well as offering many practical examples from corpora in English and many other languages: Wichmann, Fligelstone, McEnery, and Knowles (1997); Burnard and McEnery (2000); Kettemann and Marko (2002).

Another excellent book is Bernardini (2000). Bernardini offers a detailed but very accessible discussion of current theories of language description and language learning, thus providing a solid theoretical background to the use of corpora in language pedagogy as well as convincing arguments for trying out the corpora and computer tools she describes and examines.

A different kind of corpus, namely that which captures learner (inter)language rather than the language of native-speaker users, is the focus of Granger, Hung, and Petch-Tyson (2002).

Readers looking for an article-length but in-depth treatment of the relationship between corpus linguistics and language teaching would be well served by Aston (1995).

There are also further exchanges of a controversial kind which could be consulted for additional arguments in this area. These include Owen (1993) and Francis and Sinclair (1994), ideally complemented by the discussion of a very specific language teaching problem in another article by Owen: Owen (1996).

And finally, to come back to the first reference in this introduction, there is the exchange between Stubbs and Widdowson which examines the place of corpus linguistics in applied linguistics and offers a particularly rich source of problems to reflect upon: Widdowson (2000) – Stubbs (2001) – Widdowson (2001).

References

Aston, G. 1995. 'Corpora in language pedagogy: matching theory and practice' in Cook and Seidlhofer.

Aston, G. (ed.). 2001a. *Learning with Corpora*. Bologna: CLUEB and Houston, Tex.: Athelstan. (available from www.athel.com).

Aston, G. 2001b. Preface to Aston 2001a.

Bernardini, S. 2000. *Competence, Capacity, Corpora. A Study in Corpus-Aided Language Learning*. Bologna: CLUEB.

Burnard, L. and T. McEnery (eds.). 2000. *Rethinking Language Pedagogy from a Corpus Perspective*. Frankfurt: Peter Lang.

Chomsky, N. 1965. *Aspects of the Theory of Syntax*. Cambridge, Mass.: MIT Press.

Cook, G. and B. Seidlhofer (eds.). 1995. *Principle and Practice in Applied Linguistics*. Oxford: Oxford University Press.

Francis, G. and J. Sinclair. 1994. '"I bet he drinks Carling Black Label": A Riposte to Owen on Corpus Grammar'. *Applied Linguistics* 15/2: 190–200.

Gougenheim, G., R. Michea, P. Rivenc, and A. Sauvageot. 1956. *L'élaboration du français élémentaire*. Paris: Didier.

Granger, S., J. Hung, and S. Petch-Tyson (eds.). 2002. *Computer Learner Corpora, Second Language Acquisition and Foreign Language Teaching*. Amsterdam: John Benjamins.

Halliday, M. A. K., A. McIntosh, and P. Strevens. 1964. *The Linguistic Sciences and Language Teaching*. London: Longman.

Howatt, A. P. R. 1984. *A History of English Language Teaching*. Oxford: Oxford University Press.

Johns, T. and P. King (eds.). 1991. *Classroom Concordancing. English Language Research Journal* 4 (New Series), Birmingham University.

Johns, T. 1994. 'From printout to handout: Grammar and vocabulary teaching in the context of data-driven learning' in Odlin.

Kennedy, G. 1992. 'Preferred ways of putting things with implications for language teaching' in J. Svartvik (ed.). *Directions in corpus linguistics*. Berlin: Mouton de Gruyter.

Kettemann, B. and G. Marko (eds.). 2002. *Teaching and Learning by Doing Corpus Analysis*. Amsterdam: Rodopi.

Mackey, W. F. 1965. *Language Teaching Analysis*. London: Longman.

Odlin, T. (ed.). 1994. *Perspectives on Pedagogical Grammar*. Cambridge: Cambridge University Press.

Owen, C. 1993. 'Corpus-based grammar and the Heineken effect: Lexico-grammatical description for language learners'. *Applied Linguistics* 14/1: 167–87.

Owen, C. 1996. 'Do concordances require to be consulted?' *ELT Journal* 50/3: 219–24.

Palmer, H. E. 1933. *Second Interim Report on English Collocations*. Tokyo: IRET.

Palmer, H. E. 1938. *A Grammar of English Words*. London: Longman.

Palmer, H. E. and A. S. Hornby. 1937. *Thousand-Word English. What it is and what can be done with it*. London: Harrap.

Sinclair, J. 1991. 'Shared knowledge' in J. Alatis (ed.). *Georgetown University Round Table in Language and Linguistics. Linguistics and Language Pedagogy: The State of the Art*. Washington DC: Georgetown University.

Sinclair, J. 1995. (editor in chief) *Collins COBUILD English Dictionary*. London: Harper Collins.

Sinclair, J. 1997. 'Corpus evidence in language description' in Wichmann, Fligelstone, McEnery, and Knowles.

Stern, H. H. 1983. *Fundamental Concepts of Language Teaching*. Oxford: Oxford University Press.

Stubbs, M. 2001. 'Texts, corpora, and problems of interpretation: A response to Widdowson'. *Applied Linguistics* 22/2: 149–72.

Swenson, E. and M. P. West. 1934. *On the Counting of New Words in Textbooks for Teaching Foreign Languages*. Toronto: Toronto University Press.

West, M. P. 1953. *A General Service List of English Words: With Semantic Frequencies and a Supplementary Word-List for the Writing of Popular Science and Technology*. London: Longman.

Wichmann, A., S. Fligelstone, T. McEnery, and G. Knowles (eds.). 1997. *Teaching and Language Corpora*. London and New York: Longman.

Widdowson, H. G. 1991. 'The description and prescription of language' in J. Alatis (ed.). *Georgetown University Round Table in Language and Linguistics. Linguistics and Language Pedagogy: The State of the Art*. Washington DC: Georgetown University.

Widdowson, H. G. 2000. 'On the limitations of linguistics applied'. *Applied Linguistics* 21/1: 3–25.

Widdowson, H. G. 2001. 'Interpretations and Correlations: A Reply to Stubbs'. *Applied Linguistics* 22/4: 531–38.

Willis, J. D. 1990. *The Lexical Syllabus: A New Approach to Language Teaching*. London: Collins.

Section 3
Critical discourse analysis

This section is placed at the heart of this volume, and it seems appropriate that this should be so, for in many ways, the focus here is on what this whole book is essentially about, namely the encouragement of critical reading. What readers are invited to attempt in this section, then, is a critical discourse analysis of critical discourse analysis. That this is quite an ambitious undertaking will become apparent from the points raised in the articles that represent this particular controversy.

While it is intended, as in the other sections, that these papers should speak for themselves, it may nevertheless be helpful to provide at least some contextual information. It is not easy to do this in a nutshell, as it is often pointed out by critical discourse analysts themselves that there is not one homogeneous version of critical discourse analysis (henceforth CDA). Both protagonists and critics of CDA have attempted to explain just what its essence is, and particularly over the last few years a quite dense intertextual network has developed, with various authors referring and reacting to each other. Indeed, this network of exchanges would in itself constitute a fascinating object of critical study.

In a very accessible yet quite comprehensive survey, Fairclough and Wodak explain the agenda of CDA as follows:

> CDA sees discourse – language use in speech and writing – as a form of 'social practice'. Describing discourse as social practice implies a dialectical relationship between a particular discursive event and the situation(s), institution(s) and social structure(s) which frame it. A dialectical relationship is a two-way relationship: the discursive event is shaped by situations, institutions and social structures, but it also shapes them. To put the same point in a different way, discourse is both socially *constitutive* as well as socially shaped: it constitutes situations, objects of knowledge, and the social identities of and relationships between people and groups of people. It is constitutive both in the sense that it helps to sustain and reproduce the social status quo, and in the sense that it contributes to transforming it. ...
>
> CDA sees itself not as dispassionate and objective social science, but as engaged and committed. It is a form of intervention in social practice and social relationships: many analysts are politically active against racism, or as feminists, or within the peace movement, and so forth. ... What is distinctive about CDA is that it intervenes on the side of dominated and oppressed groups and against

dominating groups, and that it openly declares the emancipatory interests that motivate it.
(Fairclough and Wodak 1997: 258)

This extract gives us a clear idea of how critical discourse analysts see the relationship between language and society, and which stance they take towards the practices they analyse. What still needs some contextualization, perhaps, is the term 'critical discourse analysis' itself. One way of trying to get to grips with its meaning would be to look at its three component parts in turn, and to ask what 'critical', 'discourse', and 'analysis' mean by themselves. True, the whole is often more than the sum of its parts, but surely the meaning of the parts is relevant, otherwise they would not have been chosen to make up the combination. But here we are already approaching the problematic question as to how meanings are either read *off* or read *into* uses of language. In fact, the terms 'discourse' and 'analysis' are discussed in the articles that follow, and most readers will be aware of some of the work undertaken in the field of discourse analysis as described in the classic introductions and overviews (for example, Brown and Yule 1983; Coulthard 1985; Schiffrin 1994; Gee 1999). So it may be most useful for present purposes to ask what the first word in CDA, 'critical', is taken to signify. This is also what tends to be the focus of the explanations of CDA given in the relevant literature.

Thus van Dijk, in his contribution to Schiffrin, Tannen, and Hamilton (2001), offers a one-paragraph general introduction before moving on to examples, and in it he takes the 'discourse analytical' part for granted and thus homes in on 'critical':

> What is Critical Discourse Analysis?
> Critical Discourse Analysis (CDA) is a type of discourse analytical research that primarily studies the way social power abuse, dominance, and inequality are enacted, reproduced, and resisted by text and talk in the social and political context. With such dissident research, critical discourse analysts take explicit position, and thus want to understand, expose, and ultimately to resist social inequality.
> (van Dijk 2001: 352)

Toolan, in a paper entitled 'What is critical discourse analysis and why are people saying such terrible things about it?' asks: 'What is CDA really about? What does it purport to do that draws so many students to it? ... And why the emphasis on "critical"?' (Toolan 1997: 85). He does not answer the last question himself, but quotes a passage from the very paper by Fairclough which is reprinted in this volume:

> Calling the approach 'critical' is a recognition that our social practice in general and our use of language in particular are bound up with causes and effects which we may not be at all aware of under normal conditions (Bourdieu 1977). The normal opacity of these practices to those involved in them – the invisibility of their ideological assumptions, and of the power relations which

underlie the practices – helps to sustain these power relations. (Fairclough 1996: 54).[1]

CDA developed out of the pioneering work of Roger Fowler and his colleagues at the University of East Anglia. Fowler was co-author of the book *Language and Control*, in which the term 'critical linguistics' was coined in the late seventies (Fowler, Hodge, Kress, and Trew 1979). In this book, as well as in its companion volume *Language as Ideology* (Kress and Hodge 1979), concepts and methods chiefly associated with Halliday's functional-systemic grammar were drawn on to analyse texts in an attempt to raise consciousness about how language works in society. Although there are some important (mainly methodological) differences between critical linguistics (CL) and CDA, both can, in Wodak's words, 'be said to occupy the same "paradigmatic space"', in that

> implicit argumentations, for example, and opaque texts are deconstructed and their underlying meanings made explicit. The critical analysis also relates the analysed text to other, connected, discourses (intertextuality) and to historical and synchronic contexts.
> (Wodak 1995: 204)

A widely-quoted, more recent paper by Fowler himself, entitled 'On critical linguistics', heads Caldas-Coulthard and Coulthard's edited volume *Text and Practices. Readings in Critical Discourse Analysis*. In it, Fowler points out that critical linguists

> occupy a variety of socialist positions, and are concerned to use linguistic analysis to expose misrepresentations and discrimination in a variety of modes of public discourse: they offer critical readings of newspapers, political propaganda, official documents, regulations, formal genres such as the interview, and so on. Topics examined include sexism, racism, inequality in education, employment, the courts and so on; war, nuclear weapons and nuclear power; political strategies; and commercial practices. In relation to public discourse on such matters, the goals of the critical linguists are in general terms defamiliarisation or consciousness-raising.
> (Fowler 1996: 5)

Having looked at how some exponents of CDA explain the meaning of the term 'critical', it may be helpful to consider what some of the critics of CDA have to say about it. To start with an author who declares himself 'very much more in favour of CDA than against it' (Toolan 1997: 83), what seems to irritate him most is what he perceives as a kind of self-righteous attitude expressed in many CDA articles, which, as he points out, 'do seem to carry an excessive amount of preliminary "complaint" discourse' (p. 84). As an example, Toolan quotes van Dijk as saying:

> The bulk of research in contemporary studies of language and discourse has been decidedly 'uncritical' if not 'apolitical', even when it has focused on the social

---

[1] A note to help avoid confusion, and perhaps a welcome reminder that scepticism is an attitude that this volume seeks to encourage in its readers: Toolan does quote the passage from Fairclough like this, but it does not actually appear in 'Fairclough 1996: 54'.

dimensions of language use. Such studies typically have aimed to describe the world, and ignored the necessity to change it.
(van Dijk 1993: 131)

Toolan concludes that

> even the sympathetic observer tends to get the impression that CD analysts are attempting to garner kudos for themselves for being the first to 'really see and address' the workings of power in discourse. If there were less of this from CD analysts, I think there would be fewer people provoked to say terrible things about CDA.
> (op. cit.: 87)

While Toolan's criticism above mainly concerns the 'interpersonal' effects that the expression of certain CDA attitudes may have on some readers, Hammersley directs his criticism at the philosophical foundations of CDA (Hammersley 1997). In a section of his paper with the heading 'The meaning of "critical"', he begins by asking 'What exactly does it mean to add the word "critical" to the phrase "discourse analysis"?' He concludes with the observation that

> it is characteristic of CDA, and of much 'critical' work in the social sciences, that its philosophical foundations are simply taken for granted, as if they were unproblematic. This reflects the fact that, in many ways, the term 'critical' has become little more than a rallying cry demanding that researchers consider 'whose side they are on'. As I noted earlier,[2] the term 'critical' began life as a euphemism. And, in an important sense, it still operates as one today. ... it seems to function as an umbrella for any approach that wishes to portray itself as politically radical without being exclusive in its commitments. Indeed, as I have noted, what *could* legitimately shelter under this umbrella is very diverse.
> (Hammersley 1997: 244)

Calling the term 'critical' as used in CDA a 'euphemism' would seem to be a harsh verdict, and one that, it is hoped, will make readers want to investigate the issue with reference to some first-hand experience of reading CDA work for themselves in order to form their own judgement. Hammersley's outspoken criticism certainly needs to be included here because it indicates the broad spectrum of responses that CDA receives and so can also help place the exchange that follows below in a wider context.

The last statement Hammersley makes in the above quotation, i.e. 'what *could* legitimately shelter under this umbrella [of being "critical"] is very diverse' comes across more starkly elsewhere in his paper, when he says

[2] i.e. Hammersley (1997: 240): 'The primary source of the term "critical" in the sense being discussed in this paper is the "critical theory" developed by the Frankfurt School of Marxism. Scholem reports Walter Benjamin, an important figure on the margins of that school, to the effect that the use of the term "critical" arose when Frankfurt Marxists were exiled in the United States as a result of the Nazi takeover in Germany. The term "Marxism" was taboo in America, and so they began to refer to their work as "critical" rather than as Marxist. (Scholem 1982: 210).'

while most critical research is Leftist, it need not be; and Fairclough (1996, p. 52) acknowledges that 'a CDA of the right is quite conceivable. ... From this it should be clear that there is no reason why a 'critical' approach on decisionist foundations could not be committed to the most objectionable politics. Indeed, that seems to have been precisely the case with Heidegger and his flirtation with National Socialism. (Hammersley 1997: 243)

These observations correspond closely to comments made by Widdowson, both in the paper that follows and in his 1998 paper:

> My view would be that if a cause is just then we should look for ways of supporting it by coherent argument and well-founded (as distinct from well-funded) analysis. And I would indeed argue that to do otherwise is to do a disservice to the cause. For the procedures of ideological exposure by expedient analysis which characterize the practices of CDA can, of course, be taken up to further *any* cause, right wing as well as left, evil as well as good. They are the familiar tactics of polemic and propaganda, and they have a long history in human affairs. (Widdowson 1998: 150)

Implying something?

So far we have only been concerned with the epistemological question of how the first element in CDA, 'critical', is to be defined. But the bulk of criticism of CDA actually concerns questions of methodology. Michael Stubbs, for instance, who calls himself 'basically sympathetic' towards CDA, nevertheless levels many criticisms at it with regard to its data and its analytic procedures, and questions the extent to which work in CDA actually substantiates its claims by adherence to 'standards of careful, rigorous and systematic analysis' (Fairclough and Wodak 1997: 259, quoted in Stubbs 1997: 102). In particular, he objects to the fact that CDA provides no systematic comparisons between texts and norms in the language. As a corpus linguist (see Section 2 of this volume), Stubbs is particularly concerned to show how work in CDA could benefit from employing quantitative and comparative methods, and in order to do this, he sketches two case studies which demonstrate how observations and claims about particular uses of language can be substantiated by means of corpus linguistic methods.

Sounds good to me.

While Stubbs highlights the potential of quantitative methods for CDA, Widdowson suggests a different kind of empirical approach to strengthen its methodology. He proposes an approach that looks at how the intended recipients – that is to say, discourse participants not discourse analysts – of the texts analysed in CDA *actually* understand and interpret these texts, for instance, newspaper articles or leaflets produced by public services.[3] Widdowson argues that:

> To do this would be to take empirical ethnographic considerations into account and locate texts in their sociocultural settings. In such an ethnographic approach,

of course!

---

[3] The need to do this is, in principle, also acknowledged (but not acted upon) in various CDA publications (cf. for example, Fairclough 1995: 9): 'The principle that textual analysis should be combined with analysis of practices of production and consumption has not been adequately operationalized in the papers collected here.'

how non-analysts go about their normal pragmatic business would be the central focus of study. Rather than discount their understanding as naïve and ideologically uninformed, it would help them to an awareness of the contextual conditions that give rise to different discourse interpretations and of the essential indeterminacy of meaning. If critical discourse analysts were to explore discourses along these lines using their own partial interpretations as a stimulus for such enquiry rather than claiming a privileged status for them, their work would indeed be of considerable significance since it would be relevant to an understanding of, and intervention in, everyday uses and abuses of language.
(Widdowson 2000: 22)

It is obviously impossible in a short introduction such as this to do justice to the many important concerns that arise in discussions within, and about CDA, but it is nevertheless hoped that the few glimpses that have been offered here suffice to prime readers for a critical reading of the papers that follow, and for considering the issues that arise out of them for themselves.

To summarize, we have so far been mainly concerned to achieve an understanding of the intended meaning of 'critical'. From the various explanations offered above it is clear that 'defamiliarisation and consciousness-raising' (Fowler) are regarded as essential processes which should enable readers and listeners to recognize that 'discourse is socially constitutive as well as socially shaped' (Fairclough and Wodak), and, on the basis of this realization, to 'deconstruct' 'opaque texts' (Wodak) in order to 'understand, expose and ultimately resist social inequality' (van Dijk). These, indeed, are goals that both critical discourse analysts and their critics are agreed upon. As Widdowson puts it in a review article of three CDA books,

> What is most plainly distinctive about critical discourse analysis (henceforth CDA) is its sense of responsibility and its commitment to social justice. This is linguistics with a conscience and a cause, one which seeks to reveal how language is used and abused in the exercise of power and the suppression of human rights. In a grossly unequal world where the poor and the oppressed are subject to discrimination and exploitation such a cause is obviously a just and urgent one which warrants support.
> (Widdowson 1998: 136)

Stubbs similarly argues that:

> It is because CDA raises important social issues, that it is worthwhile trying to strengthen its analyses. ... CDA has set an important agenda, of potentially very considerable social significance. It is therefore important that both the details, and also the central logic of the argument, are as carefully worked out as possible.
> (Stubbs 1997: 101, 114)

What is at issue, then, is not what CDA *is about*, but *how it goes about it*: the issues are so important as to call for as carefully considered and

parallel to morphology

rigorous a methodology as possible so as to produce findings that are descriptively reliable and secure. And this is essentially what the argument is about.

Whereas Stubbs and Widdowson seem to think that at least some of what they see as CDA's weaknesses could, in principle, be remedied, Hammersley is more sceptical. While also acknowledging the ambitions of CDA, he sees them as a problem rather than as a strength:

> ... [CDA's] advocates argue for the superiority of their position because it is reflexive: that whereas other approaches neglect their founding assumptions and socio-historical role, critical research is self-explicating.
>
> This relates closely to what is, perhaps, the most damaging feature of CDA: the extraordinary ambition of the task that it sets itself. It aims to achieve a very great deal more than other kinds of discourse analysis. Not only does it claim to offer an understanding of discursive processes, but also of society as a whole, and what is wrong with it, and of how it can and should be changed. As a result, it faces all the methodological problems with which more conventional kinds of research have to deal, plus many others as well. ...
>
> One result of this excessive ambition is that work in this tradition takes much for granted and adopts relatively crude positions on a variety of issues. For example, it often involves the adoption of a macro-sociological theory in which there are only two parties – the oppressors and the oppressed – and only one relationship between them: dominance. ...
>
> Overambition also encourages the presentation of what can only be speculations as if they were well-grounded knowledge. In all forms of research there is considerable pressure to produce newsworthy findings. This can lead to researchers over-interpreting their data. Critical approaches institutionalise this pressure and at the same time require of research that it not only leads to an understanding of social reality but also, more or less directly, to a transformation of it. This produces a tendency to judge results according to their political implications as much if not more than their validity. And there is some evidence of this in the work of critical discourse analysis.
> (Hammersley 1997: 244–5)

The declared purpose of CDA is, as we have seen, to expose how language is used in the socio-political abuse of power. It is this that makes it such an important and influential development in applied linguistics. But clearly it does not make it immune to criticism. What Hammersley and others have questioned about CDA, however, is the validity not of the cause it espouses, but of the procedures it follows in promoting it. The following exchange between Fairclough and Widdowson will serve to bring out in clear relief issues concerning the analysis and interpretation of texts that lie at the heart of the CDA enterprise, and that need to be resolved to make it more effective. It is in this constructive spirit that the exchange which follows is offered for reflection and discussion.

Text 17

H. G. Widdowson
University of London and
University of Essex, UK

Discourse analysis: a critical view

Abstract

Discourse analysis is in vogue as a field of enquiry, particularly in the guise of critical discourse analysis, which employs procedures not essentially different from literary criticism to identify ideological bias in texts. This article argues that, perhaps as a consequence, there is a good deal of conceptual confusion in the field. One example is the uncertainty of the scope of description, which is reflected in the ambiguity of the term 'function' and the failure to distinguish between text and discourse. Another is the tendency to equate social and linguistic theory with political commitment which raises the question of the relationship between analysis and interpretation. It is argued that this confusion makes suspect some of the principles and practices of critical discourse analysis, and calls into question the validity of the notion of authentic language currently prevalent in language pedagogy.

Keywords: *analysis; authenticity; commitment, political; discourse; effect; force; function; interpretation; reference; text*

[handwritten marginal note: cynical from the beginning]

1 Discourse: in vogue and diverse

Discourse is a contentious area of enquiry, and one which rouses strong feelings. But there are two things about it which can be said at the outset without provoking disagreement. So I had better say them straightaway.

First, it is in vogue and figures prominently in discussions of language, as publishers' lists over the past ten years or so will testify. The use of the word 'discourse' will indicate that you are in tune with the trends and keeping up with the linguistic Jones's. One example. In 1982 a book appeared with the title *Language and Literature: An Introductory Reader in Stylistics* (Carter 1982). In 1989 another book appeared from the same publisher, and with the same editor: 'Language, **Discourse** and Literature: An Introductory Reader in **Discourse** Stylistics' (Carter & Simpson 1989, my emphasis). I was a contributor to the first volume and imagined that I *was* indeed doing discourse stylistics at the time. I had assumed too that discourse was conceptually included in language, and not, as it would appear by the later title, distinct from it. One reason for the second title is, one might say, that in the intervening years discourse had become popular, and therefore good for promotion. But that is perhaps too cynical – and too provocative. There is another reason for the change. As the notion of discourse became popular, so, naturally enough it took on different meanings for different people.

This brings me to the second thing to be said about discourse. Namely that it is a diverse, not to say, diffuse concept. Those who write about it acknowledge this difficulty with admirable frankness. Here, for example, is Norman Fairclough in a recent publication:

> Discourse is a difficult concept, largely because there are so many conflicting
> and overlapping definitions formulated from various theoretical and
> disciplinary standpoints.
> (Fairclough 1992: 3)▪

Very true. So we have a concept which is extremely fashionable and at the same time
extremely uncertain: widespread but spread very thin. To be cynical again, we might
say that discourse is something everybody is talking about but without knowing
with any certainty just what it is: in vogue and vague. Ignorance and popular appeal
have always been a heady and dangerous mix. As Hilaire Belloc has it:

> Oh! let us never, never doubt
> What nobody is sure about!
> (from 'The Microbe')

In view of all this it would seem sensible to begin by trying to define what we are
talking about and make a map of the terrain. Discourse may be difficult to pin
down, but this may not only be because the concept is intrinsically complex. It
may also be because discussions of it have been confused. And complexity and
confusion are not the same thing.

2 Scope and commitment of enquiry

Fairclough, in the book already cited, makes his own map. He distinguishes two
approaches to discourse: the critical and the non-critical.

> Critical approaches differ from non-critical approaches in not just describing
> discursive practices, but also showing how discourse is shaped by relations of
> power and ideologies, and the constructive effects discourse has upon social
> identities, social relations and systems of knowledge and belief, neither of
> which (*sic*) is normally apparent to discourse participants.
> (Fairclough 1992: 12)

Fairclough, of course, favours the critical: the approach which not only describes
discourse but interprets it as social practice. This distinction in effect conflates
two perspectives which, to avoid confusion, we need to separate out. The first has
to do with what we might call 'scope', with what phenomenon you think you are
analysing, and the second has to do with what we might call 'commitment' and
concerns the relationship between analysis and interpretation.

In reference to scope, there will be general agreement that the term 'discourse'
refers to the use of language in social contexts. But then you can look at your data
primarily in reference to language use, thereby bringing discourse within the
terms of reference of linguistics, or primarily in reference to social contexts,
thereby bringing discourse within the domain of sociology. Of course, you can
seek to do both and be commendably interdisciplinary – and this is indeed what
Fairclough himself claims to do. But there will always be differences in the
direction of enquiry which will inevitably privilege one perspective over the other.
In one case, you will look at social data as evidence of language processes, and in
the other case, you will look at linguistic data as evidence of social processes.
How you select the data and the significance you attach to it are bound to be in
some degree different. As I have pointed out elsewhere (Widdowson 1990a), one

tradition of discourse analysis has made statements about social attitudes and beliefs, the exercise of power, the influence of ideology, and so on, with scant reference to the linguistic data; and another tradition has made statements about the specifics of language in use without paying much attention to social factors. It ought to be possible to bring the two traditions into closer correspondence, but it is no easy matter. Particularly if the question of scope is confused with that of commitment.

It is possible to accept the need to extend the scope of discourse description by taking social factors into account without commitment to the kind of socio-political interpretation that is implied by a critical approach. Political commitment is not the same thing as social theory, although the two are easy to confuse. As has often enough been pointed out, all enquiry is of its nature partial since it is based on an idealisation of data of one kind or another. But this does not mean that there is no difference between analysis and interpretation. As I understand these terms, interpretation is a matter of converging on a particular meaning as having some kind of privileged validity. The point about analysis is that it seeks to reveal those factors which lead to a divergence of possible meanings, each conditionally valid. Whereas analysis recognises its own partiality, interpretation of its nature must suspend that recognition. Analysts may of course have their preferences, and may subsequently interpret data in one particular way after analysis. Interpreters give priority to their preferences. The argument I shall pursue is that if critical discourse analysis is an exercise in interpretation, it is invalid as analysis. The name 'critical discourse analysis', in other words, is, in my view, a contradiction in terms.

It is a contradiction which, as one might imagine, creates a good deal of confusion. It is a contradiction, too, which can be traced in a number of other concepts concerning discourse, and which has been carried over into the domain of language teaching. My main purpose in this article is to track the contradiction down. In doing so, I shall be critical as well. But the term critical can denote intellectual analysis *as distinct from* ideological interpretation. And it is in this sense that I use the term here.

As a first move, then, towards clarifying the concept of discourse, we might take our bearings on two distinctions: between analysis and interpretation in regard to commitment; and between sociological and linguistic approaches to the scope of description. Let us begin with linguistics and with a little history.

3 Sentence, text and discourse

Zellig Harris, well known as Chomsky's teacher, was responsible for introducing him to the concept of transformations. Chomsky applied the concept to the description of sentences. Harris, on the other hand, used it to discover patterns of language beyond the sentence in what, in 1952, he referred to as discourse analysis. In both cases, the interest was in discovering structural relations underlying surface forms. Discourse, for Harris, was seen as the manifestation of formal regularities across sentences in combination. A discourse was a stretch of actually occurring language data, but only treated as evidence of formal equivalences. Discourse was language in use, but Harris was not interested in the use, only in the language. Thus discourse and sentence were seen as essentially the same kind of phenomenon, different only in extent. Applying his transformations, he comes up with a number of equivalence classes of morphemes which link sentences together in his data. As he acknowledges:

> All this, however, is still distinct from an *interpretation* of the findings, which must take the meanings of the morphemes into consideration and ask what the author was about when he produced the text. Such interpretation is obviously quite separate from the formal findings, although it may follow closely in the directions which the formal findings indicate.
> (Harris 1952: 382)

Harris is, in many ways, a figure who casts a long shadow. A number of issues arise from his work on discourse analysis which have caused much of the confusion and contradiction I referred to earlier, and still remain stubbornly problematic. Let me set them out, item by item.

1 Discourse analysis is seen as the study of language patterns beyond the sentence. Thus it follows that discourse is sentence writ large: quantitively different but qualitatively the same phenomenon. It follows, too, of course, that you cannot have discourse below the sentence.

2 If the difference between sentence and discourse is not a matter of kind but only of degree, then they must signal the same kind of meaning. If sentence meaning is intrinsically encoded, that is to say, a semantic property of the language itself, then so is discourse meaning.

3 In the quotation, however, Harris talks about interpretation as involving two factors, 'the meanings of the morphemes', which presumably refers to semantics and 'what the author was about when he produced the text', which brings in pragmatic considerations like intention, and implies that interpretation is not just a matter of what the sentence means in relation to the code, but also what the author means in relation to the context. In this case interpretation cannot just be read off from the text as if it were an elongated sentence. But then if semantic and pragmatic meanings are different, *how* are they different, and by what principles can they be related?

4 Harris is talking about 'discourse' analysis. He also refers in the quotation to the production of a 'text'. Do these terms mean the same thing and is he using them, as others seem to do, in free variation? If they do denote different things, what are they, and by what principles can *they* be related?

These are four problematic issues which have, I think, caused a good deal of confusion and which, 40 years on, still do (cf. Pennycook 1994, Schiffrin 1994). Let us consider them in more detail and draw out their implications. As we shall see, they are all closely interrelated: pick at one and the others come apart as well.

The thread we might begin to pull at first is the notion that discourse analysis deals with units of language bigger than the sentence. This has become more or less established now as part of the standard definition. Thus Michael Stubbs, after sounding the usual cautionary note about the instability of the term 'discourse analysis', tells us that:

> Roughly speaking, it refers to attempts to study the organization of language above the sentence, or above the clause, and therefore to study larger linguistic units, such as conversational exchanges or written texts.
> (Stubbs 1983: 2)

The word 'text', we might note in passing, also makes an appearance here, with the implication that it refers only to written language. It would seem to follow that the discourse analysis of pieces of writing above sentence (or clause?) length is therefore text analysis: as far as written language is concerned the terms are synonymous. This leaves us with the problem of knowing whether discourse and/or text analysis is deemed to begin above the clause or above the sentence. This is not a quibble. If it begins above the clause, then it would presumably include complex and compound units which would conventionally be defined as syntactic constituents and so below the sentence. If it begins above the sentence, then there is clearly less of a continuity from conventional syntactic analysis, and you need to look (as Harris did) for other principles of ordering. If, with reference to written language, the term 'sentence' means 'orthographic sentence', then again the domain of discourse/text analysis has to be below and not above it. It is all rather vague and confusing.

A little later in the same (introductory) chapter, Stubbs tells us that the terms 'text' and 'discourse' are 'often ambiguous and confusing'. How true. One might suppose that this would be a good reason for distinguishing them more explicitly. Instead we get remarks like 'one often talks of "written text" versus "spoken discourse" and "discourse" implies length whereas a "text" may be very short'. These comments seem curiously uncritical. It is surely the purpose of intellectual analysis to counter such loose talk. As it is, the ambiguity and confusion remain, more firmly established by being so readily indulged.

Stubbs is not alone in thinking of discourse as language above the sentence, and that the distinction between discourse and text is trivial and without theoretical substance. It is, indeed, so orthodox a view that it seems perverse, not to say foolhardy, to question it. Here it is again as expressed without equivocation by Wallace Chafe in the recent *Oxford International Encyclopedia of Linguistics*: a massive and authoritative work (of which I was myself an editor):

> The term 'discourse' is used in somewhat different ways by different scholars, but underlying the differences is a common concern for language beyond the boundaries of isolated sentences. The term TEXT is used in similar ways. Both terms may refer to a unit of language larger than the sentence: one may speak of a 'discourse' or a 'text'.
> (Chafe 1992)

One may indeed so speak, and scholars do. But is it helpful so to speak? Let us consider the question.

To begin with, how do we deal with uses of language which take the form of texts which are apparently constituted of single sentences? The most obvious instances of such texts are public notices like 'TRESPASSERS WILL BE PROSECUTED', 'STICK NO BILLS', 'HANDLE WITH CARE', and so on. By the Chafe criterion, they are not texts at all since they have no other sentences to keep them company. And yet they are intuitively textual in that they are not fragments or components of any larger linguistic whole but are complete communicative units, separate speech events as Hymes (1970) might call them.

In view of this, we might concede that in certain circumstances single, isolated sentences can serve as texts. But then the question inevitably arises as to what

[marginal note:] Point out confusion / no resolution?

[marginal note:] Plays w/ words a lot.

these circumstances might be. And this in turn might lead us to suspect that perhaps it is these circumstances and not the size of the linguistic unit which determines textuality, and that whether a piece of language is larger than a sentence has little, if anything, to do with it. This suspicion is strengthened by the obvious fact that there are instances of language which have all the appearance of complete texts, but which do not even consist of separate sentences but of isolated *words*. Public notices again: 'TRAINS' 'TOILETS' 'GENTLEMEN' 'LADIES' 'SILENCE' 'PRIVATE' 'OPEN' 'CLOSED' 'IN' 'OUT' and so on. Here there is no sentence in sight, but only isolated words: nouns, adjectives, adverbs, parts of speech in grammatical limbo, constituents that have somehow declared independence from syntax and are on their own. But it is not only that parts of sentences seem to take on textual independence, parts of words do as well. The single letter 'W' signals to me where I am to register for a conference. The single letter 'P' tells me where to park my car. These are notices. Are they not therefore texts? And if not, why not? Because they are smaller than a sentence? This does not seem to be an adequate answer. So what would be?

It might be objected that I am giving unwarranted attention to relatively trivial uses of language, indulging in critical nit-picking. These are texts, if you like, but minimal texts. But the interesting question surely is how they can be texts when they *are* so minimal. One answer might be that they are a sort of shorthand, they stand for larger texts, rather like acronyms. Just as 'PTO' at the bottom of a letter stands for the sentence 'Please turn over', so 'P' stands for 'Parking'. But this is still a one word text. Well then 'Parking' in turn stands for 'Parking is permitted here' or 'Here is a place for parking your car', or something along these lines. Shorthand.

But then how do those who write such shorthand know that I will interpret it as intended? How do they know how minimal they can be? The letters 'BBC' can indeed be said to stand for the 'British Broadcasting Corporation', 'BC' for 'Before Christ', 'PC' for 'Police Constable', and so on. These are established encodings with fixed denotations, symbolically secure. But 'P' does not have the same fixity of meaning. If I see it as a notice at the side of a country road I interpret it as referring to a small space at the side of the road, a lay-by, where I can pull in for a brief halt. If I see the letter 'P' as a notice in a street in the middle of the city, I know that it refers to something entirely different: to a covered concrete place, a multi-storey edifice, where I pay to leave my car. In other words, how I interpret the 'P' depends on where I see it and what I know about the lay-by and the multi-storey car park. It depends, in other words, on relating the text to something outside itself, that is to say to the *con*text: to where it is located on the one hand, and to how, on the other hand, it keys in with my knowledge of reality as shaped and sanctioned by the society I live in – that is to say, my social knowledge. 'P' is a linguistic symbol, a letter of the alphabet, an element of English graphology. But that is not how I *interpret* it when it figures as a text. I read it not as a conventional element of the code but as an index whose function is to point away from itself to the context, and so indicate where meaning is to be found elsewhere (cf. Widdowson 1990b).

The same point can be made about the other texts we have been considering. When I see the one word 'TRAINS', for example, written on the wall of Russell Square station, I know that it refers to the trains of the Piccadilly Line proceeding westbound to Richmond. And I also know that it not only has reference to a particular direction – westwards, but it has the force of a direction in a quite different, illocutionary, sense as well – come this way to the trains. But the same word can serve as a totally different text and invoke a quite different interpretation, where reference is to other trains with the force of a warning. Similarly when I see the notice 'TRESPASSERS WILL BE PROSECUTED', its location and my familiarity with such notices will lead me to infer that it is meant to have the force of prohibition in reference to individuals who might be tempted to stray on to this particular piece of private land. I know that it is not meant to refer generically to all who trespass or to have the force of a general assertion about their fate.

How do I know all these things? Obviously because I have been socialised into a particular reality and know how to use language to engage indexically with it. I recognise a piece of language as a text not because of its linguistic size, but because I assume it is intended to key into this reality. Texts can come in all shapes and sizes: they can correspond in extent with any linguistic unit: letter, sound, word, sentence, combination of sentences. To put the matter more briskly, I identify a text not by its linguistic extent but its social intent.

But identifying something as a text is not the same as interpreting it. You may recognise intentionality but not know the intention. This is where discourse comes in, and why it needs to be distinguished from text. As I have tried to show, we achieve meaning by indexical realisation, that is to say by using language to engage our extra-linguistic reality. Unless it is activated by this contextual connection, the text is inert. It is this activation, this acting of context on code, this indexical conversion of the symbol that I refer to as discourse. Discourse in this view is the pragmatic process of meaning negotiation. Text is its product. When discourse takes the form of spoken interaction, the text is simultaneous and transitory and leaves no trace unless recorded. Since there is continual textual reflex of the discourse, it is easy to suppose that they are the same thing, although a glance at a transcription makes it immediately obvious how little of the discourse is actually made textually manifest.

Written text is different. Here we have a record made by one of the discourse participants, the writer, who is enacting the discourse on behalf of both first and second person parties, but who is, usually, only recording the first person contribution. The actual second person reader, as distinct from the projected one, then has to interpret this text, that is to say, to realise a discourse from it. The discourse which the writer intends the text to record as output is, in these circumstances, always likely to be different from the discourse which the reader derives from it. In other words, what a writer means *by* a text is not the same as what a text means *to* a reader.

4 Interpretation: reference, force, effect

So in reference to what Zellig Harris has to say, interpretation is not simply a matter of what the author was about when he or she produced the text. It is also what the reader is about when processing it. There may often, of course, be a close correspondence. This seems fairly clearly to be the case with public notices. There are, to be sure, anecdotal counter examples. There is the man who

[handwritten marginal note:] Is discourse defined or just talked about.

misunderstood the force of the notice 'DOGS MUST BE CARRIED' and declined to take the escalator because he had no dog. There is Jonathan Miller in *Beyond the Fringe* reflecting on the notice in the toilet in a train 'GENTLEMEN LIFT THE SEAT'. This, he suggests, might not actually be an injunction, but a statement of general truth about gentlemen and their habitual behaviour, or even a loyal toast ('Gentlemen, Lift the Seat!')

These are comical anecdotes: comical precisely because such incongruous instances of mistaken reference and force are rare. And indeed in most of our daily transactional uses of language we are so contracted into the schematic conventions which define them that we can fairly confidently count on an unproblematic convergence of intention and interpretation. It is hard to see how social life would be possible otherwise.

In other cases, however, convergence is less straightforward. This is particularly so when our individual identity is implicated, when the values, attitudes, and beliefs which provide us with our security are brought into play. I have talked about (locutionary) reference and (illocutionary) force as aspects of pragmatic meaning achieved in discourse. When we talk of such values, attitudes, beliefs, and individual identity, we introduce a third, and much more problematic aspect: that of (perlocutionary) *effect.*

A simple example, and a traditional one. I can make reference to the same person in a variety of ways: 'The Duke of Wellington', 'The Iron Duke', 'The Victor of Waterloo'; or, to be a little less dated, 'The previous Prime Minister', 'The Iron Lady', 'Mrs Thatcher', 'Maggie', 'the Scourge of Socialism', 'The Witch of Downing Street', and so on. The difference between these phrases lies in the attitude they appear to express, in how I seem to position myself in respect to the person referred to. So I might be deemed to indicate deference, admiration or disrespect. And of course, since communication is a matter of convergence, my choice of referring expression can be seen as an attempt to persuade my intended interlocutor into the same position. So it is that expressions can be said to be indexically the same in reference but different in effect. The same point can be made about force. I can report an event with the intention to alarm or amuse or impress, to incite your sympathy or your contempt, and you may recognise the intention and so ratify the effect intended.

But equally, of course, you may not. And there's the rub. For like reference and force, effect is not a feature of the text but a function of the discourse, either as intentionally written into the text or interpretatively read into it. You may *deem* me to have said or written something disrespectful, or rude, or ironic or racially biassed, but to do so you have to make assumptions about my intentions, which, in accordance with normal pragmatic practice, can only be partially signalled in the text. These assumptions are naturally and inevitably made on the basis of *your* conception of the world, *your* social and individual reality, *your* values, beliefs and prejudices. This is the necessary consequence of discourse conceived as social action. It is your discourse you read into my text. You can only interpret it by relating it to your reality. Where your reality corresponds to mine, or where you are prepared to co-operate in seeing things my way, then there can be convergence between intention and interpretation. Otherwise, there will be a disparity. You will be taking me out of context – out of the context of my reality.

5 Functions

These are really obvious enough pragmatic commonplaces. But they have implications which have not always been so obvious. There are three in particular that I should like to point out, and they have to do with the conceptual confusion which I referred to earlier. One relates to the term 'function', and the distinction between text and discourse. A second relates to critical discourse analysis and the distinction between analysis and interpretation. The third concerns language pedagogy and ideas about authenticity and the appropriate language for learning.

First, then, the question of function. One way of explaining the formal systems of language is to show how they have been *in*formed by function, how the code reflects the social reality of its users and their communicative requirements. Givon accounts for the code in this way (see Givon 1993). So, of course, does Halliday (1994 and *passim*), though, interestingly, they do not seem to refer to each other. The reasoning behind a functional perspective on language is persuasive. Human beings need language to establish relations between on the one hand, their first person selves and third person reality and, on the other hand their first person selves and second person others. Hence it is not surprising to find that formal systems encode these relations, and that there are systemic components in grammar corresponding to these ideational and interpersonal functions.

We may readily acknowledge that language systems are as they are because, as Halliday puts it, they reflect the functions they have evolved to serve (Halliday 1973). But we also need to note that this is a statement about historical development. Language is as it is now because of what happened in the past. It does not follow that the functions which motivated the shaping of the language are still active in the encoded forms. Social life in general is full of phenomena which have long since lost their original social significance. And so it is with the social semiotic of language. It has to be so, for otherwise language would not evolve at all. It would fail to function in the service of changing needs. It follows that you simply cannot infer what people mean by using a particular form now by invoking its functional provenance.

But nor can you infer what they mean by simply invoking the semantic which *does* have present currency. The meanings which are provided in grammars and dictionaries are records of conventional encodings, as sanctioned by a particular community as their social semiotic. They are the general semantic bearings from which language users can take their particular pragmatic fix. In any use of language, only certain aspects of the semantics of the lexico-grammar are indexically activated by the context. What we mean pragmatically is only in part a function of what the language means semantically. What the language means sets the conventional limits of common and communal agreement within which we find individual room for manoeuvre. Obviously we need to take note of these limits, but we are not bound by them: they are not so much inhibiting constraints as facilitating conditions. The pragmatic significance we achieve with linguistic forms in contexts of use, the external functions we assign to them, has to be *related to*, but cannot be *equated with* the internal functions of their semantic signification. You cannot read what people mean directly from the texts they produce. The definition of language as social semiotic can tell you about the meaning of texts as exemplification of the semantic categories in lexis and grammar, but it cannot of its nature tell you about the discourse that the texts are used to achieve. Textual data can be used as evidence for language systems as social semiotic, *or* as evidence for language use as social action. But they are not the same thing. And in both cases, the status of the data as evidence has to be demonstrated. Data as such tell us nothing whatever.

These distinctions are perhaps obvious. But they are not always very obviously recognised. Both Stubbs and Chafe, for instance, dismiss the difference between text analysis and discourse analysis as a trivial matter of terminology. Others appear to make no distinction between the internal functions of semantic signification and the external functions of pragmatic significance. This brings us to the two other instances of conceptual confusion that I referred to earlier: in the areas of critical discourse analysis and language pedagogy.

6 Critical interpretation

Critical discourse analysis (CDA) has to do with language use as social action. According to the quotation from Fairclough (1992: 12) which I gave at the beginning of this article, it concerns itself with 'how discourse is shaped by relation of power and ideologies'. Its attention, therefore, is essentially on the indexical function of *effect* as I defined it earlier. And indeed Fairclough himself uses this very term (though not, I imagine, in the same specific sense): he talks of the 'constructive *effects* discourse has upon social identities, social relations and systems of knowledge and belief'. As Pennycook points out in the article already mentioned, critical discourse analysis deals with 'the larger social, cultural, and ideological forces that influence our lives' (Pennycook 1994: 121). That is what I referred to earlier as an extension of descriptive *scope*: it now includes consideration of a broader modality, namely the attitudinal and ideological positioning of the first and second persons.

But CDA is characterised not only by a concern to describe the different *positions* which people assume in the discourse process in respect to attitude, belief and so on, but by a *commitment* to reveal the *impositions* of power and ideological influence. As Pennycook puts it, although CDA approaches differ in some degree:

> … they share a commitment to going beyond linguistic description to attempt explanation, to showing how social inequalities are reflected and created in language, and to finding ways through their work to change the conditions of inequality that their work uncovers.
> (Pennycook 1994: 121)

We should note again, however, a possible confusion creeping in here. CDA aims at explaining not how social inequalities are reflected or created in language itself, as social semiotic, but in the *use* of language as social action. You cannot explain how people express their ideology by assuming in advance that ideology is already fixed in the language. To assume that is to adopt a transmission model of communication in which meanings are semantically packaged, in which signification *is* significance, and human beings have no say in the matter. Notice too in this quotation from Pennycook that explanation would seem to imply not only the showing of social inequalities, but the correcting of them. The commitment is not only to social comprehensiveness but to social conscience as well. Now this may be seen as a laudable enterprise, but the consequence is that the scope of description is not extended but reduced because it narrows down to a single preferred interpretation. Let me expound on this a little.

I have argued that discourse is a matter of deriving meaning from text by referring it to contextual conditions, to the beliefs, attitudes, values which represent different versions of reality. The same text, therefore, can give rise to different discourses. The author Doris Lessing, in the preface to a new edition of her novel *The Golden Notebook*, has relevant things to say on this matter.

> Ten years after I wrote it [*The Golden Notebook*] I can get, in one week, three letters about it … One letter is entirely about the sex war, about man's inhumanity to woman, and woman's inhumanity to man, and the writer has produced pages and pages all about nothing else, for she – but not always a she – can't see anything else in the book.
>
> The second is about politics, probably from an old Red like myself, and he or she writes many pages about politics, and never mentions any other theme.
>
> These two letters used, when the book was, as it were, young, to be the most common.
>
> The third letter, once rare but now catching up on the others, is written by a man or woman who can see nothing in it but the theme of mental illness.
>
> But it is the same book.
>
> And naturally these incidents bring up again questions of what people see when they read a book, and why one person sees one pattern and nothing at all of another pattern, and how odd it is to have, as author, such a clear picture of a book, that is seen so differently by its readers.
>
> (Lessing 1972: xix–xx)

'But it is the same book.' Well, is it? It is in one sense, of course: it is the same *text*. But it is obviously not the same book for different readers. They derive different discourses from it depending on what they bring to the text from their own world. They read their own reality into it. This is really not odd at all. It is a natural pragmatic process.

One obvious reason for the plurality of discourses from a single text is, quite simply, because second person processers of text may not share much of the reality of the first person producer of text, and so, to that extent, may be incapable of close convergence. They are likely to give prominence to what they recognise as familiar and disregard the rest. Or they may converge on the intended reference but not on the intended effect.

But there is another reason for this plurality. Second persons may simply refuse to converge, insist on the primacy of their own ideological position, and so derive from the text the discourse which fits their preconceived ideological commitment. What this amounts to is a denial of the co-operative principle. And this, I believe, is precisely what happens with a good deal of critical discourse analysis. It presents a partial interpretation of text from a particular point of view. It is partial in two senses: first, it is not impartial in that it is ideologically committed, and so prejudiced; and it is partial in that it selects those features of the text which support its preferred interpretation.

Critical discourse analysis claims to be distinctive because it is critical, that is to say, it reveals the insinuation of ideology, the imposition of power which other people fail to recognise. But this is because, as is apparent from the quotation from Doris Lessing I cited earlier, the other people bring a different reality to bear on interpretation and so quite naturally derive different discourses from the text. There may be reasons for preferring one discourse to another, and if you are ideologically committed you will be inclined to imply that your interpretation of a text is the only one which is valid, that it is somehow *in* the text indeed, needing only to be discovered, uncovered, revealed by expert exegesis. What is actually revealed is the particular discourse perspective of the interpreter. This may be convincing perhaps, but it has no more authority than any other. To the extent that critical discourse analysis is committed, it cannot provide analysis but only partial interpretation. What analysis would involve would be the demonstration of different interpretations and what language data might be adduced as evidence in each case. It would seek to explain just how different discourses can be derived from the same text, and indeed how the very definition of discourse as the pragmatic achievement of social action necessarily leads to the recognition of such plurality. But in CDA we do not find this. There is rarely a suggestion that alternative interpretations are possible. There is usually the implication that the single interpretation offered is uniquely validated by the textual facts.

This is not to say that the work of critical discourse analysis is not of considerable interest. The interpretations are often subtle, stimulating and, paradoxically, seductively persuasive, and in this respect they bear a close resemblance to much literary criticism. But this very persuasive effect is indicative of its limitation: it is itself a critical discourse and as such it is interpretation, not analysis.

7 Authentic and appropriate language

Let me now turn finally, and briefly, to the third area of confusion I mentioned, that to be found in language education. There has been a good deal of talk in recent years about the importance of using authentic language, real English, in the language classroom. But the same difficulties arise here as with CDA. If we are talking about discourse, the use of language, then whose discourse represents the authentic response? If we are talking about real English, whose reality does it relate to? We can collect instances of language from native speaker contexts of use but its authenticity as discourse depends on those contexts and so cannot transfer to the quite different contexts of classrooms. To suppose that it can is to make the same mistaken assumption as before: that meaning resides in text and has only to be discovered. Halliday has made the point that:

> A minimum requirement for an educationally relevant approach to language is that it takes account of the child's own linguistic experience ...
> (Halliday 1973: 19)

And the linguistic experience of learners of any age, and also, one should add, their own experience of reality in general. Only then can the language be authenticated and made real. You can use native speaker text in the classroom, but you cannot replicate the conditions of native speaker discourse.

I said earlier in this article that Zellig Harris has cast a long shadow. Those working in the field still have his tendency to define the nature of discourse in terms of textual properties. It is true that they are now concerned with meaning, but it still tends to be *textual* meaning, and in this respect, in spite of the great proliferation of work on pragmatics, the underlying influence still seems to be that of a transmission view of communication. Information theory seems to cast a long shadow as well. This is not to say that there has not been exploration on a wider front. Critical discourse analysis has significantly altered the agenda by its consideration of broader social issues concerning the exercise of power and ideological positioning. This has apparently broadened the scope of enquiry. But the commitment to a particular position, I have argued, and the privileging of particular interpretations actually undermines the validity of CDA *as analysis*. Its socio-political value *as interpretation* might well be considerable. But that, I have argued, is a different matter.

Similarly, the analysis of actually occurring native speaker communication now being so impressively undertaken by computational linguistics provides factual data about real texts. But the computer cannot record the reality of the discourse of which these texts are the linguistic trace. And it cannot therefore tell us either what conditions have to be created in classrooms to make the language real for learners so that they can engage in a discourse appropriate for their learning. To suppose that texts carry with them the conditions of their own authentication as discourse is once again to espouse a context-free transmission view of communication.

8 Finally

Let me conclude with two final points. First, I have tried to indicate what I see as confused thinking in the area of discourse analysis. There has been confusion, I have argued, about the nature of discourse (as distinct from text) and about analysis (as distinct from interpretation) and I have suggested that this confusion is bred of commitment. But let me be clear that I am not therefore arguing against commitment as such: it can, and does, give impetus and inspiration to enquiry, provide a sense of purpose. What I am saying is that we need to be wary of it, because it has a way of replacing argument with persuasion and confusing cogency with conviction. The impetus needs to be controlled, the inspiration kept in check. Let me offer another literary quotation (this time from Alexander Pope: he is talking about poetic inspiration, but the point is the same):

> 'Tis more to guide, than spur the muse's steed;
> Restrain his fury, than provoke his speed;
> (*An Essay on Criticism*, lines 84–5)

The second point. You have (dear reader) been busy interpreting the text of this article, deriving from it your own discourses, authenticating it in your own terms, referring it to your reality. And naturally the discourse of your interpretation may not match the discourse of my intention. There is not much I can do about that: imperfect communication is a pragmatic fact of life. All I can hope is that in your piecing out my imperfections with your thoughts, we have arrived at some shared understanding, some mutual accommodation and convergence of worlds.

Note

1 This article is a slightly modified version of a paper given at a seminar jointly organised by the British Council and the University of Lancaster, August 1994.

References

Carter, R. A. (ed.) (1982) *Language and Literature: An Introductory Reader in Stylistics*, Allen & Unwin, London

Carter, R. A. and Simpson, P. (eds) (1989) *Language, Discourse and Literature: An Introductory Reader in Discourse Stylistics*, Unwin Hyman, London

Chafe, W. (1992) Discourse: an overview in W. Bright, (ed.) (1992) *International Encyclopedia of Linguistics*, Oxford University Press, New York, 356–8

Fairclough, N. (1992) *Discourse and Social Change*, Polity Press, Cambridge

Givon, T. (1993) *English Grammar: A Function-based Introduction*, John Benjamins, Amsterdam

Halliday, M. A. K. (1973) *Explorations in the Functions of Language*, Edward Arnold, London

Halliday, M. A. K. (1994) *An Introduction to Functional Grammar*, Edward Arnold, London

Harris, Z. (1952) Discourse analysis *Language* 28: 1–30, 474–94

Hymes, D. H. (1970) The ethnography of speaking, in J. J. Fishman, (ed.) *Readings in the Sociology of Language*, Mouton, The Hague

Lessing, D. (1972) *The Golden Notebook*, Michael Joseph, London

Pennycook, A. (1994) Incommensurable discourses, *Applied Linguistics* 15/2: 115–38

Schiffrin, D. (1994) *Approaches to Discourse*, Blackwell, Oxford

Stubbs, M. (1983) *Discourse Analysis*, Basil Blackwell, Oxford

Widdowson, H. G. (1990a) Discourses of enquiry and conditions of relevance, in J. Alatis, (ed.) (1993) *Linguistics, Language Teaching and Language Acquisition: The Interdependence of Theory, Practice and Research*, Georgetown University Press, Washington D.C.

Widdowson, H. G. (1990b) *Aspects of Language Teaching*, Oxford University Press, Oxford

Text 18

Norman Fairclough
Lancaster University, UK

A reply to Henry Widdowson's 'Discourse analysis: a critical view'[1]

I have accepted the invitation to respond to Widdowson's article in *Language and Literature* 4(3)[2] not only because it is provocative and provides a good occasion for debate, but also because I think it seriously misrepresents my work in certain ways. There are differing positions within CDA,[3] but in the notes which follow I shall refer only to my own work. One preliminary point to be made about Widdowson's article is that its target is confusingly unclear. He defines his 'main purpose' in the article as to show that the name 'critical

[handwritten margin note: Don't they always?]

my thoughts exactly

discourse analysis' is a contradiction in terms – because CDA is interpretation, and therefore not analysis (p. 159). But a large part of the article is taken up with a critique of those who fail to distinguish text and discourse. I have always made this distinction in my work, and actually in a way which is roughly similar to Widdowson's, though with important distinctions I return to. So what are we to make of this sentence: 'There has been confusion, I have argued, about the nature of discourse (as distinct from text) and about analysis (as distinct from interpretation) and I have suggested that this confusion is bred of commitment' (p. 171)? Commitment is the cardinal sin of CDA according to Widdowson, so in this summing up the confusing of text and discourse is quite illegitimately laid at the door of CDA, whereas earlier in the article it is attributed to others. It is similarly unclear how the comments on language education relate to the critique of CDA.

Widdowson's main claim is that CDA is 'an exercise in interpretation' and therefore 'invalid as analysis' (p. 159). Interpretation here is understood as 'a matter of converging on a particular meaning as having some kind of privileged validity' (p. 159). This privileging of particular meanings results from the 'ideological commitment' and 'prejudice' of CDA (p. 169). Moreover:

> There is rarely a suggestion that alternative interpretations are possible. There is usually the implication that the single interpretation offered is uniquely validated by the textual facts.
> (Widdowson 1995a: p. 169)

This is a misrepresentation of CDA. It rests upon a confusion between two senses of interpretation which are differentiated in Widdowson's main source (Fairclough 1992a: 78–86, 198–9). Let me number them. Interpretation-1 is an inherent part of ordinary language use, which analysts, like anyone else, necessarily do: make meaning from/with spoken or written texts. People make meanings through an interplay between features of a text and the varying resources which they bring to the process of interpretation-1. Interpretation-2 is a matter of analysts seeking to show connections between both properties of texts and practices of interpretation-1 in a particular social space, and wider social and cultural properties of that particular social space. Notice that interpretation-1 is part of the domain of interpretation-2; one concern of interpretation-2 is to investigate how different practices of interpretation-1 are socially, culturally and ideologically shaped. For the sake of clarity, I will now use the distinction (introduced in Fairclough 1989 but not used in Fairclough 1992a) between interpretation (=interpretation-1) and explanation (=interpretation-2). Now it is true that CDA has given particular focus to explanatory connections between texts and social relations of power, and therefore to questions of ideology. And it is true that this emphasis comes out of the particular political conjuncture within which CDA emerged (see further below) and reflects the political commitments of its practitioners. But this explanatory emphasis is very different from what CDA stands accused of in Widdowson's article – favouring particular interpretations (in the sense of interpretation-1), ignoring alternatives, and construing texts as having unique interpretations.

Let me set Widdowson's claim that 'there is rarely a suggestion that alternative interpretations are possible' against what is said in his main source (Fairclough

confusing ?

1992a). In discussing the 'critical linguistics' of Fowler *et al.* in the late 1970s,
I explicitly warn against not attending to processes of interpretation
(i.e. interpretation-1) as well as production, and write of this work that

> in practice values are attributed to particular structures (such as passive clauses
> without agents) in a rather mechanical way. But texts may be open to different
> interpretations depending on the context and interpreter, which means that
> social meanings (including ideologies) of discourse cannot simply be read off
> from the text without considering patterns and variations in the social
> distribution, consumption and interpretation of the text.
> (Fairclough 1992a: 28)

Indeed, diversity of interpretations of texts is a central assumption in the
theoretical and analytical framework of the book. This framework centres
(though Widdowson fails to point this out) upon the tension manifest in texts and
discursive events between the way in which social subjects are discursively
determined and constructed on the one hand, and the creative discursive activity
of social subjects as agents of their own discourse on the other. One aspect of this
is the claim that while some readers may interpret texts compliantly, fitting in
with positions set up for readers in texts, other readings may be resistant. In
discussing this, I wrote:

> Interpreters are ... social subjects with particular accumulated social experiences,
> and with resources variously oriented to the multiple dimensions of social life, and
> these variables affect the ways they go about interpreting particular texts ... it is
> important to take account of the ways in which interpreters interpret texts if one is
> properly to assess their political and ideological effectiveness.
> (Fairclough 1992a: 136)

Critical discourse analysis as set out in this book is committed to, and dependent
upon, the assumption of diversity of interpretations of texts. It would be fair
comment that this theoretical commitment is not carried through into
investigations of interpretative diversity (which is acknowledged on page 86 –
though see Clarke 1993), but that is a rather different matter, and such
investigations are perfectly compatible with the theory.

Widdowson's failure to distinguish interpretation and explanation also
underlies his unhelpful discussion of 'effects'. After reviewing the pragmatic
distinctions between locutionary and illocutionary acts and perlocutionary
effects, he claims that the 'attention' of CDA is:

> ...essentially on the indexical function of effect as I defined it earlier. And
> indeed Fairclough himself uses this very term (though not I imagine in the same
> specific sense): he talks of the 'constructive effects discourse has on social
> identities, social relations and systems of knowledge and belief' ...
> (Widdowson 1995a: 167)

Widdowson's hesitancy is betrayed by features of his text (*essentially, very, I imagine,
specific*). Perlocutionary effects and the constructive effects I am referring to here are
quite different things: the former are effects of features of texts on individual
interpreters and are an aspect of interpretation, whereas the latter are effects of
discursive practices on society and culture and are an aspect of explanation.

Widdowson argues that CDA (critical discourse *analysis*) is a contradiction in terms, because it is interpretation, and therefore not analysis. The actual form of the argument is: 'if critical discourse analysis is an exercise in interpretation, it is invalid as analysis'. I have argued that CDA is not an exercise in interpretation in Widdowson's sense, and if this is so his argument falls down. But I would like to comment on how Widdowson understands analysis. It involves:

> ...the demonstration of different interpretations and what language data might be adduced as evidence in each case. It would seek to explain just how different discourses can be derived from the same text.
> (Widdowson 1995a: 169)

This is a very narrow view of analysis – and in the context of the article a strategic one: CDA cannot be analysis on this definition, because this happens not to be what CDA does! But neither is it what conventional linguistic analysis of texts does – does that too cease to be analysis, then? It is more normal to define as analysis any reasonably systematic application of reasonably well-defined procedures to a reasonably well-defined body of data. On that count, CDA is analysis. It provides an analytical procedure (described for instance in Chapters 3–6 of Fairclough 1992a) and applies it systematically to various types of data (e.g. in some of the papers in Fairclough 1995).

I referred above to commitment as CDA's cardinal sin in Widdowson's eyes. It is from CDA's 'ideological commitment' that its 'prejudice' is said to come, and its privileging of particular interpretations. Practitioners of CDA are indeed generally characterised by explicit political commitments. They are people who see things wrong with their societies, see language as involved in what is wrong, and are committed to making changes through forms of intervention involving language – e.g. by working on critical language awareness programmes for schools, which can point learners towards the possibility of self-conscious language change as a form of social change. Having said that, CDA is emphatically not a political party, and the particular nature of political commitments and strategies of intervention differ widely.

CDA has developed in a particular location within a particular political situation – out of a tendency on the political left and within the new social movements (feminism, ecology, etc.) towards cultural and ideological forms of political struggle from the 1960s onwards (see Fairclough and Wodak forthcoming for more discussion). CDA has correspondingly been attracted to theories of power and ideology, and to analysis of for instance media, institutional interactions, and language and gender or ethnicity. These political positionings and priorities are not inevitable: a CDA of the right is quite conceivable, directed for instance at left-wing or feminist texts.

Is it then the case that while CDA is informed by political commitments, other approaches (such as Widdowson's) are not? According to Widdowson, analysis (and presumably analysts, such as himself) recognises its own partiality, whereas interpretation cannot; CDA is 'not impartial in that it is ideologically committed, and so prejudiced', but by implication approaches such as Widdowson's are impartial. What Widdowson is offering here is a version of the classical liberal distinction between ideology and science (or theory): on the one hand, ideology, commitment, prejudice and partiality (CDA); on the other hand, science and impartiality (e.g. Widdowson). There is, however, an issue over the meaning of ideology: Widdowson uses the term in the sense of political ideologies, explicit commitments to particular political positions; whereas the term is used in CDA – and widely in the literature on ideology – in the sense of assumptions which are built into practices (especially for CDA practices of discourse) which sustain relations of domination, usually in a covert way. CDA certainly involves explicit political commitments ('political ideologies'), but is CDA ideological in the second sense (which I shall stick with from now on)? My answer would be that it is possible that it is, because any science or social science may be ideological. What does this mean? CDA would argue that we are all – including Widdowson – writing from within particular discursive practices, entailing particular interests, commitments, inclusions, exclusions, and so forth.[4] (This claim, by the way, means that CDA is theoretically better-placed to recognise its own 'partiality' than most theories, *pace* Widdowson.) Aspects of these discursive practices may serve to sustain relations of domination and may hence be ideological – no theory or science is immune from that possibility. Whether discursive practices do or do not work ideologically needs to be established through analysis of those practices in relation to the wider social practices and relations which frame them. The implication of this is that a categorical opposition between science (or theory) and ideology cannot be sustained – even the purest of science may work ideologically (Ashmore *et al.* 1994). Both CDA and Widdowson offer theories of discourse, and do analysis of discourse. Whether they work ideologically is to be established.

I would suggest that Widdowson's theory does. Widdowson's own pragmatic account of discourse and interpretation (see below) incorporates a theory of the social subject as prior to discourse, not as discursally constituted, and a liberal theory of a society as a voluntary association of free individuals. These theories imply that discourse does *not* work ideologically in the sense that CDA claims it does. Theories which assume the non-ideological nature of social practice can do important ideological work in sustaining relations of domination, through naturalising practices of domination (see Rajagopalan 1995). However, this still leaves an apparently major difference between CDA and Widdowson with respect to politics: Widdowson has no overt political commitments. But the fact that political commitments are not overt does not of course mean that they do not exist!

The critical discourse of CDA evidently incorporates particular values. To put it crudely, the claim is that certain discursive practices are bad for certain reasons, and other alternative practices would be better. Practices may be negatively judged on the grounds for instance that they covertly sustain inequalities between doctors and patients, or women and men. Other approaches avoid such judgments and maintain a 'descriptive' stance only in so far as they evade the issue of how discourse sustains relations of dominance, how discourse works ideologically, though descriptive approaches are characterised by covert value judgements (notably in theories of 'appropriateness' – see Fairclough 1992b).

Widdowson argues that discourse is in vogue and yet vague – and warns of the dangerous mix of ignorance and popular appeal. His strategy is to 'pin down' discourse by clearing away the confusions which he claims have grown around it. Discourse is indeed fashionable, and does indeed have many meanings. But to suggest that its complexity is merely an effect of its popularity (the more people use it, the more meanings it will acquire) and of 'confusions' is superficial. Discourse has become a focus of concern within a remarkable range of disciplines and theories, whose common ground is I suggest that they are all responding to the insight of contemporary social science that language is constitutive of modern social life in a number of crucial ways. Discourse is a major transdisciplinary theme (Halliday 1993) in the humanities and social sciences, and the concept of discourse is therefore variously understood, and widely contested. Trying to 'pin it down' through definition is a hopeless and fruitless task, unless one wishes to brick oneself up within the four walls of one's discipline.

This is I think what Widdowson's own position on discourse and interpretation in effect does. He defines discourse as 'the pragmatic process of meaning negotiation', the indexical process of relating texts to the interpreter's reality, the 'acting of context on code' (p. 164). Discourse may be a matter of 'convergence' between intention and interpretation 'where your reality corresponds to mine, or where you are prepared to co-operate in seeing things my way' (p. 165). Otherwise there will be a 'disparity': interpreters 'derive different discourses' from a text depending on what they bring to it from their own world. 'They read their own reality into it ... It is a natural pragmatic process' (p. 168). Disparity is most obvious in the case of perlocutionary effects; there is generally (or is Widdowson saying always? it isn't clear) convergence on locutionary and illocutionary meanings.

Discourse analysis on this account is reduced to pragmatics, and contained within the boundaries of what we might call 'greater linguistics'. It takes on the prediscoursal theory of the subject and of context which is general in pragmatics: subjects and contexts are not constituted in discourse, they are constituted before and outside discourse – subjects use contexts to interpret discourse. This cuts discourse analysis off from exploration of the socially and culturally constitutive effects of discourse, and more generally cuts discourse analysis off from treating language as part of the social whole. It also begs the question of how the contexts which are appealed to in interpretation are themselves interpreted: 'any information we call upon to help us arrive at an interpretation of an utterance or a text ... must also receive an interpretation' (Taylor 1992: 168, see also Fairclough 1992a: 81–3).

Widdowson assumes too liberal a view of the social as a voluntary association of free individuals – notice how the conditions for convergence are specified: 'where your reality corresponds to mine, or where you are prepared to co-operate in seeing things my way'. No space here for an analysis of the social conditions under which people are 'prepared' to co-operate, the social relations of power which may explain when and where and why convergence, or disparity occur or fail to occur. Whether there is co-operation, convergence, or disparity is for Widdowson simply a matter of the circumstances or will of the individual, graced as a 'natural' pragmatic process. Yet it is consideration of these social conditions that leads to a social account of discourse which can connect the analysis of linguists to analyses in other disciplines – and inexorably to those troublesome issues of power and ideology. (Notice incidentally that for all the stress in Widdowson's article on interpretative diversity and 'negotiation', the space in his account for interpretative diversity – limited to perlocutionary effects – is actually very small. The weight seems very much towards 'convergence'.)

A galling feature of Widdowson's article is the misleading picture he gives of current work in CDA (as set out in, for instance, Fairclough 1992a, 1995), which is very much oriented to this transdisciplinary frame. I alluded above to how this work centres the dialectic of structure and action in an account of the subject in discourse. This focus is linked to the overwhelming emphasis in my recent work on showing how shifting discursive practices, manifested in texts which are heterogeneous in forms and meanings,[5] can be analysed as facets of wider processes of social and cultural change. Widdowson's article fails to mention this emphasis – he portrays the agenda of CDA as simply that of early work in critical linguistics. I have tried to develop a view of discourse analysis which goes some way to bridging the diverse disciplinary and theoretical interests in this field, by bringing together a broadly Foucaultian conception of discourses as differently positioned ways of signifying domains of practice and knowledge, and the common view in linguistics of discourse as process wherein texts are products. Widdowson's position is a variant of the latter, but an unduly restrictive one that reduces discourse processes to processes of pragmatic interpretation, and which most notably differs from mine in not including intertextual processes – the key to linking the Foucaultian tradition to the tradition in linguistics (Fairclough 1992a).

The 'interest' for linguistics of this move within CDA, if I can put it that way, is that it helps establish the case for textual analysis and therefore linguistic analysis having a substantial role in social scientific analysis. There is some evidence that social scientists in certain areas are beginning to find this persuasive, though there is a great deal of ground to be made up, given the false promise of linguistics in the past. Widdowson's reduction of discourse analysis to linguistic pragmatics would close off these interdisciplinary possibilities.

Notes

1 This article has benefited from discussion with and written comments from Erzsébet Barát, Roz Ivanic, Anna Mauranen, Sari Pietikainen, Kanavillil Rajagopalan, and members of the Language Ideology and Power Research Group at Lancaster University.
2 Widdowson has also published a review of Fairclough 1992a which contains some similar criticisms of critical discourse analysis (Widdowson 1995b).
3 CDA will be used throughout as an abbreviation for 'critical discourse analysis'.
4 These practices are however typically and normally contradictory and heterogeneous.
5 It is perhaps relevant to Widdowson's critique of CDA as analysis that CDA has arguably contributed to the literature on text analysis through its focus upon the linguistic and intertextual properties of heterogeneous texts.

References

Ashmore, M., Myers, G. and Potter, J. (1994) Rhetoric, discourse, reflexivity: seven days in the library, in S. Jasanoff *et al.* (eds) *Handbook of Science and Technology Studies*, Sage, London
Clark, R. (1993) Developing critical literacy: the gulf betwen them – the truth and other media fictions, *Changing English* 1, 1: 192–216

Fairclough, N. (1989) *Language and Power*, Longman, London

Fairclough, N. (1992a) *Discourse and Social Change*, Polity Press, London

Fairclough, N. (ed.) (1992b) *Critical Language Awareness*, Longman, London

Fairclough, N. (1995) *Critical Discourse Analysis*, Longman, London

Fairclough, N. and Wodak R. (forthcoming) Critical discourse analysis, in T. van Dijk (ed.) *Discourse: A Multidisciplinary Introduction*, Sage, London

Halliday, M. (1993) New ways of meaning: a challenge to applied linguistics, in *Language in a Changing World*, Applied Linguistics Association of Australia Occasional Paper 13, Deakin, Australia

Rajagopalan, K. (1995) Critical discourse analysis and its discontents, *Centre for Language in Social Life* 72, Linguistics Department, Lancaster University

Taylor, T. (1992) *Mutual Misunderstanding: Scepticism and the Theorising of Language and Interpretation*, Routledge, London

Widdowson, H. (1995a) Discourse analysis: a critical view, *Language and Literature* 4 (3): 157–72

Widdowson, H. (1995b) Review of Fairclough, *Discourse and Social Change*, *Applied Linguistics* 16 (4): 510–16

Text 19

H. G. Widdowson
University of London, University of Essex, UK

Reply to Fairclough: Discourse and interpretation: conjectures and refutations[1]

Norman Fairclough and I disagree about a lot of things. That much is obvious. But let me begin my comments by acknowledging the importance of his contribution to our thinking about language and society. He has brought to our attention a whole range of issues about the dialectical interplay of language and social life, not as matters for detached academic debate but as immediately implicated in practical and political affairs. He has alerted us to how language can be exploited in the manipulation of opinion and the abuse of power. His work is impressive in scope and purpose. It is highly stimulating for those who share his views, highly provocative for those who do not, and is to be valued on both counts.

It is also highly influential. Indeed it can be said to have been the main force in the establishing of the new paradigm (or episteme, to use Foucault's term?) of Critical Discourse Analysis. This can be seen as a new ideological orthodoxy and as such, paradoxically, it exerts just the kind of discursive domination which it seeks to expose in other uses of language. It is because the work of Fairclough and his colleagues has such significance as a line of enquiry, and because it has been so influential as a discursive practice in its own right, that it invites critical attention. This is why I wrote the article that Fairclough comments on. I wanted to point to what seemed to me to be fundamental problems in their approach to analysis.

His reply indicates that all I succeeded in doing was to misrepresent him. This is not what I intended. There was no deliberate distortion, but only my interpretation of what he had written. But then how could I have got it so wrong? How could I have read such mistaken meanings into his text? One reason, as

Fairclough's comments make abundantly clear, is that I do not share the same
ideological position on the nature of discourse. I do not see things his way. So I
read his text in ways other than he intended, and in ways other than those
discursively aligned with him. Just so. That is precisely the point I was trying to
make.

dif. discourse — between writer & reader

And by the same token, my own text is subject to misrepresentation. One
example. I am charged with being too liberal in supposing that the 'social' is 'a
voluntary association of free individuals', that I disregard social conditions and
see the pragmatic achievement of meaning as 'simply a matter of circumstances or
will of the individual, graced as a "natural" pragmatic process.' I should be
interested to know where there is textual warrant in my work for this bizarre
interpretation of my position. You cannot study discourse in disregard of social
factors and I do not know of anybody who claims you can. But the study of
discourse is not just the study of how it is socially constituted but of how it is
pragmatically realised, not only by conforming to its constitution, but also by
subverting it.

Norman Fairclough complains that discourse analysis, on my account, 'is
reduced to pragmatics'. Why *reduced*? Discourse, in my conception of it, cannot
be *reduced* to pragmatics. It is, for me, crucially, a function of pragmatics: the
process whereby different interpretations are drawn from the textual data. Of
course this process implicates all manner of social factors: assumptions, beliefs,
values, ideologies, which would fall within a Foucault concept of discourse. So it
would seem that we need to distinguish two senses of discourse (see Widdowson
1990). The discourse process in this pragmatic sense (Discourse 1, we might call
it) is influenced by the different discourses that participants have been socialised
in (Discourse 2). But it is not *determined* by them. To suppose that it is *is* indeed
to reduce discourse. And this is probably where my position differs most radically
from that of Norman Fairclough and his colleagues. So let me make it as explicit
as I can.

I do not believe that individuals simply act out social roles. There are socially
constituted Discourses 2 – conventions of belief, established values which
constrain the way people think and use their language to achieve meaning. But
people's activities are not determined by their ideological allegiances. They are
not bound by them. You can of course ascribe social roles to individuals and part
of their individuality can obviously be associated with this group identity.
Pragmatics would take account of this in its consideration of contextual
conditions. But to think of individuals as if they were *representative* of such
groups, as tokens of the type, is to deal in stereotypical constructs, well defined
social categories. And these are abstractions from reality analogous to those of
formalist linguistics: 'discursively constructed social subjects' seem to me to be
beings of the same order of abstraction as ideal speaker-listeners in homogenous
speech communities.

For me, discourse is individual engagement. It is individual, not social, subjects
who interact with each other. Of course, I do not mean to suggest that they are
free agents to do what they will. They are constrained by established conventions
and regulations, and restrictions are set on their initiative. But they are not
absolutely *controlled* by them: there is always room for manoeuvre. That is our
salvation. Whatever communal ideological values are institutionally in power,

they can be, and constantly are, subverted by individual initiative, for better or for worse. So it is that suppressed ideas go underground and bide their time. So it is, too, that in societies dedicated to equality, individuals are busy feathering their own nest, and in those dedicated to morality, the custodians of public probity indulge their vices in private. Individuals are never institutionalised: they retain their contradictory idiosyncracies, their impulses, fears, sensitivities and prejudices. And when they find others who share some of these, they give them institutional status, call them principles, form a group, draw up a constitution, found a party, a sect, a school.

But the very fact that individuals can bring about social change makes it clear that social forces, even the malevolent imposition of power, can have positive consequences in spite of themselves. This, I believe, is because the very constraints which inhibit freedom of thought also define the conditions which enable it to be exercised. And this is as true of language as it is of society. Language sets limits on what people can say, but those limits also allow them to exploit possibilities of meaning immanent in the language but not conventionally encoded or customarily used. Society exacts a certain conformity in the same way. But the very values and beliefs which constitute it can be exploited to realign them. Thus Norman Fairclough, as an individual thinker of considerable originality, employs an established 'mode of argumentation and mode of rationality' (as he puts it) in order to criticise the social values on which it is based. It seems to me to be entirely reasonable that he should. Indeed, he has no choice. No change, no matter how apparently revolutionary, was ever entirely innovative. Language and social change are a matter of reformulation not invention: the essential features remain in place, but differently aligned, differently expounded. This indeed is implied by Fairclough's own concept of intertextuality, whereby different modes of argumentation and rationality are created by just this kind of realignment. I am pleased to find that this concept (unless I have misrepresented it) corresponds quite closely to my own thinking (see Widdowson 1988). Happily there are some things that Norman and I can agree about.

So I certainly do not see society as 'a voluntary association of free individuals'. Of course the individuals are constrained, but they remain individuals none the less: they are not just 'subjects discoursally constituted'. This is not to deny the existence of discourses in the Foucault sense as conventionalised modes of knowledge (i.e. Discourse 2), nor the importance of studying the discursive construction of social subjects at an appropriate level of idealisation. But these discourses are abstract constructs. They can only be actualised through discourse as I have defined it, as the pragmatic process of meaning negotiation (i.e. Discourse 1). The difficulty is knowing what features of the resulting text can be adduced as evidence of the discursively constructed subject. This is where the problematic issue of interpretation comes in, of which more presently.

My position, then, is that different discourses in the Foucault sense, as ideological and idealised social constructs can only be activated through discourse in my sense: through the pragmatics of individual interaction. So it is that this present exchange between Norman Fairclough and myself is not between political values or ideological positions, Marxist versus Liberal or whatever, but between him and me, his views, sensitivities, prejudices, and mine. These are, of course, formed in part by our social history and political allegiances, expressive to some degree of the different discourse communities we belong to, but essentially this discourse we are pragmatically engaged in is a personal matter. In his comments Norman Fairclough refers to his own work rather than CDA as a whole. I would guess that it was his resentment of what he saw as my misrepresentation of his work which provoked his response. And that, in my view, is as it should be.

How then have I misrepresented his work? A key problem would seem to be that I have failed to distinguish between two senses of the term 'interpretation'. Fairclough claims that explanation (Interpretation 2) is a matter of showing how the response to a text (Interpretation 1) is influenced (perhaps determined) by social factors – how this interpretation is, in effect, socially constructed. So Interpretation 2 is an interpretation of Interpretation 1. But then we surely need to establish first what Interpretation 1 is by consulting those who practice it.

Fairclough does not see it this way. His belief is that he can gain access to Interpretation 1 through introspection. He comments:

> There is a similarity here between my account in Chapter 3 of what the analyst does, and what text interpreters do: analysts too need the resources they have as competent members of communities, even if they use them rather more systematically.
> (Fairclough 1992: 198)

This position does not seem to me to be essentially different from that taken by formal linguists: as representative members of the speech community whose language they describe, they can serve as the source of their own data and do not need to consult other informants. But, as has been pointed out often enough, they are not reliable as informants themselves precisely because they are analysts. And the idea that analysts can be competent members of the communities whose language use they analyse would seem to be in complete contradiction with Fairclough's own theoretical position, which is that there are different communities with distinct and competing discourses. People (whether 'ordinary text interpreters' or analysts) cannot be competent members of all of them. If they could, there would presumably be no covert domination, no hegemonic struggle, and indeed nothing for Critical Discourse Analysis to be critical about.

It seems to me that if the analyst provides Interpretation 1 by proxy, it is bound to get confused with Interpretation 2, and that, I think, is precisely what happens. Fairclough says that he does not just read off significance from the textual facts themselves, and has taken other critical discourse analysts to task for so doing. But it is hard to see how he can do otherwise if he relies on his own intuitions, since he cannot be a competent member of all the discourse communities whose texts he analyses. He recognises that there may, in principle, be a plurality of interpretations, and so a plurality of effects. Presumably, then, we should expect from his analysis that it would provide an explanation of what different social factors motivate this plurality. But it does not.

I want now to illustrate these difficulties in reference to a specific example of analysis. In so doing I shall subject Fairclough's own text to the same kind of close critical scrutiny that he applies to others, but without drawing conclusions about its ideological significance.

Discourse and Social Change (Fairclough 1992) develops a theory of discourse as hegemonic struggle whereby power is exercised to construct social reality by the intertextual control of discursive practices. The second part of the book provides analysis to support the theory expounded in the first part. The example I shall consider is from Chapter 6, which is entitled: 'Text Analysis: Constructing Social Reality'. The first analysis is of a text sample taken from a booklet about pregnancy. The sample is as follows:

Antenatal care
The essential aim of antenatal care is to ensure that you go through pregnancy and labour in the peak of condition. Inevitably, therefore, it involves a series of examinations and tests throughout the course of your pregnancy. As mentioned above, antenatal care will be provided either by your local hospital or by your general practitioner, frequently working in cooperation with the hospital.

It is important to attend for your first examination as early as possible, since there may be minor disorders that the doctor can correct which will benefit the rest of your pregnancy. More particularly, having seen your doctor and booked in at a local hospital, you will usually receive the assurance that everything is proceeding normally.

The first visit
Your first visit involves a comprehensive review of your health through childhood and also right up to the time you became pregnant. Just occasionally [sic] women may suffer from certain medical disorders of which they are unaware – such as high blood pressure, diabetes and kidney disease. It is important for these problems to be identified at an early stage since they may seriously influence the course of the pregnancy.

The doctor and the midwife will also want to know about all your previous health problems, as well as discussing your social circumstances. We do know that social conditions can influence the outcome of the pregnancy. For this reason, they will ask you details about your housing, as well as your present job. In addition they will need to know if you smoke, drink alcohol or if you are taking any drugs which have been prescribed by your doctor or chemists. All of these substances can sometimes affect the development of a baby.

Examination
You will be weighed so that your subsequent weight gain can be assessed. Your height will be measured, since small women on the whole have a slightly smaller pelvis than tall women – which is not surprising. A complete physical examination will then be carried out which will include checking your breasts, heart, lungs, blood pressure, abdomen and pelvis.

The purpose of this is to identify any abnormalities which might be present, but which so far have not caused you any problems. A vaginal examination will enable the pelvis to be assessed in order to check the condition of the uterus, cervix and the vagina. A cervical smear is also often taken at this time to exclude any early pre-cancerous change which rarely may be present.
(Quoted in Fairclough 1992: 170–1; originally from N. Morris (ed.) *The Baby Book*.)

CDA of
a CDA

The first thing to notice is that what we have here is a text fragment. We do not know how it functions in relation to the rest of the booklet. Furthermore, the three extracts that we have are discontinuous: a whole subsection between the second and third has been omitted. No reason is given for this. We do not know either anything about what the motivation for the text was: if, or why, it was commissioned, and by whom. There is a good deal of talk in *Discourse and Social Change* (and indeed in Fairclough's work generally) about the production and consumption of texts, but in this case, and in the case of other analyses, the actual producers and consumers are not consulted as to what their intentions or interpretations might be. Instead, these are ascribed on the sole evidence of the analysis: in other words, they are read into the text. But not only is the sample a fragment, the analysis is fragmented too, for it starts not, as one might have expected, from the first section, but from the last. Whatever reason there might be for this is not explained. We can only assume that it is random.

such a bad
thing to do?
Actual
readers will
also not
consult the
producers,
necessarily

The analysis of this section reveals that there is a predominance of sentences which consist of two clauses (referred to oddly enough as simple sentences) expounding purpose and reason relations:

Clause 1   *so that since in order to*   Clause 2
(Fairclough 1992: 171)

These are textual facts which nobody I imagine would wish to dispute. But this is what Fairclough refers to as the description dimension. The facts have now to be interpreted. There is the difficulty, though, that description itself to some degree implies interpretation. Fairclough himself points this out, but compounds the difficulty by ignoring the two senses of the term he has earlier distinguished, so we do not know whether he is talking about Interpretation 1 or 2, or both:

Description is not as separate from interpretation [2?] as it is often assumed to be. As an analyst (and as an ordinary text interpreter) one is inevitably interpreting [1? 2?] all the time, and there is no phrase of analysis which is pure description. Consequently, one's analysis of the text is 'shaped and coloured' by one's interpretation [2?] of its relationship to discourse processes and wider social processes.
(Fairclough 1992: 199, my additions in square brackets)

But here, perhaps we have an indication as to why these particular fragments were extracted from the whole text, and why the analysis starts at apparent random: these procedures are shaped and coloured in advance by the discourse processes and wider social processes that they are designed to discover. The analyst preconceives the data as evidence. Fairclough knows what he is looking for. Not surprisingly, he finds it.

But what is the interpretation of this particular description of clauses?

The message that comes across is one of re-assurance: everything that happens during antenatal care is there for a good reason.
(Fairclough 1992: 171–2)

How does Fairclough know that the readers for whom this text was designed (the consumers) are reassured by it? This conclusion does not emerge from the

Actual data! (handwritten margin note)

analysis, but is imposed upon it. One might reasonably conclude from internal textual evidence that the intended illocutionary force of this passage is explanation. But reassurance is a perlocutionary *effect*. The only way of finding out whether this is, indeed, the effect is to ask the pregnant women for whom it is written. One might even consider asking the producers whether this was intended. But you can only read such an effect off from the text like this by assuming a vicarious identity. This I would suggest is a case of Interpretation 1 masquerading as Interpretation 2.

But the analyst here not only assumes the identity of the consumer but of the producer as well. The description which follows seeks to demonstrate that the dominant discourse is a medico-scientific one, and the social reality of pregnancy is constructed in its terms. The pregnant women are positioned as compliant patients (grammatically and medically). The medical staff are in control. Evidence for this is found in the second section of the extract where there is a shift from third to first person ('The doctor and midwife' to 'We'). This apparently makes it clear that the text is produced by medical staff: it is their voice which speaks. In the next piece of text, however, we are told there is evidence of two voices in the following sentence:

> Your height will be measured, since small women on the whole have slightly a smaller pelvis than tall women – which is not surprising.

Fairclough's interpretation runs as follows:

> ...the tagged-on comment 'which is not surprising' comes across as the lifeworld voice of the prospective patient, or indeed of the medical staff in their non-professional capacities...
> (Fairclough 1992: 172)

Again, we might ask 'comes across to whom?' We just do not know whether this comes across to the prospective patients since they have not been consulted. But anyway, if this voice is indistinguishable from that of the medical staff 'in their non-professional capacities' how can we talk about two voices anyway? Are we to suppose that the medical voice is always uniform and unmodulated by lifeworld concerns, that medical staff in their professional capacities are necessarily and inevitably detached, objective, and technical in their treatment of patients? The analysis continues:

could have been more complicated (handwritten margin note)

> But notice the contrast in voices between this and the second clause of the sentence ('since small women on the whole have a slightly smaller pelvis than tall women'), which is a reason clause. This is in the medical voice: 'pelvis' is a medical term, the clause consists of an authoritative assertion, which we take to be grounded in medico-scientific evidence. It is also far more typical of the extract as a whole: most reason clauses are in the medical voice.

not quite (handwritten margin note)

What is it that characterises this medical voice? What textual evidence can we adduce to identify it? Technical vocabulary perhaps: 'pelvis' is a medical term. Is it? So what, one might ask is the non-medical equivalent? And what of 'breasts', 'heart', 'lungs', 'blood pressure', 'abdomen'? Are these all medical terms as well? The point is, surely, that you cannot talk about pregnancy at all, in any voice, without using terms like this. So if the patients were to employ them, would they too be using contrasting voices, enacting some hegemonic discursive struggle by using non-lifeworld capacities?

But if it is not lexis which is the defining feature, then what is? We are told that 'most reason clauses are in the medical voice'. Some are, then, and some are not. Which is which? We are not told, but unless we know what makes a reason clause medical as distinct from lifeworld, there is no way of knowing that the particular clause we are considering ('since small women on the whole have a slightly smaller pelvis than tall women') is 'far more typical of the extract as a whole' than the phrase 'which is not surprising'. What is it that makes it typical? We have no way of knowing because the type is left unspecified. We are told that 'this clause consists of an authoritative assertion, which we take to be grounded in medico-scientific evidence'. But the clause consists of nothing of the kind. It consists of linguistic constituents. Whether it is an assertion or not, and certainly whether it is an authoritative assertion or not, and how it is taken to be grounded, are interpretations based on an assumption of attitude assigned to the producer in advance. '… which we take as grounded …' Who is 'we'? Do the prospective patients take it in this way? This is Fairclough speaking on behalf of other readers. The explanation is an instance of Interpretation 1, but not, notice, an Interpretation 1 of the people for whom the text was written, but one vicariously assigned to them by the analyst.

But we have not yet finished with this particular clause. The phrase 'on the whole' calls for comment. This is what Fairclough says:

> The hedging of the assertion ('on the whole') is interesting. On the one hand its vagueness suggests a shift into the voice of the lifeworld, while on the other it marks the cautious and circumspect ethos we associate with scientific medicine.
> (Fairclough 1992: 173)

So in this case there is no way of knowing which voice is operative. But even if we opted for the lifeworld interpretation, it could still be taken as the voice of medico-scientific authority, but subtly modulated so that it sounds as if it was not. Fairclough goes on to provide further evidence of this ruse. First he summarises the findings of his analysis of the given extract:

> The clauses of reason or purpose, consistently cast in the voice of medicine, give the sort of rationalization and argumentation one would expect from medical staff, which contributes to the construction of medico-scientific ethos in the extract.
> (Fairclough 1992: 173)

The clauses of reason and purpose, we should note, are now represented as *consistently* expressive of the medical voice: not most, but all of them, are cast in this idiom. They contribute to 'the construction of a medico-scientific ethos'. What else contributes we are not told. But we are given an example of another text, one which contrasts with it, taken this time from a publication called *The Pregnancy Book*. This reads as follows:

> Throughout your pregnancy you will have regular check-ups … This is *to make sure that both you and the baby are fit and well, to check that the baby is developing properly*, and, *as far as possible to prevent anything going wrong…*
> (Quoted in Fairclough 1992: 173)

The italics are provided by Fairclough. He comments:

> The italicized expressions are evidently closer to the voice of the lifeworld than
> equivalent ones in *The Baby Book*…
> (Fairclough 1992: 173)

If these are evidently closer, what is the evidence? Why, one is bound to wonder, is
'check-up' not italicised as lifeworld (cf. the equivalent terms 'examination' and
'test', which figure in the medico-scientific *Baby Book*). Why, on the other hand
are 'This is' and 'and' not italicised? How can the single use of 'and' mark a shift
into a different voice? So in what respect, exactly, are these italicised expressions
'closer to the voice of the lifeworld'? To the extent that they comprise clauses of
reason and purpose one might suppose, on Fairclough's own argument, they are
just as close to the medical voice. Perhaps this is why Fairclough himself seems
uncertain about their status. He continues:

> … but I feel nevertheless that there is an ambivalence of voice in the *Pregnancy
> Book*.
> (Fairclough 1992: 173)

We might expect that reference might now be made to these clauses, or to some
other textual features to lend support to this feeling. But we get nothing of the kind:

> The reason for this is that medical staff often do shift partly into a lifeworld
> voice when talking to patients … and the italicized expressions *could* be used
> by medical staff. It therefore remains unclear whether the producer of the
> *Pregnancy Book* is writing from the patient's perspective, or from that of
> (a 'modernizing' position among) medical staff.
> (Fairclough 1992: 173)

But this is an interpretation without description. It is simply an assertion,
unfounded in this particular text. It remains unclear whether the text producer is
using one voice or another because there are no clear textual criteria which would
enable us to distinguish them. We would not know whether there is a shift or not,
and even if we had convincing linguistic reasons to suppose there was, we would
not know whether this textual shift implied a corresponding discourse shift, or
was simply a rhetorical ploy.

The medical voice is elusive, and yet it is crucial to Fairclough's argument that
it should be identified since otherwise he cannot demonstrate intertextuality, and
show how the discursive practices of authority position people by borrowing
other voices, thereby exercising deception by disguise. So medical people pretend
to adopt lifeworld values in much the same way as advertisers assume the guise of
advisers and politicians adopt the idiom of ordinary talk. Fairclough's
contention, and it is central to his theory of discourse and social change, is that
people in power shift voices in subtle ways to exert their influence. In the present
case, medical staff will assume a voice expressive of a patient perspective so as to
keep them in their place.

The whole argument depends on the assumption that there are separate and
distinguishable discourses. There is a community of social subjects, the medical
staff, which has its own distinct discourse expressive of its own distinct ethos. The
position it adopts necessarily precludes the perspective of the patient, which is a

different social subject, belonging to a different discourse – a lifeworld one. So although medical people may appear to adopt this perspective they do so only as a tactical ruse to win over the patient by a kind of covert intertextual colonisation.

You can, of course, read this significance into these texts if you are willed so to do. But this interpretation is supposed to be to some extent at least dependent on a description of the text. In the analysis I have considered here, it seems that the reverse is the case: description is provided to support a preconceived interpretation. And this interpretation is Interpretation 1. It cannot be Interpretation 2, an explanation of how a particular reading is influenced by social forces, since we have no data whatever on what significance the intended consumers *do* read into these texts. We only have the analyst taking over their role. Paradoxically, therefore, we find Fairclough indulging in the very discursive practice he sets out to expose: assuming the voice of the patient for the purpose of persuasion.

This is not to say that the interpretation is without value or without textual warrant, only that it is partial. Partiality is a necessary pragmatic feature of any interpretation, whatever term you use for it, and in my view it is the main business of analysis to explain how this partiality effects what you read into a text. These comments I have offered on Fairclough's findings are analysis in this sense. But then analysis should also reveal the essential instability of textual meaning by indicating how they can give rise to alternative interpretations. Do the texts that Fairclough deals with admit of different readings? Let us, briefly, consider the question.

These textual extracts are about pregnancy. This is both a physical process that can be seen as a third person occurence, something that involves the human body, and a personal experience, something that involves the individual human being. So there are obviously two very different ways of talking about it: objectively as fact, from the perspective of the outsider observer; and subjectively as affect from the perspective of the insider participant. Medical staff naturally take up the first position, and prospective mothers the second: naturally, because these positions are determined by the nature of the process not by any socially sanctioned assignment of role. But the purpose of the interaction between these parties is in some way to mediate between them. The prospective mothers need to know something about their bodies, the medical staff on the other hand can only talk to the human beings. Any medical text, therefore, is likely to have features which reflect this dual perspective.

So it is that in our present text we find a continual shifting from non-participant third person to participant second person reference which reflects a relative distancing from the concerns of the individual. The pregnant women are both addressed and talked about. Thus the participant phrases '*your* pregnancy', '*your* local hospital', '*your* general practitioner' co-occur with the non-participant equivalents '*the* doctor', '*a* local hospital', '*the* pregnancy'. But the participant expressions always come first and the non-participant ones take on a dependent anaphoric function. One way of interpreting these textual facts is to suggest that the writer's first concern is to acknowledge the insider perspective.

Not all non-participant expressions are anaphoric however. In the third extract, we find reference to both '*your* pelvis' and '*the* pelvis'. But the former is associated with '*your* breasts, heart, lungs, blood pressure, abdomen' and the latter with '*the* uterus, cervix and *the* vagina'. We might note that the former list becomes lexically more medical as if marking a gradual distancing into non-participant reference.

This then becomes dominant in the second paragraph where is only one single occurrence of the second person ('which so far have not caused you any problems'). In this paragraph, we might suggest, the medical perspective takes over – appropriately enough, one might suggest, since this particular extract is, by its title quite explicitly about examination. It is about human bodies, not human beings.

But the medical perspective, we should note, comes in the second paragraph. Again it is the participant perspective which comes first. This would account for the occurrence of the phrase 'which is not surprising'. For Fairclough, as we have seen, this is the interpolation of a contrasting lifeworld voice, a kind of 'slippage', like the occurrence of 'we' in the second extract. But they can also be read as support for the participant orientation which is predominant in the paragraphs they occur in. Actually the paragraph in which 'we' appears is the second paragraph of the extract, not the first, and it might seem that the principle of establishing participation before medical distancing is not evident in this case. But notice that participation is already keyed into the beginning of this first paragraph ('*Your* first visit', '*your* health', '*you* became pregnant') and then in the remaining two sentences we find a shift entirely into the non-participant mode with no second person presence whatever.

What I hope these observations indicate is that there is a pattern discernible in this text which Fairclough makes no mention of, and which gives rise to a rather different interpretation of its purpose and possible effect: one which is more co-operative than conflictual, which invokes no hegemonic struggle, and which is rather more favourable to the medical profession. I would argue that Fairclough does not notice this pattern because he is looking for something else. And of course he might argue that I have only noticed it because I am determined to be contrary. This is probably true. I would not have subjected the text to scrutiny if he had not provoked me to do so. But this is just the point. We came to the same text with different motives, assumptions, beliefs, values and so read our different discourses into it.

I make no claims for this brief analysis. It, too, is bound to be partial, and I have no idea how far my reading would be consistent with the effect it might have on the women for whom it was written. But we could try to find out. One way of doing this would be to elicit their reactions to the original texts and to versions of them in which the linguistic features I have identified have been systematically altered. One version of the first extract might be:

> The essential aim of antenatal care is to ensure that *women* go through pregnancy and labour in the peak of condition. Inevitably, therefore it involves a series of examinations and tests throughout the course of *the* pregnancy. As mentioned above, antenatal care will be provided either by *the* local hospital or by *the* general practitioner...

The beginning of the second extract might be altered to read:

> *The* first visit involves a comprehensive review of *the* patient's health through childhood and also right up to the time of *the pregnancy*...

And so on.

As Fairclough himself points out, no study of language is neutral. Idealisation implies ideology in some degree: you cast reality in your own mental image. This is bound to affect interpretation, and distinguishing two senses of the term in principle does not help if the two are conflated in practice, as I believe they are in the analysis we have considered. Fairclough's concept of distinct voices, of homogeneous groups with uniform discursive practices is well suited to his image of the hegemonic struggle: social subject against social subject, doctor against patient, man against woman, them against us.

And him against me? I think the discourse we are here enacting is a matter of individuals arguing against each other. We take up different positions, and these are of course to some degree discursively informed, expressive of different modes of thought, political beliefs, social values. And so if we feel frustrated and affronted, we might be tempted to reduce each other to 'social subjects discursively determined and constructed' and I cry 'Marxist!' and he cries 'Liberal!' and we resentfully go our separate ways. But that would be a pity. Our positions are not as polarised as all that. I am no apologist for 'greater linguistics' and totally reject the intertextual implication of the term. I agree that we need to take an interdisciplinary perspective on language study. I agree that people should be alerted to language abuse, and made aware of the ways in which it can be used to persuasive and manipulative effect. You do not have to subscribe to CDA to believe these things, and you do not have to be a critical linguist to have a social conscience. So I think there is a good deal of common ground between Normal Fairclough and myself, which both of us ought to be willing to explore.

Note

1 My thanks to Barbara Seidlhofer for comments on an earlier draft of this article.

References

Fairclough, N. (1992) *Discourse and Social Change*, Polity Press, London
Widdowson, H. G. (1988) Language spread in modes of use, in P. H. Lowenberg (ed.) *Language Spread and Language Policy*, Georgetown University Press, Georgetown USA
Widdowson, H. G. (1990) Discourses of enquiry and conditions of relevance, in J. Alatis (ed.) *Linguistics, Language Teaching and Language Acquisition: The Interdependence of Theory, Practice and Research*, Georgetown University Press, Georgetown, USA

Further reading

Analyses and counter-analyses

For readers who find actual text analyses particularly useful for formulating their own responses to CDA procedures – and whose curiosity may have been heightened by Widdowson's 'counter-analysis' in his second paper above – here are a few references to publications that offer such worked examples.

For the original text analysis referred to in the above exchange, see Fairclough (1992a).

Fairclough and Wodak (1997) analyse an extract from a radio interview with former British Prime Minister, Margaret Thatcher, with reference to 'eight principles of theory or method' (p. 268 ff.), which are:

1 CDA addresses social problems
2 Power relations are discursive
3 Discourse constitutes society and culture
4 Discourse does ideological work
5 Discourse is historical
6 The link between text and society is mediated
7 Discourse analysis is interpretative and explanatory
8 Discourse is a form of social action.

Wodak (1996) is based on research conducted by the author and her colleagues over a span of over 20 years. It summarizes several, partly longitudinal, projects, but also provides analyses of transcripts with a methodology termed 'discourse sociolinguistics', which again is part of critical discourse analysis. Examples of such analyses include the discourse of therapeutic communication in groups at the Crisis Intervention Centre in Vienna and of school committee meetings in three Viennese schools, which reflected the (very rigid) power structure of the Austrian school system.

Hodge and Kress (1993), in their concluding chapter, entitled 'Reading Power', illustrate their theory and method by analysing a set of printed and transcribed spoken media texts from the 1991 Gulf War.

Stubbs (1994) and a revised version of this in Stubbs (1996) represent an attempt to remedy weaknesses in CDA methodology (see the comments on Stubbs 1997 above) by using procedures of corpus study to analyse the language used in two school textbooks. For a critical discussion of this analysis, see Widdowson (2000). And indeed, together with Stubbs (2001) and Widdowson (2001), these exchanges form another controversy about the nature of applied linguistics and the roles and methods of critical discourse analysis and corpus linguistics within this field.

Toolan (1997: 94 ff.), in the article referred to above, offers a demonstration of how 'CDA can be kept simple, and textual' with his analysis of an advertisement by the Department of Education and Employment in a local newspaper, in which he provides 'two ideological readings of contemporary British unemployment', one sympathetic to and one sharply critical of jobless people.

Montgomery (1999) compares the reception of various televised tributes to Princess Diana after her death, in particular those by the Queen and by the British Prime Minister, Tony Blair. Cameron (2001: 133–7) offers a summary of this article and extracts from Montgomery's transcripts.

Finally, probably the richest and most varied source for examples of applications of CDA is Caldas-Coulthard and Coulthard (1996). This contains analyses of a wide range of spoken and written texts from a variety of contexts (for example, police records, psychiatric interviews, the discourse of elderly people, media discourse on immigration, and sex narratives in women's magazines) and countries (for example, Austria, Brazil, the Netherlands, the UK, Zimbabwe). For a critical review of this collection, see Widdowson (1998).

Other relevant readings

Among the general introductions to CDA, apart from the sources already mentioned above such as Fairclough and Wodak (1997) and Wodak (1996: Chapter 1), Cameron (2001) offers an even-handed, easy-to-read introduction, reminding us that '[t]here is no single "orthodox" version of CDA, and to get a sense of the range of work done under this heading, readers should look at the work of more than one scholar or "tendency"' (p. 140).

Pennycook (2001) also has a chapter on CDA.

Titscher, Meyer, Wodak, and Vetter (2000) claims in its blurb to provide 'the most comprehensive overview of linguistic and sociological approaches to text and discourse analysis currently available'; its Chapter 11 outlines CDA's theoretical background, basic assumptions, and overall goals, and then goes on to introduce 'Two Approaches to Critical Discourse Analysis' (chapter heading), namely 'critical discourse analysis in the form developed by Norman Fairclough, and the discourse-historical method of Ruth Wodak' (p. 144). This paper is also interesting because it marks what may be the beginnings of an explicit acknowledgement by CDA protagonists of the views of their critics.

Thus Titscher, Meyer, Wodak, and Vetter (pp. 163–4) mention criticism coming from conversations analysis (notably Schegloff 1998) and Widdowson (1995). Richardson (1987) is another example of constructive criticism of CDA 'from within'.

Critical points from within the ranks of CDA are also raised by Clark and Ivanič (1997) and Norton (1997). Clark and Ivanič mainly expound on the educational application of CDA in the form of Critical Language Awareness (as exemplified in Fairclough 1992b), and one point which they make is a problem already discussed above, namely the lack of empirical research into the reactions of 'ordinary people' to the texts analysed by CDA. Another issue briefly discussed by Clark and Ivanič is one specific to (language) education:

> Learners often argue that they, as people without social status, do not have the power to contribute to social change, and therefore have no option other than to conform to discourse conventions and thereby reproduce the existing social order. … There is a tension between the pedagogical objective of helping learners to use statusful discourses which will be to their immediate advantage, and that of giving them the means to challenge those conventions which are disrespectful to

or disempowering of any social group, thereby contributing to discoursal and social change. Some learners may not want to challenge the conventions, only to gain access to them. Associated with this is the unpalatable truth that raising awareness of the empowering and disempowering characteristics of discourses can have the opposite of the intended effect, giving people tools with which to linguistically abuse or oppress others.
(Clark and Ivanič 1997: 224)

Norton, concerned with critical discourse research in the field of education, gives a compact and accessible overview of some important work in the area. Of particular interest for this volume are the problems and difficulties she addresses, such as the lack of commitment of some critical discourse researchers to engage with the complexities of actual classrooms, and the 'gendered division of labour in mainstream educational research', which is also to be found in CDA. As an example, Norton mentions the collection edited by Caldas-Coulthard and Coulthard (1996), pointing out that 'all the contributors to the theory section of the collection, "critical discourse theory", are males (Fowler, Kress, van Leeuwen, Fairclough, van Dijk) while the women in the collection (Wodak, Ribeiro, Gough, Talbot, Caldas-Coulthard) are concentrated in the "applications" section' (Norton 1997: 212ff.). Norton also observes that

> critical discourse research has been unable to shake the hegemony of the English language in educational research internationally. While many of the leading theorists and researchers in this field are not anglophones (Bourdieu, Foucault, Wodak), their work has reached a wider audience only after being translated into English. In this respect, there is dramatic irony that the work of critical discourse researchers concerned with the hegemony of English internationally is published exclusively in English (see Peirce 1989; Pennycook 1994; Phillipson 1992; Tollefson 1991). Critical discourse researchers cannot be complacent about complicity in the perpetuation of unequal relations of power in a variety of academic, social, and political relationships. (p. 213)[4]

With these comments and caveats, Norton provides us with a link both with Section 1 of this volume on Global English, and also with the following section on second language acquisition, in which she figures (under the name Bonny Norton Peirce) as a participant in one of the controversies presented and discussed there – a welcome reminder of how closely the controversies included in this volume relate to each other, despite the different headings under which they may appear.

---

[4] Norton makes an important point here, but at the same time demonstrates the difficulty of breaking through the hegemony of English, for she is writing in English herself, and for an eight-volume encyclopedia of language and education published entirely in English. Also, it might be noted that hegemony has to do not only with the *production* but also the *reception* of texts, and that it is also the lack of reception of work in languages other than English that leads to the (wrong) impression that 'the work of critical discourse researchers concerned with the hegemony of English internationally is published exclusively in English'.

References

Brown, G. and **G. Yule.** 1983. *Discourse Analysis.* Cambridge: Cambridge University Press.

Caldas-Coulthard, C. R. and **M. Coulthard** (eds.). 1996. *Texts and Practices: Readings in Critical Discourse Analysis.* London: Routledge.

Cameron, D. 2001. *Working with Spoken Discourse.* London: Sage.

Coulthard, M. 1985. *An Introduction to Discourse Analysis.* 2nd edition. London: Longman.

Clark, R. and **R. Ivanič.** 1997. 'Critical discourse analysis and educational change' in L. van Lier and D.Corson (eds.). *Encyclopedia of Language and Education. Volume 6: Knowledge about Language.* Amsterdam: Kluwer

Fairclough, N. L. 1992a. *Discourse and Social Change.* Cambridge: Polity Press.

Fairclough, N. L. 1992b. *Critical Language Awareness.* London: Longman.

Fairclough, N. L. 1995. *Critical Discourse Analysis: The Critical Study of Language.* Harlow: Longman.

Fairclough, N. L. 1996. 'A reply to Henry Widdowson's "Discourse analysis: a critical view"'. *Language and Literature* 5/1: 49–56.

Fairclough, N. L. and **R. Wodak.** 1997. 'Critical discourse analysis' in T. A. van Dijk (ed.). *Discourse Studies. A Multidisciplinary Introduction. Vol. 2. Discourse as Social Interaction.* London: Sage.

Fowler, R. 1996. 'On critical linguistics' in Caldas-Coulthard and Coulthard.

Fowler, R., R. Hodge, G. Kress, and **T. Trew.** 1979. *Language and Control.* London: Routledge and Kegan Paul.

Gee, J. P. 1999. *An Introduction to Discourse Analysis: Theory and Method.* London: Routledge.

Hammersley, M. 1997. 'On the foundations of critical discourse analysis'. *Language and Communication* 17/3: 237–48.

Hodge, R. and **G. Kress.** 1993. *Language as Ideology.* London: Routledge. [2nd edition of Kress and Hodge 1979].

Kress, G. and **R. Hodge.** 1979. *Language as Ideology.* London: Routledge and Kegan Paul.

Montgomery, M. 1999. 'Speaking sincerely: public reactions to the death of Diana'. *Language and Literature* 8/1: 5–33.

Norton, B. 1997. 'Critical discourse research' in N. Hornberger and D. Corson (eds.). *Encyclopedia of Language and Education. Volume 8: Research Methods in Language and Education.* Amsterdam: Kluwer.

Peirce, B. N. 1989. 'Toward a pedagogy of possibility in the teaching of English internationally: People's English in South Africa'. *TESOL Quarterly* 23/3: 401–20.

Pennycook, A. 1994. *The Cultural Politics of English as an International Language.* London and New York: Longman.

Pennycook, A. 2001. *Critical Applied Linguistics: A Critical Introduction.* Mahwah, New Jersey and London: Lawrence Erlbaum Associates.

Phillipson, R. 1992. *Linguistic Imperialism.* Oxford: Oxford University Press.

Richardson, K. 1987. 'Critical linguistics and textual diagnosis'. *Text* 7/2: 145–63.

Schegloff, E. 1998. 'Text and context paper'. *Discourse and Society* 3: 4–37.

Schiffrin, D. 1994. *Approaches to Discourse.* Oxford: Basil Blackwell.

Schiffrin, D., D. Tannen, and H. Hamilton (eds.). 2001. *The Handbook of Discourse Analysis*. Malden, Mass.: Blackwell.

Stubbs, M. 1994. 'Grammar, text, and ideology: Computer-assisted methods in the linguistics of representation'. *Applied Linguistics* 15/2: 201–23.

Stubbs, M. 1996. *Text and Corpus Analysis. Computer-Assisted Studies of Language and Culture*. Oxford: Basil Blackwell.

Stubbs, M. 1997. 'Whorf's children: critical comments on critical discourse analysis (CDA)' in A. Ryan and A. Wray (eds.). *Evolving Models of Language*. Clevedon: Multilingual Matters.

Stubbs, M. 2001. 'Texts, corpora, and problems of interpretation: A response to Widdowson'. *Applied Linguistics* 22/2: 149–72.

Titscher, S., M. Meyer, R. Wodak, and E. Vetter. 2000. 'Two approaches to critical discourse analysis' in *Methods of Text and Discourse Analysis*. London: Sage.

Tollefson, J. 1991. *Planning Language, Planning Inequality*. London and New York: Longman.

Toolan, M. 1997. 'What is critical discourse analysis and why are people saying such terrible things about it?' *Language and Literature* 6/2: 83–103.

van Dijk, T. A. 1993. 'Principles of Critical Discourse Analysis'. *Discourse and Society* 4(2): 249–83.

van Dijk, T. A. 2001. 'Critical discourse analysis' in Schriffrin, Tannen, and Hamilton.

Widdowson, H. G. 1995. 'Discourse analysis: a critical view'. *Language and Literature* 4/3: 157–72.

Widdowson, H. G. 1998. 'The theory and practice of critical discourse analysis'. *Applied Linguistics* 19/1: 136–51.

Widdowson, H. G. 2000. 'On the limitations of linguistics applied'. *Applied Linguistics* 21/1: 3–25.

Widdowson, H. G. 2001. 'Interpretations and Correlations: A Reply to Stubbs'. *Applied Linguistics* 22/4: 531–38.

Wodak, R. 1995. 'Critical linguistics and critical discourse analysis' in J. Verschueren, J.-O., Östman, and J. Blommaert (eds.). *Handbook of Pragmatics. Manual*. Amsterdam: Benjamins.

Wodak, R. 1996. *Disorders of Discourse*. London: Longman.

Section 4
Second language acquisition

Considering what a young field of research second language acquisition (SLA) is, it can already look back at quite an eventful history and development. It would therefore seem helpful to clarify what is intended by the term 'second language acquisition' here, and how the controversies that follow in this section fit into this collection as a whole.

In the most general formulation for non-specialists I could find, SLA is paraphrased as 'the study of the way in which people learn a language other than their mother tongue' (Ellis 1997, cover blurb). But even this formulation, straightforward though it seems, encapsulates implications that are open to question: that 'SLA' stands for 'the *study* of SLA'; that 'second language' includes such notions as 'foreign language' and 'third, fourth, ... nth language'; that the 'A' in SLA covers both 'acquisition' and 'learning' (which, for some researchers, are terms for processes which are very different and in contrast to one another); that, lastly, 'learning' refers to different kinds of learning (for example, inside a classroom or by living in the country where the target language is spoken). There is considerable complexity and a lack of clarity behind the acronym and this raises expectations of all sorts of potential disagreements – expectations which are amply fulfilled when one consults the literature.

The beginnings of SLA are usually dated in the late 1960s or early 1970s, with Corder (1967) being the most-quoted publication marking the decisive break from the then prevailing behaviourist view of language acquisition. This, coupled with the contrastive analysis hypothesis, posited a direct causal relationship between the difficulties learners encountered in trying to master features of the L2 and differences between the learners' L1 and target language. Accordingly, where L1 and L2 converged, i.e. where a rule or feature existed in both, 'positive transfer' would be expected to happen, whereas in areas of divergence, i.e. where L1 and L2 rules or features conflicted, or only existed in one of the two languages, 'negative transfer' would occur, with the learner inappropriately transferring the L1 rule or feature to the L2.

When Corder discussed 'the significance of learners' errors' (the title of his 1967 article), however, he did so not in terms of interference. Instead he argued that these errors were evidence of the underlying systems learners built and the processes and strategies they used, and thus indicative not of failure but of the learning process itself. With this shift in perspective, away from the differences between languages to the characteristics of learners, a theoretical base for examining L2 acquisition had been proposed and the field of SLA was born.

However, while there is practically unanimous agreement that Corder's article constitutes the origins of SLA as a field of research, this accord is in stark contrast to the multitude of ways in which the domain and methodology of SLA are defined by different scholars working in the area (which of course begs the question just what 'the area' is). Rod Ellis, one of the most authoritative and objective commentators on the discipline as a whole in all its various guises, sketches developments in SLA as being characterized by

- the addition of a sociolinguistic-pragmatic perspective to the former linguistic (particularly grammatical) one
- the strengthening of the mutual relationship between SLA research and linguistic theory
- the increase of theory-led, 'confirmatory' research (as opposed to 'interpretative' research starting from empirical findings and resulting in post hoc interpretations)
- the parallel development of the study of 'learning' as a phenomenon with universal properties and 'learners' and their individual differences
- the proliferation of studies investigating classroom L2 acquisition (as opposed to L2 acquisition in natural settings).

(cf. Ellis 1994: 1ff.)

Ellis concludes that all these developments have contributed to making SLA research 'a rather amorphous field of study with elastic boundaries' (1994: 2). There is considerable disagreement among researchers in the field, however, about how elastic such boundaries should be, as the readings in this section will demonstrate.

In view of the claimed relevance of this book to language (teacher) education, an appropriate starting point for sketching the context for the exchanges below might be the relationship between SLA, applied linguistics and (foreign) language teaching.

It is precisely this relationship and its significance for university contexts in the United States that an article by Claire Kramsch deals with. She points out that

[t]he current popularity of the term second language acquisition (SLA) has created some confusion about the nature of SLA as a domain of research and the way in which it contributes to the teaching and learning of foreign languages.

(Kramsch 2000: 311)

In order to get a handle on what SLA means in universities in the United States, Kramsch compares three definitions given by different US representatives of the field in the 1990s. The scope of these definitions differs very markedly: at the narrow end, SLA is described as an 'internally driven, individual phenomenon that is largely independent of the context in which it takes place' (Kramsch 2000: 314); in a broader definition, SLA includes not just language acquisition but also language use, and a distinction is made between 'basic SLA research', which investigates what the first definition encompasses, and 'applied SLA research', which 'explores the effects of social identity, schooling, and cultural integration on the learning and teaching of FLs [foreign languages]' (ibid.). The third definition also covers 'basic' and 'applied' SLA, but adds to this 'societal concerns', particularly 'the role that language learning ... plays in multicultural societies' (ibid.). Kramsch summarizes her comparison of definitions thus:

> From definition 1 to definition 3, we note an increase in the perceived scope of the field of SLA, from a phenomenon that is purely internal to the learner, to an interaction between the learner and an educational context, to the individual and societal aspects of multilingualism.
> (p. 314)

This summary is a useful primer for the controversies which follow below (particularly for the first one), for even though other issues get variously foregrounded in the different exchanges, it is the question of scope which can be seen as the most common, and the most contentious, concern among the different researchers in the field.

This may also be why Larsen-Freeman entitles her earlier state-of-the-art overview 'Second language acquisition research: Staking out the territory', and identifies two themes which help her characterize SLA:

> the alternate broadening and narrowing of perspective on the focus of enquiry and the movement from description (or what learners do) to explanation (or how they learn to do it).
> (Larsen-Freeman 1993: 133ff.)

Larsen-Freeman explains that 'the focus has alternately broadened as researchers became more aware of the complexity of the issues and narrowed as greater depth of analysis was required' (ibid.). It would be interesting to know whether the authors in the controversy below would share this view, and indeed whether they see the issue of 'broadening and narrowing' as central to their differences.

These issues of scope and focus are relevant to work in second language acquisition that has been undertaken outside the Anglo-American tradition, and here they tend to be seen from a rather different perspective. In Germany, for example, we encounter the notion of *Sprachlehr- und-lern-forschung* (language teaching and learning research, usually abbreviated to

Sprachlehrforschung) as a well-established academic area of enquiry. What is of particular interest about this field in the present context is its insistence that it studies the teaching and learning of foreign languages (mostly in an institutional context) 'holistically and in its complete complexity' (Grotjahn 2000: 570), as opposed to other disciplines such as linguistics, psycholinguistics, sociolinguistics, and pedagogy, 'which usually only focus on a partial dimension of the topic "foreign language teaching and learning"' (ibid.), and that it is therefore based on the a priori inclusion of other, related, neighbouring disciplines. The practical aim of *Sprachlehr- und-lernforschung* is 'to make well-founded recommendations for action with respect to the teaching and learning of foreign languages which take into consideration the political and societal context' (Grotjahn 2000: 569). These are, then, very clearly declared broad aims which contrast with much of what goes on in Anglo-American SLA research. Indeed, Grotjahn points out that 'the establishment of *Sprachlehrforschung* can be seen, in terms of academic history, as a reaction against discipline-specific reductions of the object "foreign language teaching and learning"' (p. 570).

'Discipline-specific reductions' could be regarded as the key to and main target of criticism characterizing both Firth and Wagner's and Norton Peirce's 'stimulus articles' below: as already spelt out in Firth and Wagner's abstract, they argue for a 'reconceptualization' of SLA research that would 'enlarge the ontological and empirical parameters of the field' and for a 'broadening of the traditional SLA data base', while Norton Peirce's central argument is that 'SLA theorists have not developed a comprehensive theory of social identity that integrates the language learner and the language learning context' (p.12). The question of scope, then, although also present in the other controversies in this book, is given particular prominence in these SLA readings.

In the sense that these readings are mostly about what is normally *not* included in SLA but, according to them, should be, they raise questions about 'the very nature of the beast' (Long 1997: 319) – what (to change the metaphor) should or should not form part of 'mainstream SLA'. Given that the term is employed (if not defined) by authors with as diverse views about it as Kramsch (2000), Long (1997), and Pennycook (2001), as well as Firth and Wagner below, the question also arises, of course, as to who decides, and on what criteria, which work in the field is mainstream, as distinct from merely a tributary, or even a backwater.

A short note about the exchanges which follow: SLA research has quite a few controversies to offer about specific disputed questions in the field: the role of comprehensible input/output, L1 interference, interlanguage, and fossilization, task-based instruction, field dependence/independence, and so on. While these 'traditional' topics are all interesting and instructive for people working in the field, it seemed desirable in the context of this collection to choose controversies which concentrated more on the scope and nature of SLA as such. At this meta-level, the questions of which theories SLA should draw on and what links to other research areas can usefully be made become the focus. At a fairly high level of generality, what the source papers have in common is that they have to do with proposals for a reconceptualization of SLA. At the same time, they have the added advantage of containing references to numerous SLA studies which are considered important, and of involving several of the protagonists in the field.[1]

The first controversy, sparked off by Firth and Wagner, though very varied, is also compact in that the 'stimulus paper' and all but one of the responses appeared in the same issue of *Modern Language Journal*. Not all of the responses are reproduced below – only the papers by those authors whose work had been criticized by Firth and Wagner, and who directly expressed (fairly) strong disagreement with points they make. The papers omitted from the present collection are Joan Kelly Hall's 'A consideration of SLA theory of practice: A response to Firth and Wagner', Anthony Liddicoat's 'Interaction, social structure, and second language use: A response to Firth and Wagner', and Ben Rampton's 'Second language research in late modernity: A response to Firth and Wagner', which all appeared in the same volume of *Modern Language Journal* as Firth and Wagner's paper. The main reason for omitting them is that they are, generally speaking, in broad agreement with Firth and Wagner.

Text 20

Alan Firth and Johannes Wagner

On Discourse, Communication, and (Some) Fundamental Concepts in SLA Research

This article argues for a reconceptualization of Second Language Acquisition (SLA) research that would enlarge the ontological and empirical parameters of the field. We claim that methodologies, theories, and foci within SLA reflect an imbalance between cognitive and mentalistic orientations, and social and contextual orientations to language, the former orientation being unquestionably in the ascendancy. This has resulted in a skewed perspective on discourse and

---

[1] For more 'traditional topics' of SLA, readers are referred to the journals which publish 'SLA research proper', for instance *Studies in Second Language Acquisition*, *Language Learning*, and *Second Language Research*. There are, as one of the anonymous reviewers for the proposal for the present volume also pointed out, academic disagreements of a less 'adversarial' kind with contributors representing different SLA theories, such as L. Eubank (ed.) (1983) and T. Huebner (ed.) (1991).

communication, which conceives of the foreign language speaker as a deficient communicator struggling to overcome an underdeveloped L2 competence, striving to reach the 'target' competence of an idealized native speaker (NS). We contend that SLA research requires a significantly enhanced awareness of the contextual and interactional dimensions of language use, an increased 'emic' (i.e., participant-relevant) sensitivity towards fundamental concepts, and the broadening of the traditional SLA data base. With such changes in place, the field of SLA has the capacity to become a theoretically and methodologically richer, more robust enterprise, better able to explicate the processes of second or foreign language (S/FL) acquisition, and better situated to engage with and contribute to research commonly perceived to reside outside its boundaries.

> Native speakers and nonnative speakers are multiply handicapped in conversations with one another.
> Varonis & Gass (1985b, p. 340)

This article examines critically the predominant view of discourse and communication within second language acquisition (SLA) research.[1] We argue that this view is individualistic and mechanistic, and that it fails to account in a satisfactory way for interactional and sociolinguistic dimensions of language. As such, it is flawed, and obviates insight into the nature of language, most centrally the language use of second or foreign language (S/FL) speakers. As part of this examination, we discuss the status of some fundamental concepts in SLA, principally *nonnative speaker* (NNS), *learner*, and *interlanguage*. These concepts prefigure as monolithic elements in SLA, their status venerated and seemingly assured within the field. We claim that, for the most part, they are applied and understood in an oversimplified manner, leading, among other things, to an analytic mindset that elevates an idealized 'native' speaker above a stereotypicalized 'nonnative,' while viewing the latter as a defective communicator, limited by an underdeveloped communicative competence.

Our critical assessment of some of SLA's core concepts is, in part, a reaction to recent discussions on theoretical issues within the field. Long (1990), for example, inaugurated a discussion on the perceived proliferation of theories in SLA, and argued the need for 'theory culling.' Subsequent contributions from Beretta (1991), Crookes (1992), Beretta and Crookes (1993), Long (1993), Ellis (1994, p. 676ff.), and Gregg (1990, 1993) similarly engage problems of theory and paradigm formulation. Such discussions reflect a desire to keep apace with an expanding and increasingly diversified field, and to introduce 'quality control' on the basis of 'established' and 'normal' scientific standards.

In a recent paper, Block (1996) has challenged many of the assumptions upon which these discussions are predicated, not least the assumption that there is a 'normal science,' as well as the assumption that the existence of multiple theories in SLA is inherently problematic (in that a multitude of theories is said to prevent SLA from becoming a 'normal science'), and the assumption that there exists an 'ample body' of 'accepted findings' within SLA research.

Long (1993) claims that a theoretically 'slimmed down' SLA would allow for knowledge accumulation and the prevention of a 'wild-flowering' of disparate and 'rivalling' theories (p. 235). Such a process, it is felt, will bolster the theoretical foundations of SLA. In Long's view, knowledge production in 'normal' science 'becomes cumulative, details can be attended to, and applications of theory can be harvested' (p. 230). And yet, as introductory SLA texts such as Larsen-Freeman and Long (1991), Lightbown and Spada (1993), and Ellis (1990, 1994) demonstrate, there is a strong tendency within SLA to accumulate large quantities of heterogeneous research. The problem is that the accumulation is done largely without critical assessment of the presuppositions underpinning the research. As we argue below, although SLA research is imbalanced in favour of cognitive-oriented theories and methodologies, the fact remains that the branch of the discipline dealing with discourse and communication is, and always has been, of necessity multitheoretical in its adopted approaches and conceptual apparatus. Hence, SLA would appear to require not so much a 'theory culling,' but rather a more critical discussion of its own presuppositions, methods, and fundamental (and implicitly accepted) concepts. This article engages in such a discussion.

By challenging prevailing views, presuppositions, and concepts, and by examining critically theoretical assumptions and methodological practices, our ultimate goal is to argue for a reconceptualization of SLA as a more theoretically and methodologically balanced enterprise that endeavours to attend to, explicate, and explore, in more equal measures and, where possible, in integrated ways, both the *social* and *cognitive* dimensions of S/FL use and acquisition.

We are aware of the growing number of SLA studies, mainly of an ethnographic nature, that are socially and contextually oriented (e.g., Aston, 1993; Blyth, 1995; Kramsch, 1995; Hall, 1995). Although such studies are beginning to impact SLA in general, and have begun questioning and exploring the fundamental notions of learner, nonnative, native speaker, and interlanguage, most tend to take the formal learning environment (i.e., the S/FL classroom) as their point of departure. Thus, although S/FL interactions occurring in noninstructional settings are everyday occurrences (e.g., in the workplace), they have not, as yet, attracted the attention of SLA researchers (see, though, Rampton, 1995a; Bremer, Roberts, Vasseur, Simonot, & Broeder, 1996).

Although many findings and theories in SLA have been important and even groundbreaking, we submit that, on the whole, work that purports to examine nonnative/learner discourse and communication is impaired. This is a result of an imbalance of theoretical concerns and methodologies. It is an imbalance that hinders progression within the field. The reconceptualization we call for, which would redress this imbalance, requires three major changes in SLA: (a) a significantly enhanced awareness of the contextual and interactional dimensions of language use, (b) an increased emic (i.e., participant-relevant) sensitivity towards fundamental concepts, and (c) the broadening of the traditional SLA data base. If we begin to accomplish such goals, we believe that the field of SLA has the capacity to become a theoretically and methodologically richer, more robust enterprise, better able to explicate the processes of S/FL acquisition, and better placed to engage with and contribute to research commonly perceived to reside outside its boundaries.

In the sections that follow, we trace, first, the origins of the perceived imbalance in SLA research practices, arguing that it has led to the prioritizing of the individual-as-'nonnative speaker'/'learner' over the participant-as-language-'user' in social interaction. In order to consider the theoretical and methodological implications of this prioritization, we (re)analyse previously published data extracts, upon which we offer alternative insights and conclusions.

Discourse and communication

Researchers within SLA have a relatively long history of recording and analysing 'learner' discourse; that is, language 'above the sentence,' produced in spoken encounters with others. In SLA, such recordings are commonly labelled 'performance data.' The aim is to explicate the processes of S/FL acquisition, while (at least implicitly) acknowledging the social basis of language. In large measure, this practice of collecting data from interactive encounters is rooted in the 'communicative' turn within anthropology and linguistics in the mid-1960s, represented most notably by Hymes's (1961; 1962; 1974, p. 90ff.) critique of Chomsky's (1957) formalistic, context-free, 'grammatical competence' programme for linguistics.[2] By stressing the centrality of communicative competence rather than grammatical competence, Hymes was instrumental in launching a more social and contextual view of language, which permeated, in greater or lesser degrees, a number of disciplines, SLA included.[3] This view is predicated on the conviction that language – as a social and cultural phenomenon – is acquired and learned through social interaction (see, e.g., Halliday, 1978, p. 18; Gass & Varonis, 1985a, p. 150; Ellis, 1990, p. 99; Yano, Long, & Ross, 1994, pp. 192–193). As such, it can, and should, be profitably studied in interactive encounters. Long (1981), for example, takes the position that '… participation in conversation with N[ative]S[peaker]s, made possible through the modification of interaction, is the *necessary* and sufficient condition for SLA' (p. 275, emphasis added). Gass and Varonis (1985a) contend that '[a]ctive involvement is a necessary aspect of acquisition, since it is through involvement that the input becomes "charged" and "penetrates" deeply' (p. 150).

Hymes's influential critique notwithstanding, Chomsky's impact was too powerful to resist. His distinction between competence (the ideal speaker-listener's abstract knowledge of grammar of his own language) and performance (language as actual utterance) parallelled, reinforced, and extended Saussure's dichotomy of *langue* and *parole*, and maintained the priority of the former over the latter (see Sampson, 1980, p. 50). But it was Chomsky's theory of a language instinct (Pinker, 1994), an innate 'mental structure' or 'language acquisition device' within the brain, enabling language acquisition to take place, that had a cataclysmic effect on linguistics, an effect that reverberated in research in child development, speech perception, neurology, genetics, psycholinguistics – and SLA. Chomsky's legacy is clearly evident in groundbreaking SLA work, including Corder (1967) on learners' errors, Selinker (1971) on the notion of 'interlanguage,' and Dulay, Burt, and Krashen's (1982) model of SL speech processing.

The Chomskyan paradigm – its roots traceable to Plato and Descartes's rationalistic theories of the mind (see Chomsky, 1976, pp. 6–8) – was to manifest and subsequently establish itself within SLA as a central concern with language as an aspect of individual cognition. According to Chomsky (1968), linguists should 'establish certain general properties of human intelligence,' the reason being that '[l]inguistics is simply the sub-field of psychology that deals with these aspects of the mind' (1968, p. 24). For Corder (1973), a leading figure in SLA for a generation, the consequence was that SLA must subscribe to a view of language 'as a phenomenon of the individual,' while being 'principally concerned with explaining how we acquire language ... its relation to general human cognitive systems, and ... the psychological mechanisms underlying the comprehension and production of speech' (p. 24). Moreover, such an approach would be 'much less [concerned] with the problem of what language is for, that is, its function as communication, since this necessarily involves more than a single individual' (ibid). For many within SLA, the strength of this conviction has not diminished with passing years. In a recent paper, Gregg (1993) contends:

> In SLA, for reasons that I (and others) have given elsewhere ... and which I for one find totally compelling, the overall explanandum is the acquisition (or non-acquisition) of L2 competence, in the Chomskyan sense of the term. (p. 278)

Gregg continues:

> SLA theory is a theory of the acquisition of linguistic knowledge, and thus requires a property theory or functional analysis of that knowledge. But it is also a theory of the acquisition of linguistic knowledge ... Our property theory asks 'How is L2 knowledge instantiated in the mind/brain?' (p. 279)

According to these views, acquisition is an individual phenomenon, its locus being the individual's 'mind' or 'brain.' Thus social, discursive approaches to the nature of mind, as well as competence and knowledge (e.g., Bakhtin, 1981; Wertsch, 1991; Sampson, 1993; Harré & Gillett, 1994), are beyond the purview of SLA.

The consequences of the rapid development during the 1960s of these two strands of language research – let us call them the 'social-anthropological' and the 'cognitive' – were of great importance, because while in an embryonic state, SLA was subjected to a tension between, on the one hand, an acknowledgement of the *social*, contextual dimensions of language, language acquisition and learning, and on the other, the centrality of the *individual's* language cognition and mental processes. This tension is, to some extent, still prevalent within SLA. And yet, as Gregg's observations (above) intimate, the centripetal forces of the individual-cognitive orientation remain irresistible for SLA. The field was to become if not firmly embedded within, then at least an important adjunct of, psycholinguistics (Clark & Clark, 1977; Stern, 1983), which by the mid-1960s had largely adopted Chomsky's programmatic statements on the cognitive, autonomic nature of the mind as its research agenda.

Benefits have accrued from the tension between these two perspectives. For example, researchers have attempted to investigate the influence of a range of contextual factors on language acquisition (e.g., the influence of task, conversational topic, prior acquaintance with one's interlocutor), and have at times sought to embellish their research by invoking ethnographic information on data. The most lasting benefit is that SLA is an applied field of research, where learners' competence (in both a Hymesian and a Chomskyan sense) has been studied through investigations of performance in verbal interaction (see the overviews in Ellis, 1990; Larsen-Freeman & Long, 1991; Ellis, 1994).

But this tension is by no means one of equipoise or counterbalance. It is a tension weighted against the social and the contextual, and heavily in favour of the individual's cognition, particularly the development of grammatical competence. This has led to an imbalance of adopted theoretical interests, priorities, foci, methodologies, perspectives, and so on, resulting in distorted descriptions of and views on discourse, communication, and interpersonal meaning – the quintessential elements of language. Moreover, this has occurred even in SLA work that is concerned with discourse and interaction (e.g., communication strategies [CS] and input modification [IM] research), as we discuss below.

Indeed, the imposition of an orthodox social psychological hegemony on SLA has had the effect of reducing social identities to 'subjects,' or at best to a binary distinction between natives and nonnatives/learners. It gives preeminence to the research practice of coding, quantifying data, and replicating results. It prioritizes explanations of phenomena in terms of underlying cognitive processes over descriptions of phenomena. It assigns preference to (researcher manipulation of) experimental settings rather than naturalistic ones. It endorses the search for the universal and underlying features of language processes rather than the particular and the local. It views communication as a process of information transfer from one individual's head to another's. It prioritizes etic (analyst-relevant) concerns and categories over emic (participant-relevant) ones. At best it marginalises, and at worst ignores, the social and the contextual dimensions of language.

We do *not* argue that such theoretical predilections or methodological practices are in and of themselves erroneous or flawed, and that, as such, they should be eschewed. Rather, we point out their striking predominance within the field, leading to a general methodological *bias* and theoretical *imbalance* in SLA studies that investigate acquisition through interactive discourse.

Communications strategies

A case in point is much of the work conducted under the rubric of 'communication strategies' (CS), as represented by Færch and Kasper (1983) and, more recently, Poulisse (1993), and Kasper & Kellerman (1997).[4] In a trenchant critique, Rampton (1997) argues that CS research constitutes the quintessential L2 moment. It bears many of the hallmarks of an orthodox psycholinguistic/social-psychological hegemony as outlined above, but an additional element, peculiar perhaps to SLA, is also prominent. This is SLA's general preoccupation with the *learner*, at the expense of other potentially relevant social identities. For SLA, the learner identity is the researcher's taken-for-granted *resource*, rather than, or as well as, a *topic* of investigation.[5] (In most cases, 'learner' is implicitly taken to be an adult receiving formal education in a S/FL.) The emic relevance of the learner identity is not an issue in SLA. More important, the learner is viewed as a defective communicator. So the focus and emphasis of research – a reflection of the quintessential SLA 'mindset,' we venture – is on the foreign learner's *linguistic deficiencies* and *communicative problems*. Indeed, CS are defined as 'potentially conscious plans for solving what to an individual presents itself as a problem in reaching a particular communicative goal' (Færch & Kasper, 1983, p. 36).

In some senses this view is understandable: feelings of incompetence and difficulty when learning a FL are surely commonplace, and often psychologically salient. The problem as we see it, however, is that studies of 'difficulties' and 'problems' predominate. Moreover, the study of problems in S/FL communication is implicitly taken to cast more light on SLA than does a focus on, say, communicative 'successes.' Yet although largely neglected by SLA in general and CS studies in particular, the fact is that people often do succeed in communicating in a FL even with quite limited communicative resources; successful communication, however, is perhaps less psychologically salient, and this may, in part, explain its disregard in SLA research. Nevertheless, we suggest that a study of communicative successes – in addition to studies of perceived failures and problems – may provide new and productive insights into SLA. We return, briefly, to this issue below.

Within CS research, we see social processes being interpreted from the perspective of cognition, which is prejudged to be hindered by the demands of a L2. For example, in Poulisse and Bongaert's (1990) CS work, the FL speaker's anomalous word formations (actually Dutch L1 lexical items) are viewed as erroneous features, explained solely in terms of the individual's lack of lexical competence (through the concept of 'automatic transfer'). Explanations are not sought in terms of interactional or sociolinguistic factors. Yet as Rampton (1997) suggests, the identified lexical items may equally well have discourse organizing functions – as 'contextualization cues' (in the sense of Gumperz, 1982) – or 'the speakers might … be code-switching in order to explore a mixed Anglo-Dutch identity' (p. 22). In either case, it is problematic to view the L1 lexical items as exclusively erroneous artefacts of cognition.

The CS model of communication is characteristic of both psycholinguistic and transformational grammar approaches to language in that it implicitly draws upon the 'mechanistic' (Shannon & Weaver, 1949) or 'telementational' concept of message exchange. Here communication is viewed as a process of transferring thoughts from one person's mind to another's (see, e.g., Harris, 1981). According to the transformational grammarian Katz (1966), for example, 'linguistic communication consists in the production of some external, publicly observable acoustic phenomenon whose phonetic and syntactic structure encodes a speaker's inner private thoughts or ideas' (p. 98). In CS research, then, speakers are viewed as having a preverbalised message or goal (the 'information source' in Shannon and Weaver's model) equated with the speech act (Færch & Kasper, 1983, p. 24). This message or goal, known a priori by the putative speaker, is converted into a 'plan,' which is the locus of the selected communication strategy (op. cit., p. 30). The strategy is then executed through speech. In this way, meaning and social interaction are viewed as essentially separate and discrete entities.

Færch and Kasper (1983) present the following extract involving two 17-year-old females – a Danish learner (L) and a native speaker (NS) of English – as an example of a CS. The CS occurs at lines 4 and 6 (arrowed):

1 NS: ((pause)) what do you read at home ((pause)) what what do you
    er read
2 L: mmmm
3 NS: what er subjects do you read about
4 L: → er historie
5 NS: mhm

6 L: → and ((laugh)) I read 'historie' home and sometimes in my school –
and – er
7   not more
8 NS: mm – do you like er history – in school – do you like learning
history
9   ((pause))
10 NS: do you have history lessons in school –
11 L: er yes
12 NS: I mean when you learn about er I don't know
13 L: kings
14 NS: old kings yes
15 L: oh yes I have that
16 NS: do you like it
17 L: no ((laugh)) ((extract continues))

Færch and Kasper (1983) observe that the conversation:

> illustrates various aspects of interlanguage (IL) communication: the learner has
> difficulty in expressing in English what she could easily have expressed in
> Danish (namely that she likes reading stories); her attempt to communicate
> leads to a misunderstanding on the part of the native speaker which then gets
> clarified at a later time. (p. 21)[6]

The CS in this extract is the word 'historie,' produced by L at lines 4 and 6.
Presumably, Færch and Kasper would refer to this as an achievement strategy of
'code switching' (p. 46), since 'historie,' reproduced by the authors inside
quotation marks (at line 6, though not at line 4, the reason for this being unclear),
is likely uttered (in standard Danish at least) as /his'dɔːʔjə/, which the authors
recognize as a Danish word, the English equivalent here being 'stories.' Færch
and Kasper see the uttering of the word 'historie' as marking a point of 'difficulty'
for the learner and of causing misunderstanding. They do so, it would appear, on
the basis of what transpires several turns later (not reproduced above), where the
learner declares that her interests are 'not with this old things you know kings or
all that,' from which the native speaker responds 'oh you mean a story, just a
story about people, not necessarily in the past' (p. 20).

To begin with, it is at least debatable whether L does in fact experience difficulty
at lines 4 and 6. The filled pause – 'er' – at line 4 is hardly compelling evidence of
difficulty. (If this is the authors' reason for identifying difficulty, would they apply
the same yardstick and declare that NS, in line 1, is experiencing difficulty in
enunciating the word 'read' in her 'what do you er read'? We doubt this.) Færch
and Kasper's assessment seems to be based on an etic view that sees language
encoded in a 'marked' (e.g., L1) form as an indicator of difficulty for the speaker.
This learner-as-defective-communicator mindset has seemingly prevented the
authors from considering the possibility that, in code switching, L has avoided
difficulty and preempted a problem, not solved or experienced one.

A more emically based perspective would allow the authors to explicate the
competencies through which the participants conjointly accomplish meaningful
communication with the resources – however seemingly imperfect – at their
disposal. For example, although L's pronunciation of 'historie' is marked, the

interlocutor, NS, is able to make sense of the utterance-as-pronounced (see Firth, 1996). This is so because, in this instance, both L and NS rely upon the nonnative status as a resource for sense-making: L in the way she can, knowingly, use a marked form in the knowledge that her interlocutor will take account of her NNS status in the interpretive work of making sense of the marked form; and NS in the way she focuses on the substrate of message content, rather than on the marked form of L's speech. In this extract, the identities of NNS and NS are not concomitant with linguistic 'handicaps' or communicative deficiencies. On the contrary, they are resources that have aided communication.

Although L may have intended 'story' and not 'history' – as NS clearly interprets 'historie' – the point is that the meaning or sense is that which is conjointly negotiated and implicitly agreed upon in the talk.[7] Contrary to Lockean principles of communication, people cannot say what they mean in an absolute sense; meaning is ineluctably negotiated. Moreover, in order to make sense, people are obliged to do ceaseless interpretive work.[8]

The negotiated meaning in the above extract – the meaning conjointly established in an apparently unproblematic way – is 'history.' How does this come about? How have we moved from 'historie' (lines 4 and 6) to 'history' (lines 8 and 10)? Færch and Kasper propose that this is caused by a misunderstanding resulting from L's reduced competence in English. We offer an alternative analysis. NS has used the word 'history' in line 8 because L's answer 'historie' in line 4 is assumed to be topically relevant vis-à-vis the preceding question, namely 'what er subjects do you read about' (line 3). The question, as a 'first pair part' of an 'adjacency pair' (Schegloff & Sacks, 1973), establishes a set of expectations as to what will occur in the following turn, one central expectation being that the next turn will be occupied with topically relevant materials vis-à-vis the preceding turn (Sperber & Wilson, 1986, p. 162), another expectation being that it will answer the posed question; that is, it will have an actional relationship.[9] NS has thus inferred that L's 'historie,' though enunciated in a marked way, is intended as the English 'history,' since 'subject' (line 3) and 'history' (line 4) are (in this specific sequential configuration) topically interrelated ('history' is a school 'subject' that can be read about). By reacting in this way, by 'searching for a normal form' (Cicourel, 1973), NS has made the abnormal, anomalous form 'normal' (see Firth, 1996, pp. 245–247).

The misunderstanding that Færch and Kasper claim resulted from the use of the word 'historie' is thus questionable. Note that after L's use of the word at line 4, NS does not intimate misunderstanding (line 5). Rather, the 'mhm' is interpreted by L as a token of understanding and as a signal to continue on topic. This is borne out by L's on-topic turn at line 6, which not only elaborates the topic with a voluntary disclosure on where she (L) reads 'historie' ('home and sometimes in my school,' line 6), but also reuses the word 'historie.' Lacking a public display of non-understanding from NS, then, in line 6 L makes the common-sense, default assumption that she has been understood. NS's subsequent triple-deployment of the word 'history'[10] (lines 8 and 10), and L's affirmative answers (lines 11, 13, & 15) show that for these participants 'historie' is *not* a problem.[11] If there is a misunderstanding on NS's part, L is either unaware of it, or she lets it pass at lines 9 and 11 – sequential 'slots' that offer clear opportunities for L to carry out a 'third-turn repair' (see Schegloff, 1992) of

NS's erroneous interpretation.[12] If L did see it as a misunderstanding on NS's part, at this moment in the conversation it was deemed to be nonfatal or irrelevant.

Meaning, from this perspective, is not an individual phenomenon consisting of private thoughts executed and then transferred from brain to brain, but a social and negotiable product of interaction, transcending individual intentions and behaviours (see Streek, 1980, pp. 147–149; Goodwin, 1979). This transcendence is possible because talk is organized on a turn-by-turn basis, thereby providing participants with a resource – a 'procedural infrastructure of interaction' (Schegloff, 1992, p. 1338) – for accomplishing, demonstrating, and transforming meaning in an ongoing fashion. Each speaking turn, then, is a locus for the display of understanding of the prior turn (see, e.g., Schegloff, 1992, pp. 1300–1301). Participants orient to this feature, and in so doing are able to construct a transcendental 'architecture of intersubjectivity' (Heritage, 1984, p. 254).

By extension, we would want to at least question Færch and Kasper's (1983) claim that 'although problems in interaction are necessarily "shared" problems and can be solved by joint efforts, they *originate* in either of the interactants' (p. 50; emphasis added). Because interaction and communication are per definition conjointly and publicly produced, structured, and made meaningful, communicative 'problems,' we suggest, are likely to be recognized as problems in interaction. In this sense, it may be more useful to view problems in communication as contingent social phenomena, as *inter*subjective entities, and not invariably as 'things' possessed by individuals.

Input modification studies

The mindset that views learners/nonnatives as inherently defective communicators is not restricted to CS research, but encompasses a wide range of 'interactional' studies in SLA, included in which are influential papers by Varonis and Gass (1985a, 1985b) and Gass and Varonis (1985a, 1985b).[13] These authors investigated communication between native speakers and nonnative speakers, a major impetus of their work being Long's (1981) claim that 'participation in conversation with NSs [native speakers] … is the *necessary and sufficient condition* for SLA' (p. 275, emphasis added). Summarising work in the field, Varonis and Gass (1985b) write:

> … native speakers (NSs) respond differently to non-natives (NNSs) than they do to natives. Specifically, there are more clarification requests, repetitions, expansions and elaborations, and a greater incidence of transparency in conversation with nonnatives than with natives. (p. 328)

Research that investigates the way participants accomplish mutual understanding has been termed 'input modification studies.' As alluded to in Varonis and Gass (1985b), this work focuses almost exclusively on interactions involving NSs and NNSs, the modifications being made by the NSs (resulting in 'foreigner talk'). Modifications include slower speech rate, shorter and simpler sentences, more questions and question tags, greater pronunciation articulation, and less use of contractions (Zuengler, 1992). Even when nonnatives interact together, that is, when natives are not involved, the language and forms of interaction are compared (by the researcher) to NS interactions, the supposition being that NS interactions are the norm. Indeed, the general notion of modification presupposes that there is a standard or normal way of talking and interacting; it is this standard or normal way that is modified.

Native and Nonnative Speakers

Prior to discussing input modification studies directly, we wish to comment briefly on the status of the concept of NS in input modification research, although our comments will be relevant to SLA in general.

(a) Consonant with Chomskyan linguistics, in input modification research, and in SLA as a whole, the NS is a seemingly omniscient figure. In SLA, as Mey (1981, p. 73) sardonically puts it, the NS's status as 'the uncrowned King of linguistics' is upheld.[14] NS data are thus viewed as the warranted baseline from which NNS data can be compared, and the benchmark from which judgements of appropriateness, markedness, and so forth, can be made.

(b) As a logical extension, NNSs are unproblematically viewed as the NSs' subordinates, with regard to communicative competence (the negative connotation of the 'non-' prefix is hardly coincidental).

(c) The SLA researcher approaches NS and NNS interactions in an overwhelmingly a priori fashion, viewing them as inherently problematic encounters. Thus Varonis and Gass (1985b) say: 'even with earnest nonnatives and cooperative native speakers, misunderstandings are inevitable,' (p. 328) and 'NSs and NNSs are multiply handicapped in conversations with one another' (p. 340). At the very least, NS – NNS interactions are prejudged to be somehow unusual, anomalous or extraordinary. Richards and Sukwiwat (1983), for example, claim that '[f]or the speaker of a foreign language, *any* conversational exchange with a native speaker of the target language is a form of cross-cultural encounter' (p. 113, emphasis added).

(d) NS and NNS are blanket terms, implying homogeneity throughout each group, and clearcut distinctions between them. So a NS is assumed unproblematically to be a person with a mother tongue, acquired from birth. How bilingualism, multilingualism, 'semi-lingualism,' and (first) language loss relate to the concept of NS are in large measure ignored, as is the question of whether one can become a NS in a S/FL (some of these issues are discussed in Davies, 1991).

(e) The identity categorizations NS and NNS are applied exogenously and without regard for their emic relevance. The fact that NS or NNS is only one identity from a multitude of social identities, many of which can be relevant simultaneously, and all of which are motile (father, man, friend, local, guest, opponent, husband, colleague, teacher, teammate, intimate acquaintance, stranger, brother, son, expert, novice, native speaker, uninitiated, joke teller, speaker, caller, overhearer ad infinitum) is, it seems fair to conclude, a nonissue in SLA. For the SLA researcher, only one identity *really matters*, and it matters constantly and in equal measure throughout the duration of the encounter being studied.[15]

(f) The ascendancy of NS and the assumed subserviency of NNS in SLA reflects not only a mindset of learner/nonnative-as-defective-communicator, it also illustrates the prevailing monolingual orientation of SLA (and, to some, the monolingual orientation of linguistics in general; see, e.g., Romaine, 1989, p. 1; Blyth, 1995), where monolingual NSs are taken to be the numerically (and, by implication, politically) dominant and identifiable group with which the NNS is to interact (see Blyth, 1995, p. 148; also Pennycook, 1994, pp. 136–137).[16,17] Indeed, for some, interactions with NS are seen to be the 'preferred' conditions for SLA to occur (recall that they are 'necessary and sufficient' conditions, in Long's [1981] view). This orientation fails to take account of the multilingual reality of communities (see Edwards, 1994) and the reality of more transient, interacting groups, throughout the world. In the case of English, the international status of the language means that a vast number of NS routinely interact with other NNS, in which cases English is a lingua franca.[18] In most cases, such interactions are not, at least ostensibly, undertaken for educational, instructional, or learning purposes, but are a quotidian part of life, the range of purposes, like the social settings in which they occur, varying widely. Given this state of affairs, newcomers to SLA may be surprised to discover that the study of FL use (involving both NS – NNS and NNS – NNS) in naturally occurring, everyday (noneducational) settings constitutes a small fraction of SLA research.[19]

(g) Even where NNS – NNS interactions are the object of study, a common practice within SLA is to compare observed features of interaction with 'comparable' NS interactions (i.e., so-called 'baseline' data; see, e.g., Trosborg, 1994, pp. 177–186). In the majority of cases, the NNSs being studied are unacquainted (college) students engaged in a formal learning programme and interacting in a quasi-experimental setting.

Interlanguage

It appears that people who are demonstrably not engaged in the formal learning of a L2, but who nevertheless voluntarily use a L2 in their everyday affairs (e.g., at work or play), are essentially uninteresting from the perspective of SLA research – judging by the paucity of what we may term 'everyday L2 use' studies. However, in the few studies where interest in noneducational settings is shown (e.g., Varonis & Gass, 1985a), NNSs tend to be cast in the same light as 'learners.' Thus, users of a L2 are deemed to be in a phase of transition, in terms of language. That is, their language skills and competencies are seen to be underdeveloped. Once again, the NS is brought into the picture as the definitive object of comparison. Moreover, this transitional phase is regarded as more or less systematic and predictable – as a 'system' in its own right. The system is seen to be on the move, the goal being 'target' (NS) competence. Implicit here is the (at least disputable) assumption that target or NS competence is constant, fully developed, and complete.

Therefore, apparently regular though anomalous linguistic (phonological, syntactic, morphological, etc.) features of NNS speech are termed 'fossilizations;' these are areas where movement in the system is seen to have been suspended, thus inducing linguistic petrification.[20] In a similar fashion, 'anomalous' speech acts have been deemed to result in 'pragmatic failure' (e.g., Thomas, 1983). Completion is achieved and failures are avoided (the argument goes) once the NNS has reached NS competence.

These views on a NNS/learner language system are representative of the extraordinarily influential concept of interlanguage (IL) (Selinker, 1971), described by Larsen-Freeman and Long (1991) as 'a continuum between the L1 and L2 along which all learners traverse' (p. 60). This concept, like the work undertaken under the rubric of CS, is predicated on a range of metatheoretical assumptions on what it means to be a FL speaker, the nature of a 'native' language, the nature of cognition, and the desirability of achieving native competence (though not NS status).[21] And once again, within studies of IL, what may be – and often are – social dimensions of language use tend to be viewed through the optics of individual cognition. The tensional imbalance reemerges.

This imbalance is particularly discernible in IL research because, as Rampton (1987) points out, IL studies are placed at the intersection of SLA and sociolinguistics, in the sense that both fields are concerned with language variability. Rampton's (1987) concern is with SLA's myopia in IL research, which 'runs the risk of remaining restrictively preoccupied with the space between the speaker and his grammar, rather than with the relationship between speakers and the world around them' (p. 49). The 'world around' speakers (and, presumably, hearers) is a myriad of factors, for example social relations, identities, task, physical setting, and both global and turn-by-speaking-turn agenda, each instantiated through language yet potentially influential on the way language is used. Research on speech genres, ethnography of speaking, and sociolinguistics in its many guises has irrefutably established and documented this reflexive relationship between language use and social context. Nevertheless, IL studies remain locked into a pattern of explaining variability and anomalous usage by recourse to notions of underdeveloped grammatical competence.

Yet as both Rampton (1987) and Firth (1996) show, NNSs' marked or deviant forms are not of necessity fossilizations of IL, nor can they on each and every occasion be accounted for by interference or a reduced L2 competence. Such forms may be deployed resourcefully and strategically, to accomplish social and interactional ends – for example, to display empathy, or to accomplish mutual understanding. IL studies in large measure do not appear to recognize that FL speakers are not simply at the mercy of their L2 (in)competence. The incompetence – if we wish to call it that – may in some instances also be a resource.[22] Anomalous forms of talk may be accounted for not by incompetence but by the notion of recipient design, that is, speakers purposively designing their talk in anomalous ways in response to their specific, local circumstances, for *this* coparticipant, at *this* particular sequential moment (Sacks, [1970]1992, p. 230ff.; Firth, 1996). And not only utterances are recipient designed; interpretations of others' utterances also may be said to be recipient designed. Features of talk that are initially perceived and categorized as interference or fossilizations may be more appropriately viewed as adroit, local responses to practical and discursive exigencies that have arisen in the unfolding talk, resulting, on occasions, in purposive 'codeswitching.'[23]

There are interesting connections between IL and 'input modification' research. One of these is that, in order to effect meaningful interaction, the NS appears to adopt IL-like behaviour – in the way language is simplified and adjusted to the perceived (lower) level of the NNS. The following extract was reproduced in Larsen-Freeman and Long (1991) to illustrate input modification.

Here the NS 'is female, Caucasian American, in her late twenties, and a speaker of "educated West Coast (Los Angeles) English." ' The NNS 'is a male Japanese office worker in his mid-twenties [...] He is a "beginner." This is their first meeting, which has been arranged by the researcher':

```
 1 NS:   are you a student in Japan?
 2 NNS:  no I am no (. . .) I am worker
 3 NS:   you're a worker what kind of work do you do?
 4 NNS:  uh I'm a /oSs'/ (.) /oSs'/
 5 NS:   official [official
 6 NNS:           [Official of (.) (pu.) public
 7 NS:   ah you work for the government
 8 NNS:  uhm (pref-?) (..) no?
 9 NS:   (I don't understand) no. [pre?
10 NNS:                           [/prlfek prif ker/
11 NSS:  s-Japan has uh (. . . .) many / prifkers/
12 NS:   factory (.) [factory?
13 NNS:              [no
14 NS:   what is it? can you tell me? what is that? (extract continues;
        pp. 146–147)
```

Larsen-Freeman and Long (1991) observe that the participants talk about 'here-and-now' topics, use interactional modification, produce repetitions, paraphrase, and check for confirmation. We ask: If this is 'modified' interaction, what would be the 'baseline' conversation? We do not take issue with the analysts' observations on what the participants are seen to be doing – paraphrasing, repeating, and so forth; more pressing is that data of this kind are taken to be a representation of FL interaction per se and 'foreigner talk' (i.e., NSs' actions) in general. Thus Yano, Long, and Ross (1994) offer the following overview:

> Conversational adjustments affect both the content and interactional structure of foreigner talk discourse. Where content is concerned, conversation with NNSs tends to have more of a here-and-now orientation and to treat a more predictable, narrower range of topics more briefly, for example by dealing with fewer information bits and by maintaining a lower ratio of topic-initiating to topic-continuing moves. The interactional structure of NS-NNS conversation is marked by abrupt topic-shifts, more use of questions ... more repetition of various kinds. (pp. 193–194)

Our concerns are with the validity of such claims, and with the built-in assumption that a baseline form of interaction would be different from foreigner talk solely as a result of it involving NS. We question the implication that, in initial encounters between NSs and NNSs, interaction is over-ridingly patterned as depicted above – for example, that natives and nonnatives, when interacting for the first time, routinely restrict themselves to 'here-and-now topics,' and that natives invariably adopt the role of 'information gatherer' – as is the case in the extract above.

It appears that, as a result of an urge to generalize across interactions between groups of NS and NNS, and as a result of a focus on experimental settings to the detriment of naturalistic, real-life encounters, researchers neglect the constraints and effects of setting and setting-related tasks on the structure of discourse. This raises the possibility that participants may not behave at the behest of their native or nonnative competencies and identities, but as a result of the (quasi-experimental) setting, their unfamiliarity with each other, and the setting-imposed task they have agreed to undertake.

It may be illuminating to consider why certain activities in the talk above appear to be differentially assigned, such that NS adopts the role of information gatherer, while NNS orients to and instantiates the role of information provider. Input modification researchers would most likely explain this as a result of NS's superior language competence; that is, NS is simply 'taking the initiative' (by, e.g., controlling topic). What we might allow for, however, is the possibility – borne out, we believe, in this extract – that NS is not *taking* the initiative; NS is being *given* the initiative by NNS, and is taking it on this basis. That is, both NS and NNS are collaborating in constructing meaningful discourse, and a mainstay of this collaboration is an effective 'division of labour,' based on the resources that the two parties bring to and make relevant in the interaction. This is shown in the way NSS, in line 4, produces a marked form, and repeats it in rapid succession. The repetition of a marked utterance, we suspect, may be a methodic way in which speakers can implicitly seek assistance from their interlocutor (further research is clearly requisite on this matter). This appears to be the effect here, as NS in line 5 offers a 'candidate hearing' of NNS's marked pronunciation in line 4. This is followed by NNS's acceptance of the candidate hearing and his incorporation of NS's pronunciation (*official*) into his own turn (line 6). The phenomenon is repeated at lines 10, 11, and 12. Rather than dominance, incompetence, and underdeveloped FL ability (i.e., IL), we are witness to collaboration, sharing, resourcefulness, the skillful and artful application of a mechanism to effect collaboration in talk, and thus an efficient division of labour between the participants.

The materials considered in Zuengler (1993), Zuengler and Bent (1991), and Wagner (1996) also appear to challenge the 'modification' researcher's reliance on an assumption of inequalities in competence to explain features of NS – NNS interactions. Zuengler and Bent refer to the importance of content knowledge for the level of participation in conversations. Wagner's data hints at the importance of factors such as social and institutional roles, and setting. In Wagner's study, the NNS is a customer, conversing with a (NS) salesman in her (the NNS's) own home. In this case it is the 'customer' and 'salesman' identities that appear to come to the fore, with NNS doing the information gathering and the NS salesman doing the providing – this despite NNS's demonstrably limited syntactic and phonologic competence in the L2. Here, then, the NNS/NS identities are overridden (they appear, if anything, to be exchanged), while alternative identities – instantiated in the talk – are made relevant.

The type and incidence of modifications in NS – NNS interactions, indeed *all* types of interactions, are intricately related to the interactants' local agenda, the social and institutional identities that are made relevant and instantiated in the actual encounter and, not least, the demands and contingencies that become relevant in the minutiae of the talk itself. In short, it is at least debatable whether there is such a thing as 'interlanguage per se,' and it is problematic to hold that there exists a general, universal set of rules for how NS and NNS – *as* NS and

NNS – converse. Equally questionable is the notion of there being a comparable baseline of NS – NS interactions. This simplification is once again predicated on a tendentious assumption that NSs represent a homogeneous entity, responding on each and every occasion in a patterned and predictable fashion.

The Notion of 'Faultless' Discourse

This final section examines briefly another manifestation of the mindset of the 'learner' or 'nonnative' as per definition a deficient communicator, while casting critical light on the prevailing SLA view of discourse processes. Gass and Varonis (1985a) present the following two extracts involving two NNSs:

> (extract 1)
> 1 NNS1: My father now is retire
> 2 NNS2: retire?
> 3 NNS1: yes
> 4 NNS2: oh yeah
> (extract 2)
> 1 NNS1: This is your two term?
> 2 NNS2: Pardon me?
> 3 NNS1: Two term, this is this term is t term your two term? (p. 151)

Gass and Varonis (1985a) view these extracts as exemplifications of 'exchanges in which there is some overt indication that understanding between participants has not been complete.' According to the authors, lines 1 from each extract contain 'unaccepted input' that act as 'triggers.' These serve to 'stimulate or invoke incomplete understanding on the part of the hearer' (p. 151). However, in the case of extract 1, it is at least debatable whether the interlocutor (NNS2) demonstrates any kind of 'incomplete understanding,' or that the preceding turn is somehow 'unaccepted.' A more convincing case can surely be made for the interpretation that NNS2's reuse of the word 'retire' (line 2) is seen – by NNS1 – as a request for confirmation, rather than as indicating 'misunderstanding' or 'unacceptance.' NNS1 provides confirmation in the subsequent turn (line 3). Further along, NNS2 displays the acceptability of this interpretation in line 4 ('oh yeah'). Similar to the Faerch and Kasper (1983) extract above, Gass and Varonis appear to be basing their judgement of acceptability and understandability of line 1 on an implicit assumption that marked usage (i.e., the marked word order of 'my father now is retire') is problematic. This view distorts the analyst's interpretations of what is going on in the talk, such that NNS2's repetition of the word – here, 'retire' (line 2) – is taken to indicate a problem in understanding.

The same applies to extract 2. Here NNS2's 'pardon me' (line 2) is adjudged to be indicative of a problem in understanding on NNS2's part, or that NNS1's turn 1 is unacceptable. Other interpretations are not considered. For example, NNS2's 'pardon me' is not considered indicative of NNS2's preoccupation with other things during the uttering of NNS1's line 1, or indicative of an acoustics-related problem. Reduced competence is seemingly *the* metric upon which discourse is interpreted by the analysts – regardless of interactants' interpretations, which suggest that other factors may be at play.

Related to this is Gass and Varonis's (1985a) discourse model, predicated on an assumption of the existence of a 'normal' form of discourse that is free of misunderstandings and such unaccepted input routines as above. Gass and Varonis (1985a) present the following extract:

1 NNS1: I'm living in Osaka
2 NNS2: Osaka?
3 NNS1: yeah
4 NNS2: yeah Osaka, Osaka
5 NNS1: What do you mean?
6 NNS2: Osaka (Japanese word)
7 NNS1: oh
8 NNS2: I'm not really mean Osaka city. It's near city.
9 NNS1: near city? (p. 152)

According to Gass and Varonis, the 'trigger' is NNS1's turn at line 1. This 'initiates a "push-down" in the conversation, which continues until interlocutors have resolved the difficulty and "pop" back up to the main discourse' (p. 152). What we question here is the implication there is a main discourse devoid of 'triggers,' 'repairs,' and 'misunderstandings,' one where progression is concomitant with problem-free interaction. This notion represents an erroneous conception of discourse processes – produced by NS or NNS. Misunderstandings and repair sequences like the one above are not aberrations. Rather, they are integral parts of the progression of normal, conversational discourse, regardless of the social identities of the actors involved.

Concluding remarks

By critiquing what we take to be prevailing SLA views on discourse and communication, this article has sought to argue for a reconceptualization of SLA that would significantly – though, we feel, justifiably and necessarily – enlarge the ontological and empirical parameters of the field. The reconceptualization we call for is based on a belief that methodologies, theories, and foci within SLA reflect an imbalance between cognitive and mentalistic orientations, and social and contextual orientations to language, the former orientation being unquestionably in the ascendancy. This has resulted in a skewed perspective on discourse and communication, one that is accompanied by an analytic mindset that conceives of the FL speaker as a deficient communicator struggling to overcome an underdeveloped L2 competence, striving to reach the 'target' competence of an idealized NS. For SLA, then, FL learning and interaction are inherently problematic undertakings. What SLA tends to overlook, however – perhaps because it is less psychologically salient – is that people do, often, succeed in communicating (in a FL) by using whatever competencies they have at their disposal. It is the explication of the successful deployment of communicative resources – as indicators of the dynamics of S/FL acquisition – that should, among other things, be added to SLA's research agenda.

In essence, we call for work within SLA that endeavours to adopt what we have referred to as a holistic approach to and outlook on language and language acquisition, an approach that problematizes and explores the conventional binary distinction between 'social' and 'individual' (or cognitive) approaches to language use and language learning, that attends to the dynamics as well as the summation of language acquisition, that is more emically and interactionally attuned, and that is critically sensitive towards the theoretical status of fundamental concepts (particularly 'learner,' 'native,' 'nonnative,' and 'interlanguage'). Such a call for a reconceptualized SLA lends support to like-minded sentiments expressed recently by Hall (1995), Rampton (1987, 1995b, 1997), Pennycook (1994), Kramsch (1995), Blyth (1995), Roberts (1996), and Block (1996). This article attempted to point out some of the existing theoretical, methodological, and conceptual problems – as we perceive them – within SLA, and to sketch, albeit briefly, the ramifications of a reconceptualized SLA. A crucially important and challenging next step is to develop, in much greater detail, the theoretical bases, a research agenda, and a set of methodological approaches that are aligned with the 'reconceptualization' here espoused.

SLA is directly concerned with the nature of FL acquisition and the development of language-based knowledge and competencies. It has firmly established interests in matters of language education and pedagogy. More obliquely, it is concerned with multilinguality, language socialization, linguistic variability, 'foreignness' and 'nativeness.' As such, SLA is part of the nexus of approaches to the wider, interdisciplinary study of language, discourse, and social interaction. It thus has the potential to make significant contributions to a wide range of research issues conventionally seen to reside outside its boundaries. Yet that potential is not being realised while the field in general perpetuates the theoretical imbalances and skewed perspectives on discourse and communication exemplified above.

Researchers working with a reconceptualized SLA will be better able to understand and explicate how language is used *as it is being acquired through interaction*, and used resourcefully, contingently, and contextually. Language is not only a cognitive phenomenon, the product of the individual's brain; it is also fundamentally a social phenomenon, acquired and used interactively, in a variety of contexts for myriad practical purposes. The time has come for SLA to recognize fully the theoretical and methodological implications of these facts, a crucial implication being a need to redress the imbalance of perspectives and approaches within the field, and the need to work towards the evolution of a holistic, bio-social SLA.

Acknowledgments

Alan Firth gratefully acknowledges financial support for this research provided by the C. W. Obel Family Foundation. For discussions and detailed comments on this paper we are indebted to Jack Bilmes and Dennis Day. The paper was first presented at the International Applied Linguistics Association (AILA) conference in Jyväskylä, Finland, in August, 1996. Particular thanks to our official respondents at the conference, Gabriele Kasper, Joan Kelly Hall, Tony Liddicoat, Nanda Poulisse, and Ben Rampton, as well as to members of the audience, for their stimulating remarks and criticisms, many of which have been incorporated into the published version of the paper. The authors alone take responsibility for the article's remaining shortcomings.

Please address all correspondence regarding this paper to Dr. Alan Firth.

Notes

1 At the risk of overgeneralizing, we conceive SLA to be a discrete and institutionalized field of study; we do not deny that research within the field is varied in terms of theoretical approaches and methodologies, as is the case in all collective endeavours within developing fields. Nevertheless, our critique of SLA is based on the view that the field has core interests, theoretical predilections, methodologies, and basic assumptions. It is this SLA 'core' that has the focus of our attention here.

2 Other important and related influences at that time were John L. Austin's (1962) ('ordinary language') theories of speaking as a form of action, and H. P. Grice's 'William James Lectures' (1960, subsequently published in part as Grice, 1975). Both Austin's and Grice's work, like Hymes's, extended the scope of linguistics into language use, that is, language beyond grammar (see Hanks, 1996, p. 92).

3 The debate about the 'individual' and the 'social' aspects of language predated Hymes and Chomsky, of course. See, for example, Saussure's (1916/1959) contention that speech was individual, that it 'depended on the free will of the speaker' (p. 19), and Volosinov's (1930/1973) outright rejection of this, including his claim that '[t]he immediate social situation and the broader social milieu *wholly* determine – and determine from within, so to speak – the structure of an utterance' (p. 86, emphasis added). Hymes's predecessors who promulgated a more 'contextual' view of language included Malinowski (1923) and Firth (1937), and more immediately, Jakobson (1960) and Goodenough (1957). See also Brown, Malmkjaer, and Williams (1996).

4 Our observations on CS research are a condensed form of Wagner and Firth (1997).

5 On the distinction between researcher's *resources* and *topics*, see Zimmerman and Pollner (1971).

6 The transcription format has been altered from Faerch and Kasper's original, though no detail has been omitted. In passing, we may point out the lack of detail in the transcript (e.g., on features such as pause length, word and/or syllable stress, intonation, and precise onset of overlaps – features that are reproducible, see, e.g., Sacks, Schegloff, & Jefferson, 1974, pp. 731–733) hinders others' reanalysis of the transcript, inasmuch as such features may have important consequences for the way discourse is interpreted.

7 A caveat on the notion of 'negotiation': The term 'conjoint negotiation' of meaning is not meant to imply that in order to talk openly and explicitly parties attempt to reach some kind of definitive agreement on the meaning of a word or utterance (although such 'negotiations' may take place [e.g., between lawyers drafting a contract], in everyday circumstances they are rare). Normally, such negotiations are done implicitly, in the way an interlocutor will display acceptance or understanding of the meaningfulness of the other's turn or utterance by producing an appropriate response. There are strong sceptical arguments – put forward by Schutz (1932/1967), for example – that agents cannot, in any theoretical sense, be said to fully understand one another, since no two people share identical interpretational schemes. However, in practice people *do* make common sense assumptions that they understand one another (see Pollner, 1987).

8 On notions of understanding in discourse, see Taylor's (1992) outstanding exposition.

9 This is the basic proposition of the notion of 'adjacency pair' relationships in discourse, also encapsulated in what Schegloff (1968) termed 'conditional relevance'; see also Levinson (1983, p. 306).

10 Jefferson (1987) has referred to this as 'embedded repair': This is the activity of covertly repairing others' perceivedly anomalous or marked usage in one's own subsequent talk. Thus L's 'historie' is subsequently repaired in an embedded way by NS as 'history.'

11 Also, the very fact that NS continued to use the word 'history' in the three questions at lines 7 and 9, in spite of L's lack of responses to the first two questions, strongly suggests that NS assumes that L knows the word and, moreover, intended to use it in its sense of a school subject. If NS did see 'history' as being a problem for L, presumably she would not have used the word repeatedly in her three questions.

12 Firth (1996) analysed how parties to (foreign language) talk are skillfully and differentially able to assess the gravity of misinterpretations, misspeakings, anomalous usage, and so forth, in their endeavours to construct coherent, meaningful discourse.

13 Although these papers were published over a decade ago (as was also the case with Faerch and Kasper, 1983), we feel that their influence on the field in general, and the contemporary currency of the views expressed within them, warrant their inclusion and examination here.

14 A useful collection of papers on the concept of native speaker in linguistics is Coulmas (1981). See also Davies's (1991) study *The Native Speaker in Applied Linguistics*.

15 The extension of this is *not* that the SLA researcher must, on all occasions, refrain from using the categorization NS or NNS. Categorizations such as these (and a multitude of others, e.g., speaker, hearer, male, female, caller, doctor, patient) are necessary shorthands for the analyst-observer. What we point out, once again, is the predominance of the binary NS/NNS distinction, as well as the *possibility* that greater emic sensitivity towards identity categorizations *may*, at specific analytical moments, or in general, prove to be profitable for the SLA researcher.

16 That monolingualism is viewed as the norm, and multi- or bi-lingualism the exception (even aberration), is borne out in the premise of the *one language only* policy underpinning the so-called 'Natural Method' of (foreign) language teaching; see Kachru (1990, p. 16).

17 On the whole, SLA researchers implicitly view NNS as being synonymous with 'learner' (see, e.g., Bardovi-Harlig & Hartford, 1995, p. 125).

18 McCrum, Cran, and MacNeil (1986, p. 19) note that 'English is used by at least 750 million people, and barely half of those speak it as a mother tongue.' A 1988 survey (Hesselbeg-Møller, 1988) of over 500 Danish businesses operating internationally revealed that English was the chosen foreign language in over 80% of all contacts. Contacts with Anglophone countries made up no more than 20% of all business interactions. English is the official language of international air and sea travel; it has been described as the lingua franca sine qua non in the European Union headquarters in

Brussels (Dinyon & Greaves, 1989); members of the Free Trade Association conduct their business in English, even though no English-speaking countries are represented (Bryson, 1990, p. 2).

19 'Naturally occurring' in the sense that the interactions take place, or would have taken place, regardless of the researcher's interest, involvement, or presence.

20 The 'anomalies' are invariably characterized as such due to a comparison with a (often idealized) NS.

21 'Metatheoretical' in the sense that such assumptions are rarely, if ever, openly discussed, presented or debated within SLA; they remain tacit. On metatheoretical assumptions in sociolinguistics in general, see Figueroa (1994).

22 Davey (1993), for example, describes how L1 (Dutch) lexical items were creatively deployed as 'nonce' forms in interactions involving Dutch and Danish business personnel, speaking English as a lingua franca.

23 Rampton (1987) compared the approaches to linguistic variability in sociolinguistics and SLA, and noted how the two approaches perceived identical linguistic phenomena in different ways, such that '[c]ode-switching in sociolinguistics winds up as interference in SLA' (p. 55).

References

Aston, G. (1993). Notes on the interlanguage of comity. In G. Kasper & S. Blum-Kulka (Eds.), *Interlanguage pragmatics* (pp. 224–250). New York: Oxford University Press.

Austin, J. L. (1962). *How to do things with words*. Oxford: Clarendon Press.

Bakhtin, M. M. (1981). *The dialogic imagination*. Austin: University of Texas Press.

Bardovi-Harlig, K., & Hartford, B. S. (1995). The construction of discourse by nonnative speakers: Introduction. *Studies in Second Language Acquisition, 17*, 125–128.

Beretta, A. (1991). Theory construction in SLA: Complimentary and opposition. *Studies in Second Language Acquisition, 13*, 495–511.

Beretta, A., & Crookes, G. (1993). Cognitive and social determinants of discovery in SLA. *Applied Linguistics, 14*, 250–275.

Block, D. (1996). Not so fast: Some thoughts on theory culling, relativism, accepted findings and the heart and soul of SLA. *Applied Linguistics, 17*, 63–83.

Blyth, C. (1995). Redefining the boundaries of language use: The foreign language classroom as a multilingual speech community. In C. Kramsch (Ed.), *Redefining the boundaries of language study* (pp. 145–183). Boston, MA: Heinle.

Bremer, K., Roberts, C., Vasseur, M., Simonot, M., & Broeder, P. (1996). *Achieving understanding: Discourse in intercultural encounters*. London: Longman.

Brown, P., Malmkjær, K., & Williams, J. (Eds.). (1996). *Performance and competence in second language acquisition*. Cambridge: Cambridge University Press.

Bryson, B. (1990). *Mother tongue: The English Language*. Harmondsworth, England: Penguin.

Chomsky, N. (1957). *Syntactic structures*. The Hague, Netherlands: Mouton.

Chomsky, N. (1965). *Aspects of the theory of syntax*. Cambridge, MA: MIT Press.

Chomsky, N. (1968). *Language and mind*. New York: Harcourt, Brace, Jovanovich.

Chomsky, N. (1976). *Reflections on language*. New York: Temple Smith.

Cicourel, A. (1973). *Cognitive sociology*. Harmondsworth, England: Penguin.

Clark, H., & Clark, E. (1977). *Psychology and language: An introduction to psycholinguistics*. New York: Harcourt, Brace, Jovanovich.

Crookes, G. (1992). Theory format and SLA theory. *Studies in Second Language Acquisition, 14*, 425–449.

Corder, S. P. (1967). The significance of learners' errors. *International Review of Applied Linguistics, 5*, 161–169.

Corder, S. P. (1973). *Introducing applied linguistics*. Harmondsworth, England: Penguin.

Coulmas, F. (Ed.). (1981). *A festschrift for native speaker*, The Hague, Netherlands: Mouton.

Davey, W. (1993). *An interaction analysis of a reconnaissance interview in which English is used as a 'lingua franca' between non-native speakers, with particular reference to two varieties of cooperation: collaboration and collusion*. Unpublished master's thesis, University of Birmingham, England.

Davies, A. (1991) *The native speaker in applied linguistics*. Edinburgh: Edinburgh University Press.

Dinyon, M., & Greaves, W. (1989). Articles in *The Times*, (1989, 23–24 October), p. 14.

Dulay, H., Burt, M., & Krashen, S. (1982). *Language two*. New York: Oxford University Press.

Edwards, J. (1994). *Multilingualism*. London: Routledge.

Ellis, R. (1990). *Instructed second language acquisition*. Oxford, England: Blackwell.

Ellis, R. (1994). *The study of second language acquisition*. Oxford: Oxford University Press.

Figueroa, E. (1994). *Sociolinguistic metatheory*. Oxford, England: Pergamon.

Firth, A. (1996). The discursive accomplishment of 'normality:' On lingua franca English and Conversation Analysis. *Journal of Pragmatics, 26*, 237–259.

Firth, J. R. (1937). *The tongues of men*. Oxford: Oxford University Press.

Færch, C., & Kasper, G. (1983). Plans and strategies in foreign language communication. In C. Færch & G. Kasper (Eds.), *Strategies in interlanguage communication* (pp. 20–60). London: Longman.

Gass, S. M., & Varonis, E. M. (1985a). Task variation and nonnative/nonnative negotiation of meaning. In S. M. Gass & C. G. Madden (Eds.), *Input in second language acquisition* (pp. 149–161). Rowley, MA: Newbury House.

Gass, S. M., & Varonis, E. M. (1985b). Variation in native speaker speech modification to non-native speakers. *Studies in Second Language Acquisition, 7*, 37–57.

Goodenough, W. H. (1957). Cultural anthropology and linguistics, *Georgetown University Monograph Series on Language and Linguistics, 9*, 167–173.

Goodwin, C. (1979). The interactive construction of a sentence in natural conversation. In G. Psathas (Ed.), *Everyday language: Studies in ethnomethodology* (pp. 77–121). New York: Irvington.

Gregg, K. (1990). The variable competence model for second language acquisition, and why it isn't. *Applied Linguistics, 11*, 364–383.

Gregg, K. (1993). Taking explanation seriously; or, let a couple of flowers bloom. *Applied Linguistics, 14*, 276–294.

Grice, H. P. (1975). Logic and conversation. In P. Cole & J. Morgan (Eds.), *Syntax and semantics: Vol. 3, Speech acts* (pp. 41–58). London: Academic.

Gumperz, J. J. (1982). *Discourse strategies*. Cambridge: Cambridge University Press.

Hall, J. K. (1995). (Re)creating our worlds with words: A sociohistorical perspective of face-to-face interaction. *Applied Linguistics, 16*, 206–232.

Halliday, M. A. K. (1978). *Language as a social semiotic: The social interpretation of language and meaning*. London: Edward Arnold.

Hanks, W. F. (1996). *Language and communicative practices*. Boulder, CO: Westview Press.

Harré, R., & Gilletz, G. (1994). *The discursive mind*. London: Sage.

Harris, R. (1981). *The language myth*. London: Duckworth.

Heritage, J. (1984). *Garfinkel and ethnomethodology*. Oxford, England: Polity.

Hesselberg-Møller, N. (1988). *Eksport og uddannelse*. Copenhagen: Industrirådet (The Danish Council of Trade and Industry).

Hymes, D. (1961). Functions of speech: The evolutionary approach. In F. Gruber (Ed.), *Anthropology and education* (pp. 55–83). Philadelphia: University of Pennsylvania Press.

Hymes, D. (1962). The ethnography of speaking. In T. Gladwin & W. Sturteant (Eds.), *Anthropology and human behavior* (pp. 15–53). Washington, DC: Anthropological Society of Washington.

Hymes, D. (1974). *Foundations in sociolinguistics: An ethnographic approach*. Philadelphia: University of Pennsylvania Press.

Jakobson, R. (1960). Concluding statement: linguistics and poetics. In T. Sebeok (Ed.), *Style in language* (pp. 350–373). Cambridge, MA: MIT Press.

Jefferson, G. (1987). On exposed and embedded correction in conversation. In G. Button & J. R. E. Lee (Eds.), *Talk and social organisation* (pp. 86–100). Clevedon, England: Multilingual Matters.

Kachru, B. (1990). World Englishes and applied linguistics. *World Englishes, 9*, 3–20.

Kasper, G., & Kellerman, E. (Eds.). (1997). *Communication strategies: Psycholinguistic and sociolinguistic perspectives*. London: Longman.

Katz, J. J. (1966). *The philosophy of language*. New York: Harper & Row.

Kramsch, C. (1995). Introduction: Making the invisible visible. In C. Kramsch (Ed.), *Redefining the boundaries of language study* (pp. ix–xxxiii). Boston: Heinle.

Larsen-Freeman, D., & Long, M. (1991). *An introduction to second language acquisition research*. London: Longman.

Levinson, S. C. (1983). *Pragmatics*. Cambridge: Cambridge University Press.

Lightbown, P., & Spada, N. (1993). *How languages are learned*. Oxford: Oxford University Press.

Long, M. H. (1981). Input, interaction and second language acquisition. In H. Winitz (Ed.), *Native language and foreign acquisition* (sic). *Annals of the New York Academy of Sciences, 379*, 259–278.

Long, M. H. (1990). The least a second language acquisition theory needs to explain. *TESOL Quarterly, 24*, 649–666.

Long, M. H. (1993). Assessment strategies for SLA theories. *Applied Linguistics, 14*, 225–249.

Malinowski, B. (1923). The problem of meaning in primitive languages. In C. K. Ogden & I. A. Richards (Eds.), *The meaning of meaning* (pp. 295–336). New York: Harcourt, Brace, & World.

McCrum, R., Cran, W., & MacNeil, R. (1986). *The story of English*. London: Faber.

Mey, J. (1981). 'Right or wrong, my native speaker:' Estant les régestes du noble souverain de l'empirie linguistic avec un renvoy au mesme roy. In F. Coulmas (Ed.), *A festschrift for native speaker* (pp. 69–84). The Hague, Netherlands: Mouton.

Pennycook, A. (1994). *The cultural politics of English as an international language*. London: Longman.

Pinker, S. (1994). *The language instinct*. London: Allen Lane.

Pollner, M. (1987). *Mundane reason*. Cambridge: Cambridge University Press.

Poulisse, N. (1993). A theoretical account of lexical communication strategies. In R. Schreuder & B. Weltens (Eds.), *The bilingual lexicon* (pp. 157–189). Amsterdam: John Benjamins.

Poulisse, N., & Bongaerts, T. (1990, April). *A closer look at the strategy of transfer*. Paper presented at the 9th AILA Conference, Thessaloniki, Greece.

Rampton, B. (1987). Stylistic variability and not speaking 'normal' English: Some post-Labovian approaches and their implications for the study of interlanguage. In R. Ellis (Ed.), *Second language acquisition in context* (pp. 47–58). Englewood Cliffs, NJ: Prentice Hall.

Rampton, B. (1995a). *Crossing*. London: Longman.

Rampton, B. (1995b). Politics and change in research in applied linguistics. *Applied Linguistics, 16*, 233–256.

Rampton, B. (1997). A sociolinguistic perspective on L2 communication strategies. In G. Kasper & E. Kellerman (Eds.), *Communication strategies: Psycholinguistic and sociolinguistic perspectives*. London: Longman.

Richards, J., & Sukwiwat, M. (1983). Language transfer and conversational competence. *Applied Linguistics, 4*, 113–125.

Roberts, C. (1996). Taking stock: contexts and reflections. In K. Bremer, C. Roberts, M. Vasseur, M. Simonot, & P. Broeder, *Achieving understanding: Discourse in intercultural encounters* (pp. 207–238). London: Longman.

Romaine, S. (1989). *Bilingualism*. Oxford, England: Blackwell.

Sacks, H. (1970/1992). *Lectures on conversation*. (Gail Jefferson, Ed.). Oxford, England: Blackwell.

Sacks, H., Schegloff, E. A., & Jefferson, G. (1974). A simplest systematics for the organization of turn-taking for conversation. *Language, 50*, 696–735.

Sampson, E. E. (1993). *Celebrating the other*. Hemel Hempstead, England: Harvester Wheatsheaf.

Sampson, G. (1980). *Schools of linguistics: Competition and evolution*. London: Hutchinson.

Schegloff, E. A. (1968). Sequencing in conversational openings. *American Anthropologist, 70*, 1075–1095.

Schegloff, E. A. (1992). Repair after next turn: The last structurally provided defense of intersubjectivity in conversation. *American Journal of Sociology, 98*, 1295–1345.

Schegloff, E. A., & Sacks, H. (1973). Opening up closings. *Semiotica, 7,* 289–327.

Schutz, A. (1967). *The phenomenology of the social world* (G. Walsh & F. Lehnert, Trans.), Evanston, IL; Northwestern University Press (original work published in 1932).

Selinker, L. (1971). Interlanguage. *International Review of Applied Linguistics, 10,* 209–231.

Shannon, C., & Weaver, W. (1949). *The mathematical theory of communication.* Champaign, IL: University of Illinois Press.

Sperber, D., & Wilson, D. (1986). *Relevance.* Cambridge, MA: Harvard University Press.

Stern, H. H. (1983). *Fundamental concepts of language teaching.* Oxford: Oxford University Press.

Streek, J. (1980). Speech acts in interaction: A critique of Searle. *Discourse Processes, 3,* 133–153.

Taylor, T. J. (1992). *Mutual misunderstanding.* London: Routledge.

Thomas, J. (1983). Cross-cultural pragmatic failure. *Applied Linguistics, 4,* 91–112.

Trosborg, A. (1994). *Interlanguage pragmatics: Requests, complaints and apologies.* Berlin: Mouton.

Varonis, E. M., & Gass, S. M., (1985a). Non-native/Non-native conversations: A model for negotiation of meaning. *Applied Linguistics, 6,* 71–90.

Varonis, E. M., & Gass, S. M. (1985b). Miscommunication in native/non-native conversation. *Language in Society, 14,* 327–343.

Volosinov, V. N. (1973). *Marxism and the philosophy of language.* (L. Matejka & J. R. Titunik, Trans.). New York: Seminar Press (original work published 1930).

Wagner, J. (1996). Foreign language acquisition through interaction: A critical review of research on conversational adjustments. *Journal of Pragmatics, 23* (8), 215–235.

Wagner, J., & Firth, A. (1997). Communication strategies at work. In G. Kasper & E. Kellerman (Eds.), *Communication strategies: Psycholinguistic and sociolinguistic perspectives.* London: Longman.

Wertsch, J. V. (1991). *Voices of the mind.* Hemel Hempstead, England: Harvester-Wheatsheaf.

Yano, Y., Long, M. H., & Ross, S. (1994). The effects of simplified and elaborated texts on foreign language reading comprehension. *Language Learning, 44,* 189–219.

Zimmerman, D. H., & Pollner, M. (1971). The everyday world as a phenomenon. In J. Douglas (Ed.), *Understanding everyday life* (pp. 80–103). London: Routledge & Kegan Paul.

Zuengler, J. (1992). Accommodation in native–nonnative interactions: Going beyond the 'what' to the 'why' in second language research. In H. Giles, N. Coupland, & J. Coupland (Eds.), *The Context of accommodation: Developments in applied sociolinguistics* (pp. 223–244). Cambridge: Cambridge University Press.

Zuengler, J. (1993). Explaining NNS interactional behavior: The effect of conversational topic. In G. Kasper & S. Blum-Kulka (Eds.), *Interlanguage progmatics* (pp. 184–195). New York: Oxford University Press.

Zuengler, J., & Bent, B. (1991). Relative knowledge of content domain: An influence on native – non-native conversations. *Applied Linguistics, 12*, 394–415.

Text 21

Gabriele Kasper

'A' Stands for Acquisition: A Response to Firth and Wagner

Firth and Wagner's (F&W) paper raises important issues about second language (L2) studies. Its call for a more critical examination of taken-for-granted concepts in L2 research is well taken, and so is the admonition to tighten up our transcription practices when we work with conversational data. In my comments, I will focus on some positions advanced by the authors that I find problematic.[1]

First, I shall ruthlessly exploit my privileged knowledge of the first transcript that F&W reanalyzed. The continuation of this transcript was published in Færch, Haastrup, and Phillipson (1984, p. 31). It reads as presented in Table 1:

Table 1
Transcript of *historie* Conversation

```
NS but you like reading books about                          aha –
L                               not about hist er this history –      you

NS
L    know – er er young histories – er not not with this old thing you know

NS      aha                  (laugh) in er in er for example – what
L    kings or – all that – but er (laugh)

NS – 1930– or so – do you mean – recent – in more recent years like that
L                                                  yes er maybe

NS – er I mean in years which aren't so far away – from us now –
L                                                  er – a

NS
L    book er – a a history is – maybe on a boy – girl and – er this er young

NS               oh you mean a story –     maybe-just a story – about
L    people life and              yer –           yer

NS people –     yes not not necessarily not – in the past   no – I see yes
L        yer –                                 no

NS – no now I understand you (laugh)
L                  (laugh)
```

Note. NS = Native Speaker: L = Learner

I am unable to detect any evidence in this data that the Danish learner changed her mind about what she wanted to talk about – reading stories or reading about history. From the videotape, which is available from the English Department of the University of Copenhagen and has been shown in Denmark and throughout Scandinavia on many occasions, there is every evidence in the first part of the conversation that the Danish student used the Danish word *historie*, knowing that this was not a good solution for what she wanted to express: She spoke more slowly, more softly, and looked at her interlocutor for confirmation. Granted, this information is not included in the transcript and hence it is not publicly available. The transcript is all the reader can go by.

This small point of contention raises a number of bigger issues more important than quibbling about multiple interpretations of this particular transcript. First of all, there is a lot of conversational data around in L2 research, but not all conversational data require equal treatment. As has been said repeatedly, all transcription is necessarily selective. How data is transcribed, analyzed, and presented depends on the research objective, the researcher's theoretical commitment, and not least, the context of presentation. For instance, adjacency pairs were identified by Sacks as a conversational unit on the basis of very carefully transcribed conversations, following a particular method of transcription suited for the project of Conversation Analysis (CA), that is, demonstrating how social order is constructed at the microlevel of conversational interaction. Any textbook on discourse analysis examines adjacency pairs, but usually the exchanges presented for illustration are either plausible inventions or, when extracted from authentic conversation, presented in an extremely reductive fashion, as in the standard examples for greeting-greeting (A: Hello. – B: Hi.) and question-answer pairs (A: How are you? – B: Fine.) (e.g., Brown & Yule, 1983, p. 230). I do not think there is anything wrong with this. A more data-loyal presentation could obscure the purpose at hand, which is to demonstrate a structural relationship between utterances in adjacent turns. The *historie* example is placed at the beginning of a theoretical article on communication strategies, which is a chapter in a book on communication strategies. Its purpose is to illustrate different categories of communication strategies, and it so happened that the phenomena we categorized as communication strategies, according to the adopted model of speech production, conveniently occurred in a continuous stretch of interactional talk. We could just as well have used data from a picture description task or other noninteractional data, but then we would not have contributed to this enjoyable controversy.

A more interesting and important point is the theory-dependency of transcription. Ochs (1979) discussed this issue in a well-known paper, demonstrating, among other things, that transcript arrangements may privilege certain interlocutors over others. Ehlich and Rehbein's HIAT system (*halb-interpretative Arbeitstranskriptionen*, 'semi-interpretive work transcription,' e.g., Ehlich, 1993), adopts as its organizational principle that of a musical score, which represents each interlocutor's speech activity on continuous horizontal lines; thus preconceived categorizations of verbal production as turns are avoided. A simplified version of the HIAT system is illustrated in the *historie* transcript above. Of course, any turn-based transcript makes assumptions about the definition and identification of turns; whether these turn assignments are consonant with interlocutors' perceptions, that is, whether they reflect emic categorization, is not at all clear. In the CHAT system, the transcription system of the CHILDES database (MacWhinney, 1995), the unit per line is the utterance, reflecting a consensus among many first language (L1) acquisition researchers that the utterance is an appropriate unit of analysis for studying the development of children's linguistic knowledge. For L2 data, a similar point has been made by Crookes (1990). An attempt to adapt CHAT to written speech act data proved unsuccessful because the utterance is *not* an adequate unit of analysis for speech act data. The point is that there is no transcription system that is privileged over others in and of itself. Transcription adequacy is always relative to the adopted theory and research goals. This point has also been emphasized in Edward and Lampert's (1993) book *Talking data*, which discusses a number of the most frequently used transcription systems, including the HIAT system.

There is thus a three-way dependency – theory shapes transcripts, transcripts shape results, the results shape theory. I fully join F&W's complaint that, in L2 research, this circle of dependencies has not always received the attention it deserves. But this complaint is not new, and it may be helpful to remind ourselves that more careful transcription was advocated in the past by L2 researchers representing very different traditions. In continental European second and foreign language classroom research, researchers like Wagner (1983), Rehbein (1984), Bolte and Herrlitz (1986) and others used the HIAT system because intrinsically interactional discourse activities such as repair, elicitations, and feedback require a transcript that clearly represents the flow of participants' speech activity relative to each other, without predetermining fundamental categories such as turns. The other example of a research tradition that has paid even closer attention to the finer details of speech activity than the transcription conventions in CA or HIAT comes from the quarters that are among the targets of F&W's critique, namely psycholinguistic research on L2 speech production. Especially in the Kassel project, scholars like Dechert, Möhle, and Raupach (1984) used very fine-grained transcription that is capable of capturing temporal characteristics of speech, such as different kinds of pauses, false starts, drawls, changes in the rate of articulation, and so on. The theoretical assumption underlying such detailed notation is that temporal variables provide a window to both the representation of linguistic knowledge and the processes of speech production. In communication strategy (CS) research, for example, these features of speech production, together with retrospective reports, have been interpreted as indicators of planning decisions and lexical search (e.g., Færch & Kasper, 1983; Poulisse, Bongaerts, & Kellerman, 1987). In L2 *acquisition* research, it would indeed be helpful to pay closer attention to the temporal characteristics of speech because they may be one indicator of interlanguage development. So, with regard to transcription, we should transcribe adequately to the research purpose at hand. CA conventions have no inherent superiority over other notation systems.

Moving onwards and upwards to the conceptual level, F&W critique three fundamental concepts of L2 (acquisition) research: those of non-native speaker, learner, and interlanguage (IL). Again, I share their viewpoint to some extent, as I have written in several places (e.g., Kasper, 1995) and elaborated in my 1993 AILA keynote. But because I have already aligned myself in that way, I will now take a critical stance towards F&W's positions, in celebration of the dialogic principle.

To start with learner and nonnative speaker, these are constructs invented by practitioners of L2 studies in order to talk about the kinds of agents that are the object of their inquiry. As such, these notions are highly reductionist in that they abstract from the complex multiple identities that constitute real people. Of course, all social sciences, even disciplines such as anthropology that favor holistic and socially situated approaches to research, such as ethnography, construct their idealized agents by reducing away what seems trivial in terms of the adopted theory. Surely academic disciplines, and approaches within them, differ according to the degree to which they operate in a holistic and contextualized manner versus a particularizing and isolating fashion, but I think it is debatable whether the conversation analyst's 'conversationalist' is any less reductionist than the cognitive psychologist's 'limited capacity information processor.' The constructs 'nonnative speaker' and 'learner' focus upon the aspect that is *common* to the studied agents, and relevant in the global research context (or discourse universe) of L2 study generally and L2 acquisition (SLA) specifically. As F&W note, the generic notions 'learner' or 'nonnative speaker' are more or less specified in studies, mostly in terms of L1, L2 proficiency level, length of residence in the target community, age, gender, and sometimes but not often, social class; if the focus is on individual differences, we find all sorts of cognitive and affective variables specified as well. These learner variables are *not* included in studies because they are relevant to the interlocutors in the ongoing interaction (to the extent that the data is interactional), but because the researcher has theoretically or empirically motivated reason to believe that such variables may influence L2 use and learning in some way. Of course, interlocutors *may* attend to these or any other categories, for instance, culture-specific notions of self and face. Identifying such emic categories has been one of the traditional goals of ethnography. In SLA, we have recently seen an increase in ethnographic or ethnographically inspired studies that situate L2 learners in the sociocultural context where L2 acquisition takes place. These studies are quite different though from what, I think, F&W have in mind. I will come back to them shortly.

I am not too concerned that generic terms such as 'learner' and 'nonnative speaker' suggest to anybody that all learners or all nonnative speakers are the same. What they do suggest is a researcher's focus on human agents. Perhaps such terms should be seen more as indexical than as referential in function: When we open an article and notice that people are referred to as learners or nonnative speakers, we have good reason to believe that the article is about L2 research. If the article were talking about consumers, patients, or passengers, we would contextualize it differently.

Now about interlanguage (IL). When the construct was first introduced with a different term – for instance, as 'transitional competence' by Corder (1967) –, it was conceptualized as a construct parallel to children's developing language. Corder argued that just as it was pointless to assess child language in terms of adult language and talk about 'errors' when child forms were different from adults', it was also pointless to set off learners' 'errors' against native speakers' 'correct' forms because such a view ran counter to the idea that learners creatively construct their IL. Therefore, what Corder advocated was actually a very emic view, a view that informs many longitudinal studies modeled on child language acquisition research. The comparative focus was introduced through Selinker's

(1972) recipe for research designs in IL study: performance data in the learners' IL, their L1, and L2, that is, one set of nonnative speaker data paralleled with two different sets of native speaker data. This design was inherited from Contrastive Analysis (note that the acronym CA has shifted its meaning since). Bley-Vroman (1983) warned against the 'comparative fallacy' in IL research; I cautioned against the same problem in the context of interlanguage pragmatics (e.g., Kasper, 1992), but no one has listened much to either of us (including myself). Perhaps F&W will be able to make their case more effectively, but I am not too hopeful. SLA researchers have legitimate and important interests in assessing learners' IL knowledge and actions not just as achievements in their own right but measured against some kind of standard. The solution to the comparative fallacy that I envision does not renounce on comparison but selects more appropriate baselines. For instance, when you study the phonological development and ultimate attainment of Anglocanadians learning French, do not choose as a baseline monolingual speakers of Canadian French; choose highly competent French-English bilinguals. Careful choices of baselines are not just crucial for obtaining valid research results but also highly consequential in applied contexts, such as L2 teaching and assessment and speech pathology.

Finally, I shall address what in my view is the most nagging problem with the F&W paper. The paper purports to redirect the field of SLA, but has in fact very little to say about L2 *acquisition*. Any theory of language acquisition has to make explicit what the conditions and mechanisms of learning are. In other words, it has to address the question of how learners' interlanguage knowledge progresses from stage A to stage B, and what events promote or hinder such progress. F&W do not address these questions. What they seem to call for are socially situated studies of second language *use*. Yet as they also note, there are already a number of such studies, which adopt approaches such as interactional sociolinguistics, critical discourse analysis, and – especially in the work of Firth and Wagner themselves – Conversation Analysis (CA). But none of these approaches has anything to say about L2 learning. It would be fruitful to explore how discourse analysis in its different incarnations could be combined with (some) theories of L2 acquisition; however, F&W do not offer any suggestions to that effect – perhaps because CA, their discourse approach of choice, is strictly anti-cognitive? On the other hand, Gregg's (1993) view of the project of SLA succinctly identifies 'the acquisition (or non-acquisition) of L2 competence' as 'the overall explanandum' in SLA (Gregg, p. 278, cited in F&W, p. 287). One does not have to subscribe to Gregg's theoretical commitment to Universal Grammar as the only compelling approach to SLA, nor to the narrow definition of L2 knowledge as competence in the Chomskyan sense, in order to accept the (rather obvious) proposition that SLA is about what its name suggests. If the 'A' of 'SLA' is dropped, we are looking at the much wider field of second language studies, which spans as diverse endeavors as intercultural and cross-cultural communication, second language pedagogy, micro- and macrosociolinguistics with reference to second languages and dialects, societal and individual multilingualism, and SLA.

Notwithstanding my interest in pragmatics, sociolinguistics, and discourse analysis, I am comfortable with an essentially cognitivist definition of SLA. This is because in the final analysis, learning or acquiring anything is about establishing new knowledge structures and making that knowledge available for effective and efficient use. Issues of knowledge representation, processing, and recall have to be central to any discipline that is concerned with learning. A noncognitivist discipline that has learning as its central research object is a contradiction in terms.

But this being said, there is a whole range of issues about SLA that cognitive theory does not tell us anything about, nor does any formal (as opposed to functional, not informal) theory of language, for that matter. Because SLA, just as L1 acquisition, always takes place in a social context, one can suspect that the social context in some way influences SLA. Furthermore, because language learners are not passive recipients of input but actively participate in different kinds of interaction, they also construct their own identities and those of their respective other; these experiences are likely to be reflected in different parts of learners' developing L2 competence. Among the 'at least forty' theories of SLA counted by Larsen-Freeman and Long (1991, p. 227), there are many that address these aspects of SLA, and from different theoretical vantage points. Vygotsky's (1934/1964) theory of cognitive development has been applied to L2 development (Lantolf & Appel, 1994); specifically, Vygotsky's construct of a Zone of Proximal Development has been connected to the input and practice opportunities afforded by different participation structures (Shea, 1994). As a social-psychological approach, Communication Accommodation Theory (Giles, Coupland, & Coupland, 1991) has the potential to explain interlocutors' convergence and divergence in terms of interactional dynamics and attitudinal factors, and to relate the conversational practices of learners and their interlocutors to the learning opportunities provided in different kinds of encounters. Different ethnographic approaches to L2 classroom research have been adopted in recent work by Atkinson and Ramanthan (1995), Duff (1995), and to sojourners' (Siegal, 1996) and immigrants' development of communicative competence in the target community (Peirce, 1995a); theoretical discussion of ethnography in L2 research has been offered by Watson-Gegeo (1988), Davis (1995), Lazaraton (1995), and Peirce (1995b). Language socialization theory (e.g., Schiefflin & Ochs, 1986) examines the dialectic relationship between linguistic and cultural practices in the interaction between experts (caretakers, teachers, native speakers) and novices (child or adult learners) from a developmental perspective. Studies applying language socialization theory to L2 acquisition have shown how linguistic and pragmatic competence, sociocultural knowledge, and learner identity are shaped by novice-expert interaction in various contexts (e.g., Poole, 1992; Duff, 1995; Willett, 1995; Pallotti, 1996; Siegal, 1996; He, 1997). Although compatible with the previously mentioned approaches, language socialization theory has a particularly rich potential for SLA because it is inherently developmental and requires (rather than just allows) establishing links between culture, cognition, and language, between the macrolevels of sociocultural and institutional contexts, and the microlevel of discourse. A good example is Poole's (1992) reinterpretation of interactional modification and feedback in ESL classroom discourse.

To conclude on a heretic note, if the excellent microanalytic tools of CA were incorporated into a language socialization approach to SLA, we might be able to reconstruct links between L2 discourse and the acquisition of different aspects of communicative competence that have been largely obscure thus far.

Note

1   This text is based on the original oral draft, presented as an invited response to F&W's paper at the symposium on Discourse Analysis at the 1995 AILA Congress. I have tried to retain some of its original stylistic flavor in the written version.

References

Atkinson, D., & Ramathan, V. (1995). Cultures of writing: An ethnographic comparison of L1 and L2 university writing/language programs. *TESOL Quarterly, 29,* 539–566.

Bley-Vroman, R. (1983). The comparative fallacy in interlanguage studies: The case of systematicity. *Language Learning, 33,* 1–17.

Bolte, H., & Herrlitz, W. (1986). Language learning processes and intervention in the foreign language classroom: A reconstructive and interventive model. In G. Kasper (Ed.), *Learning, teaching and communication in the foreign language classroom* (pp. 195–223). Arhus, Denmark: Aarhus University Press.

Brown, G., & Yule, G. (1983). *Discourse analysis.* Cambridge: Cambridge University Press.

Corder, S. P. (1967). The significance of learners' errors. *International Review of Applied Linguistics, 5,* 161–170.

Crookes, G. (1990). The utterance, and other basic units for second language discourse analysis. *Applied Linguistics, 11,* 183–199.

Davis, K. A. (1995). Qualitative theory and methods in applied linguistics research. *TESOL Quarterly, 29,* 427–453.

Dechert, H. W., Möhle, D., & Raupach, M. (Eds.) (1984). *Second language productions.* Tübingen, Germany: Narr.

Duff, P. A. (1995). An ethnography of communication in immersion classrooms in Hungary. *TESOL Quarterly, 29,* 505–537.

Edwards, J. E., & Lampert, M. D. (Eds.), *Talking data.* Hillsdale, NJ: Erlbaum.

Ehlich, K. (1993). HIAT: A transcription system for discourse data. In J. E. Edwards & M. D. Lampert (Eds.), *Talking data* (pp. 123–148). Hillsdale, NJ: Erlbaum.

Færch, C., Hasstrup, K., & Phillipson, R. (1984), *Learner language and language learning.* Copenhagen, Denmark: Gyldendal.

Færch, C., & Kasper, G. (1983). On identifying communication strategies in interlanguage production. In C. Færch & G. Kasper (Eds.), *Strategies in interlanguage communication* (pp. 210–238). London: Longman.

Gregg, K. (1993). Taking explanation seriously; or, let a couple of flowers bloom. *Applied Linguistics, 14,* 276–294.

Giles, H., Coupland, J., & Coupland, N. (Eds.) (1991). *Contexts of accommodation.* Cambridge: Cambridge University Press.

He, A. W. (1997). Learning and being: Identity construction in the classroom. In L. Bouton (Ed.), *Pragmatics and language learning,* Vol. 8. (pp. 201–222). University of Illinois at Urbana-Champaign.

Kasper, G. (1993, August). A bilingual perspective on interlanguage pragmatics. Keynote held at the 10th AILA Congress, Amsterdam.

Kasper, G. (1992). Pragmatic transfer. *Second Language Research, 8*, 203–251.

Kasper, G. (1995). Wessen Pragmatik? Für eine Neubestimmung sprachlicher Handlungskompetenz. *Zeitschrift fur Fremdsprachenforschung, 6*, 1–25.

Lantolf, J. P., & Appel, G. (1994). *Vygotskyan approaches to second language research*. Norwood, NJ: Ablex.

Larsen-Freeman, D., & Long, M. H. (1991). *An introduction to second language acquisition research*. London: Longman.

Lazaraton, A. (1995). Qualitative research in applied linguistics: A progress report. *TESOL Quarterly, 29*, 455–472.

MacWhinney, B. (1995). *The CHILDES project* (2nd ed.). Hillsdale, NJ: Erlbaum.

Ochs, E. (1979). Transcription as theory. In E. Ochs & B. Schieffelin (Eds.), *Developmental pragmatics* (pp. 43–72). New York: Academic.

Pallotti, G. (1996). Towards an ecology of second language acquisition: SLA as a socialization process. In E. Kellerman, B. Weltens, & T. Bongaerts (Eds.), *EuroSLA 6: A selection of papers (= Toegepaste Taatwetenschap in Artikelen, 55)*, 121–143.

Peirce, B. N. (1995a). Social identity, investment, and language learning. *TESOL Quarterly, 29*, 9–31.

Peirce, B. N. (1995b). The theory of methodology in qualitative research. *TESOL Quarterly, 29*, 569–576.

Poole, D. (1992). Language socialization in the second language classroom. *Language Learning, 42*, 593–616.

Poulisse, N., Bongaerts, T., & Kellerman, E. (1987). The use of retrospective reports in the analysis of compensatory strategies. In C. Færch & G. Kasper (Eds.), *Introspection in second language research* (pp. 213–229). Clevedon, England: Multilingual Matters.

Rehbein, J. (1984). Reparative Handlungsmuster und ihre Verwendung im Fremdsprachenunterricht. *ROLIGpapir* 30.

Schieffelin, B. B., & Ochs. E. (1986). Language socialization. *Annual Review of Anthropology, 15*, 163–191.

Selinker, L. (1972). Interlanguage. *International Review of Applied Linguistics, 105*, 209–231.

Shea, D. P. (1994). Perspective and production: Structuring conversational participation across cultural borders. *Pragmatics, 4*, 357–390.

Siegal, M. (1996). The role of learner subjectivity in second language sociolinguistic competency: Western women learning Japanese. *Applied Linguistics, 17*, 356–382.

Vygotsky, L. S. (1964). *Denken und Sprechen*. Stuttgart: Fischer. (Russian original 1934).

Wagner, J. (1983). Indføring i centrale problemstillinger. In J. Wagner & U. Helm Petersen (Eds.), *Kommunikation i fremmedsprogsundervisning* (pp. 10–66). Copenhagen, Denmark: Gjellerup.

Watson-Gegeo, K. A. (1988). Ethnography in ESL; Defining the essentials. *TESOL Quarterly, 22*, 575–592.

Willett, J. (1995). Becoming first graders in an L2: An ethnographic study of L2 socialization. *TESOL Quarterly, 29*, 437–505.

Text 22

Michael H. Long

Construct Validity in SLA Research: A Response to Firth and Wagner

Firth and Wagner (F&W) set out to critique what they claim is the dominant view of 'discourse and communication' in SLA research. Its analyses are oversimplistic, F&W assert, because they have generally considered the L2 acquirer as a 'nonnative speaker' of the L2, as a 'learner,' and as someone whose L2 repertoire and underlying grammar is an 'interlanguage' (the psycholinguistic L2 equivalent of an 'idiolect' in sociolinguistics, a construct to which F&W presumably also object), and as a 'deficient communicator, struggling to overcome an L2 competence' when interacting with an 'idealized native speaker,' who is attributed elevated status by researchers. They assert that this view is 'individualistic,' 'mechanistic,' and

> fails to account in a satisfactory way for interactional and sociolinguistic dimensions of language. As such, it is flawed, and obviates insight into the nature of language, most centrally the use of second or foreign language (S/FL) speakers. (p. 285)

And therein lies the fundamental problem with F&W's case. SLA, as the name indicates, is the study of L2 *acquisition*, not (except indirectly) of 'the nature of language' in general or 'most centrally the language use of second or foreign language speakers' – especially not 'most centrally' – interesting though those subjects may be. Most SLA research, F&W complain (echoing Rampton), is preoccupied with the relationship between a speaker and his or her interlanguage grammar, not that between speakers and the world around them, this despite research in sociolinguistics having 'irrefutably established and documented [a] reflexive relationship between *language use and social context*' (p. 293, emphasis added). And who would deny it? The question, again, however, is what any of this has to do with the appropriate focus for research on SLA.

Few would dispute that SLA takes place in an interactional and sociolinguistic context. A persistent question in the field, however, is the relevance of that context, and of different dimensions of it, to *acquisition*. Answers currently vary among researchers working within different theoretical frameworks or who hold different interpretations of the empirical findings, or both. For example, some view linguistic input to the learner as degenerate and underspecified; others think the same corpus is often tailored for acquisition in various ways. Some view negative evidence and negative feedback, for example, in the form of recasts, as nonexistent, unusable, unused, or nonuniversal (and thus nonessential); others take a very different view, claiming to have shown such feedback is available and at least facilitative of acquisition. These are empirical matters, surely, not to be settled by fiat.

It is ironic that the very SLA researchers who F&W claim have ignored context are among those who have most often explicitly focused on at least some dimensions of it in their work. The current cast of villains, Faerch and Kasper, Poulisse, Gass and Varonis, and Long, for example, along with Hatch, Sato, Freed, Gaies, Porter, Bygate, Derwing, Skehan, Schachter, Pica, Doughty, Swain,

Chaudron, Ishiguro, Oliver, Watson-Gegeo, Muranoi, Linnell, Iwashita, and many others, have all, and often, studied various dimensions of conversations between people acquiring a L2 and their interlocutors, be they other L2 acquirers or native speakers of the target language – specifically, again, the dimensions of conversation that both L1 and L2 research to date suggest are important for *acquisition*.[1] Several targets of F&W's displeasure have been among the strongest proponents of the idea that (S)LA occurs crucially through participation in conversation of certain kinds, including conversation with 'native speakers' and with other 'learners' of the L2 (if one may still use the terms), that is, of the relevance for some aspects of SLA of 'talking to learn.' F&W are aware of this, of course, and their initial sweeping claim that the accused have failed to address the interactional and sociolinguistic dimensions of language is later reduced (p. 287 et infra) to the lesser, more defensible, although not inevitably interesting, one that we have failed to focus on the dimensions F&W consider relevant for sociolinguistic studies of L2 use, for example, as a lingua franca in telephone conversations between Danish and German businessmen, or to do so in the way F&W prefer. More important than whether we are guilty as charged, however, is the deeper underlying issue F&W wish to raise: the very nature of the SLA beast. Whether F&W like it or not (they do not), most SLA researchers view the object of inquiry as in large part an internal, mental process: *the acquisition of new (linguistic) knowledge*.[2] And I would say, with good reason. SLA is a process that (often) takes place in a social setting, of course, but then so do most internal processes – learning, thinking, remembering, sexual arousal, and digestion, for example – and that neither obviates the need for theories of those processes, nor shifts the goal of inquiry to a theory of the settings. A theory of memory, for example, deals with such matters as relationships among the frequency and intensity of instances of the phenomena an individual experiences and the subset that are remembered, storage and retrieval of same, and so on, but not, or not 'centrally,' at least, with the social events, for example, courtroom testimony or storytelling in a pub, during which memories are put to use. The result of that communicative experience – and/or of the interaction of linguistic input with certain innate (linguistic or general) knowledge structures and/or neural networks – does not evaporate when an interlocutor leaves the room or when the learner goes to sleep at night; it remains, memory permitting, in the form of a modified, individual, partly idiosyncratic, internal, mental representation of the L2. The goal of research on SLA, qualitative or quantitative, inside or outside the classroom, in the laboratory or on the street, is to understand how changes in that internal mental representation are achieved, why they sometimes appear to cease (so-called 'fossilization'), and which learner, linguistic, and social factors (and where relevant, which instructional practices) affect and effect the process.

Given, then, that most SLA researchers are, in my view, correctly, endeavoring to understand a mental process and a changing mental representation of the L2, or interlanguage grammar, *cognitive* variables are for them inevitably and justifiably a central focus, and what F&W call 'cognitive oriented theories and methodologies' are inevitably and appropriately those researchers' central theories and methodologies. Perhaps the reason F&W find this difficult to understand or accept is that, again, as noted above, they are as interested, more interested, or perhaps in some cases only interested in the study of L2 *use*, and, following Hymes, see language first and foremost as 'a social and cultural phenomenon' (p. 287). That is all well and good, and the research they conduct will no doubt have theoretically interesting and socially beneficial results, but it is hardly a basis for attacking the work of researchers with different goals, a partly different understanding of the explanandum, and an at least partly different domain of inquiry. Social and affective factors, the L2 *acquisition* literature suggests, are important, but relatively minor in their impact, in both naturalistic and classroom settings, and most current theories of and in SLA reflect that fact, although by no means do all of them (fortunately, as clearly it would be dangerous and counterproductive to succumb to a single paradigm at this relatively early stage in the field's development). Simply asserting that this is not so, that there are no widely (not universally, of course) accepted findings in SLA, or that a greater 'balance' between cognitive and other 'more holistic' social views is needed, as F&W do, will not make it so. Nor will repeating the assertions, however often, as opposed to producing some evidence for them.

So what evidence do F&W provide in support of the claimed superiority of their approach, or for their assertions that research on discourse and communication 'always has been, of necessity multitheoretical in its adopted approaches and conceptual apparatus' (p. 286 et passim), and that this all shows the need for a 'reconceptualization of SLA'? Well, to be charitable, very little. And even that speaks at most to the considerably reduced, though surely still rather blunt, charge that 'on the whole, work that purports to examine nonnative/learner discourse ... is impaired' (p. 286). Three brief conversational excerpts from studies by Faerch and Kasper,[3] Long, and Gass and Varonis, are reanalyzed (at some length). Because the other researchers concerned have been invited to respond to F&W's reanalyses of their work, I will limit myself to F&W's comments on mine (although F&W level some of the same criticisms at SLA discourse work in general). The following, with my responses attached, appear to be their major complaints:

1   A distinction between native speakers (NSs) and nonnative speakers (NNSs), or learners, in my and others' work (a) objectively ignores, and (b) by assertion, underestimates the importance for understanding SLA of, other separate or simultaneous speaker social identities (father, friend, business partner, etc.) to which both parties may be giving expression when they talk. My response is that (a) is clearly correct, and F&W's reanalyses show this, and that (b) is an empirical matter, about which it will be interesting to see some data.

2   The claim (Long, 1981) that certain kinds (not any kinds) of interactions with NNSs are the necessary and sufficient condition for SLA assumes that NS – NS baseline data are the relevant norm, and ignores the existence of language learning in multilingual communities, where a learner's interlocutors may all be other NNSs of the L2. (Ignoring their own admonition, F&W appear to consider 'learner,' 'NS,' and 'NNS' relevant 'identities' and legitimate terms in this discussion.) My response is that 'NNS' was the relevant label in Long (1981), given the study being presented there. There are, however, of course, numerous multilingual

settings in which most, even all, L2 users that a learner encounters will be other NNSs. The so-called Interaction Hypothesis (for a recent up-date, see Long, 1996) has always concerned the experience by learners (yes, 'learners') of interactionally modified discourse through negotiation for meaning, be the *source* other NSs, other NNSs (for review, see, e.g., Pica, Lincoln-Porter, Paninos, & Linnell, 1996), spoken or written (see, e.g., Long, & Ross, 1993; Yano, Long, & Ross, 1994), 'authentic' or contrived for language learning (Long, 1997).

3 Use of NS and NNS data wrongly assumes that there is such a thing as a 'standard' or 'normal' way of talking, and that this is the 'norm' that is modified for learners. My response is that I agree that there is no normal or standard way of talking. It is precisely for that reason, among others, however, that it is incumbent upon researchers to collect comparable baseline data (e.g., when analyzing conversation in pairs of individuals, from NS – NS dyads, not just NS – NNS or NNS – NNS dyads, and preferably from a goodly number of each). This is especially the case if a researcher wishes to make more than purely impressionistic claims about certain linguistic or conversational modifications attributable to one speaker in a dyad being a NNS (or a 'father' or 'business partner,' for that matter), about both being NNSs using the L2 as a lingua franca, or whatever the case may be. For the same reasons, it is important that any likely confounding learner, setting, or task variables either be controlled or systematically manipulated. The use of baseline data, although always open to the charge that variable X or Y also should have been controlled, is a *strength* of the kind of work F&W attack; the typical absence of such data is a serious weakness in much of the kind of work they propose in its place, as is the frequent (often unnecessary) absence of such data in sociolinguistically oriented naturalistic studies of any quantification, the lack even of descriptive statistics pertaining to the normalcy and variation of isolated cited examples and excerpts, and the consequent unknown typicality or status of those examples. My own view is that both kinds of data can shed useful light on many issues in SLA and L2 use, but that the strengths and relevance of the former for studies of *acquisition* are far greater.

4 With reference to the brief excerpt that F&W discuss (p. 293) from a NS – NNS conversation included in Larsen-Freeman and Long (1991, pp. 146–147), one of 36 (18 NS – NS & 18 NS – NNS) in the original study, each lasting about 5 minutes, F&W say they do not take issue with the original analysis, but ask rhetorically, 'if ["here-and-now" topics, interactional modification, repetitions, paraphrase, confirmation checks, and so forth.] is "modified" interaction, what would be the "baseline" conversation?' and wonder how it can be 'taken to be a representation of foreign language interaction per se and "foreigner talk" (i.e., NSs' actions) in general' (p. 293), as summarized in Yano et al. (1994, pp. 193–194) and elsewhere. My response, first, is that in the original study, conducted in 1978, from which the NS – NS excerpt F&W discuss was taken, the baseline data consisted of an equal number of 5-minute conversations in 18 NS – NS dyads given identical instructions and meeting under identical conditions to the 18 NS – NNS dyads. As indicated in my response to point 3, above, it is precisely the collection and analysis of *comparable* baseline data – not just one brief decontextualized excerpt from

one dyad – that, in my view, would justify (on the basis of one study) *only* limited and tentative generalizations about foreigner talk (FT) or foreigner talk discourse (FTD). The more confident tone and broader generalizations summarized in Yano et al. (1994) and elsewhere reflected the accumulation of dozens of studies with fairly consistent findings (the work of numerous researchers) over the intervening 15-year period by the time that paper was written. A recent and far more extensive review of research on the role of the linguistic environment in SLA (Long, 1996) gave me no reason to modify the claims, incidentally. The generalizations F&W cite were quite clearly specified as pertaining to FT, that is, NS – NNS interaction, not *foreign language interaction*, and *relative*, that is, as concerning trends, patterns, and tendencies for FT and FTD to exhibit more or less of feature X or Y than comparable NS talk. They were not presented, there or elsewhere, as unique to FT or FTD, but always as reflecting statistically different frequencies of certain features and patterns in FT or FTD and comparable NS baseline data. There is also considerable recognition in my own work and that of many other researchers of the individual variation often found in such data. There is no statement I am aware of to the effect that the patterns are universal or unaffected by such variables as the proficiency of the speakers or the purpose of their talk, for example, no suggestion that a specific pair of European businessmen using English as a lingua franca will always maintain a here-and-now orientation or always treat topics briefly, which in any case, would be an absolute, not a relative claim.

5   F&W suggest that findings on NS – NNS interactions may be an artifact of the frequent use of 'experimental' settings and may not generalize to 'naturalistic' encounters, nor to other populations of NSs, contrary to the 'tendentious assumption that NSs represent a homogeneous entity, responding on each and every occasion in a patterned and predictable fashion' (p. 294). My response is that, with the possible exception of the frequency (still relatively low) with which ungrammatical FT is used (possibly rather more in naturalistic settings), over 20 years and dozens of studies show that findings in 'laboratory' and 'natural' settings have generally been very similar (for review, see Long, 1996). This is not to say that studies showing systematic effects for setting, conversational purpose, interlocutor role, and other factors may not or will not eventually be reported, but simply that the patterns to date for the most part hold across experimental and naturalistic settings. (Should such differences come to light, of course, it will still not necessarily mean that they are relevant for a theory of SLA.) As for the issue of 'tendentious assumptions' about NS homogeneity and invariant responses, see my response to point 4, above. This is an unsupported and baseless charge about work in the field in general, not just my own.

In a revealing aside, F&W state that their critical assessment of 'mainstream' SLA research is in part due to their (negative) reaction to recent discussions of SLA theory construction and evaluation by some of the current sinners and others – Beretta, Crookes, Gregg, and Long – whom they see as (a) wrongly having problematized theory proliferation, (b) wrongly not having problematized 'normal science,' and (c) wrongly believing that there are some generally (not universally) accepted findings in SLA.[4] They note that Block (1996) 'has challenged' (p. 286) those authors' assumptions, something apparently constituting evidence for F&W's own assertions. In other words, like Block, whose position they endorse, F&W would have us believe that they, too, oppose the standard rationalist understanding of scientific research in favor of some unspecified, but inevitably hopeless brand of relativism (for a trenchant critique, see Laudan, 1996). This, of course, they would be perfectly entitled to do. In fact, however, the rest of F&W's paper shows that this is *not* their view at all. Their arguments really concern the (surely still large enough) issues of *which* goals, methods, and styles of *rationalist* research and theory construction they favor, the claim being the perfectly reasonable and empirically testable one that their approach will yield more insightful understandings of L2 discourse than current practice – more insightful for their own interests in SL *use*, at least, although not necessarily for the interests of the original researchers in *acquisition*.

In other words, unlike Block, F&W are not against replication, not against control of variables, not in denial of the very possibility of falsification and of comparative theory assessment, not against the principle of accountability to data, and certainly not in favor of an 'anything goes' relativist position. F&W's painstaking efforts to demonstrate that their analyses of published data are more insightful, more valid, than those of the original analysts demonstrates this. Nor are they against experimental research, something which, after all, is essential for addressing many crucial issues in SLA (on this topic, see the forthcoming 1997 thematic issue of *Studies in Second Language Acquisition*), nor against coding and quantifying data, nor an interest in universals, and nor (it comes as a relief to hear, otherwise what interest would research findings have?) a prioritization of explanations over descriptions of phenomena. They are instead concerned about what they see as a 'methodological *bias* and theoretical *imbalance*' in SLA studies (p. 288), one that should be modified, not abandoned altogether, they believe, in order to give greater emphasis to naturalistic data, the local and the particular, emic rather than etic views, and a broader view of communication than (what they allege is) simply one of 'information transfer.' Few would deny the potential of such an approach for offering insights into SLA, although as indicated above, most would continue to emphasize the psycholinguistic approach, given the object of inquiry and given (to the best of my knowledge, and lacking any evidence from F&W to the contrary) that to date insights into SL *acquisition* from sociolinguistically oriented research have been relatively minor. It is unsettling and disappointing, therefore, to see in F&W's article some of the same confusions about the assumptions underlying the discussions of SLA theory construction and assessment they refer to by Beretta et al. that are evident in Block's unhappy piece (and in Lantolf's recent postmodernist commentaries on the debate also endorsing relativism; see Lantolf, 1996a, 1996b), and to see those issues introduced irrelevantly in the current context.[5]

In sum, in my view, F&W are perfectly justified, and probably right, in arguing that a broader, context-sensitive, participant-sensitive, generally sociolinguistic orientation might prove beneficial for SLA research. They are, of course, also correct to caution about generalizations of research findings from (mostly) NS – NNS conversation, often (but by no means only) in 'laboratory' settings, to as yet rarely studied populations, for example, multilingual speech communities in which the L2 of interest may be used as a lingua franca by a wide range of different types of speakers, few of them NSs, for different purposes not intrinsically or obviously related to *acquiring* the L2. On the other hand, F&W need to show how *they* plan to deal with some obvious methodological problems in the kind of research they propose, namely, the representativeness, verifiability, and relevance to theory of cited examples and of analyses, however detailed and careful, of isolated, 'local,' 'particular' events. Aside from some strawman arguments, arguments by assertion, rather sweeping claims about the state of the field based on very limited data, and an unfortunate, irrelevant (and for their own position, misleading) endorsement of Block's confusions about philosophy of science issues, the major problem I have with F&W's polemic remains my skepticism as to whether greater insights into SL *use* will *necessarily* have much to say about SL *acquisition*.

Notes

1 I will not cite references and take space to document such statements. Because so much of F&W's argument is by assertion, and since space constraints limit my response. I will be obliged, and feel free, occasionally to make some unsupported assertions of my own, leaving it to those familiar with the refereed SLA literature to judge each side's assertions on their merits.

2 A major source of confusion in their article is that F&W appear to equate any conception of SLA that includes the acquisition of new knowledge and/or involves an individual, internal, mental (as opposed to 'social') process, with a Universal Grammar (UG) position, when this is obviously unwarranted. See, for example, their potted history of the influence of Chomskyan linguistics on SLA (p. 287), and their misuses of the citations from Gregg, 1993, about the goals and assumptions of UG-based work, implying that UG positions are representative of all current 'cognitivist' SLA, on p. 287, and again on p. 288, where they write, 'as Gregg's observations (above) intimate, the centripetal forces of the individual-cognitive orientation to language remains irresistible for SLA.' UG-ers hold the 'narrow,' 'cognitivist' view, it is true (although arguably, even in the opinion of many critics, have the single most coherent, some would say the only coherent, research program in the field). But, like so many quadrupeds not of the canine persuasion, by far the majority of 'cognitively oriented' SLA researchers are not UG-ers; they include, for example, general nativists and, to the best of my knowledge, all of the 'cognitive/social interactionists' that F&W are attacking here. As if this confusion were not enough, F&W conclude their section attacking Chomskyites and psycholinguistically oriented researchers by bemoaning 'the imposition of an orthodox social psychological hegemony on SLA' (p. 288). UG-ers in SLA have been called many names in the past, but surely this is going too far.

3 As part of their critique of work on communication strategies, F&W propose adoption of an understanding of 'meaning' that:

> transcending individual intentions and behaviours ... This transcendence is possible because talk is organized on a turn-by-turn basis, thereby providing participants with a resource – a 'procedural infrastructure of interaction' ... – for accomplishing, demonstrating, and transforming

meaning in an ongoing fashion. Each speaking turn, then, is a locus for the display of understanding of the prior turn ... Participants orient to this feature, and in so doing are able to construct a transcendental 'architecture of intersubjectivity.' (pp. 290–291)

One could be forgiven for wondering whether adoption of such a 'transcendental' analysis might not 'problematize' a number of other things, including researchers' ability to obtain acceptable inter-rater reliability coefficients.

4 F&W (p. 286) quote Long (1993) as opposing 'a "wild-flowering" of disparate and "rivaling" theories' (p. 235). The reader of page 235, or indeed any page, of Long (1993) or any other paper of mine, will find neither this view (which I do not hold), nor use of either term.

5 For a detailed critique of Block's (and Lantolf's) misunderstandings of the SLA field and of the relevant philosophy of science issues, see Gregg, Long, Beretta, and Jordan (in press).

References

Block, D. (1996). Not so fast: Some thought on theory culling, relativism, accepted findings and the heart and soul of SLA. *Applied Linguistics, 17,* 63–83.

Gregg, K. (1993). Taking explanation seriously; or, let a couple of flowers bloom. *Applied Linguistics, 14,* 276–294.

Gregg, K., Long, M. H., Beretta, A., & Jordan, G. (in press). Rationality and its discontents in SLA. *Applied Linguistics, 18,* 1997.

Laudan, L. (1996). *Beyond positivism and relativism. Theory, method, and evidence.* Boulder, CO: Westview Press/Harper-Collins.

Lantolf, J. (1996a). Second language acquisition theory building? In G. M. Blue & R. Mitchell (Eds.). *Language and education: British Studies in Applied Linguistics, 11,* (pp. 16–27). BAAL and Clevedon, England: Multilingual Matters.

Lantolf, J. (1996b). SLA theory building: 'Letting all the flowers bloom!' *Language Learning, 46,* 713–749.

Long, M. H. (1981). Input, interaction and second language acquisition. In H. Winitz (Ed.). *Native and foreign language acquisition. Annals of the New York Academy of Sciences, 379* (pp. 259–278). New York: New York Academy of Sciences.

Long, M. H. (1993). Assessment strategies for SLA theories. *Applied Linguistics, 14,* 225–249.

Long, M. H. (1996). The role of the linguistic environment in second language acquisition. In W. Ritchie & T. Bhatia (Eds.), *Handbook of second language acquisition* (pp. 413–468). San Diego, CA: Academic.

Long, M. H. (1997). Authenticity and learning potential in L2 classroom discourse. In G. M. Jacobs (Ed.), *Language classrooms of tomorrow. Issues and responses* (pp. 148–169). Singapore: SEAMEO Regional Language Centre.

Long, M. H., & Ross, S. (1993). Modifications that preserve language and content. In M. L. Tickoo (Ed.). *Simplification: Theory and application* (pp. 29–52). Singapore: SEAMEO Regional Language Centre.

Pica, T., Lincoln-Porter, F., Paninos, D., & Linnell, J. (1996). Language learners'
interaction: How does it address the input, output, and feedback needs of
language learners? *TESOL Quarterly, 30*, 59–84.

Yano, Y., Long, M. H., & Ross, S. (1994). The effects of simplified and
elaborated texts on foreign language reading comprehension. *Language
Learning, 44*, 189–219.

Text 23

Nanda Poulisse

Some Words in Defense of the Psycholinguistic Approach: A Response to Firth and Wagner

The article written by Firth and Wagner (F&W) seeks to reconceptualize SLA 'as
a more theoretically and methodologically balanced, "holistic" enterprise' in
which there is 'a significantly enhanced awareness of the contextual and
interactional dimensions of language use,' and 'an increased "emic" (i.e.,
participant relevant) sensitivity towards fundamental concepts' like nonnative
speaker, learner, and interlanguage (p. 286). The reason for F&W's article is the
imbalance that they have perceived in SLA studies. SLA studies, they say, are
psycholinguistic rather than sociolinguistic in nature and focus on the individual
nonnative speaker or learner in conversation, who is often regarded as an
incompetent native speaker rather than as a language user who is one of the
participants in social interaction.

Although it is perfectly laudable to promote SLA research from a
sociolinguistic perspective, there appear to be some problems with some of
the arguments presented in their article. The present response seeks to comment
on these.

However, let us first consider the role of psycholinguistically and
sociolinguistically oriented research in SLA. In this respect it is important to bear in
mind that the acquisition and learning of skills are generally considered to be
psychological processes, as are the production and perception of language. Hence,
it is no wonder that many studies of second language acquisition and use take a
psycholinguistic approach. If one is studying psycholinguistic processes, one should
relate one's findings to psycholinguistic theories. Naturally, this psycholinguistic
approach could – and should – be expanded by also taking a look at outside factors
influencing the conditions for language learning, namely the opportunity to practise
(which includes both receiving input and producing output) and to obtain either
explicit or implicit feedback. Examples of factors determining the opportunities for
practice and feedback would be the language situation (L2 vs. FL), the teaching
method (e.g., drills, communicative teaching, gapfill exercises), the learner's
emotional status within that situation (e.g., whether he feels at ease or not), the
presence of a cooperative interlocutor, and so forth. It seems that with respect to
SLA both the psycholinguistic and the sociolinguistic approaches are important. I
would consider the psycholinguistic approach to be primary though, and the
sociolinguistic approach to be secondary. You first need to describe the basic
processes of learning and using language, and then to discuss the contextual factors
that may influence these processes.

My first comment on the F&W article concerns the paragraph that states that 'the imposition of an orthodox social psychological hegemony on SLA' (which is the result of SLA's strong affinities with psycholinguistics) has had the effect of, among other things, giving 'preeminence to the research practice of coding, quantifying data, and replicating results;' of prioritizing 'explanations of phenomena ... over descriptions of phenomena;' of assigning 'preference to ... experimental settings rather than naturalistic ones;' of endorsing 'the search for the universal and underlying features of language processes rather than the particular and the local' (p. 288). Although F&W say that they 'do not wish to argue that such theoretical predilections or methodological practices are *in and of themselves* erroneous or flawed' and therefore to be eschewed, the tone of this paragraph is decidedly negative. It suggests that these practices, though not erroneous, are the *negative* results of a psychological approach. I would rather argue though, that no matter what paradigm one uses, psychological or sociological, it makes good sense to follow such practices.

First, it seems that any research method, including F&W's, requires a theoretical perspective on the data that allows one to develop a coding system that adequately describes the data and catches generalizations. Coding forces researchers to be explicit about what they consider to be the most relevant features of the data and to motivate their decisions to assign particular codes. Similarly, quantifying may serve to give an empirical validation of the categories distinguished. It helps to give an objective picture of the importance of particular phenomena in the data and keeps the researcher from presenting just one, juicy part. If anything, therefore, coding and quantifying data make the results of research more concrete, so that it is clearer what needs to be explained.

Second, it seems that no matter which paradigm one follows, it is useful to replicate research results. Of course, replication does put high demands on the report of the original study. It requires a carefully described procedure, a well-defined coding system and clearly presented results. Once these requirements are met, replication is an excellent way to establish the reliability of research.

Third, it seems to be the task of all researchers to not only describe, but also explain and predict phenomena. Hence, it is not clear why explanations should not be prioritized over descriptions. After all, researchers should go beyond the description of their findings and develop and test theories that can explain (and predict) their observations.

Fourth, it seems that experimental studies, in which the researcher manipulates the factor of interest, can contribute to both psycholinguistic and sociolinguistic research. Surely, experimental research needs to be complemented by naturalistic research, but once a theory that yields precise hypotheses has been developed, experiments are a very efficient way to test them, precisely because they allow one to control contextual and situational dimensions that so often blur the results of naturalistic research.

Fifth, irrespective of one's research paradigm, it seems useful to search for universal and underlying features of language processes. Clearly, it is the task of researchers to develop parsimonious theories explaining as many features of language processes as possible. It would definitely not do to just look at particular and local phenomena and find specific explanations for each of them.

To conclude, it seems that if these theoretical and methodological practices have been the effect of SLA researchers adopting a psycholinguistic approach, then we may be grateful that they did, because they all appear to be very sound and fruitful to the study of language, whether this study takes place in a psycholinguistic or a sociolinguistic paradigm.

My second set of comments on F&W's paper concerns their discussion of Communication Strategies (CS) research. F&W begin by pointing out that this research has been preoccupied with the foreign language learner's linguistic deficiencies and communicative problems. This is true, and there is a good reason for it. Linguistic deficiencies and communicative problems are relatively frequent in the speech of foreign language learners. And typically, foreign language learners are very successful in solving these problems. The strategies they employ for doing so have become known as CS. Although the use of CS is not restricted to L2 speech, as many researchers have pointed out, the phenomenon is very frequent in L2 speech, and hence of interest to researchers of SLA and L2 use. To distinguish strategic language use from ordinary, nonstrategic, L2 speech, Faerch and Kasper (1983, p. 36) defined CS as 'potentially conscious plans for solving what presents itself as a problem in reaching a particular communicative goal.' Following this position, I characterized compensatory strategies (i.e., those CS that are aimed at achievement) as 'processes ... which are adopted by language users [so not just learners] in the creation of alternative means of expression when linguistic shortcomings make it impossible for them to communicate their intended meanings in the preferred manner' (Poulisse, 1990, p. 193). By limiting the object of study to those processes to which the language users resort when the preferred processes cannot be executed, Faerch and Kasper and those who adopted or adapted their definition, managed to focus their research on an area of interest to SLA. They definitely did not mean to say that L2 speech is full of problems, degenerate, unsuccessful, or inferior to L1 speech.

In what follows, F&W (following Rampton, 1997) misrepresent Poulisse and Bongaerts' (1990) CS work, saying that 'the foreign language speaker's anomalous word formations (actually Dutch L1 items) are viewed as 'erroneous' features, explained solely in terms of the individual's lack of lexical competence (through the concept of 'automatic transfer'), rather than, or as well as, in terms of interactional and/or sociolinguistic factors' (p. 289). This is simply not true. The paper referred to dealt with the use of L1 in L2 speech and distinguished between several types of transfer, one of which was transfer as a CS (as defined above), and another one was the use of 'automatic transfer,' which was defined as 'the automatic, and unintentional, use of a Dutch word without any morpho-phonological adaptations to make it sound more English.' In our revision of this paper, published in *Applied Linguistics* in 1994, we noted the similarity between these cases of automatic transfer and slips of the tongue in which semantically related lexical items like 'summer' and 'winter' are unintentionally substituted. Unfortunately, F&W do not distinguish between the strategic and the automatic types of transfer. With respect to the strategic type of transfer, it should be noted that this does indeed *result from* the individual's lack of lexical competence – the L1 word is used because the required L2 word is not available – but it is not *explained* by it. The choice for a particular strategy, I have argued, is determined by contextual factors (like task demands, the availability of a linguistic context, the presence of an interlocutor, the language that the interlocutor speaks) (Poulisse, 1990; Poulisse & Schils, 1989). In using CS, 'speakers generally follow Grice's Cooperative Principle and the Economy Principle which is entailed by it. Together these principles require the speakers to produce intelligible messages on the one hand, and to minimize both their own and their listeners' processing effort on the other hand' (Poulisse & Bongaerts, 1990, p. 2). So, although we do describe the use of CS in psycholinguistic terms, we have also explained the use of particular types of CS in terms of general communicative principles, referring to contextual factors influencing the operation of these principles. Therefore, just as the conceptualization of any message is influenced by outside factors in Levelt's (1989) model of speaking, so too the use of CS is influenced by these same outside factors. This seems to me just as F&W would have it.

Automatic transfer is a different issue. It results, not from lack of lexical competence as suggested by F&W, but from lack of automatization of L2 production processes. Less automatic processes require more attention. Attention is limited. Hence one needs to slow down so that the attentional resources can be replenished, or if this is impossible or undesirable, one needs to divide one's attention. Dividing one's attention may result in slips of the tongue. The results of our study suggest that the L2 speakers devoted most attention to the contents of their speech and less to function words, which resulted in the unintentional use of a substantial number of L1 function words (Poulisse & Bongaerts, 1994).

With respect to Rampton's suggestion that the identified lexical items may be seen as well to have discourse organizing functions or that the speakers might be code-switching in order to explore a mixed Anglo-Dutch identity, it can only be said that L1 use may have these functions, but that in the instances we identified as automatic transfer this is unlikely to be the case. The Dutch words involved in the following examples are a highly frequent filler (1), part of a set phrase (2 & 3) and a frequently used adverb, corrected immediately afterwards (4). What these words have in common is their frequency, and in some cases the fact that they have no straightforward translation in English (1 & 2) or the fact that their use is triggered by another word (2 & 3). None of the words in the examples have a discourse organizing function or reveal a mixed Anglo-Dutch identity. The latter would be strange anyway, because the subjects were all born and bred in the Netherlands and had little or no prior contact with native speakers of English:

1 yes uh one brother, and uh 1 my elders *dan hè*. (Dutch: *dan hè* = literally: then uh)
2 and then my mother said *van*, so uh 1 uh. (Dutch: *zeggen van* = say)
3 yes it's also a book *vol* uh 1 with uh, like uh Donald Duck. (Dutch: *een boek vol* = a book full of)
4 I have *ook*, I have uh, a brother too. (Dutch: *ook* = too)

The discussion of Faerch and Kasper's work on CS is limited to one example that they gave as an introduction to their 1983 article to illustrate various aspects of interlanguage communication, namely the learner having difficulty in expressing herself in English, and the misunderstanding which results from her use of the Danish word *historie*. F&W devote more than five pages to this example. In these five pages they give a very detailed analysis of it, focussing on the joint efforts of the two participants to interact. Much of what F&W say here is very insightful, and most people, including Faerch and Kasper, would probably agree with it. That Faerch and Kasper themselves were less detailed in their discussion can hardly be held against them. Their point was merely to introduce the notion of lexical problems so that they could anchor their discussion of CS. The point of F&W's discussion appears to be to define meaning not as 'an individual phenomenon – private thoughts, executed and then transferred from brain to brain, but a social and negotiable product of interaction' (p. 290). I have no problem with this. What I do have a problem with, however, is that they seem to deny that in planning their speech, individual speakers, taking into account external factors like the speaker's knowledge of the world, of the situation (including the interlocutor), and of the preceding discourse, conceptualize their message, which includes determining a meaning. Of course, the intended meaning may not get across in its entirety, but it seems incorrect to say that meaning does not originate in the speaker. Hence problems in encoding the intended meaning may also originate in the speaker, just as problems in decoding may originate in the listener. I agree that both participants may contribute to the solution to these problems and both participants may be responsible for ensuring that as much as possible of the meaning gets across, but the origin of a problem may well lie with only one of the participants.

Finally, I would like to comment briefly on the discussion of the input modification studies. These studies have revealed differences between NS – NS conversations and NS – NNS conversations. The latter are reported to contain 'more clarification requests, repetitions, expansions and elaborations, and a greater incidence of transparency' (Varonis & Gass, 1985, p. 328). F&W quite rightly point out that modifications like this are due to the speakers following the normal rules of conversation. They result from 'collaboration, sharing, resourcefulness, the skillful and artful application of a mechanism to effect collaboration in talk, and thus an efficient division of labour between the participants' (p. 294). In other words, F&W emphasise that NNS know the rules of the game, the principles of conversation. Again, nobody would disagree with them on this. The point of studies by Varonis and Gass (1985), Zuengler (1992), Larsen-Freeman and Long (1991), and others is to illustrate that following the rules of the game results in more repetitions, requests for confirmation, comprehension checks, and so forth in interactions involving NNS than in interactions only involving NSs.

This brings us to the point that NNS are usually compared to NS, a comparison with which F&W appear to find fault. It could be argued though that since language learning is a gradual process, in which the learner's L2 behaviour continually changes in the direction of that of the L1 speaker (until learning stops), it makes perfect sense to compare the two behaviours. Obviously, this does not mean that NNS are defective communicators. Considering their limited L2 vocabulary and considering the fact that their L2 production and reception skills are not yet fully developed and automatized, they do a wonderful job. But to mark the development in L2 learners' behaviour, their performances at different stages need to be compared. And if there is no time for such a longitudinal study, it makes good sense to compare learners at different proficiency levels and to compare learners with NS.

I fully agree with F&W that other factors besides one's proficiency in the language determine one's linguistic behaviour, as Wagner's (1996) study has clearly shown. For this reason, it would be interesting to study the effect of the speaker's social identity (as a father [or mother], man [or woman], friend, local, guest, opponent, etc., see p. 292). However, SLA researchers happen to be interested in L2 learners, and for this reason it is no wonder that to them the most important identity is that of being a L2 learner. If the research is to be valid, it takes into account the proficiency level of the L2 learner and it controls for all other possible variables affecting linguistic behaviour, including the speaker's other social identities. Of course, comparisons with NSs should only be made if they are tested under exactly the same conditions, which means that the social identities of the NNS and NS must be matched too. It is only in that case that the precise effect of the learner's proficiency level in the L2 can be determined.

Notwithstanding the points raised above, it is obvious that F&W have a point when they plea for 'an enhanced awareness of the contextual and interactional dimensions of language use' and a more positive view of the NNS's attempts to interact in the L2. It is clear that there is room for a more sociolinguistically oriented approach toward SLA. Let us not, however, throw away the baby with the bathwater. There is also a continued need for good, methodologically sound, psycholinguistically oriented research.

Acknowledgements

I would like to thank my colleague Jet van Dam van Isselt for her thoughtful comments on an earlier version of this paper.

References

Færch, C., & Kasper, G. (1983). Plans and strategies in foreign language communication. In C. Faerch & G. Kasper (Eds.). *Strategies in interlanguage communication* (pp. 20–60). London: Longman.

Levelt, W. J. M. (1989). *Speaking. From intention to articulation*. Cambridge, MA: Bradford/MIT.

Larsen-Freeman, D., & Long, M. (1991). *An introduction to second language acquisition research*. London: Longman.

Poulisse, N, (1990). *The use of compensatory strategies by Dutch learners of English*. Dordrecht. The Netherlands: Foris.

Poulisse, N., & Bongaerts, T. (1990). *A closer look at the strategy of transfer*. Paper presented at the 9th AILA conference, Thessaloniki, Greece.

Poulisse, N., & Bongaerts, T. (1994). First language use in second language production. *Applied Linguistics, 15*, 36–57.

Poulisse, N., & Schils, E. (1989). The influence of task-and proficiency-related factors on the use of compensatory strategies: A quantitative analysis. *Language Learning, 39*, 15–48.

Rampton, B. (1997). A sociolinguistic perspective on L2 communication strategies. In G. Kasper & E. Kellerman (Eds.), *Communication strategies: Psycholinguistic and sociolinguistic perspectives*. London: Longman.

Varonis, E. M., & **Gass, S. M.** (1985). Miscommunication in native/non-native conversation. *Language in Society, 14*, 327–343.

Zuengler, J. (1992). Accommodation in native–nonnative interactions: Going beyond the 'what' to the 'why' in second language research. In H. Giles, N. Coupland, & J. Coupland (Eds.), *The context of accommodation: Developments in applied psycholinguistics* (pp. 223–244). Cambridge: Cambridge University Press.

Text 24

Susan Gass

Apples and Oranges:
Or, Why Apples Are Not Orange and Don't Need to Be
A Response to Firth and Wagner

This is a response to the article by Firth and Wagner (F&W) 'On Discourse, Communication, and (Some) Fundamental Concepts in SLA Research' that appeared in MLJ 81.3. The present article deals with three areas discussed by F&W. First, I point out that F&W misinterpret my own work as well as that by others who have written within the input/interactionist framework (and within SLA in general); claims that are attributed to certain researchers were not ones made by those researchers. In particular, the scope of inquiry that F&W attribute to some SLA research is quite different from the actual area of inquiry. Second, I deal with the notion of 'learners as deficient communicators,' arguing that F&W's attribution of this concept to SLA researchers is flawed. Finally, I discuss F&W's reanalysis of data that originally appeared in some of my earlier publications.

I have read with interest the article by Firth and Wagner (F&W) and welcome this opportunity to respond to some of the issues that they raise. My remarks will focus on three areas: (a) I will elaborate on what I see as some fundamental misinterpretations of the scope and goal of my research and the research of others who work within the framework F&W critique, (b) I will deal with the concept of learners as deficient communicators, and (c) I will discuss F&W's interpretation of data that originally appeared in my own work. I have selected these three areas as points of discussion because they are ones that permeate in the entire paper.[1]

The scope of inquiry

Second language acquisition (SLA) is a broad field, often practiced by individuals who at times, because of their different academic backgrounds and orientations, appear to be talking past one another. This diversity has been noted by many, including Gass & Selinker (1994):

> [SLA] is the study of how second languages are learned. It is the study of how learners create a new language system with only limited exposure to a second language. It is the study of what is learned of a second language and what is not

learned; it is the study of why most second language learners do not achieve the same degree of proficiency in a second language as they do in their native language; it is also the study of why only some learners appear to achieve native-like proficiency in more than one language. Additionally, second language acquisition is concerned with the nature of the hypotheses (whether conscious or unconscious) that learners come up with regarding the rules of the second language. Are the rules like those of the native language? Are they like the rules of the language being learned? Are there patterns that are common to all learners regardless of the native language and regardless of the language being learned? Do the rules created by second language learners vary according to the context of use? (p. 1)

As is apparent, there are many ways of approaching the field of SLA. It is also presumably clear from reading the totality of my own work that my primary interest is in the determination of the linguistic systems of learners (sometimes known as nonnative speakers) and in the determination of how that knowledge evolves. In short, the central question relates to how nonprimary acquisition takes place. It therefore strikes me as odd, to say the least, that F&W categorize my work over the past 15 years as attempting to account for 'interactional and sociolinguistic dimensions of language' (p. 285). And it also strikes me as odd that the framework within which some of my work has been categorized (discourse and communication – although this is not a phrase that I would use) 'obviates insight into the nature of language, most centrally the *language use* of second or foreign language (S/FL) speakers' (p. 285, emphasis added). This strikes me as odd because the goal of my work (and the work of others within the input/interaction framework, e.g., Doughty & Pica, 1986; Ellis, Tanaka, & Yamazaki, 1994; Long, 1980, 1981, 1983a, 1983b; Long, Inagaki, & Ortega, in press; Loschky, 1994; Mackey, 1995; Mackey & Philp, in press; Oliver, 1995, in press; Pica, 1987, 1988, 1994; Pica & Doughty, 1985; Pica, Doughty, & Young, 1986; Pica, Holliday, Berducci, & Newman, 1991; Pica, Holliday, & Morgenthaler, 1989; Pica, Young, & Doughty, 1987; Polio & Gass, in press; Sato, 1986, 1990; Swain & Lapkin, in press) has never been to understand language use per se (i.e., use is not an end in itself), but rather to understand what types of interaction might bring about what types of changes in linguistic knowledge (see Ellis, 1984; Gass & Varonis, 1994; Wagner-Gough & Hatch, 1975). Nevertheless, it is true that in order to examine these changes, one must consider language use in context. But in some sense this is trivial; the emphasis in input and interaction studies is on the *language* used and not on the act of communication. This may appear to be a small difference, but to misunderstand the emphasis and the research questions within my own framework can result (as in the case of the F&W article) in fundamental misinterpretations and naïve criticism. In fact, the result is the proverbial (and not very useful) comparison between apples and oranges.

F&W portray cognitive approaches and communication/discourse emphases as mutually incompatible when the real questions about how second languages (L2) are acquired should involve an exploration of how they might relate. For example, how do conversational interactions relate to learning? In what ways does input interact with some innate module? Gass (1988, 1997) examines precisely these questions, laying out a view of acquisition in which the study of interaction relates to linguistic knowledge (with the role of attention receiving primary focus).

The confusion between *learners* as opposed to *users* becomes clear when F&W state: 'although S/FL interactions occurring in noninstructional settings are everyday occurrences (e.g., in the workplace), they have not, as yet, attracted the attention of SLA researchers'[2] (p. 286) and '... it has led to the prioritizing of the individual-as-"nonnative speaker"/"learner" over the participant-as-language-"user" in social interaction' (p. 286). Here again there seems to be general confusion as to what the scope of inquiry is of many (including myself) conducting research in SLA. In fact, the approach that F&W advocate is not actually part of SLA, but part of the broader field of L2 studies[3] (of which SLA is a subset).

The issue of 'scope of inquiry' is to a large degree responsible for the confusion inherent in the F&W article. When they argue that more research should be conducted with L2[4] speakers in a noninstructional setting, there is little with which one can disagree. But there are two avenues that one can take: First, one could use this population to study L2 use as part of the broader field of L2 studies, or one could use this population to study acquisition. With this latter goal in mind, one must remember that many of the individuals in a workplace setting, for example, are not learners in the sense that is of interest to researchers in SLA. They do not evidence change in grammatical systems.[5] Thus, when F&W state that this population is 'uninteresting from the perspective of SLA research,' (p. 292) they may in some instances be correct, if such speakers are for all intents and purposes not 'learners.' In that same discussion, F&W point out that when noneducational studies are used (and here they point to Varonis & Gass, 1985b), the participants are 'cast in the same light as learners.' In Varonis & Gass (1985b) it was not a matter of casting them in the same light as learners, but rather they *were* learners inasmuch as these individuals were students at the English Language Institute of the University of Michigan where they were paying rather large sums of money in order to learn.[6]

The question then arises: Have F&W misunderstood the basic aim of SLA (as opposed to L2 studies) or are they saying that I and others should not be conducting the research that we are conducting (i.e., only a discourse and communication perspective should be taken)?[7] I seriously hope that it is not the latter for many reasons, not the least of which is the fact that it would run counter to the arguments they present earlier in their article.

Thus, F&W's criticism of 'SLA's general preoccupation with the *learner*' (p. 288) makes as much sense as would a criticism of primatologists' general preoccupation with primates. The research question central to SLA that I and others ask is: How do people *learn* a L2? – The question is not: How do people *use* a L2, unless the latter question is a means of getting at the former. If one is talking about learning or acquisition,[8] then how can one not be preoccupied with learners? Learners are, after all, the sine qua non of acquisition.

Learners as deficient communicators

Throughout the article by F&W, there is a criticism – sometimes overt and sometimes subtle – of the field of SLA for elevating 'an idealized "native" speaker above a stereotypicalized "non-native," while viewing the latter as a defective communicator, handicapped by an underdeveloped communicative competence' (p. 285). I assume by this comment that being unable to communicate in a L2 is viewed as something derogatory. In the context within which I have worked, I interpret (and intended) as descriptive the quote at the beginning of F&W's article, which was taken from my own writing (Varonis & Gass, 1985a): 'Native speakers and nonnative speakers are multiply handicapped in conversations *with one another*' (p. 340, emphasis added). Both individuals in a two-party conversation are equally handicapped. It is certainly not a pejorative evaluation of one party over another. This is made clear in Varonis & Gass (1985b): 'Because the fault of non-understanding may reside with either the speaker or the hearer or both, the interlocutors have a shared incompetence' (p. 71). But more to the point, the emphasis in SLA is not on deficiencies qua deficiencies. Rather the emphasis is on the nature of linguistic systems qua systems of learners; the so-called deficiencies (not a term in common use in the SLA literature) may provide insight into systems, but then so do 'correct forms' (see Corder, 1967; Selinker, 1972). This is the whole point of looking at learner systems.

In a similar vein, F&W engage in a discussion of the status of the terminology of native speaker (NS) and nonnative speaker (NNS). They see the 'non'[9] of nonnative as somehow indicating lower status or even the evaluative 'subordination.'[10] How one goes from the descriptive 'non' to subordination is, in my view, a leap in logic. They do acknowledge in note 15 that this terminology may be just a shorthand, and also point out that there may be times when greater precision is needed. There is no doubt that this is correct, but it is not the case that the need for precision is ignored in the SLA literature. Rather, the need for greater precision is frequently and generally reflected in the descriptive and often biographical information given about those from whom language samples are taken (see, e.g., Zobl, 1992, for a study that specifically manipulates the factor of the number of languages known). With regard to specific definitions, a NS of language X simply refers to those who have grown up with language X as their first (and often only) language. In many studies, those with multiple languages (true bilinguals) are often excluded from the database, as are those whose native language or linguistic background is unclear. Within this discussion, F&W express concern with the fact that conversations involving NSs and NNSs are viewed as 'problematic' encounters and that, as a result, they are 'prejudged to be somehow "unusual," anomalous or extraordinary.'[11] (p. 291) The logic here once again escapes me. I assume that by 'unusual, anomalous or extraordinary,' F&W refer to frequency. If that is the case, then it is clear that these conversations are not unusual because they occur with great frequency in the classroom, outside of the classroom, in daily interactions, in the workplace, and so forth. However, frequency has little or nothing to do with problematicity; they can be problematic even while being frequent.

F&W also discuss the implication of homogeneity within groups (i.e., NS groups and NNS groups). They point out, correctly, that the concept of NS can be a problematic one, because, as mentioned above, issues of bilingualism or multilingualism are important considerations. It is true that these issues are often glossed over in determining the nature of linguistic knowledge of potential participants. But it is also the case, as mentioned earlier, that potential 'participants' in experimental work are often excluded in the final pool precisely because some of these issues are unresolved. It is a simplification to state that homogeneity is implied within groups inasmuch as in many studies, characteristics of the individuals within the groups (e.g., exposure to the target language, age, other languages known, years of study) are provided and manipulated when they are deemed relevant. Other categories specifically mentioned by F&W, such as 'father, man, friend, local, guest, opponent, husband, colleague, teacher, teammate, intimate, acquaintance, stranger, brother, son, expert, novice, native speaker, uninitiated, joke teller, speaker, caller, overhearer ad infinitum' (p. 292) (and perhaps others that designate women rather than men) are not included because they are not deemed to be relevant[12] to the question at hand, which is, how are L2s acquired and what is the nature of learner systems? As F&W note, there are many categories that individuals can be placed into, some of which they do not mention, for example, hair color or hand preference. It is a basic assumption of experimental work that categories, such as hair color, that have no theoretical bearing on the question at hand are not part of a design, whereas categories, such as hand preference, that might be relevant might be part of a research design. In other words, relevance has to be established theoretically insofar as it affects the acquisition of a L2.

A final area of concern within this context is the concept of baseline data. Here, too, I find some confusion. It is not so much that NS interaction is the 'norm,' if by that it is meant that NNSs are involved in something subnormal or abnormal. The point is that baseline data reflect data from those who are not involved in *learning*. The crucial variable is the presence or absence of learning. Researchers may need to describe (a) the input to learners and (b) the interactions in which learners are involved, in order to determine what features might affect the cognitive dimension, that is, learning. Further, again because one is studying learning, an assumption is made that what individuals do is in some sense aimed at what the object of learning is, in this case the language and language behaviors of speakers of the target language (in most cases, NSs).[13] But what makes their discussion even more unclear is that F&W do recognize the need for gathering baseline data as the 'norm' when, in a discussion of data presented by Larsen-Freeman and Long (1991), they question the type of talk that occurs in NS – NNS initial interactions as being different from NS – NS interactions, presumably because the latter in this instance represents some sort of 'norm.'

Data analysis

F&W point to specific examples where they question the analysis of the researchers, including mine and that of others. At one point F&W state that one cannot know what the 'constraints and effects of setting and setting-related tasks on the structure of discourse [are]. This raises the possibility that participants may not behave at the behest of their native or nonnative competencies and identities, but as a result of the (quasi-experimental) setting ...' (p. 294). But this is precisely why one needs baseline data, that is, to differentiate what is a factor of being a NNS who is also a learner from what is a factor of the setting or research design.

One example of a questionable reanalysis on the part of F&W comes from their discussion of data that come from Gass & Varonis (1985), repeated here:

1 NNS1: My father now is retire
2 NNS2: retire?
3 NNS1: yes
4 NNS2: oh yeah
1 NNS1: This is your two term?
2 NNS2: Pardon me?
3 NNS1: Two term, this is this term is term your two term? (p. 151)

The point made by Gass & Varonis (1985) is that there is some indication of nonunderstanding on the part of NNS2 in both examples. F&W see the second example as less problematic (I return to this below), in the sense that they agree with the interpretation of nonunderstanding given by Gass & Varonis. In the first example, however, F&W state that 'a more convincing case can surely be made for the interpretation that NNS2's reuse of the word "retire" (line 2) is seen – by NNS1 – as a request for confirmation, rather than as indicating "misunderstanding" or "unacceptance." ' (p. 295). They further argue that Gass & Varonis base their interpretation on the 'marked' usage (i.e., the marked word order). However, we never said anything about word order and second, until I read F&W's article, I had never even considered word order as being the issue. Rather, the word 'retire,' because it is the echoed word, is what I believe (and have believed all along) stimulated the lack of comprehension, likely because of (a) pronunciation or (b) lack of familiarity with the meaning of the word 'retire.' The minor variation in word order would probably not in and of itself interfere with comprehension. But it is important to note that a request for confirmation does come about because there has been some question about what was heard, either linguistically or contextually. In other words, whether it is a total lack of comprehension or only partial comprehension, the point is still the same as the one we made in the 1985 article: There is evidence here of 'incomplete understanding.' A second point to make about this example comes from the fact that F&W do not cite the entire example that is analyzed in Varonis and Gass (1985b). If one considers the end of this extract, NNS1 'reenters' the conversation at exactly this point, but using a slight change of words. After having gone through a lengthy explanation of her father's work, she returns to the issue of retirement by saying '... but now he is old.' Hence, her change in wording may indicate that she took the echo of 'retire' as signifying a lack of understanding of that word.

Finally, I am in sympathy with F&W's point about other possible interpretations of data. In fact, this possibility was discussed in Gass & Varonis (1985) and to a greater extent in Varonis & Gass (1985b). One cannot always determine when a particular form or echo is functioning as a conversational continuant, a request for confirmation with partial comprehension, or an indicator of no comprehension. It is clear that, in this case, there was enough comprehension for NNS2 to repeat the two syllables more or less accurately.

With regard to the second example, F&W point out that perhaps it was not a matter of nonunderstanding, but rather a matter of nonattention or even an acoustics-related problem. With regard to the first, nonattention is always a possibility (however, without some verification from the speaker herself, it seems to me only a researcher's 'cop out,' i.e., a weak interpretation); with regard to the second, it is highly unlikely because we would have heard some noise on the tape that muffled the words and this would have been indicated on the transcript by 'XXX.' But these alternative explanations miss the point. The point is that these signals of nonunderstanding (whatever their origins) provide NNS1 with some indication that some modification needs to be made in order to make herself understood. It is a way of indicating to the speaker that there is something that is interfering with her comprehensibility. Furthermore, learners are definitely aware of their own limitations. Often NNSs, when beginning data elicitation, identify themselves as 'learners' and as 'incompetent' vis à vis the target language and admit this freely, often as a way of apology.

The second piece of data that F&W examine comes from Varonis & Gass (1985b):

1 NNS1: I'm living in Osaka
2 NNS2: Osaka?
3 NNS1: yeah
4 NNS2: yeah Osaka, Osaka
3 NNS1: What do you mean?
4 NNS2: Osaka (Japanese word)
5 NNS1: oh
6 NNS2: I'm not really mean Osaka city. It's near city.
7 NNS1: near city?

F&W use these data to exemplify the model that was proposed in Varonis & Gass (1985b). In that model, we did distinguish units of conversation, labeling them with terms such as *triggers* and *push-downs* and the *main discourse*. F&W question that there could be a 'main discourse devoid of "triggers," "repairs," and "misunderstandings," one where progression is concomitant with problem-free interaction' (p. 295). However, what Varonis and I attempted to do is define 'main discourse' as that part of the discourse that does not have triggers, repairs, or misunderstandings. We did not claim that NS discourse does not have these features or that NS discourse is qualitatively different (in fact, our data in that paper showed that these same features are indeed present in NS discourse). Rather, we defined, for the sake of our model, the top horizontal progression as that part of the discourse that moves along without 'interruptions' for clarification. Of course, misunderstandings and repair sequences, such as those that we presented, are exemplified in all types of conversation. That was the point of our paper – that is, to demonstrate that these units of conversation exist in discourse whether or not learners are involved, and that certain features exist to a greater extent and are qualitatively more complex in discourse between individuals who do not share the same language or the same background. The following example (and ones that we presented in our 1985b article) shows that these so-called 'interruptions' or triggers do occur in discourse with individuals of the same language (and perhaps even more so with individuals who are from different cultural backgrounds but who share the same language background).

Australian: I'll see you this arvo.
American: What?
Australian: Oh, sorry, I'll see you this afternoon.

Conclusion

I find the perspective that F&W have taken to be somewhat perplexing.
I do not disagree that it is a good thing for data to be considered from different
perspectives, but I do believe that in order to make comparisons between or
among approaches, at the minimum one has to be asking the same questions.
Views of language that consider language as a social phenomenon and views of
language that consider language to reside in the individual do not necessarily
have to be incompatible. It may be the case that some parts of language are
constructed socially, but that does not necessarily mean that we cannot
investigate language as an abstract entity that resides in the individual. Further, as
many have argued, there are parts of what we know about language (e.g., what is
grammatical and what is ungrammatical) that cannot come from social
interaction. The establishment of a rigid dichotomy (see Gregg, 1990; Ellis,
1990; Tarone, 1990) is perhaps misguided.

Acknowledgments

I am grateful to Josh Ard and Alison Mackey for helpful comments on an earlier
draft of this paper. I alone am responsible for all errors that remain.

Notes

1 It is necessary to point out from the outset that some of the references F&W
   use to bolster their claims (e.g., Long's 1981 claim about necessary and
   sufficient conditions for learning) are outdated (see, e.g., Long, 1996).
2 It is difficult to see how foreign language interactions take place frequently in
   daily contexts (e.g., the workplace) because by definition foreign language
   learning takes place in the environment in which the foreign language is not
   spoken natively. That nonclassroom interactions take place frequently may be
   the case for L2 contexts, but not to any great degree in FL contexts.
3 Within the category of L2 studies (but not necessarily SLA) I would include
   areas of research such as communication strategies, conversational analysis of
   NNSs, or descriptions of L2 speech acts, unless these can be shown to be
   directly related to how L2s are learned. One might want to diagram this
   relationship something like Figure 1.
4 F&W point out correctly the inappropriate use of the cover-term of *second*
   language acquisition inasmuch as in many instances it is not the L2. This has
   been discussed by Gass & Selinker (1994, p. 4).
5 This does not mean that there would not be any interesting population to
   study from the knowledge perspective, only that the evidence of change is
   often not present.
6 Alison Mackey (personal communication) has pointed out that there may be
   some confusion about the distinction between naturalistic versus classroom
   versus (quasi) experimental research. In fact, as mentioned earlier, it is not

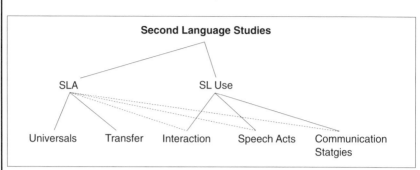

Figure 1
A Characterization of Research in 'SLA'

clear to me why F&W state that the research conducted in Varonis & Gass, 1985b is noneducational when we clearly state in the article that 'All members of the NNS – NNS dyads were students at the English Language Institute of the University of Michigan' (p. 72).

7 On page 288, where F&W discuss the bias of quantitative, cognitive-oriented, experimental, and universal-based research, they do acknowledge that these are not to be interpreted as erroneous or flawed and therefore to be eschewed. What they seem to be arguing is that there are other perspectives and that the field is unbalanced. If that is the case, then F&W's treatise is more of a straw-person treatise rather than one involving true argumentation.

8 I use the terms learning and acquisition more or less without differentiation.

9 This is part of F&W's general discussion in which they characterize the field of SLA as one in which a NS is in an elevated position and as one which ignores the multilinguality of the world. As evidence of this, they point to Long's (1980) work in which he argues for the need for interaction for language learning. His argument is that *interaction* is needed; F&W interpret this as meaning that interaction with NSs is needed. Long's work only dealt with NS – NNS interactions, but to my knowledge, he did not claim that it was that type of dyad which was necessary. In fact, Varonis and Gass (1985b) extended Long's work and argued that NNS – NNS interactions might have greater benefit for learners than NS – NNS interactions. The important point is that interaction is needed – the emphasis in Long's work was not on whom the interaction is with.

10 The issue of subordination and dominance permeates the F&W paper. For example, in the discussion on p. 294, in referring to a conversation presented in Larsen-Freeman and Long (1991), F&W state that 'Input modification researchers would most likely explain this [the NS as information gatherer] as a result of NS's superior language competence; that is, NS is simply "taking the initiative" (by, e.g., controlling topic).' For some reason, F&W feel that the most common interpretation would be one of 'dominance, incompetence, and undeveloped FL ability' (p. 294) (which they say is *interlanguage*, a very strange definition of interlanguage, indeed!). First, it is not clear that 'input modification' researchers would interpret this interaction in that way. In fact, in my collaborative work with Varonis, we often described conversations in

which there appeared to be differential roles for participants (see Gass & Varonis, 1986). Further, in my collaborative work with Houck (e.g., Gass & Houck, forthcoming; Houck & Gass, 1996, 1997), it is clear that I have looked at conversation as being coconstructed, with both parties contributing in different ways.

11 This, of course, holds only for those conversations in which both parties are not fluent in the same language or in which they do not have at least a reasonable degree of fluency in the same language. For example, a conversation between Henry Kissinger and President Clinton would probably not exhibit any of the features described in many of the interactional studies, or at least not any more than occur between two NSs of a language. It must also be noted that the studies to which F&W refer are based by and large on data from individuals who are truly learners and who are conversing in a language to which they have had little exposure and little productive experience.

12 In other words, no previous research studies suggest that these are considerations that need to be taken into account and no theories are dependent on these concepts.

13 The extent of NNS knowledge is of some theoretical concern. Can a L2 learner ever acquire the same kind of knowledge as the knowledge gained by L1 speakers? (see work by Birdsong, 1992; Coppietiers, 1987; Long, 1990; White & Genesee, 1996)

References

Birdsong, D. (1992). Ultimate attainment in second language acquisition. *Language, 68,* 706–755.

Coppieters, R. (1987). Competence differences between native and fluent non-native speakers. *Language, 63,* 544–573.

Corder, S. P. (1967). The significance of learner's errors. *International Review of Applied Linguistics, 5,* 161–170.

Doughty, G., & Pica, T. (1986). 'Information Gap' tasks: Do they facilitate second language acquisition? *TESOL Quarterly, 20,* 305–325.

Ellis, R. (1984). *Classroom second language development.* Oxford, England: Pergamon.

Ellis, R. (1990). A response to Gregg. *Applied Linguistics, 11,* 118–131.

Ellis, R., Tanaka, Y., & Yamazaki, A. (1994). Classroom interaction, comprehension, and the acquisition of L2 word meanings. *Language Learning, 44,* 449–491.

Gass, S. (1988). Integrating research areas: A framework for second language studies. *Applied Linguistics, 9,* 198–217.

Gass, S. (1997). *Input, interaction and the second language learner,* Mahwah, NJ: Lawrence Erlbaum.

Gass, S., & Houck, N. (forthcoming). Interlanguage refusals: A cross-cultural study in Japanese-English refusals.

Gass, S., & Selinker, L. (1994). *Second language acquisition: an introductory course.* Hillsdale, NJ: Lawrence Erlbaum.

Gass, S., & Varonis, E. (1985). Task variation and nonnative/nonnative negotiation of meaning. In S. Gass & C. Madden (Eds.), *Input in second language acquisition* (pp. 149–161). Rowley, MA: Newbury House.

Gass, S., & Varonis, E. (1986). Sex differences in nonnative speaker-nonnative speaker interactions. In R. Day (Ed.), *Talking to learn: Conversation in second language acquisition* (pp. 327–351). Rowley, MA: Newbury House.

Gass, S., & Varonis, E. (1994). Input, interaction and second language production. *Studies in Second Language Acquisition, 16*, 283–302.

Gregg, K. (1990). The variable competence model of second language acquisition, and why it isn't. *Applied Linguistics, 11*, 364–383.

Houck, N., & Gass, S. (1996). Non-native refusals: A methodological perspective. In. S. Gass & J. Neu (Eds.), *Speech acts across cultures* (pp. 45–64). Berlin, Germany: Mouton.

Houck, N., & Gass, S. (1997). Cross-cultural back channels in English refusals: A source of troubles. In A. Jaworski (Ed.), *Silence* (pp. 285–308). Berlin, Germany: Mouton.

Larsen-Freeman, D., & Long, M. H. (1991). *An introduction to second language acquisition research*. Harlow, England: Longman.

Long, M. (1980). Input, interaction, and second language acquisition. Unpublished doctoral dissertation, University of California, Los Angeles.

Long, M. (1981). Input, interaction, and second language acquisition. In H. Winitz (Ed.), *Native language and foreign language acquisition: Annals of the New York academy of sciences, 379* (pp. 259–278). New York: New York Academy of Sciences.

Long, M. (1983a). Linguistic and conversational adjustments to non-native speakers. *Studies in Second Language Acquisition, 5*, 177–193.

Long, M. (1983b). Native speaker/non-native speaker conversation and the negotiation of comprehensible input. *Applied Linguistics, 4*, 126–141.

Long, M. (1990). Maturational constraints on language development, *Studies in Second Language Acquisition, 12*, 251–285.

Long, M. (1996). The role of the linguistic environment in second language acquisition. In W. Ritchie & T. Bhatia (Eds.), *Handbook of second language acquisition* (pp. 413–468). San Diego: Academic.

Long, M., Inagaki, S., & Ortega, L. (in press). The role of implicit negative feedback in SLA: Models and recasts in Japanese and Spanish. *Modern Language Journal, 82* (3).

Loschky, L. (1994). Comprehensible input and second language acquisition: What is the relationship? *Studies in Second Language Acquisition, 16*, 303–324.

Mackey, A. (1995). Stepping up the pace: Input, interaction and interlanguage development, an empirical study of questions in ESL. Unpublished doctoral dissertation, University of Sydney, Australia.

Mackey, A., & Philp, J. (in press). Conversational interaction and second language development: Recasts, responses, and red herrings. *Modern Language Journal, 82* (3).

Oliver, R. (1995). Negative feedback in child NS-NNS conversation. *Studies in Second Language Acquisition, 17*, 459–481.

Oliver, R. (in press). Negotiation of meaning in child interactions. *Modern Language Journal, 82* (3).

Pica, T. (1987). Second language acquisition, social interaction, and the classroom. *Applied Linguistics, 8*, 3–21.

Pica, T. (1988). Interlanguage adjustments as an outcome of NS–NNS negotiated interaction. *Language Learning, 38*, 45–73.

Pica, T. (1994). Research on negotiation: What does it reveal about second-language learning conditions, processes, and outcomes? *Language Learning, 44*, 493–527.

Pica, T., & Doughty, C. (1985). Input and interaction in the communicative language classroom: A comparison of teacher-fronted and group activities. In S. Gass & C. Madden (Eds.), *Input in second language acquisition* (pp. 115–132). Rowley, MA: Newbury House.

Pica, T., Doughty, C., & Young, R. (1986). Making input comprehensible: Do interactional modifications help? *ITL Review of Applied Linguistics, 72*, 1–25.

Pica, T., Holliday, L., Lewis, N., Berducci, D., & Newman, J. (1991). Language learning through interaction: What role does gender play? *Studies in Second Language Acquisition, 13*, 343–376.

Pica, T., Holliday, L., Lewis, N., & Morgenthaler, L. (1989). Comprehensible output as an outcome of linguistic demands on the learner. *Studies in Second Language Acquisition, 11*, 63–90.

Pica, T., Young, R., & Doughty, C. (1987). The impact of interaction on comprehension. *TESOL Quarterly, 21*, 737–758.

Polio, C., & Gass, S. (in press). The role of interaction in native speaker comprehension of nonnative speaker speech. *Modern Language Journal, 82* (3).

Sato, C. (1986). Conversation and interlanguage development: Rethinking the connection. In R. Day (Ed.), *Talking to learn* (pp. 23–45). Rowley, MA: Newbury House.

Sato, C. (1990). *The syntax of conversation in interlanguage development.* Tübingen, Germany: Gunter Narr Verlag.

Selinker, L. (1972). Interlanguage. *International Review of Applied Linguistics, 10*, 209–231.

Swain, M., & Lapkin, S. (in press). An anatomy of interaction and second language learning: Two adolescent French immersion students working together. *Modern Language Journal, 82* (3).

Tarone, E. (1990). On variation in interlanguage: A response to Gregg. *Applied Linguistics, 11*, 392–399.

Varonis, E., & Gass, S. (1985a). Miscommunication in native/non-native conversation. *Language in Society, 14*, 327–343.

Varonis, E., & Gass, S. (1985b). Non-native/non-native conversations: A model for negotiation of meaning. *Applied Linguistics, 6*, 71–90.

Wagner-Gough, J., & Hatch, E. (1975). The importance of input data in second language studies. *Language Learning, 2*, 297–307.

White, L., & Genesee, F. (1996). How native is near-native? The issue of ultimate attainment in adult second language acquisition. *Second Language Research, 12*, 233–265.

Zobl, H. (1992). Prior linguistic knowledge and the conservation of the learning procedure: Grammaticality judgments of unilingual and multilingual learners. In S. Gass & L. Selinker (Eds.), *Language transfer in language learning* (pp. 176–196). Amsterdam: John Benjamins.

Text 25

Alan Firth and Johannes Wagner

SLA Property: No Trespassing!

We are grateful for the considered and thought-provoking responses of our colleagues, both those supporting our views and those opposing them. In general, we feel that the response articles lend support to our position (stated in detail in *MLJ 81,3*) that conceptual and methodological tensions in Second Language Acquisition (SLA) do exist, and that they indicate that the field is in need of conceptual and methodological broadening and is thus more or less ready and willing to reconsider concepts which have generally been unquestioningly accepted and well established (specifically, the concepts of learner, nonnative, and interlanguage). We sincerely hope that our *MLJ* article and its responses will provide a framework upon which fruitful debates may be conducted in the years to come.

The critics of our article hold that our views are, in general, not relevant to SLA (see Long, *MLJ 81,3*, 1997; Poulisse, *MLJ 81, 3*, 1997; and to some extent, Kasper, *MLJ 81,3*, 1997) or are naïve (Gass, this issue). The consensus of our critics seems to be that our arguments have been stated from 'outside' SLA proper; that is, that our position is related to research in second language use, but not to acquisition per se. As Gass points out, research in language use is considered useful for, though ultimately secondary to, psycholinguistic research into acquisition, because – it is claimed – language use provides the context for psycholinguistic processes which are the real and bona fide focus of SLA.

This position is not entirely unproblematic. To begin, what constitutes 'acquisition' is essentially unclear; we cannot be sure where 'use' ends and 'acquisition' begins. There is surely no easily distinguishable dividing line between psycholinguistics and sociolinguistics. More important for the current debate, the emphasis on the centrality of acquisition, rather than use, is a view that erects barriers, sealing off the area of SLA as a kind of intellectual 'private property' of documented, card-carrying SLA researchers (the 'villains' referred to by Long, p. 318). Based particularly on the responses of Long and Poulisse, we cannot help but register a sense of 'Trespassers will be prosecuted!'

Before we sum up our arguments, which have been presented in different papers,[1] we look at two issues which, on a metatheoretical level, are relevant for the current debate.

The competence argument

If, as we argue, language competence is a fundamentally transitional, situational, and dynamic entity, then any language users will always be 'learners' in some respects. New or partly known registers, styles, language-related tasks, lexical items, terminologies and structures, routinely confront language users, calling for the contingent adaption and transformation of existing knowledge and competence, and the acquisition of new knowledge. As we make clear in our *MLJ* article, we are unable to accept the premises of 'interlanguage' – namely, that language learning is a transitional process that has a distinct and visible 'end' (in SLA's case, the end being acquisition of 'native-like' competence). Two consequences thus arise: (a) that the notion of 'acquisition' is far less clear-cut than Kasper, Long, and Poulisse appear to assume in their responses; (b) that the study of foreign language interaction in a variety of natural, social contexts – outside the formal educational environment – must be regarded as centrally relevant for the study of acquisition. Acquisition and learning do not stop; certainly they do not stop outside the classroom.

It is in relation to the competence debate that we find a major difference between our position and that of most of our critics. Our own interpretation of 'functionalist' evidence[2] (from first language acquisition and from the modelling of cognitive processes) follows Vytgotsky (as outlined by Hall, *MLJ 81,3*, 1997) and holds that cognitive structures are influenced and, indeed, developed through engagement in social activity (see Wertsch, 1991). From this perspective, it can be said that language use forms cognition. This effectively renders the notion of competence (remember, it has been defined in contrast to performance) obsolete; one simply cannot unproblematically separate one from the other. In our view, SLA seems to be dominated by Chomskian thinking to such a degree that others' frames of reference for the understanding of language and cognition have become inconceivable. We are surprised that this structural, cognitive paradigm is advocated by researchers who actually study interactional aspects of SLA. For example, we are puzzled that Gass maintains a clear-cut distinction between language used in interaction and the act of communication. Whereas Poulisse and Gass argue that language competence is system plus its use, we believe that both are indistinguishable. This is a major difference in the view of language per se. We maintain that a 'functionalist' model of language, firmly rooted in contingent, situated, and interactional experiences of the individual as a social being, is better suited to understand language and language acquisition in the long run than a structural model, even though it may become a very long run.

The expert argument

Studies of naturally occurring foreign language interaction are relevant for SLA in that they describe what speakers of foreign (or as Rampton [*MLJ 81,3*, 1997, p. 329] prefers, 'other' or 'additional') languages are doing in a variety of everyday contexts. In these cases, studies of foreign/other/additional language use will specify the research goals of language acquisition studies. This is where the (to us) problematic concept of 'baseline data' creeps in. If there is a need for comparison between the learner population and the population which has in some nontrivial ways mastered what the learners are attempting to do (though we are extremely uneasy about this view of learners), then it is surely advanced foreign/other/additional language speakers, not natives, that would constitute the relevant baseline. (Though again, we are uneasy about the distinction between 'advanced speakers' and 'natives' because these distinctions are far from clear-cut).

Our argument in several papers has been that SLA – as an apparently hermetically sealed area of study – is in danger of losing contact with research on language and social interaction. This state of affairs is visible in three ways: (a) the narrow spectrum of data types and contexts examined in SLA studies, (b) the methods of analysis and the underlying analytic assumption of 'learner-deficient interactant,' and finally (c) the theoretical understanding of what constitutes discourse and communication. On all three levels, we pointed in our article to what we perceive to be serious problems in current SLA. In what follows, it may be useful to adumbrate our position again before it becomes lost in the specific criticisms targeted at our paper.

The data

SLA has collected data mainly in lab-like situations. There is reason to believe that this quasi-experimental situation triggers a certain set of interactional activities which – and here our critics are correct – have been shown to occur systematically in a large number of studies (see Liddicoat's [*MLJ 81,3*, 1997] comments). Because we do not find comparable evidence in our data from naturally occurring, everyday, or workplace interactions between speakers of different languages,[3] our conclusion is that experimental, elicited data may provoke the nonnative speaker into acting as an interactional guinea pig (see Wagner, in press). For this reason, such data cannot unproblematically be taken as a basis for generalizations. We are astonished that SLA research has, in general, resisted data types from a variety of mundane, everyday, or professional social contexts in actual speech communities.

The method

Interaction analysis uncovers and explicates the locally sensitive use of the resources deployed by interactants. A L2 is surely one of several resources deployed by interactants. For some, the L2 may be perceived as being underdeveloped, inchoate, imperfect, and faulty, and indeed, interactants may display an orientation to this. Although we subscribe to Long's (1983a, 1983b; Larsen-Freeman & Long, 1991) previously published views on the importance of studying interaction as a way of gaining insight into the acquisition and use of resources, we do not subscribe to SLA's generally adopted methodology for the analysis of interaction. As we were at pains to point out in our article, the adopted methodologies are overridingly and a priori deficit oriented. Even though we would not wish to exclude all analyses of data elicited in experimental settings, we would maintain that such data types are useful once they have been subjected to a deficit-free description of the interactional features in the data.

The theory

The whole SLA issue of interactionally modified discourse presupposes a notion of nonmodified, somehow 'pure' or 'real' communication. In SLA, communication appears to be viewed as the transfer of information that can be accomplished appropriately (i.e., paralleling or mirroring the native speaker 'baseline') or in an inappropriate, deficient manner. Only if one adopts this 'deficient' model does the notion of interactional modification of meaning make sense. Unfortunately, though, this view of communication cannot be upheld when looking at interactions empirically, without preconceived ideas of what is 'normal' or 'appropriate.' Communication is not simply transfer of information in a 'normal,' that is, native-speaker-equivalent, manner. What may appear 'abnormal' to observer-analysts may be regarded as appropriate and 'normal' by the interactants themselves. Communicative meaning is created incrementally; it is locally situated and emerges between participants. Because we say this repeatedly in our article, it may begin to sound like a riddle, but repetition of the riddle may be necessary as long as SLA subscribes to an empirically flawed theory of interaction.

Our arguments and recommendations for a 'reconceptualized' SLA are not by any means the end of the debate, as the various responses to our article make abundantly clear. Nor do we feel that our position is watertight; Long and Kasper are right to point out the centrality of acquisition, and the need to keep our eye on the proverbial ball. But such arguments must also acknowledge that the notion of acquisition is itself not clearly defined. It overlaps with notions of contingent application, modification, transformation, 'local' design, and situational adaption. Hence, as we argue above, it is surely pertinent to ask where 'use' and 'acquisition' stand in relation to one another. Although Kasper reminds us in the title of her article that ' "A" stands for acquisition,' we take this opportunity to venture that acquisition will not occur without use. It is surely time to take seriously the possibility of deconstructing such dichotomies as use versus acquisition, sociolinguistics versus psycholinguistics, and language use versus communicative act. There is more than one way to skin a cat, as the old adage says. Likewise, there will be more than one way to conduct effective and insightful SLA research on acquisition through interaction. We urge SLA practitioners to open their conceptual and methodological gates and to make 'trespassers' welcome.

Notes

1 See Firth (1996), Wagner (1996), Firth & Wagner (1997), Wagner & Firth (1997). Wagner (in press).
2 Length limitations on this response prevent us from longer argumentation for this case. Elman et al. (1996) may serve as a general reference.
3 We have access to data from Danish companies who use English, German, Danish, and Swedish and, in some instances, French, Italian, and Spanish with speakers from a number of different European and non-European countries.

References

Elman, J., Bates, E. A., Johnson, M. H., Karmiloff-Smith, A., Parasi, D., & Plunkett, K. (1996). *Rethinking innateness: A connectionist perspective on development*. Cambridge, MA: M.I.T. Press.

Firth, A. (1996). On the discursive accomplishment of 'normality:' On lingua franca English and conversation analysis. *Journal of Pragmatics, 26*, 237–259.

Firth, A., & Wagner, J. (1997). On Discourse, communication, and (some) fundamental concepts in SLA Research. *Modern Language Journal, 81*, 285–300.

Gass, S. (1997). Apples and oranges; Or, why apples are not oranges and don't need to be. *Modern Language Journal, 82*, 83–90.

Hall, J. K. (1997). A consideration of SLA as a theory of practice: A response to Firth and Wagner. *Modern Language Journal, 81*, 301–306.

Kasper, G. (1997). 'A' stands for acquisition: A response to Firth and Wagner. *Modern Language Journal, 81*, 307–312.

Larsen-Freeman, D., & Long, M. H. (1991). *An introduction to second language acquisition research*. London: Longman.

236 Controversies in Applied Linguistics

Liddicoat, A. (1997). Interaction, social structure, and second language use: A response to Firth and Wagner. *Modern Language Journal, 81*, 313–317.

Long, M. H. (1983a). Native speaker/non-native speaker conversation and the negotiation of comprehensible input. *Applied Linguistics, 4*, 126–141.

Long, M. H. (1983b). Native speaker/non-native speaker conversation in the second language classroom. In M. Clarke & J. Handscombe (Eds.), *On TESOL '82* (pp. 207–225). Washington, DC: TESOL.

Long, M. H. (1997). Construct validity in SLA research: A response to Firth and Wagner. *Modern Language Journal, 81*, 318–323.

Poulisse, N. (1997). Some words in defense of the psycholinguistic approach: A response to Firth and Wagner. *Modern Language Journal, 81*, 324–328.

Rampton, B. (1997). Second language research in late modernity: A response to Firth and Wagner. *Modern Language Journal, 81*, 329–333.

Schegloff, E. A. (1993). Reflections on quantification in the study of conversation. *Research on Language and Social Interaction, 26*, 99–128.

Wagner, J. (1996). Foreign language acquisition through interaction: A critical review of research on conversational adjustments. *Journal of Pragmatics, 26*, 215–235.

Wagner, J. (in press). On doing 'being a guinea pig.' A response to Seedhouse. *Journal of Pragmatics.*

Wagner, J., & Firth, A. (1997). Communication strategies at work. In G. Kasper & E. Kellerman (Eds.), *Advances in communication strategies research* (pp. 323–344). London: Longman.

Wertsch, J. V. (1991). *Voices of the mind.* Hemel Hempstead, England: Harvester-Wheatsheaf.

While texts 20 to 25 represent a controversy with numerous participants, the second SLA-related exchange in this section has a more straightforward structure: Bonny Norton Peirce addresses issues of social identity and of investment, two notions not commonly encountered in 'traditional' SLA. Her theorizing of social identity is then called into question by Stephen Price. In Bonny Norton Peirce's response, the very nature of reading and responding to texts is foregrounded in a way that seems particularly suitable to the present volume. And as always, readers are invited to consider specific aspects of this exchange with the help of (some of) the study questions on pp 325ff.

Text 26

Bonny Norton Peirce:
Ontario Institute for Studies in Education

Social Identity, Investment, and Language Learning*

The author argues that second language acquisition (SLA) theorists have struggled to conceptualize the relationship between the language learner and the

---

* Earlier drafts of this paper were presented at the Social Issues/Social Change Conference in Toronto, Canada, in July 1993; and the 28th Annual TESOL convention in Baltimore, United States, in March 1994.

social world because they have not developed a comprehensive theory of social identity which integrates the language learner and the language learning context. She also maintains that SLA theorists have not adequately addressed how relations of power affect interaction between language learners and target language speakers. Using data collected in Canada from January to December 1991 from diaries, questionnaires, individual and group interviews, and home visits, the author illustrates how and under what conditions the immigrant women in her study created, responded to, and sometimes resisted opportunities to speak English. Drawing on her data analysis as well as her reading in social theory, the author argues that current conceptions of the individual in SLA theory need to be reconceptualized, and she draws on the poststructuralist conception of social identity as multiple, a site of struggle, and subject to change to explain the findings from her study. Further, she argues for a conception of investment rather than motivation to capture the complex relationship of language learners to the target language and their sometimes ambivalent desire to speak it. The notion of investment conceives of the language learner, not as ahistorical and unidimensional, but as having a complex social history and multiple desires. The article includes a discussion of the implications of the study for classroom teaching and current theories of communicative competence.

> Everybody working with me is Canadian. When I started to work there, they couldn't understand that it might be difficult for me to understand everything and know about everything what it's normal for them. To explain it more clearly I can write an example, which happened few days ago. The girl [Gail] which is working with me pointed at the man and said:
> 'Do you see him?' – I said
> 'Yes, Why?'
> 'Don't you know him?'
> 'No. I don't know him.'
> 'How come you don't know him. Don't you watch TV. That's Bart Simpson.'
> It made me feel so bad and I didn't answer her nothing. Until now I don't know why this person was important.
> Eva, February 8, 1991[1]

> No researcher today would dispute that language learning results from participation in communicative events. Despite any claims to the contrary, however, the nature of this learning remains undefined.
> Savignon, 1991, p. 271

How would second language acquisition (SLA) theorists conceptualize the relationship between Eva, an immigrant language learner, and Gail, an anglophone Canadian, both of whom are located in the same North American workplace in the 1990s? Because they have struggled to conceptualize the relationship between the individual language learner and larger social processes, a question such as this poses a problem for SLA theorists. In general, many SLA theorists have drawn artificial distinctions between the language learner and the language learning context. On the one hand, *the individual* is described with

---

[1] Quoted in Peirce, 1993, p. 197. Eva explained that the man her co-worker pointed to had a 'Bart Simpson' t-shirt on. Spelling mistakes in the original have been corrected.

respect to a host of affective variables such as his/her motivation to learn a second language. Krashen (1981, 1982), for example, has hypothesized that *comprehensible input* in the presence of a low *affective filter* is the major causal variable in SLA. In Krashen's view, this affective filter comprises the learner's motivation, self-confidence, and anxiety state – all of which are variables that pertain to the individual rather than the social context. Furthermore, the personality of the individual has been described unidimensionally as introverted or extroverted, inhibited or uninhibited, field dependent or field independent.[2] With reference to these theories, Eva might be described as someone who is unmotivated with a high affective filter; perhaps an introverted personality who is unable to interact appropriately with her interlocutors. Or she might be portrayed as a poor language learner who has not developed sociolinguistic competence.

Other theories of SLA focus on social rather than individual variables in language learning. The *social* frequently refers to group differences between the language learner group and the target language group (Schumann, 1976). In this view, where there is congruence between the second language group and the target language group, what Schumann (1976) terms *social distance* between them is considered to be minimal, in turn facilitating the acculturation of the second language group into the target language group and enhanced language learning. Where there is great social distance between two groups, little acculturation is considered to take place, and the theory predicts that members of the second language group will not become proficient speakers of the target language. Supporters of the Acculturation Model of SLA (Schumann, 1978) might argue that despite the fact that Eva and Gail are in contact, there is great social distance between them because there is little congruence between Eva's culture and that of Gail. For this reason, Eva might struggle to interact successfully with members of the target language community.

Because of the dichotomous distinctions between the language learner and the social world, there are disagreements in the literature on the way affective variables interact with the larger social context. For example, although Krashen regards motivation as a variable independent of social context, Spolsky (1989) regards the two as inextricably intertwined. Although Krashen draws distinctions between self-confidence, motivation, and anxiety, Clement, Gardner, and Smythe (quoted in Spolsky, 1989) consider motivation and anxiety as a subset of self-confidence. Although Krashen considers self-confidence as an intrinsic characteristic of the language learner, Gardner (1985) argues that self-confidence arises from positive experiences in the context of the second language: 'Self-confidence ... develops as a result of positive experiences in the context of the second language and serves to motivate individuals to learn the second language' (p. 54).

Such disagreements in the SLA literature should not be dismissed, as Gardner (1989) dismisses them, as 'more superficial than real' (p. 137). I suggest that this confusion arises because artificial distinctions are drawn between the individual and the social, which lead to arbitrary mapping of particular factors on either the individual or the social, with little rigorous justification. In the field of SLA, theorists have not adequately addressed why it is that a learner may sometimes be

---

[2] See Brown (1987) for an overview of the literature on personality variables and language learning.

motivated, extroverted, and confident and sometimes unmotivated, introverted, and anxious; why in one place there may be social distance between a specific group of language learners and the target language community, whereas in another place the social distance may be minimal; why a learner can sometimes speak and other times remains silent. Although muted, there is an uneasy recognition by some theorists that current theory about the relationship between the language learner and the social world is problematic. Scovel (1978) for example, has found that research on foreign language anxiety suffers from several ambiguities, and Gardner and MacIntyre (1993) remain unconvinced of the relationship between 'personality variables' (p. 9) and language achievement.

The central argument of this paper is that SLA theorists have not developed a comprehensive theory of social identity that integrates the language learner and the language learning context. Furthermore, they have not questioned how relations of power in the social world affect social interaction between second language learners and target language speakers. Although many SLA theorists (Ellis, 1985; Krashen, 1981; Schumann, 1978; Spolsky, 1989; Stern, 1983) recognize that language learners do not live in idealized, homogeneous communities but in complex, heterogeneous ones, such heterogeneity has been framed uncritically. Theories of the good language learner have been developed on the premise that language learners can choose under what conditions they will interact with members of the target language community and that the language learner's access to the target language community is a function of the learner's motivation. Thus Gardner and MacIntyre (1992), for example, argue that 'the major characteristic of the informal context is that it is voluntary. Individuals can either participate or not in informal acquisition contexts' (p. 213). SLA theorists have not adequately explored how inequitable relations of power limit the opportunities L2 learners have to practice the target language outside the classroom. In addition, many have assumed that learners can be defined unproblematically as motivated or unmotivated, introverted or extroverted, inhibited or uninhibited, without considering that such affective factors are frequently socially constructed in inequitable relations of power, changing over time and space, and possibly coexisting in contradictory ways in a single individual.

Drawing on a recent study (Peirce, 1993) as well as my reading in social theory, I will propose a theory of social identity that I hope will contribute to debates on second language learning. This theory of social identity, informed by my data, assumes that power relations play a crucial role in social interactions between language learners and target language speakers. In March 1991, for example, when I asked Eva why the communication breakdown between her and Gail had taken place, Eva indicated she had felt humiliated at the time. She said that she could not respond to Gail because she had been positioned as a 'strange woman.' What had made Eva feel strange? When I analyzed Eva's data more closely, I realized that Gail's questions to Eva were in fact rhetorical. Gail did not expect, or possibly even desire a response from Eva: 'How come you don't know him. Don't you watch TV. That's Bart Simpson.' It was Gail and not Eva who could determine the grounds on which interaction could proceed; it was Gail and not Eva who had the power to bring closure to the conversation. If, as Savignon (1991) argues, language learning results from participation in communicative events, it is important to investigate how power relations are implicated in the nature of this learning.

I therefore take the position that notions of the individual and the language learner's personality in SLA theory need to be reconceptualized in ways that will problematize dichotomous distinctions between the language learner and the language learning context. I argue that SLA theory needs to develop a conception of the language learner as having a complex social identity that must be understood with reference to larger, and frequently inequitable social structures which are reproduced in day-to-day social interaction. In taking this position, I foreground the role of language as constitutive of and constituted by a language learner's social identity. It is through language that a person negotiates a sense of self within and across different sites at different points in time, and it is through language that a person gains access to – or is denied access to – powerful social networks that give learners the opportunity to speak (Heller, 1987). Thus language is not conceived of as a neutral medium of communication but is understood with reference to its social meaning. I support these arguments with findings from a longitudinal case study of the language learning experiences of a group of immigrant women in Canada (Peirce, 1993).

The study: immigrant women as language learners

From January to June 1990 I helped teach a 6-month ESL course to a group of recent immigrants at Ontario College in Newtown, Canada.[3] After the course was complete, I invited the learners to participate in a longitudinal case study of their language learning experiences in Canada. Five women agreed to participate in the study: Mai from Vietnam, Eva and Katarina from Poland, Martina from Czechoslovakia, and Felicia from Peru. My research questions were divided into two parts:

Part I

> How are the opportunities for immigrant women in Canada to practice ESL socially structured outside the classroom? How do immigrant women respond to and act upon these social structures to create, use, or resist opportunities to practice English? To what extent should their actions be understood with reference to their investment in English and their changing social identities across time and space?

Part II

> How can an enhanced understanding of natural language learning and social identity inform SLA theory, in general, as well as ESL pedagogy for immigrant women in Canada? (Peirce, 1993, p. 18)

The study lasted 12 months – from January to December 1991. A major source of data collection was a diary study: From January to June 1991, the participants kept records of their interactions with anglophone Canadians and used diaries to reflect on their language learning experiences in the home, workplace, and

---

[3] The names of places and participants have been changed to protect the identities of participants.

community. During the course of the study, we met on a regular basis to share some of the entries the women had made in their diaries and to discuss their insights and concerns. I also drew a substantial amount of data from two detailed questionnaires I administered before and after the study, as well as personal and group interviews, and home visits.

One of the assumptions on which I based my research questions was that practice in the target language is a necessary condition of second language learning. As Spolsky (1989) argues, extensive exposure to the target language, in relevant kinds and amounts, and the opportunity to practice the target language are essential for second language learning: Learning cannot proceed without exposure and practice. These conditions, furthermore, are graded: The more exposure and practice, the more proficient the learner will become. Spolsky (1989) argues that the language learner can have exposure to and practice in the target language in two qualitatively different settings: the natural or informal environment of the target language community or the formal environment of the classroom. The focus of my research was on the natural language learning experiences of the women in their homes, workplaces, and communities.

The theory: social identity, investment, and the right to speak

Social Identity as Multiple, a Site of Struggle, and Changing Over Time

In examining the relationship between the language learners in my study and the social worlds in which they lived, I drew in particular on Weedon's (1987) conception of social identity or subjectivity. Feminist poststructuralism, like much postmodern educational theory (Cherryholmes, 1988; Giroux, 1988; Simon, 1992), explores how prevailing power relations between individuals, groups, and communities affect the life chances of individuals at a given time and place. Weedon's work, however, is distinguished from that of other postmodern theorists in the rigorous and comprehensive way in which her work links individual experience and social power in a theory of subjectivity. Weedon (1987) defines subjectivity as 'the conscious and unconscious thoughts and emotions of the individual, her sense of herself and her ways of understanding her relation to the world' (p. 32). Furthermore, like other poststructuralist theorists who inform her work (Derrida, Lacan, Kristeva, Althusser, and Foucault), Weedon does not neglect the central role of language in her analysis of the relationship between the individual and the social: 'Language is the place where actual and possible forms of social organization and their likely social and political consequences are defined and contested. Yet it is also the place where our sense of ourselves, our subjectivity, is constructed' (p. 21).

Three defining characteristics of subjectivity, as outlined by Weedon, are particularly important for understanding my data: the multiple nature of the subject; subjectivity as a site of struggle; and subjectivity as changing over time. First, Weedon (1987) argues, the terms *subject* and *subjectivity* signify a different conception of the individual from that associated with humanist conceptions of the individual dominant in Western philosophy. Whereas humanist conceptions of the individual – and most definitions of the individual in SLA research – presuppose that every person has an essential, unique, fixed, and coherent core (introvert/extrovert; motivated/unmotivated; field dependent/ field independent), poststructuralism depicts the individual as diverse, contradictory, and dynamic; multiple rather than unitary, decentered rather than centered. By way of example (and at the risk of oversimplification) a humanist might be attracted by a book with the title *How to Discover Your True Self*. A poststructuralist, on the other hand, might prefer a book titled *It's OK to Live with Contradictions.*

Second, the conception of social identity as a site of struggle is an extension of the position that social identity is multiple and contradictory. Subjectivity is produced in a variety of social sites, all of which are structured by relations of power in which the person takes up different subject positions – teacher, mother, manager, critic – some positions of which may be in conflict with others. In addition, the subject is not conceived of as passive; he/she is conceived of as both subject of and subject to relations of power within a particular site, community, and society: The subject has human agency. Thus the subject positions that a person takes up within a particular discourse are open to argument: Although a person may be positioned in a particular way within a given discourse, the person might resist the subject position or even set up a counterdiscourse which positions the person in a powerful rather than marginalized subject position. Third, in arguing that subjectivity is multiple, contradictory, and a site of struggle, feminist poststructuralism highlights the changing quality of a person's social identity. As Weedon (1987) argues, 'the political significance of decentering the subject and abandoning the belief in essential subjectivity is that it opens up subjectivity to change' (p. 33). This is a crucial point for second language educators in that it opens up possibilities for educational intervention.

I will demonstrate below that although it might be tempting to argue that Eva was essentially an introverted language learner, the data which follows provides convincing evidence that Eva's social identity was not fixed; it was a site of struggle and changed dramatically over time – as did her interactions with anglophone Canadians. At the time of the Bart Simpson exchange, however, Gail was in a powerful subject position and Eva did not actively resist being positioned as 'strange.' Because of the construction of Eva's social identity in Canada as immigrant, the social meaning of Gail's words to her were understood by Eva in this context. Had Eva been, for example, an anglophone Canadian who endorsed public rather than commercial television, she could have set up a counterdiscourse to Gail's utterance, challenging Gail's interest in popular culture. However, because of the unequal relations of power between Gail and Eva at that point in time, it was Gail who was subject *of* the discourse on Bart Simpson; Eva remained subject *to* this discourse. Thus while Eva had been offered the opportunity to engage in social interaction, to 'practice' her English, her subject position within the larger discourse of which she and Gail were a part undermined this opportunity: 'It made me feel so bad and I didn't answer her nothing.' This discourse must be understood not only in relation to the words that were said, but in relationship to larger structures within the workplace, and Canadian society at large, in which immigrant language learners often struggle for acceptance in Canadian society.

From Motivation to Investment

A logical extension of reconceptualizing notions of the individual in SLA theory is the need to problematize the concept of motivation. In the field of second language learning, the concept of motivation is drawn primarily from the field of social psychology, where attempts have been made to quantify a learner's commitment to learning the target language. The work of Gardner and Lambert (1972) and Gardner (1985) has been particularly influential in introducing the notions of *instrumental* and *integrative* motivation into the field of SLA. In their work, instrumental motivation references the desire that language learners have to learn a second language for utilitarian purposes, such as employment, whereas integrative motivation references the desire to learn a language to integrate successfully with the target language community.

Such conceptions of motivation, which are dominant in the field of SLA, do not capture the complex relationship between relations of power, identity, and language learning that I have been investigating in my study of immigrant women. In my view, the conception of investment rather than motivation more accurately signals the socially and historically constructed relationship of the women to the target language and their sometimes ambivalent desire to learn and practice it. My conception of investment has been informed by my reading in social theory, although I have not as yet found a comprehensive discussion of the term in these contexts. It is best understood with reference to the economic metaphors that Bourdieu (1977) uses in his work – in particular the notion of *cultural capital*. Bourdieu and Passeron (1977) use the term cultural capital to reference the knowledge and modes of thought that characterize different classes and groups in relation to specific sets of social forms. They argue that some forms of cultural capital have a higher exchange value than others in a given social context. I take the position that if learners invest in a second language, they do so with the understanding that they will acquire a wider range of symbolic and material resources,[4] which will in turn increase the value of their cultural capital. Learners will expect or hope to have a good return on that investment – a return that will give them access to hitherto unattainable resources. Furthermore, drawing on Ogbu (1978), I take the position that this return on investment must be seen as commensurate with the effort expended on learning the second language.

It is important to note that the notion of investment I am advocating is not equivalent to instrumental motivation. The conception of instrumental motivation generally presupposes a unitary, fixed, and ahistorical language learner who desires access to material resources that are the privilege of target language speakers. In this view, motivation is a property of the language learner – a fixed personality trait. The notion of investment, on the other hand, attempts to capture the relationship of the language learner to the changing social world. It conceives of the language learner as having a complex social identity and multiple desires. The notion presupposes that when language learners speak, they are not only exchanging information with target language speakers but they are

---

[4] By *symbolic resources* I refer to such resources as language, education, and friendship, whereas I use the term *material resources* to include capital goods, real estate, and money.

constantly organizing and reorganizing a sense of who they are and how they relate to the social world. Thus an investment in the target language is also an investment in a learner's own social identity, an identity which is constantly changing across time and space.

Communicative Competence and the Right to Speak

Given the position that communication and social interaction are implicated in the construction of a language learner's social identity, my research on immigrant women in Canada develops questions I have raised in earlier research (Peirce, 1989) about the way Hymes' (1971) views on communicative competence have been taken up by many theorists in the field of second language learning over the past 15 years. I have argued (Peirce, 1989) that although it is important for language learners to understand the rules of use of the target language, it is equally important for them to explore whose interests these rules serve. What is considered appropriate usage is not self-evident but must be understood with reference to relations of power between interlocutors. I take the position that theories of communicative competence in the field of second language learning should extend beyond an understanding of the appropriate rules of use in a particular society, to include an understanding of the way rules of use are socially and historically constructed to support the interests of a dominant group within a given society. Drawing on Bourdieu (1977), I argue in this paper that the definition of competence should include an awareness of the right to speak – what Bourdieu calls 'the power to impose reception' (p. 75). His position is that the linguist takes for granted the conditions for the establishment of communication: that those who speak regard those who listen as worthy to listen and that those who listen regard those who speak as worthy to speak. However, as Bourdieu argues, it is precisely such assumptions that must be called into question.

The analysis: identity, investment, and language learning

Although the findings from my study are extensive (Peirce, 1993), I wish to highlight data that address the question, How can an enhanced understanding of natural language learning and social identity inform SLA theory? First, I will address how the notion of investment helps explain the contradictions between the women's motivation to learn English and their sometimes ambivalent desire to speak it. Second, I highlight data from two of the participants – Martina and Eva – to analyze the relationship between investment, social identity, and language learning.

Investment and Social Identity

All the participants in the study were highly motivated to learn English. They all took extra courses to learn English; they all participated in the diary study; they all wished to have more social contact with anglophone Canadians; and all of them, except Martina, indicated that they felt comfortable speaking English to friends or people they knew well. It is significant, however, that all the women felt uncomfortable talking to people in whom they had a particular symbolic or material investment. Eva, who came to Canada for 'economical advantage',[5] and was eager to work with anglophones, practice her English and get better jobs, was silenced when the customers in her workplace made comments about her accent. Mai, who came to Canada for her life in the future and depended on the wishes of management for her job security and financial independence, was most uncomfortable speaking to her boss. Katarina, who came to Canada to escape a communist and atheistic system, and had a great affective investment in her status as a professional, felt most uncomfortable talking to her teacher, the doctor, and other anglophone professionals. Martina, who had given up a surveyor's job to come to Canada 'for the children,' was frustrated and uncomfortable when she could not defend her family's rights in the public world. Felicia, who had come to Canada to escape 'terrorism,' and had great affective investment in her Peruvian identity, felt most uncomfortable speaking English in front of Peruvians who speak English fluently.

The concept of motivation as currently taken up in the SLA literature conceives of the language learner as having a unified, coherent identity which organizes the type and intensity of a language learner's motivation. The data indicate that motivation is a much more complex matter than hitherto conceived. Despite being highly motivated, there were particular social conditions under which the women in my study were most uncomfortable and unlikely to speak (See also Auerbach & McGrail, 1991; Cumming & Gill, 1992; Goldstein, 1991; Peirce, Harper, & Burnaby, 1993; Rockhill, 1987). The data suggest that a language learner's motivation to speak is mediated by investments that may conflict with the desire to speak. Paradoxically, perhaps, the decision to remain silent or the decision to speak may both constititue forms of resistance to inequitable social forces. For example, although Felicia resisted speaking English in front of strangers because she did not want to be identified as an immigrant in Canada, other immigrant language learners are anxious to speak English for the express purpose of resisting unscrupulous social practices. For example, in his Toronto-based study of Spanish-speaking immigrants, Klassen (1987) found that some language learners wanted to learn English as a means of defence in their daily lives. An understanding of motivation should therefore be mediated by an understanding of learners' investments in the target language – investments that are closely connected to the ongoing production of a language learner's social identity. This position will be defended more comprehensively in the following discussion of Martina and Eva's experiences of learning English in Canada. In the following discussion, I demonstrate how the conception of social identity as multiple, a site of struggle, and subject to change helps to explain the conditions under which Martina and Eva spoke or remained silent.

Martina: Social identity as Multiple and a Site of Struggle

Martina was born in Czechoslovakia in 1952. She came to Canada in March 1989 when she was 37 years old, with her husband Petr and their three children (Jana 17, Elsbet 14, Milos 11 at the time). She came to Canada for a 'better life

---

[5] The only alterations that have been made to the written contributions of the participants are spelling corrections.

for children.' Neither she nor her husband knew any English before they came to Canada, but her children had received some English language training in Austria where the family had spent 19 months waiting for Canadian visas. Although Martina had a professional degree as a surveyor, she worked as a 'cook help' at a restaurant, Fast Foods, before she started the ESL course in January 1990.

Initially, Martina was dependent on her children to perform the public and domestic tasks of settling into a new country. When Martina went looking for a job, she took her eldest daughter with her, even though her daughter would become distressed because nobody wanted to employ her mother. When Martina wanted to help serve customers at Fast Foods, she asked her daughters to tell her what words to use. As Martina's English improved, she took on more of the parental tasks in the home. Many of Martina's diary entries describe the way that she used English to perform a wide variety of tasks in the home and community. It was Martina rather than her husband Petr who did most of the organization in the family, like finding accommodations, organizing telephones, buying appliances, finding schools for the children. Martina also helped her husband to perform public tasks in English. When Petr was laid off work, he relied on Martina to help him get unemployment insurance and he asked Martina to help him prepare for his plumber's certificate by translating the preparation book from English to Czech.

I wish to argue that Martina's investment in English was largely structured by an identity as primary caregiver in the family. It was important that she learn English so that she could take over the parental tasks of the home from her children. The very reason why Martina and Petr came to Canada was to find a 'better life for children.' Martina was anxious not to jeopardize the children's future by having them take on more public and domestic tasks than were absolutely necessary. Furthermore, because Martina had the responsibility for dealing with the public world, she was also anxious to understand the Canadian way of life – how things get done in Canadian society.

The poststructuralist view that social identity is nonunitary and contradictory helps to explain how Martina responded to and created opportunities to practice English. To illustrate this point, I will address some of the multiple sites of Martina's identity formation: She was an immigrant, a mother, a language learner, a worker, a wife. As a socially constructed immigrant woman (Ng, 1987; Boyd, 1992), Martina never felt comfortable speaking. Despite the fact that Martina showed remarkable resourcefulness and progress in her language learning, she frequently referred to herself as 'stupid' and 'inferior' because she could not speak English fluently. As she wrote in December 1991:

1 I feel uncomfortable using English in the group of people whose English language is their mother tongue because they speak fluently without any problems and I feel inferior.

Significantly, however, despite feelings of inferiority and shame, despite what could be described as a high affective filter, Martina refused to be silenced. I suggest that the reasons why Martina refused to be silenced were because her social identity as a mother and primary caregiver in the home led her to challenge what she understood to be appropriate rules of use governing interactions between anglophone Canadians and immigrant language learners. The multiple sites of identity formation explain the surprises in Martina's data – occasions when Martina would speak despite the fact that she was not a 'legitimate speaker' (Bourdieu, 1977, p. 650) in the particular discourse. To mention only two occasions: First, Martina surprised her children (and no doubt her landlord and herself) by entering into a long conversation with her landlord on the phone in which she insisted that her family had not broken their lease agreement. In her diary of March 8, 1991, she wrote:

2   The first time I was very nervous and afraid to talk on the phone. When the phone rang, everybody in my family was busy, and my daughter had to answer it. After ESL course when we moved and our landlords tried to persuade me that we have to pay for whole year, I got upset and I talked with him on the phone over one hour and I didn't think about the tenses rules. I had known that I couldn't give up. My children were very surprised when they heard me.

Second, Martina surprised customers at Fast Foods (who looked at her strangely) and co-workers (who were surprised, but said nothing) by taking the initiative to serve the customers while the other workers were playing a video game in the manager's office. Consider the following entry from her diary on March 7, 1991.

3   My experiences with young Canadians were very bad, maybe I didn't have fortune. Usually I worked only with my manager, but when was P. A. day or some holidays for students, the manager stayed in his office and I worked with some students. Very often I worked with two sisters Jennifer (12 years) and Vicky (15 years) and the assistant manager who was at a cash [register]. These two girls loved talking but not with me. Even though I was very busy, they talked with young customers and laughed and sometime looked at me. I didn't know, if they laughed at me or not. When we didn't have any customers, they went to the manager office and tried to help the manager with 'wheel of fortune' on the computer. Later when some customers came in and I called these girls, they went but they made faces. I felt bad and I wanted to avoid this situation. In the evening I asked my daughter what I have to tell the customer. She answered me 'May I help you' then 'pardon' and 'something else.' When I tried first time to talk to two customers alone, they looked at me strangely, but I didn't give up. I gave them everything they wanted and then I went looking for the girls and I told them as usually only 'cash.' They were surprised but they didn't say anything.

I suggest that Martina's perseverance with speaking ('I couldn't give up,' 'I didn't give up') and her courage to resist marginalization intersect with her social identity as a mother in two ways. First, as a primary caregiver, she could not rely on her husband to deal with the public world and defend the family's rights against unscrupulous social practices. Martina had to do this herself, regardless of her command of the English tense system, the strange looks she received from her interlocutors, and her feelings of inferiority. Second, Martina drew on her symbolic resources as a mother to reframe the power relations between herself and her co-workers. Thus, instead of conceding to their power as legitimate speakers of English, she reframed their relationship as a domestic one in which, as children they had no authority over her, as a parent. Consider the following extract taken from an interview with Martina on March 17, 1991:

4 In restaurant was working a lot of children, but the children always thought that I am – I don't know – maybe some broom or something. They always said 'Go and clean the living room.' And I was washing the dishes and they didn't do nothing. They talked to each other and they thought that I had to do everything. And I said 'No.' The girl is only 12 years old. She is younger than my son. I said 'No, you are doing nothing. You can go and clean the tables or something.'

Martina's social identity was a site of struggle. By setting up a counterdiscourse in her workplace and resisting the subject position immigrant woman in favor of the subject position mother, Martina claimed the right to speak. It is precisely this ability to claim the right to speak that I suggest should be an integral part of an expanded notion of communicative competence.

Eva: Social Identity as Changing Over Time

Eva was born in Poland in 1967 and came to Canada as a refugee in 1989 when she was 22 years old. She immigrated because she wanted 'economical advantage.' Eva had finished high school and worked as a bartender before she left Poland. She chose to come to Canada because it is one of the few industrialized countries that encourages immigration. She came alone, with no family or friends, but did know one person in Newtown before she arrived. Before Eva came to Canada, she spent 2 years in Italy where she became fluent in Italian. She knew no English before she arrived in Canada.

When Eva arrived in Newtown, she found employment at what she calls 'The Italian store' which is situated in the heart of an established Italian neighborhood in Newtown. Eva herself lived in this neighborhood, as do many recent immigrants to Newtown. Eva was given the job at the Italian store because she was a fluent speaker of Italian. Eva was happy at the Italian store but was concerned because she wanted to learn English and had little opportunity to practice English while working in this store. After she finished the ESL course in June 1990, she began looking for another job in earnest, at a place where she could become a more proficient speaker of English. She found employment at a restaurant in Newtown called Munchies, where she was the only employee who could not speak English fluently. Eva was a full-time employee whose main job was to clean the store and prepare the food for cooking.

The conception of social identity as subject to change helps explain the way Eva over time responded to and created opportunities to practice English in her workplace. The central point I wish to make here is that it was only over time that Eva's conception of herself as an immigrant – as 'illegitimate' speaker of English – changed to a conception of herself as a multicultural citizen with the power to impose reception. When Eva first started working at Munchies, she did not think it was appropriate for her to approach her co-workers and attempt to engage them in conversation. As she said in an interview on March 7, 1991,

5 When I see that I have to do everything and nobody cares about me because –
then how can I talk to them? I hear they doesn't care about me and I don't feel
to go and smile and talk to them.

Note that Eva does not complete a crucial part of her sentence. 'Nobody
cares about me because –.' The data suggest that nobody acknowledged Eva
because she had the subject position immigrant in the workplace: As Eva put it,
she was someone who was not fluent in English; she was 'not Canadian,' she
was 'stupid,' she had 'the worst type of work' in the store. To speak under such
conditions would have constituted what Bourdieu (1977) calls *heretical usage*
(p. 672). Eva accepted the subject position immigrant; she accepted that she
was not a legitimate speaker of English and that she could not command
reception of her interlocutors. As she herself said, when she first arrived in
Canada, she assumed that if people treated her with disrespect, it was because
of her own limitations. She conceded to these rules of use in her workplace,
rules that Eva herself accepted described as normal. As she said in an interview
on January 23, 1991,

6 I think because when I didn't talk to them, and they didn't ask me, maybe they
think I'm just like – because I had to do the worst type of work there. It's
normal.

As Eva's sense of who she was, and how she related to the social world began
to change, she started to challenge her subject position in the workplace as an
illegitimate speaker of English. An extract from an interview on January 23,
1991, indicates how Eva claimed spaces in conversations with co-workers. Her
purpose was to introduce her own history and experiences into the workplace in
the hope that her symbolic resources would be validated. This surprised her co-
workers.

7 (*B* refers to Bonny and *E* refers to Eva.)
   B: You were saying Eva that you are starting to speak to other people?
      The other people who work [at Munchies]?
   E: Ya. Because before –
   B: Is everybody there Canadian?
   E: Ya. Because there everybody is Canadian and they would speak to each
      other, not to me – because – I always was like – they sent me off to do
      something else. I felt bad. Now it's still the same but I have to do
      something. I try to speak.
   B: How are you doing that?
   E: For example, we have a half-hour break. Sometimes – I try to speak.
      For example, they talk about Canada, what they like here, the places
      which they like –
   B: Like to visit? Vacations?
   E: Ya. Then I started to talk to them about how life is in Europe. Then they
      started to ask me some questions. But it's still hard because I cannot
      explain to them how things, like –
   B: How do you actually find an opportunity in the conversation to say
      something. Like, if they're talking to each other, do you stop them?
   E: No.

B: You wait for a quiet – Then what do you say?

E: No. I don't wait for when they are completely quiet, but when it's the moment I can say something about what they are talking about.

B: When you started doing that, were they surprised?

E: A little bit.

As Eva continued to develop what I have called an identity as a multicultural citizen, she developed with it an awareness of her right to speak. If people treated her with disrespect, it was their problem and not her problem. Thus when, after a year's experience in the workplace, a male customer said to her in February 1992,[6] 'Are you putting on this accent so that you can get more tips?' Eva had been angry, rather than ashamed; she had spoken out, rather than been silenced. When she said to him, 'I wish I did not have this accent because then I would not have to listen to such comments,' she was claiming the right to speak as a multicultural citizen of Canada. Over time, then, Eva's communicative competence developed to include an awareness of how to challenge and transform social practices of marginalization.

The implications: classroom-based social research

Although it is beyond the scope of this article to offer a comprehensive analysis of ways in which my research might inform second language teaching, I take in good faith Savignon's (1991) comment that communicative language teaching looks to further language acquisition research to inform its development. I have argued thus far that SLA theorists have struggled to define the nature of language learning because they have drawn artificial distinctions between the individual language learner and larger, frequently inequitable social structures. I have drawn on Martina and Eva's data to argue that the individual language learner is not ahistorical and unidimensional but has a complex and sometimes contradictory social identity, changing across time and space. I have drawn on my data to argue that motivation is not a fixed personality trait but must be understood with reference to social relations of power that create the possibilities for language learners to speak. I have suggested that even when learners have a high affective filter, it is their investment in the target language that will lead them to speak. This investment, in turn, must be understood in relation to the multiple, changing, and contradictory identities of language learners.

An important implication of my study is that the second language teacher needs to help language learners claim the right to speak outside the classroom. To this end, the lived experiences and social identities of language learners need to be incorporated into the formal second language curriculum. The data indicates, however, that students' social identities are complex, multiple, and subject to change. What kind of pedagogy, then, might help learners claim the right to speak? Drawing on insights from my research project in general and the diary study in particular (see Peirce, 1994), as well as a wide range of classroom research (e.g., Auerbach, 1989; Cummins, 1994; Heath, 1983, 1993; Heller & Barker, 1988;

---

[6] Although the diary study was officially over by February 1992, I continued to maintain contact with the participants.

Morgan, 1992; Stein & Janks, 1992; Stein & Pierce, in press), I suggest that what I call *classroom-based social research* might engage the social identities of students in ways that will improve their language learning outside the classroom and help them claim the right to speak. It may help students understand how opportunities to speak are socially structured and how they might create possibilities for social interaction with target language speakers. Furthermore, it may help language teachers gain insight into the way their students' progress in language learning intersects with their investments in the target language.

I define classroom-based social research (CBSR) as collaborative research that is carried out by language learners in their local communities with the active guidance and support of the language teacher. In many ways, language learners become ethnographers in their local communities. Like the students in Heath's (1983) study, learners will develop their oral and literacy skills by collapsing the boundaries between their classrooms and their communities. Adult immigrants, however, differ from native-born students in that they do not have easy access to the linguistic codes or cultural practices of their local communities. The emphasis on CBSR, therefore, is to focus precisely on these aspects of social life, with a view to enhancing language learning and social interaction. As will be discussed below, a crucial component of CBSR is the use of the written word for reflection and analysis. As Ngo (1994) has convincingly argued from her personal experience of immigration, writing can build bridges not only across geographic space but across historical time:

> Through my writing I found myself again after a long time of being lost. I learned who I was in the past, who I was then, and who I wanted to be in the future. There I finally found freedom in writing. I flew in the sky with my pencil and notebook.

CBSR might include the following objectives and methodologies.

Objective 1:
Investigative Opportunities to Interact with Target Language Speakers

Learners can be encouraged to investigate systematically what opportunities they have to interact with target language speakers, whether in the home, the workplace, or the community. To this end, they might make use of observation charts or logbooks.

Objective 2:
Reflect Critically on Engagement with Target Language Speakers

Learners can be encouraged to reflect critically on their engagement with target language speakers. That is, learners might investigate the conditions under which they interact with target language speakers; how and why such interactions take place; and what results follow from such interaction. This might help learners develop insight into the way in which opportunities to speak are socially structured and how social relations of power are implicated in the process of social interaction. As a result, they may learn to transform social practices of marginalization.

Objective 3:
Reflect on Observations in Diaries or Journals

Learners can be encouraged to reflect on their observations in diaries or journals.
This will create opportunities for learners to write about issues in which they have a
particular investment, and in so doing, develop their talents as writers. Specifically,
learners could use their diaries to examine critically any communication
breakdowns that may have occurred with target language speakers. These diaries
could be written in the target language and collected regularly by the teacher. The
diaries might give the language teacher access to information about the students'
opportunities to practice the target language outside the classroom, their
investments in the target language, and their changing social identities. The teacher
could help students critically reflect on findings from their research and make
suggestions for further research, reflection, and action where necessary.

Objective 4:
Pay Attention to and Record Unusual Events

Learners could be encouraged to pay particular attention to those moments when an
occurrence, action, or event, surprises them or strikes them as unusual. By recording
their surprises in the data collection process, the learners may become conscious of
differences between social practices in their native countries and those in the target
language community. Given the subject position student researcher rather than
language learner or immigrant, learners may be able to critically engage their
histories and their experiences from a position of strength rather than a position of
weakness. With this enhanced awareness, learners may also be able to use the
language teacher as an important resource for further learning.

Objective 5:
Compare Data with Fellow Students and Researchers

Students could use the data they have collected as material for their language
classrooms, to be compared with the findings of their fellow students and
researchers. In comparing their data with other learners, the students will have an
investment in the presentations that their fellow students make and a meaningful
exchange of information may ensue. Students may begin to see one another as part
of a social network in which their symbolic resources can be produced, validated,
and exchanged. The teacher may also be able to use this information to structure
classroom activities and develop classroom materials that will help learners claim
the right to speak outside the classroom. Drawing on Heath (1993), the teacher
could make use of drama to help students develop confidence in interacting with
target language speakers. Furthermore, the teacher may be able to guide classroom
discussion from a description of the findings of the research, to a consideration of
what the research might indicate about broader social processes in the society. In
this way, the teacher could help students interrogate their relationship to these
larger social processes, understand how feelings of inadequacy are frequently
socially constructed, and find spaces for the enhancement of human possibility.

   In sum, second language theorists, teachers, and students cannot take for
granted that those who speak regard those who listen as worthy to listen, and
that those who listen regard those who speak as worthy to speak.

Acknowledgments

I would like to acknowledge and thank the participants in my study, who generously allowed me to bring their personal insights into public debate. I would also like to thank Roger Simon, Monica Heller, Jim Cummins, Barbara Burnaby, Sandra Silberstein, Kathleen Troy, and two *TESOL Quarterly* reviewers for their diverse contributions to my research and analysis. The research on which this article is based was supported by the Social Sciences and Humanities Research Council of Canada. This support is gratefully acknowledged.

The author

Bonny Norton Peirce is a postdoctoral fellow in the Modern Language Centre, Ontario Institute for Studies in Education, Canada. She is interested in the relationship between social theory and language learning, teaching, and testing internationally. Recent research has been accepted for publication in *Applied Linguistics* and the *Harvard Educational Review*.

References

Auerbach, E. R. (1989). Toward a social-contextual approach to family literacy. *Harvard Educational Review, 59*, 165–181.

Auerbach, E., & McGrail, L. (1991). Rosa's challenge: Connecting classroom and community contexts. In S. Benesch (Ed.), *ESL in America: Myths and possibilities* (pp. 96–111). Portsmouth, NH: Heinemann.

Bourdieu, P. (1977). The economics of linguistic exchanges. *Social Science Information, 16*, 645–668.

Bourdieu, P., & Passeron J. (1977). *Reproduction in education, society, and culture*. Beverley Hills, CA: Sage Publications.

Boyd, M. (1992). Immigrant women: Language, socio-economic inequalities, and policy issues. In B. Burnaby & A. Cumming (Eds.), *Socio-political aspects of ESL in Canada*. (pp. 141–159). Toronto, Canada: OISE Press.

Brown, H. D. (1987). *Principles of language learning and teaching*. Englewood Cliffs, NJ: Prentice Hall.

Cherryholmes, C. (1988). *Power and criticism: Poststructuralist investigations in education*. New York: Teachers College Press.

Cumming, A. & Gill, J. (1991). Motivation or accessibility? Factors permitting Indo-Canadian women to pursue ESL literacy instruction. In B. Burnaby & A. Cumming (Eds.), *Socio-political aspects of ESL education in Canada* (pp. 241–252). Toronto, Canada: OISE Press.

Cummins, J. (1994). Knowledge, power, and identity in teaching English as a second language. In F. Genesee (Ed.), *Educating second language children: The whole child, the whole curriculum, the whole community* (pp. 33–58). Cambridge: Cambridge University Press.

Gardner, R. C. (1985). *Social psychology and second language learning. The role of attitudes and motivation*. London: Edward Arnold.

Gardner, R. C. (1989). Attitudes and motivation. *Annual Review of Applied Linguistics, 1988, 9*, 135–148.

Gardner, R. C., & Lambert, W. C. (1972). *Attitudes and motivation in second language learning*. Rowley, MA: Newbury House.

Gardner, R. C., & MacIntyre, P. D. (1992). A student's contributions to second-language learning. Part I: Cognitive variables. *Language Teaching, 25*, 211–220.

Gardner, R. C., & MacIntyre, P. D. (1993). A student's contributions to second-language learning. Part II: Affective variables. *Language Teaching, 26*, 1–11.

Giroux, H. A. (1988). *Schooling and the struggle for public life: Critical pedagogy in the modern age.* Minneapolis: University of Minnesota Press.

Goldstein, T. (1991). *Immigrants in the multicultural/multilingual workplace: Ways of communicating and experience at work.* Unpublished doctoral dissertation, Ontario Institute for Studies in Education/University of Toronto, Canada.

Heath, S. B. (1983). *Ways with words: Language, life, and work in communities and classrooms.* Cambridge: Cambridge University Press.

Heath, S. B. (1993). Inner city life through drama: Imagining the language classroom. *TESOL Quarterly, 27*, 177–192.

Heller, M. (1987). The role of language in the formation of ethnic identity. In J. Phinney & M. Rotheram (Eds.), *Children's ethnic socialization* (pp. 180–200). Newbury Park, CA: Sage.

Heller, M., & Barker, G. (1988). Conversational strategies and contexts for talk: Learning activities for Franco-Ontarian minority schools. *Anthropology and Education Quarterly, 19*, 20–46.

Hymes, D. (1971). On communicative competence. In C. J. Brumfit & K. Johnson (Eds.), *The communicative approach to language teaching* (pp. 5–26). Oxford: Oxford University Press.

Klassen, C. (1987). *Language and literacy learning: The adult immigrant's account.* Unpublished masters thesis, Ontario Institute for Studies in Education/University of Toronto, Canada.

Krashen, S. (1981). *Second language acquisition and second language learning.* Oxford: Pergamon.

Krashen, S. (1982). *Principles and practice in second language acquisition.* Oxford: Pergamon.

Morgan, B. (1992). Teaching the Gulf War in an ESL classroom. *TESOL Journal, 2*, 13–17.

Ng, R. (1987). Immigrant women in Canada: A socially constructed category. *Resources for Feminist Research/Documentation sur la recherche feministe, 16*, 13–15.

Ngo, H. (1994, March). *From learner to teacher: Language minority teachers speak out.* Paper presented at the 28th Annual TESOL Convention, Baltimore, Maryland.

Ogbu, J. (1978). *Minority education and caste: The American system in cross-cultural perspective.* New York: Academic Press.

Peirce, B. N. (1989). Toward a pedagogy of possibility in the teaching of English internationally: People's English in South Africa. *TESOL Quarterly, 23*, 401–420.

Peirce, B. N. (1993). *Language learning, social identity, and immigrant women.* Unpublished doctoral dissertation. Ontario Institute for Studies in Education/University of Toronto, Canada.

Peirce, B. N. (1994). Using diaries in second language research and teaching. *English Quarterly, 26*, 22–29.

Peirce, B. N., Harper, H., & Burnaby, B. (1993). Workplace ESL at Levi Strauss: 'Dropouts' speak out. *TESL Canada Journal, 10*, 9–30.

Rockhill, K. (1987). Literacy as threat/desire: Longing to be SOMEBODY. In J. Gaskill & A. McLaren (Eds.), *Women and education: A Canadian perspective* (pp. 315–331). Calgary, Canada: Detselig Enterprises.

Savignon, S. (1991). Communicative language teaching: State of the art. *TESOL Quarterly, 25,* 261–278.

Schumann, J. (1976). Social distance as a factor in second language acquisition. *Language Learning, 26,* 135–143.

Schumann, J. (1978). The acculturation model for second-language acquisition. In R. C. Gringas, (Ed.), *Second language acquisition and foreign language teaching* (pp. 27–50). Washington, DC: Center for Applied Linguistics.

Scovel, T. (1978) The effect of affect on foreign language learning: A review of the anxiety research. *Language Learning, 28,* 129–42.

Simon, R. (1992). *Teaching against the grain: Texts for a pedagogy of possibility.* New York: Bergin & Garvey.

Spolsky, B. (1989). *Conditions for second language learning.* Oxford: Oxford University Press.

Stein, P., & Janks, H. (1992). The process syllabus: A case study. *Perspectives in Education, 13,* 93–105

Stein, P., & Peirce, B. N. (in press). Why the Monkeys Passage bombed: Tests, genres, and teaching. *Harvard Educational Review.*

Stern, H. H. (1983). *Fundamental concepts of language teaching.* Oxford: Oxford University Press.

Weedon, C. (1987). *Feminist practice and poststructuralist theory.* London: Blackwell.

Text 27

Stephen Price:
Monash University

Comments on Bonny Norton Peirce's 'Social Identity, Investment, and Language Learning'
A Reader Reacts ...

Peirce's central concern in her *TESOL Quarterly* article (Vol. 29, No. 1) is to contribute to an overcoming of the 'artificial distinctions [drawn] between the language learner and the language learning context' (p. 10) and the 'arbitrary mapping of particular factors on either the individual or the social' (p. 11). Her central argument is that 'SLA theorists have not developed a comprehensive theory of social identity that integrates the language learner and the language learning context. Furthermore, they have not questioned how relations of power in the social world affect social interaction between second language learners and target language speakers' (p. 12).

I believe Peirce advances our understanding of the way in which power relations have a direct effect on language use and learning, and her attempt to deal with challenges raised by poststructural thought for language learning is gratifying. However, I wish to raise several questions concerning her theorising of *social identity,* whether it actually does overcome the dichotomy she addresses and make consequent comments on agency, power, and practice in the application of poststructural thinking to SLA.

Social identity and the cases of Martina and Eva

Peirce clearly shows that power is embedded in the social relations Martina and Eva are engaged in. Martina's position as an 'immigrant' induced silence. However, because Martina's 'investment in English was largely structured by an identity as primary caregiver in the family' (p. 21), she claimed the right to speak 'by setting up a counterdiscourse in her workplace and resisting the subject position "immigrant woman" in favour of the subject position "mother" ' (p. 23). Peirce's concern with learners exercising their right to speak in order to practice their target language underpins the classroom objectives she suggests in the last section of her article.

Whether Peirce overcomes the dichotomy of language learner/learning context is questionable, as is, consequently, whether she raises the most pertinent and pressing questions that poststructural theory raises for second language acquisition (SLA) theory.

Borrowing from Weedon, Peirce asserts 'the multiple nature of the subject; subjectivity as a site of struggle; and subjectivity as changing' (p. 15). Fundamental to her argument is the application of these characteristics to social identity. But this theoretical conflation of subjectivity and identity weakens her own position because it blinds her to the practical distinction she in fact necessarily continues to make. She asserts, following Weedon, that 'language is the place ... where our sense of selves, our subjectivity is constructed' (p. 15). Yet, in her interpretation of Martina's case, she asserts that 'despite feelings of inferiority and shame ... Martina refused to be silenced' (p. 21). This was because 'her social identity as a mother and primary caregiver in the home led her to challenge' (p. 21) the prevailing expectations of the discursive contexts she found herself in. Somehow then, Martina finds the resources to maintain her identity as mother despite the 'multiple sites of Martina's identity formation [as] immigrant, a mother, a language learner, a worker, a wife' (p. 21).

The problem here is that Martina somehow can insist on one identity (mother) over others, despite the way discourse might construct her (e.g., immigrant) at any given moment. Peirce seems obliged to appeal to an ongoing identity (mother) that seems in fact remarkably constant, reaching back even to the decision to migrate to Canada.[1] There is no sense here that identity is multiple and a site of struggle. Indeed, mother, migrant woman, and other identities are all presented as remarkably unitary. The multiplicity and site of struggle that Peirce argues for exists between the options which present themselves to Martina, as she struggles to take up one or another alternative identity. That is, a pre-given Martina, decides between these alternative options according to her own pre-given interests (e.g., her investment as a mother). In Peirce's account, there is no sense that these identities (mother, migrant) and Martina's interests change as

---

[1] It might be better to argue that Martina identifies with the *signifier* mother. However, Peirce is suggesting that she identifies with the *signified*, as if this remains constant. But it is not within Martina's or any other subject's capacity to insist on a constant signified; this is stressed by much poststructural thought (Lacan's theory particularly utilises the distinction between signifier and signified. Jacques-Alain Miller, 1991, a leading exponent of Lacan, states, 'The subject is nothing more than the effect of the combination of the signifiers' (p. 33).

a function of ongoing discursive practices. Whereas discourse presents the options, choice between them and the sustaining of their meaning is presented as a function of individual capacities, not of discourse practices.

I am suggesting then that for Peirce, discourse and power facilitates or impedes the taking up of different identities/positions but does not seem to be involved in the construction of them. There is no indication of how Martina's identity as mother varies in meaning and significance according to ongoing discourse practices. The meaning of mother seems to be given by Martina herself, which she safeguards despite the changing discursive and social contexts to which she is subject.

Precisely how Martina maintains certain meanings or what power she draws on to insist on them remains unclear, but Peirce's argument does seem to point toward a subject-agent that is capable of circumventing the constitutive role of discourse and resisting the power relations, through an act of will, an act of courage, of determination, thus setting up a counterdiscourse. And this leaves us with the possibility that some learners will simply lack the fortitude to insist. If my reading is valid, then it would seem that the dichotomy between language learner and context remains fundamental to Peirce's account.

I am suggesting then that Peirce's argument places discourse as a medium through which subject interests may be facilitated or impeded, but that she fails to adequately incorporate into her account how those interests themselves, and the subject as such, is constructed by discourse. The identity the learner takes up and the resistance offered to alternative positions are presented as depending on meanings maintained individually, rather than socially. The danger here is of reducing (social) language use to (individual) language competence. Consequently, there is no indication that in challenging the discourse practices themselves, the subject identity and motivating interests are at the same time brought into question.

I want next to suggest how Peirce's theorising makes insistent appeal to such a pre-given subject and indicate possible alternative directions suggested by poststructuralist thinking.

Investment and agency

Peirce substitutes the term *investment* for motivation, arguing that it better signals 'the socially and historically constructed relationship of the women to the target language' (p. 17). Yet investment does seem to be a function of a dominant and enduring identity (e.g., mother in the case of Martina) rather than of prevailing practices and which, like motivation, seems the dominant factor in determining whether or not the subject will insist on speaking. Although Peirce shows the importance of circumstance in shaping the relative ease or difficulty with which the right to speak can be claimed (in contrast to the concept of motivation that she claims provides no space for such variability), not only does her argument rely on the concept of a continuing identity (mother in Martina's case) that resists prevailing practices because it insists on a meaning independent of those practices, but she also grounds investment itself in a noncontingent, ahistorical subject.

Thus, she argues that 'if learners invest in a second language, they do so with the understanding that they will acquire a wider range of symbolic and material resources' (p. 17). She adds, 'learners will expect or hope to have a good return on that investment' and further that 'this return on investment must be seen as commensurate with the effort expended on learning the second language' (p. 17). There is no suggestion this a priori calculative rationality directing investment changes across cultures and over time. That is, it is not constructed in discourse but is an inherent quality of all human subjects. This is a very contentious claim and yet central to Peirce's argument. The assumption of such a given, rational subject has been a central object of criticism by much poststructural and critical thinking alike.[2]

I am suggesting that on the one hand Peirce resorts to a pre-given subject-agent, yet on the other argues that 'subjectivity is produced in a variety of social sites, all of which are structured by relations of power' (p. 15). The place of the subject-agent needs further clarification, especially if the dissolution of agency into social/discourse determinism is to be avoided.[3]

Peirce deals with agency simply by asserting 'the subject has human agency' and that consequently 'the subject positions a subject takes up within a particular discourse are open to argument' (p. 15) by the subject. However, whether the subject who resists does so according to interests and faculties that are discourse mediated or pre-given remains very unclear. Despite Peirce's intention of overcoming the dichotomy between pre-given learner and language learning context, I am suggesting she remains locked into the impasse.

Practice

Peirce addresses the issues of social identity and power relations from an SLA perspective that emphasises the importance of practice. She draws on two different concepts of practice. These two are exemplified perhaps in the statement: 'While Eva had been offered the opportunity to engage in social interaction, to 'practice' her English, her subject position within the larger discourse of which she and Gail were a part undermined this opportunity' (p. 16). Practice on the one hand refers to rehearsal and to the learner developing competence in systematic aspects of language use. On the other hand, language use entails a realisation of social practice, which in the above quote involves Eva in enacting a social identity and relations that ensured her silence. Practice in the former sense accentuates systematic aspects of language use that cut across context, 'rules' that can be properly internalised, autonomised, and applied appropriately. Practice in the latter sense accentuates the moment of realisation of meaning and its contingency. Eva takes up her position and is silent because she can already respond to the discourse. In this sense an important aspect of acquisition has already taken place. How remains unexplored. To resist being silenced, she must oppose one identity to another.

Peirce at this point appeals to a pre-given subject rather than looking for resistance that is rooted in factors inherent in the discourse itself. Such inherent resistance may or may not lead to speech. Claiming the 'right to speak' in itself is

---

[2] One attempt to understand the subject as a function of the structuring of desire, and hence historically contingent, rather than being essentially rational and ahistorical, can be found in Henriques, Hollway, Urwin, Venn, & Valkerdine (1984). See also comments by McCarthy (1993, p. 11).

[3] McCarthy (1993) discusses this risk in Foucault's thinking.

not necessarily the desired goal. Silence can be 'produced in ways other than that of victimisation and suffering ... . being insurgent is not to trade one form of knowledge/power for another, but to move transversal to the logic of what is. To move, that is, and to speak, *across* and *through* the symbolic, while remaining fully, yet reflexively, *implicated in it*.' (Schenke, 1991, p. 49, italics in original).[4]

The relationship between the two views of practice I have mentioned is problematic. Bourdieu (1977) suggests they are not compatible. He argues that there is an 'abstraction in the concept of competence' (p. 646) which suggests the autonomisation of 'linguistic production.' This 'competence can be autonomised neither *de facto* nor *de jure*.' Language, he asserts, is a praxis, by which he means one acquires a 'practical competence.' 'Understanding is not a matter of recognising invariable meaning, but of grasping the singularity of a form which only exists in a particular context' (p. 647).

Peirce's concern is not with how a learner takes up a position according to 'the particularity of the form ... in a particular context.' Rather, she is concerned with exercising the right to speak, with individual resistance to power relations once such meanings and positions have been recognised and taken up; resistance in order to maximise language practice and pre-given interests. Her argument presupposes that learners have responded to changing identities offered by different discourses in specific contexts, yet how this occurs seems to be the more interesting problematic that poststructural thinking raises. Peirce neglects this problem, instead framing her problematic in terms of competency and fluency development. Her stance distracts us from recognising the problematic nature of silence, and the complex process of recognising and utilising meaning in novel circumstances, and of how language is not only something we master and use (as subjects using a tool to achieve our interests) but as integral to the practice of an ongoing construction of social reality and identity.

Conclusion

Although the practical suggestions Peirce makes in the last section of her article seem of great value, I have questioned how far they respond to and grow out of issues raised by poststructural thought and how far her argument does in fact integrate the language learner and language learning context. I have questioned how far Peirce moves beyond the concept of a unitary subject. I have argued that her concern with resistance, power, and silence rests ultimately on an appeal to individual capacities and does not explore far enough the way the individual subject/learner is implicated in social and discourse practices. If attention is directed more to the radical contingency of subject identity, interests, and desires (and rationality), which are formed within discourse practices; if this is the focus of attention, then from an SLA perspective, the ways in which learners respond to the specificity of discourses and take up positions and the ways in which resistance itself can be grounded in such practices will take on greater prominence and urgency.

The focus shifts from the ways in which learners might come to exercise the right to speak and develop competence in order to realise individually given and

---

[4] Schenke's article provides, amongst other things, valuable comments on the complexity of silence in language acquisition and use.

sustained pre-given interests to how interests and discourse positions are structured and taken up by learners in ever changing contexts.

Acknowledgments

I would like to express my gratitude to Alastair Pennycook and the students in his graduate course The Politics of Language Education/Critical Applied Linguistics for comments made on a first draft of this response. I would also like to thank Brian Lynch for very helpful comments made on subsequent drafts.

References

Bourdieu, P. (1977). The economics of linguistic exchanges, *Social Sciences Information, 16*, pp. 645–668.

Henriques, J., Hollway, W., Urwin, C., Venn, C., & Valkerdine, V. (1984). *Changing the subject*. London: Methuen.

McCarthy, T. (1993). *Ideals and illusions: On reconstruction and deconstruction in contemporary critical theory*. Cambridge, MA: MIT Press.

Miller, J. (1991). Language: Much ado about what? In E. Ragland-Sullivan & M. Bracher (Eds.), *Lacan and the subject of language*. London: Routledge.

Schenke, A. (1991). The 'Will to Reciprocity' and the work of memory: Fictioning speaking out of silence in ESL and feminist pedagogy.' *Resources for Feminist Research, 20*, 47–55

Text 28

Bonny Norton Peirce:
University of British Columbia

Interpreting Data: The Role of Theory

In some schools of poststructuralist theory, advocates celebrate the 'death of the author' (Foucault, 1977, p. 117). In its strong version, advocates argue that the author's intentions and objectives are not central to the meaning of a text and that the meaning of a text shifts with every reading. It is clear that Price does not support this school of poststructuralist theory because he has questioned whether his reading of my article, 'Social Identity, Investment, and Language Learning,' (Peirce, 1995a) is a valid one. Further, he has given me, the author, the opportunity to elaborate on my research and clarify my objectives. I value this opportunity to engage in debate on postmodern thought and its relationship to the field of language learning and teaching.

As an author, I am in the privileged position of determining whether Price's reading of my article is indeed a valid one. Because he raised some critical questions, there is, to some extent, a conflict of interest. I am both the accused and the judge of his critique. As I sought to distance myself from these conflicting identities and read Price's critique as a disinterested scholar, it struck me that the process I was going through served to validate further the theories of social identity and investment I was exploring in my article. My identity was multiple – I was accused, judge, and scholar. By extension, my identity also shifted over time as I reread the critique from different subject positions and with different investments. In sum, the complex relationship between me and the social world mediated my engagement with Price's text.

But this is not the central argument I wish to make to support the theories of social identity and investment explored in my article. Rather, I defend the position that Price's reading was structured by an a priori assumption that was not consistent with the objectives of my research. This assumption is made explicit in the conclusion of his commentary. Price asserts that although the practical suggestions I make in my article seem of great value, he questions the extent to which they 'grow out of issues raised by poststructural thought.' In conducting my research and in writing the article, it was never my intention to serve as an apologist for poststructuralist theories. Instead, I drew on poststructuralist theories to help me make sense of my data and to examine how they might inform second language acquisition theory. Whereas I recognize that there is a complex relationship between theory and research (Peirce, 1995b), I do not believe a researcher should tailor her or his analysis to suit a particular theoretical orientation. Thus the question I asked in my research was as follows: 'To what extent can poststructuralist theory help me to understand my data?' The question was not, as Price assumes, 'To what extent does my data support poststructuralist theory?'

To defend this argument, I would like to address the questions Price raises about my interpretation of the Bart Simpson exchange between Eva, one of the participants in my research, and Gail, one of Eva's co-workers. When Eva is silenced in the course of the exchange, I argue as follows, 'This discourse must be understood not only in relation to the words that were said, but in relationship to larger structures in the workplace, and Canadian society at large, in which immigrant language learners often struggle for acceptance in Canadian society' (Peirce, 1995a, p. 16). Price questions this interpretation, arguing that I did not theorize Eva's silence as a form of resistance. 'Peirce at this point appeals to a pre-given subject, rather than looking for resistance that is rooted in factors in the discourse itself.'

In this regard, there are two issues that I need to address. First, Price has challenged me to be accountable for my interpretation of Eva's silence. This, I believe, is essential for scholarly inquiry, and I welcome the opportunity to elaborate on my analysis. The second issue, however, is more problematic. Without having met Eva, spoken to her, or read any of her work, Price feels qualified to interpret her actions. As he argues, 'Eva takes up her position and is silent because she can already respond to the discourse. In this sense, an important aspect of acquisition has already taken place ... Such inherent resistance may or may not lead to speech.' He provides little evidence to support this analysis, resorting only to secondary sources.

To return then to the first issue: How can I defend my interpretation of Eva's silence? In a more comprehensive account of my research (Peirce, 1994) I had consulted Eva on this topic, attempting to establish why she had turned silent during the course of the exchange. I was unable to find evidence to support the view that her silence was a covert form of resistance. Groping for words, Eva explained her humiliation to me by describing herself through the eyes of her interlocutor, '"You don't watch TV?" And I felt, "What are you doing." I was thinking like, "This strange woman."' (Peirce, 1994, p. 197). Tempting though it was, I could not sustain the interpretation that her silence was a covert form of resistance. The only defensible argument I could make was that Eva had remained silent because she had, like many immigrant women in Canada, felt 'strange' and marginalized in her anglophone workplace. Under such conditions, it was her anglophone co-worker Gail who was in a position of power relative to Eva, and it was Gail who could structure the conditions under which Eva could speak.

It was only much later – a year later – that I was able to find evidence that Eva's identity as an immigrant women had changed, and with it, the extent to which she claimed the right to speak. First, she explained that she had reached a point where she felt that if people treated her with disrespect it was 'their problem' and not her problem. Second, she described an encounter with an anglophone customer who had accused her of 'putting on an accent' to get more tips. Rather than remaining silent, Eva had defiantly responded, 'I wish I did not have this accent because then I would not have to listen to such comments' (Peirce, 1994, p. 118). Although I did not find evidence of resistance in the Bart Simpson exchange, I could find such evidence in the second exchange, a year later. In addition, I could find evidence that Eva had a changing conception of herself, her relationship to the wider community, and her insistence on her right to speak. Poststructuralist theories of identity, which theorize identity as changing over time, helped me to make sense of this data.

Notwithstanding this evidence that identities change over time, Price chides me for being unable to provide evidence from Martina (another participant) that 'identities are changeable over time.' Again, the central question for me is not whether my research can support poststructuralist theories, but whether poststructuralist theories can help me to understand the conditions under which language learners will speak. In the case of Martina, the poststructuralist theory that identity is multiple and a site of struggle helped me to understand Martina's complex identities and the surprising conditions under which she spoke. Although she said that as an immigrant she frequently felt 'inferior,' she drew on her resources as a mother to claim the right to speak. The fact that Martina's identities as mother, immigrant woman, worker, and wife do indeed appear, as Price argues, 'remarkably unitary' over time, is not necessarily inconsistent with the view that identities are changeable. The data collection period was limited to the duration of a year, during which time Martina's children remained dependent on her as the primary caregiver of the family, notwithstanding social and economic changes in their lives. Had my project continued for a few more years, I may well have found that the meaning of 'mother' had changed dramatically for Martina – along with her relationship to the wider community and the conditions under which she spoke.

In response to Price's critique, I have argued that I am more concerned about investigating the conditions under which language learners speak than with validating the central tenets of poststructuralist theory. Whether my theorising of social identity and investment helps to explain the conditions under which learners speak is subject to further inquiry. Nevertheless, I hope that my research makes a contribution to a highly complex set of questions about the relationship between the language learner and the social world. Further research (see, e.g.,

McKay & Wong, in press) is necessary to refine, extend, or refute the theories presented. I hope that Price's interest in theory is complemented by a passion for research.

References

Foucault, M. (1977). What is an author? In M. Foucault, *Language, counter-memory, practice: Selected essays and interviews* (pp. 113–138). Ithaca, NY: Cornell University Press.

McKay, S., & Wong, S. L. (in press). Multiple discourses, multiple identities: Investment and agency in second language learning among Chinese adolescent immigrant students. *Harvard Educational Review*.

Peirce, B. N. (1994). *Language learning, social identity, and immigrant women.* Unpublished doctoral dissertation. Ontario Institute for Studies in Education/University of Toronto.

Peirce, B. N. (1995a). Social identity, investment, and language learning. *TESOL Quarterly, 29,* 9–31.

Peirce, B. N. (1995b). The theory of methodology in qualitative research. *TESOL Quarterly, 29,* 569–576.

For readers who have been following the controversies in this volume it will be easy to see how the plot thickens: concerns raised in the SLA exchanges above connect with issues discussed in all of the previous sections. For instance, with reference to Section 1 on global English, we might note that the term 'SLA', although it has a fairly specific, technical ring to it, is actually not defined any more clearly than the denomination 'English', as in 'English as a native language', 'English as a foreign language', or 'English as a lingua franca'. Also, some of the points Firth and Wagner make in Text 20 above become particularly significant when we bear in mind the increasing worldwide use of English as a lingua franca. Here approximating to a native-speaker norm is often simply not an issue – unlike for most of SLA. In this sense, the important and continuing debate about the relationship between 'mainstream SLA' and its assumption about norms of competence, and the recognition of the legitimacy of indigenized varieties of English (for example, Y. Kachru 1994; Sridhar 1994; Sridhar and Sridhar 1986), will have to be extended to contexts where English is used as a lingua franca. (Cf. Seidlhofer 2002.)

As for connections with Section 2 on corpus linguistics and language teaching, it is clear that the target that SLA researchers have in mind for second language learners will inevitably have to depend on the available descriptions of the target language, and these of course have undergone a revolution since the advent of corpus linguistics. For instance, Mitchell and Myles (1998: 12) point out that

> Work in corpus linguistics has led us to the increasing recognition that formulas and routines play an important part in everyday language use by native speakers;

when we talk, our everyday L1 utterances are a complex mix of creativity and pre-fabrication (Sinclair 1991). ... Analysis of L2 data produced by classroom learners in particular seems to show extensive and systematic use of chunks to fulfil communicative needs in the early stages. ... Studies of informal learners also provide some evidence of chunk use. This phenomenon has attracted relatively little attention in recent times, compared with that given to learner creativity and systematicity (Weinert 1995). However, we believe it is common enough in L2 spontaneous production ... to need some more sustained attention from L2 learning theory.

The SLA controversies above would seem to make contact too with a number of issues concerning critical discourse analysis in Section 3. For one thing, in both we find (re)analyses of texts from different points of view, bringing home the point that texts can never have a unitary, fixed meaning but will be interpreted in different ways by people with different views, mindsets, agendas, etc. Also, the concerns of individual vs. social identities and the (questioning of the) validity of any idealization and generalization in a postmodern era are particularly prominent in both of these controversies.

These last issues are also highlighted in the exchange that follows in the next section on the nature of applied linguistics, and this is further testimony to the considerable overlap among these controversies. In the case of SLA and applied linguistics, the two areas themselves seem to overlap completely in some people's minds, with the two terms used interchangeably. As Kramsch observes, 'SLA' has become a kind of euphemism for 'Applied Linguistics' in some US university contexts:

> The politics of academia often introduce hidden hierarchies in a field with such porous boundaries as those found in Applied Linguistics. Some institutions are reluctant to call their program *Applied Linguistics*, fearing the negative connotations associated with the adjective *applied*, and prefer the name *Second Language Acquisition*, instead. Others, concerned that the term *education* might be perceived in the United States as less prestigious than *acquisition*, or that *foreign* as in *foreign language* might raise political red flags, also prefer the phrase *Second Language Acquisition*. Hence we see the proliferation of the term *Second Language Acquisition* to cover many areas of research that are, in fact, subsumed under Applied Linguistics.
> (Kramsch 2000: 323, n. 6)

Apart from this institutional point of view, SLA as an area of research is usually included as a matter of course in applied linguistics conferences and books which give an introduction to or overview of applied linguistics. However, for many people, the case for the inclusion of SLA within applied linguistics is not at all self-evident, and the ways in which it is viewed vary greatly. As an illustration, and as a convenient transition to the next, and last, controversy, here are two quotations from two recently published introductions to applied linguistics. Of course, these are just short extracts to whet readers' appetites for the next section, and they are offered here with the urgent invitation to consult their sources for the complete context and a fuller picture:

Starting then from a problem, what error means, SLA research has developed its study of the learner's language (or 'interlanguage') into the most abstract of applied-linguistic projects. So much so that applied linguists (not just language teachers) have begun to query what the current paradigm has to offer to the amelioration and improvement of communication, which we have suggested is the overall aim of applied linguistics.

It may be that indeed SLA research has shifted from being an applied linguistic activity to being more of a linguistic-applied one and that would explain the increasing research time given to investigating cognitive models based on L1 universal grammar theory. If this is the case then SLA research is no longer part of applied linguistics, and it may be that this is a natural process whereby language problems when studied can become formalised, a kind of colonisation by linguistics, a widening of its empire.
(Davies 1999: 83ff.)

Unfortunately, studies of how people learn a second language have been constricted by the narrow purview of mainstream second language acquisition (SLA) work. The issues of language learning have been cast as questions to do with the acquisition of morphemes, syntax, and lexis, with pronunciation or communicative competence, and the learner has been cast as a one-dimensional acquisition device. From this perspective, learners are viewed according to a mechanistic metaphor, as a sort of language learning machine. The writing on this topic is full of metaphors such as *input, output, information processing*, and so on. It has also operated with a positivistic research methodology in which the emphasis has been on the quantification of results achieved by experimental or quasi-experimental studies. Typically from this perspective, an attempt is made to study minute aspects of learning in a controlled environment. As a result, studies in second language acquisition have tended to ignore the context of learning, viewing learning environments and learners as setting in which 'variables' need to be controlled. From this perspective, issues to do with identity would be sidelined under a category such as 'learner variables'. Furthermore, language tends to be seen as a fixed object to be acquired rather than as a semiotic system full of variations and struggles. Even basic considerations of variability posed by sociolinguistics pose challenges to the fixed code fallacy of SLA; the broader considerations raised by a world Englishes perspective ... pose more serious challenges, especially in terms of norms, targets, and interlanguage (Sridhar and Sridhar 1986); and, the more radical postcolonial performative vision of language I am trying to develop here makes the whole paradigm look very suspect.
(Pennycook 2001: 143)

It is clear from these quotations that views about the place of SLA in applied linguistics, or indeed whether it has a place at all, are so varied and conflicting that there is plenty of scope for further controversies in the future.

Further reading

The literature on second language acquisition as such is of course vast. For readers new to the field who would like to get a very brief overview, the following are excellent accessible introductions: Ellis (1997) and Spada and Lightbown (2002).

The current standard reference works of the more comprehensive kind include Ellis (1994) and Ritchie and Bhatia (1996).

A medium-length introduction to SLA is Larsen-Freeman and Long (1991).

For readers interested in *Sprachlehr- und-lernforschung* (second language teaching and learning research) there is more to read in German than in English, notably the classic introduction by Edmondson and House (2000). A brief description of *Sprachlehrforschung* is provided by Grotjahn (2000).

Other controversies

As I indicated earlier, there are a number of controversies about particular issues in SLA which are not the concern of this book. There is, however, one other controversy (a particularly animated one) on the more general question of the theoretical bases of SLA research which is worth noting: Block (1996) – Gregg, Long, Jordan, and Beretta (1997) – Sheen (1999). The references in these papers indicate where to go if readers want to trace its origins. Another paper which provides more context for this controversy is Lantolf (1996).

Another controversial topic concerns the relationship between the status of indigenized varieties of English vis-à-vis the concept of interlanguage, which is so central to SLA thinking, and generally the problem of defining the notion of competence. This is discussed in particular in Sridhar and Sridhar (1986). Related questions are also discussed, under the heading 'Sources of bias in SLA Research', in *TESOL Quarterly* 28 in: Y. Kachru (1994) and Sridhar (1994), as well as in Selinker (1993). These papers provide a link with Section 1 dealing with the global spread of English, as does Cook (1999).

References

Block, D. 1996. 'Not so fast: Some thoughts on theory culling, relativism, accepted findings, and the heart and soul of SLA'. *Applied Linguistics* 17/1: 63–83.

Cook, V. 1999. 'Going Beyond the Native Speaker in Language Teaching'. *TESOL Quarterly* 33/2: 185–209.

Corder, S. P. 1967. 'The significance of learners' errors'. *International Review of Applied Linguistics* 5: 161–9.

Davies, A. 1999. *An Introduction to Applied Linguistics. From Practice to Theory.* Edinburgh: Edinburgh University Press.

Edmondson, W. and J. House. 2000. *Einführung in die Sprachlehrforschung.* 2nd edition. Tübingen: Francke.

Ellis, R. 1994. *The Study of Second Language Acquisition*. Oxford: Oxford University Press.

Ellis, R. 1997. *Second Language Acquisition* in the series 'Oxford Introductions to Language Study'. Oxford: Oxford University Press.

Eubank, L. (ed.). 1983. *Point Counter-Point: Universal Grammar in Second Language Acquisition*. Amsterdam: John Benjamins.

Gregg, K., M. Long, G. Jordan, and A. Beretta. 1997. 'Rationality and its Discontents in SLA'. *Applied Linguistics* 18/4: 538–58.

Grotjahn, R. 2000. Sprachlehrforschung' in M. Byram (ed.). *Routledge Encyclopedia of Language Teaching and Learning*. London: Routledge. 569–72.

Huebner, T. (ed.). 1991. *Crosscurrents in Second Language Acquisition and Linguistic Theories*. Amsterdam: John Benjamins.

Kachru, Y. 1994. 'Monolingual bias in SLA research'. *TESOL Quarterly* 28/4: 795–800.

Kramsch, C. 2000. 'Second Language Acquisition, Applied Linguistics, and the teaching of foreign languages'. *The Modern Language Journal* 84/3: 311–26.

Lantolf, J. 1996. 'SLA Theory building: "Letting all the flowers bloom!"' *Language Learning* 46/4: 713–49.

Larsen-Freeman, D. and M. Long. 1991. *An Introduction to Second Language Acquisition Research*. London/New York: Longman.

Larsen-Freeman, D. 1993. 'Second language acquisition research: Staking out the territory' in S. Silberstein (ed.). *State of the Art TESOL Essays*. Alexandria, Va. TESOL.

Long, M. 1997. 'Construct validity in SLA research: A response to Firth and Wagner'. *The Modern Language Journal* 81/3: 318–23.

Mitchell, R. and F. Myles. 1998. *Second Language Learning Theories*. London: Arnold.

Pennycook, A. 2001. *Critical Applied Linguistics: A Critical Introduction*. Mahwah, New Jersey and London: Lawrence Erlbaum Associates.

Ritchie, W. and T. K. Bhatia (eds.). 1996. *Handbook of Second Language Acquisition*. New York: Academic Press.

Schmitt, N. (ed.). 2002. *An Introduction to Applied Linguistics*. London: Arnold.

Seidlhofer, B. 2002. '*Habeas corpus and divide et impera: 'Global English' and applied linguistics*' in K. Spelman Miller and P. Thompson (eds.). *Unity and Diversity in Language Use*. London: Continuum.

Selinker, L. 1993. 'Fossilization as simplification?' in Tickoo.

Sheen, R. 1999. 'A response to Block's (1996) paper, "Not so fast": Some thoughts on theory culling, relativism, accepted findings and the heart and soul of SLA'. *Applied Linguistics* 20/3: 368–75.

Sinclair, J. 1991. *Corpus, Concordance, Collocation*. Oxford: Oxford University Press.

Spada, N. and P. Lightbown. 2002. 'Second Language Acquisition' in Schmitt.

Sridhar, K. K. and S. N. Sridhar. 1986. 'Bridging the paradigm gap: second language acquisition theory and indigenised varieties of English'. *World Englishes* 5/1: 3–14.

Sridhar, S. N. 1994. 'A reality check for SLA theories'. *TESOL Quarterly* 28/4: 800–5.

Tickoo, M. (ed.). 1993. *Simplification: Theory and Application*. Singapore: SAMEO Regional Language Centre.

Weinert, R. 1995. 'The role of formulaic language in second language acquisition: a review'. *Applied Linguistics* 16/2: 180–205.

Section 5
The nature of applied linguistics

The title of this volume, *Controversies in Applied Linguistics*, suggests that there is something definable as applied linguistics, within which these controversies take place. Certainly, applied linguistics (henceforth AL) has been institutionalized as a field of academic enquiry. There are academic departments and courses that bear its name, and there are associations such as the International Association of Applied Linguistics (or, rather, Association Internationale de Linguistique Appliquée (AILA)). AL appears in the titles of books, and has journals exclusively devoted to it. But the impression all this gives of comfortable stability is in many ways an illusion. As with the other areas this collection deals with, so also with AL any impression we might have of settled certainty and agreement quickly disappears as we look behind the label.

In fact, the field of AL has been plagued by self-doubt, identity crises, and the fear of fragmentation since very early on in its history. When AL was given nominal recognition in the late 1940s, it was taken to be something like the 'academic arm' of English language teaching, both in Britain and in the United States, and in 1948 the journal *Language Learning: A Quarterly Journal of Applied Linguistics* was founded. In the decades that followed, the term 'applied linguistics' gradually broadened, the first addition being what was then referred to as 'automatic translation'. Institutions such as the School of Applied Linguistics under Ian Catford at Edinburgh University and the Center for Applied Linguistics in Washington, D.C., with Charles Ferguson as its first director were founded. In 1964 the first international AILA congress was held, with two programme strands: foreign language teaching and automatic translation.

If we look at the claimed scope of AL as reflected in the titles of the 25 AILA scientific commissions today (listed below), it is clear how diverse the field has become:

- Adult Language Learning
- Child Language
- Communication in the Professions
- Contrastive Linguistics and Error Analysis
- Discourse Analysis
- Educational Technology and Language Learning

- Foreign Language Teaching Methodology and Teacher Education
- Forensic Linguistics
- Immersion Education
- Interpreting and Translating
- Language and Ecology
- Language and Education in Multilingual Settings
- Language and Gender
- Language and the Media
- Language Contact and Language Change
- Language for Special Purposes
- Language Planning
- Learner Autonomy in Language Learning
- Lexicography and Lexicology
- Literacy
- Mother Tongue Education
- Psycholinguistics
- Rhetoric and Stylistics
- Second Language Acquisition
- Sign Language.

It is not clear from the list itself, of course, which of the areas it specifies have already been extensively studied, and which, more speculatively, are staked out as claims for subsequent exploration. At all events, the specification has a very wide range, from Psycholinguistics at the most general end of the spectrum, to Learner Autonomy in Language Learning at the other.

What also comes across from this list is that it is indeed difficult to see any unifying principles or defining criteria for what is to be included in AL: one might ask why Discourse Analysis and Psycholinguistics should be represented but not Pragmatics or Sociolinguistics; why Learner Autonomy is deemed to be autonomous in the field of Language Learning (but not, say, Needs Analysis) and why Language Disorders and Language Attrition, once included, are not there any more. It seems easy to see, then, why Meara comes to the conclusion that

> Applied Linguistics is now so fragmented in its range of interests that one can no longer rely on a common basis of shared assumptions between people who are called 'Applied Linguists'.
> (Meara 1989: 66)

This is, of course, reminiscent of Ellis' dictum about SLA research constituting 'a rather amorphous field of study with elastic boundaries' (1994: 2) quoted in Section 4. And indeed (as Claire Kramsch is also quoted as observing in Section 4 above), for some people AL and SLA are co-terminous, anyway:

> Research in applied linguistics consists of comparisons of materials and methods, with student progress in L2 performance as the dependent variable.
> (Krashen 1980: 13)

Equating AL with SLA has the convenient effect of reducing its confusing diversity, but only, of course, by greatly diminishing its scope.

A common factor in all these areas of AL, diverse as they are, is the assumption that linguistics, in some shape or form, can provide insights of potential relevance in the practical domain. But even this is controversial. With regard to language teaching, for example, the scepticism expressed by Sampson in 1980 would still strike a chord in many people's minds:

> I do not believe that linguistics has any contribution to make to the teaching of English or the standard European languages. The many people who claim that it has seem to me to deceive themselves and others. This would not matter were it not for the extent to which the *applied linguistics* industry, like so many other dubious enterprises, is financed not by those who see it as having some value but by taxpayers helpless in the grip of a voracious and tyrannical state.
> (Sampson 1980: 11)

Others would add that one needs to question the relevance, or at least the primary significance of linguistics in other areas of AL study as well.

So far we have been looking at ways of defining AL by reference to scope or coverage. But it may be that simply to specify the various topical areas of AL is not the most helpful way of going about defining it. Perhaps we need to look for more powerful procedural definitions of what AL attempts to do and how it attempts to do it. For instance, one would expect the journal entitled *Applied Linguistics* to be able to operationalize what its title signifies in order to decide which submissions to accept and which to reject. So here is the journal's 'mission statement' published on the webpage (and, with some differences in the listing of 'current areas of enquiry' in the pages of the journal itself):

> The aim of this journal is to promote a principled approach to language education and other language-related concerns by encouraging inquiry into the relationship between theoretical and practical studies. The journal is less interested in the ad hoc solution of particular problems and more interested in the handling of problems in a principled way by reference to theoretical studies.
> *Applied linguistics* is viewed not only as a relation between theory and practice, but also as the study of language and language-related problems in specific situations in which people use and learn languages. Within this framework the journal welcomes contributions in such areas of current inquiry as first and second language learning and teaching, multilingualism and multilingual education, language in education, critical linguistics, discourse analysis, translation, language testing, language teaching methodology, language planning, the study of interlanguages, stylistics, and lexicography.
> http://www3.oup.co.uk/applij/instauth (accessed 6 September 2002)

What seems to be foregrounded in this description is not so much the *areas* of enquiry of AL as the *mode of enquiry* that is employed: how it involves the principled exploration of the relationship between theory and practice. And here we come close to the view expressed by Widdowson and Brumfit, and referred to by Rampton in the first paper below as the 'Widdowson/Brumfit stance on AL'. While the very existence of such a joint stance is denied by Brumfit in his paper below, it might still be helpful to quote here the most concise definitions of AL I could find by these two authors:

> The theoretical and empirical investigation of real-world problems in which language is a central issue. ... This definition enables application to centre on problems which require resolution.
> (Brumfit 1995: 27)

> An area of enquiry which seeks to establish the relevance of theoretical studies of language to everyday problems in which language is implicated.
> (Widdowson 1996: 125)

Looked at closely, these formulations only make very modest claims: the emphasis is on investigating, *understanding* problems, and trying to establish the relevance of theory, and no assertions are made about AL being able to actually *solve* problems. This is emphasized even more strongly in Widdowson (2000), where he says that a prerequisite for AL is

> the recognition that linguistic insights are not self-evident but a matter of interpretation; that ideas and findings from linguistics can only be made relevant in reference to other perceptions and perspectives that define the context of the problem. Applied Linguistics is in this respect a multilateral process which, of its nature, has to relate and reconcile different representations of reality, including that of linguistics, without excluding others.
> (p.5)

Such a view, one might think, should sit well with observations Rampton, the third author represented in this controversy, made about what he regarded (in 1995) as

> quite a fundamental change in applied linguistics in Britain. Compared with the situation ten years ago, it is much less common today for applied linguists to feel isolated and remote from the users of their research. ... it certainly looks as though there has been a shift in interest over the last ten years, away from language pedagogy, linguistics, and psychology towards language and more general social phenomena and processes, drawing on anthropology, sociology, and media studies.
> (Rampton 1995: 233–4)

The shift of interest that Rampton refers to can be understood in two ways. One would be that, as different practical problems involving language emerge and impress themselves on the attention of applied linguists, so they call for the consideration of the potential relevance of different theoretical perceptions and perspectives. The other reason why interests can shift is that there may be developments within the disciplines themselves, particularly perhaps in linguistics, that provoke us to think again about language problems in the 'real world' and suggest ways of reformulating them. One such development is the electronic processing of language data in corpus linguistics, which reveals all manner of information about language usage which can be drawn upon in AL work (see Section 2 above).

It is by no means self-evident, however, how developments in disciplinary enquiry are relevant to the practical domain, or whether they are relevant at all. One might argue, for example, that models of language description which are outmoded and discredited from the perspective of linguistics, may still retain some relevance for language teaching. In view of this, it is interesting to note what Paul Meara (whose very sceptical, even resigned remarks about the state of AL as he saw it in 1989 are quoted above) has to say in his entry on 'Applied Linguistics' in the *Routledge Encyclopedia of Language Teaching and Learning*:

> The current situation seems to be that few people expect modern theoretical linguistics to make a serious contribution to language teaching. Modern linguistics deals with language at an abstract level, and tends to ignore language as interaction or performance, and this means that the claims it makes have little immediate relevance and cannot be applied in any obvious way. However, the insights of structural linguistics – particularly contrastive linguistics – are still with us, and they still inform the way we teach languages. In a way, the enduring legacy of applied linguistics is that it has preserved, and continues to make use of, a body of knowledge about language which was in danger of being lost to mainstream linguistics. These ideas are no longer at the cutting edge of research, but they still form part of the basic training of most language teachers – particularly TEFL (English as a Foreign Language) teachers, though perhaps less so for teachers of other languages. In a way, the fact that these once-radical and innovative ideas are now part of basic training – a set of shared assumptions that professional language teachers and textbook writers can usually take for granted – is a measure of the impact that applied linguistics has made on language teaching.
> (Meara 2000: 35)

With this quotation from Meara we return to the issues of the relationship between theory and practice, which direction it should take, and how its relevance can be established. These are the issues that all those engaged in the controversy presented here are, in their different ways, essentially concerned with.

Text 29

Ben Rampton
Thames Valley University, London

Retuning in applied linguistics

What do we now mean by the term 'applied linguistics'? Can we provide a coherent characterisation that says it's more than simply all and anything that isn't 'autonomous'/'core'? Should we even try? Nik Coupland's paper, 'Language, ageing and ageism: a project for applied linguistics?', provides a focus for reflection on this issue, and the present paper serves as an introduction, setting up some of the context for the subsequent discussion. As its point of departure, the paper cites the Widdowson-Brumfit view that AL should serve as a point of interdisciplinary synthesis where theories with their own integrity are developed in close interaction with users and professionals. There are, however, reasons for doubting how far this has succeeded in the area that is sometimes regarded as most typically AL (SLA research and L2 teacher education), and so it's important to look to other fields of AL. In fact, a good model can be found in Hymes' 1972 vision of a linguistics that is 'socially constituted', and the relevance and force of this has now been enhanced by much wider developments in social science. A serious commitment to dialogue outside the academy is now characteristic of a great many programmes of basic, specialist *research, and while there is still great value in Strevens' view of AL as a relatively open space where a large variety of practical interest groups, researchers and development projects can meet, there are no longer any grounds for assuming that the* generalist *in applied linguistics should hold the central place.*

Introduction

Rather than simply borrowing theories from linguistics to try to solve language-related problems in the real world, applied linguistics (AL) should serve as a point of interdisciplinary synthesis where theories with their own integrity develop in close interaction with language users and professionals. This view of what applied linguistics ought to be dates back at least 15 years (Widdowson [1981] 1984; Brumfit 1981), and it is worth asking now how far it has actually held water.

In the areas of activity which are often regarded as prototypically applied linguistic – second language acquisition (SLA) research and second language (L2) teacher education – progress towards the vision which Widdowson and Brumfit programmatically sketched out has in fact been far from clear. On the one hand, SLA researchers are insisting on more theoretical autonomy (Lightbown 1985: 184; Beretta & Crookes 1993: 271), while on the other, Widdowson (1992: 267–8) has more recently argued for *pedagogy* rather than applied linguistics as a domain of enquiry, characterising applied linguistics rather disparagingly as a 'patchwork of insights stitched together' that is engaged in top-down imposition insensitive to 'the possible validity of homegrown ways of thinking'. Indeed, in this situation, van Lier's observation (1994a: 5) seems to be quite apt:

> the linguistics in AL has veered off in the direction of theory (in a sense, therefore, has left AL), leaving pedagogy to cope with the practical side of things. The mutually strengthening relationship between theory and practice described by Halliday et al, in 1964 ... seems therefore to have disappeared. There has thus occurred a sort of 'double split' – linguistics (and SLA) with theory in one direction, and education with practice in another – and this split needs to be resolved before we can once again speak of a healthy AL.

SLA and SL teacher education are, however, only two areas within a broader understanding of applied linguistics,[1,2] and to establish whether or not there has been any movement either towards or indeed beyond the early vision of AL as a productive interdisciplinary dialogue between theory and practice, it is essential to look around more widely. In fact a number of coherent interdisciplinary research programmes have emerged and/or been consolidated over the last 10 to 20 years which combine (a) the empirical investigation of fundamental communicative processes with (b) a commitment to using research knowledge to improve communicative relationships in everyday life. For example (from where I stand in the sociolinguistic corner of applied linguistics):

> interactional sociolinguistics and the micro-ethnography of institutional settings (Gumperz 1982a, b; Erickson & Shultz 1982); ethnographic studies of socialisation, education and literacy (Cazden 1986; Heath 1983; Hewitt 1986; Street 1984; Barton 1994); systemic linguistics and genre theory (Halliday 1985; Christie (ed.) 1989; Kress 1994); critical discourse analysis (Fairclough 1989, 1992); the social psychology of language and speech accommodation theory (Coupland, Coupland, Giles & Henwood 1988); and, increasingly, institutionally oriented conversation analysis (Drew & Heritage 1992).

Within and across these programmes of research, there are of course important differences in kinds and amounts of interdisciplinarity as well as in the strength of their interest in influencing life outside the academy; and whether, how and how far they actually achieve such influence is itself a complex and open question (cf. e.g. Cook-Gumperz & Gumperz 1992: 173–4). Nevertheless, for anyone broadly in sympathy with the earlier Widdowson-Brumfit vision of applied linguistics, research programmes such as these merit close attention. In precisely what ways do they (attempt to) integrate the investigation of fundamental linguistic processes with dialogue with the community and the professions? How can their trajectories be characterised, and what are the philosophical assumptions that sustain them? Do they actually point to a broad philosophical field of ideas about language, knowledge and action which can nourish a variety of programmes committed to both discovery and usefulness?

To address questions like these, to discuss whether, how and where progress has been made either towards or beyond the early Widdowson-Brumfit programme for applied linguistics, this peer commentary collection looks closely at work within one of the research programmes mentioned above – the social psychology of language and speech accommodation theory. Nik Coupland provides an account of the development of ground-breaking work that he and his colleagues have undertaken on language and ageing. This then provides a context for a more general discussion of the development and character of applied linguistics (or whatever else it ought to be called), with contributions from Karin Aronsson, Christopher Brumfit, Christopher Candlin, Monica Heller, Sinfree Makoni, Celia Roberts and Leo van Lier.

To begin with, though, it is probably worth anchoring the present discussion in a very brief sketch of a little of the recent history of debate about the nature of applied linguistics.[3]

'Linguistics applied' vs 'applied linguistics': AL as SLA + ELT

According to Corder (1973: 10–11):

> The application of linguistic knowledge to some object – or applied linguistics, as its name implies – is an activity. It is not a theoretical study. It makes use of the findings of theoretical studies. The applied linguist is a consumer or user, not a

producer of theories ... The pace of [linguistic] investigation has quickened in
recent years and the methods of investigation have increasingly been made more
rigorous, to the point that we can now, with some justification and within certain
defined boundaries, claim that linguistic studies are scientific.

The challenge to this position – characterised as 'linguistics applied' rather than
'applied linguistics' – was, among others, clearly formulated by Widdowson
([1980] 1984: 8):

> The relevance of linguistics cannot, I think, be taken for granted because it is
> not obvious that the way linguists conceive of language is the most appropriate
> for teaching purposes. I want to suggest that the main business of applied
> linguistics should be the establishing of appropriate concepts or models of
> language in the pedagogic domain without prejudging the issue by supposing
> that a relevant model of language must inevitably derive from a formal model
> of linguistic description.[4]

The critique took an explicitly philosophical turn in a rejection of natural science
as the most relevant model of inquiry. Citing Dilthey, Brumfit argued for the
importance of interpretation, of holistic *Verstehen* and of the participants'
'knowledge of what it is to ...' (e.g. 1984: ch. 1). In a slightly different idiom,
Widdowson ([1981] 1984: 22) argued that

> [l]inguistics claims to be science, like physics. It must, therefore, conform to the
> general principles of scientific enquiry, and in particular, it must avoid intuitive
> contamination in the interpretation of its findings. And it is here that we come
> against a major problem ... What I have been trying to show is that the
> analyst's description and the user's experience of language are necessarily quite
> different ... For analysis to be valid it must be precise: for communication to be
> effective it must be imprecise. Precision in analysis is achieved by the observer
> taking up a detached position, by disassociating ... from participation.

Although the claims to an *alternative* kind of *scientific* status are relatively
muted, there is an orientation towards culturally contextualised interpretation
and towards an important role for dialogue with non-researchers that is shared
by at least some of the research programmes listed in the preceding section.
However, for what are no doubt a number of very complex reasons (to do, among
other things, with commitments in teacher education and the backgrounds and
positions of applied linguists in British higher education),[5] the Widdowson-
Brumfit stance on AL seems to have worked out *as a declaration of independence
from basic linguistic research, rather than as a challenge or alternative claim to it.*
Much more than the production of original analyses reported in journals of
theoretical and descriptive research, the applied linguist's key activities generally
involve the responsible (and often creative) reinterpretation/mediation of theories
and findings from elsewhere. At least partly in line with this, immersion in
particular data-bases doesn't appear to figure prominently in the repertoire of
relationships in which applied linguists engage, and rather than dogged
dedication to the accurate representation of specific corpora, flexibility and
breadth are the key intellectual values within this particular strand of applied
linguistics.[6] The concern is with formulating accounts of language learning and

use that are appropriate to pedagogy and accessible to teachers, drawing on a wide range of different kinds of knowledge, and in this version, AL is a field for *generalists*. Most recently, its identity as such has been resoundingly endorsed by Cook & Seidlhofer (1995; see also van Lier 1994b: 332).[7]

Admittedly, in another part of the study of second language teaching and learning – what people often see as the heart of applied linguistics – there has been a lot of data-based research on basic linguistic processes, and this has come together under the banner of second language acquisition research. The vast bulk of SLA research is, however, generally rather incompatible with the philosophical assumptions outlined by Widdowson and Brumfit.[8] Certainly there has been a very substantial tradition of interest in the relevance of SLA research to teaching, but in SLA there is an overwhelming emphasis on the *difference* between doing research and using research to influence ordinary life. Researchers produce findings, and then 'what is known about SLA' (Ellis 1985: 1 and 1994: 38) is relayed to practitioners, who, it is often acknowledged, may or may not find this knowledge helpful (Lightbown 1985; Klein 1986: 2, 18; Ellis 1994: 686–90; Long 1993: 229).[9] The interaction crucial to the production of knowledge about SLA occurs *within* the academy, where indigenous methodological and social processes 'disengage researchers from their findings' (Long 1990: 656 and 1993: 233) and 'have much the same effects as if the enterprise were utterly selfless and rational' (Berreta 1993: 223; Beretta & Crookes 1993). The assumption in the mainstream of SLA is that science separates fact from value, rationality from interest – indeed theory from practice – and far from research being socio-historically located, with different priorities in different settings, the dream of reaching a complete and definitive theory of SLA remains a central inspiration. Doing and using research are seen as fundamentally distinct.

In much of the study of second language teaching and learning, then, the division between (a) speculative/non-empirical inquiry committed to teacher education and (b) empirical analysis of language learning, amounts to rather more than some people wanting to think and work with teachers and others wanting to think and look at data. The assumptions about knowledge underpinning their reflections are themselves radically different, and while one group regards contingency and multi-party dialogue as essential to their activity, these are compromising for the other group which instead 'strives for the [academy's] right to soliloquy' (Bauman 1990: 126). All this makes a lot of the SLA-ELT nexus rather unpropitious as a site for discussion of the ways that the relationship between theory and practice might be constituted in applied linguistics, and if applied linguistics were to be construed like this as just SLA+ELT, a return to Corder's 'linguistics applied' seems almost inevitable. Anyone interested in studying closely how people learn an L2 will almost inevitably have to immerse themselves in a tradition aspiring to the natural sciences,[10] while all the talk of dialogue and interpretation seems to come from teacher education, where it is easily overlooked as a set of rival claims about the nature of knowledge and reality, being instead most easily seen as something like 'the inevitable reflex of people looking to involve their students and to cope with lots of uncontrolled variables (and be academically respectable as well)'. Within this kind of intellectual configuration, AL-as-ELT+SLA can quickly slip back into some kind of dichotomy along the lines of 'theory = science versus practice and art'.

Other kinds of applied linguistics

To break out of this impasse, it is worth taking a broader view of the issues and approaches falling within AL's remit. Looking beyond SLA+ELT, there are traditions of research in which interpretation and dialogue are actually seen as vital ingredients not just in persuading people about the significance of research findings but also in coming to understand linguistic objects and processes themselves. Within sociolinguistics, the possibility of combining usefulness with discovery is articulated particularly clearly in the writings of Hymes and Bernstein (and indeed Halliday).

Hymes, in an illuminating discussion of the relationship between 'scientific and practical need' ([1972] 1977: 194), identifies three positions on linguistics in society. The first, encompassing for example 'Sapir's semantic research for an international auxiliary language, Bloomfield's work in the teaching of reading, Swadesh's literacy work, the "Army method" of teaching foreign languages', he designates *the social as well as the linguistic*:

> For the most part, this work is conceived as an application, lacking theoretical goals, or else as pursuing theoretical goals that are in addition to those of normal linguistics, or perhaps even wholly unrelated to them. When 'sociolinguistics' serves as a legitimizing label for such activity, it is ... not conceived as a challenge to normal linguistics. (pp. 195–6)

There is a clear parallel here with Corder's notion of linguistics applied, and also perhaps the Brumfit-Widdowson position to the extent that the latter holds back from challenging the mainstream.

Hymes' second approach is called *socially realistic linguistics*:

> This term is apt for work that extends and challenges existing linguistics with data from the speech community. The challenge, and indeed the accomplishment, might be summed up with the two words, 'variation' and 'validity'. A salient example is the work of William Labov ... The expressed theoretical goals are not distinct from those of normal linguistics, e.g. the nature of linguistic rules, the nature of sound change, but the method of work and the findings differ sharply. Here might also be put work which recognises dependence of the analysis of meaning and speech acts on social context. (p. 196)

An obvious parallel here is with SLA research on variability and interaction (cf. Ellis 1994: chs 4–7).

The third and last position is the one that Hymes himself identifies with, and though he considers 'applied linguistics' as one possible designation,[11] he prefers to call this *socially constituted linguistics* (cf. 1977: 196–209). This amounts to a vision of a kind of social and cultural semiotics which brings cultural and social organisation centre-stage, and which construes language in the first instance not as grammar but as a repertoire of ways of speaking shaped through the part it plays in social action and communicative conduct (see also Halliday 1964). Rather than setting out to identify universal relationships from the outset, socially constituted linguistics holds the comprehensive comparative and historical analysis of difference and particularity as its explanatory goal (p. 203), and this in turn serves higher ethical objectives – achieving *Liberté, Egalité,*

Fraternité (pp. 205, 206) – since it 'prepares [sociolinguists] to speak concretely to actual inequalities' (p. 204):

> If linguistic research is to help as it could in transcending the many inequalities in language and competence in the world today, it must be able to analyse these inequalities. In particular, a practical linguistics so motivated would have to go beyond means of speech and types of speech community to a concern with [both] persons and social structure. (pp. 204–5)

Hymes wonders whether Mao Tse-tung was right:

> If you want to know a certain thing or a certain class of things directly, you must personally participate in the practical struggle to change reality, to change that thing or class of things, for only thus can you come into contact with them as phenomena. (p. 209)

and elsewhere ([1973] 1980: 21), he sketches out the kinds of question that a socially constituted, 'practical linguistics' would need to work through, beginning well beyond the walls of the academy:

> it is unusual today to think of language as something to be overcome, yet four broad dimensions of language can be considered in just that way: diversity of language, medium of language (spoken, written), structure of language, and functioning of language. Of each we can ask,
> 1 when, where, and how it came to be seen as a problem;
> 2 from what vantage point it is seen as a problem (in relation to other vantage points from which it may not be so seen);
> 3 in what ways the problem has been approached or overcome as a practical task and also as an intellectual, conceptual task;
> 4 what its consequences for the study of language itself have been;
> 5 what kinds of study, to which linguists might contribute, are now needed.
> I cannot do more than raise such questions here; limitations of knowledge would prevent my doing more, if limitations of space did not. To raise such questions may, I hope, help to stimulate the development of a general perspective.

Elsewhere in social science, a broadly compatible view, tempered by the same sense of standing on the threshold of an approach to research which had yet to bear fruit, can be found in Bernstein's 1972 discussion of the development of the sociology of education (reprinted 1975). Rather than being principally directed by questions formulated exclusively within any particular school of research, Bernstein (p. 160) seeks a mode of inquiry which develops

> a sense of the possible, that is, [of] the construction and analysis of the alternative forms [that] social relationships can take, ... through openness to the variety of social experience ... This may require a widening of the focus of the sociology of education, less an allegiance to an approach, and more a dedication to a problem.

Growing sociological attention to discourse would play a key role in the problem-oriented inquiry that Bernstein (pp. 151–2) advocates:

> From the mid-1960s onwards ... new sociological perspectives were attaining influence in the USA. From different sources, Marxist, Phenomenological,

Symbolic-Interactionist and Ethnomethodological viewpoints began to assert themselves. Although there are major differences between these approaches, they share certain common features:

1 A view of man as a creator of meanings.
2 An opposition to macro-functional sociology.
3 A focus on the assumptions underlying social order, together with the treatment of social categories as themselves problematic.
4 A distrust of forms of quantification and the use of objective categories.
5 A focus upon the transmission and acquisition of interpretative procedures.

Within this though, *contra* 2 and 4 above, Bernstein also insists on recognising what quantitative macro-sociology can contribute since, in his view at the time, (a) the empirical value of discursive sociology remained still to be seen,[12] and (b) macro-sociology provides an indispensible account of the larger social relations within which interaction takes place. So in the problem-addressing sociology which Bernstein sees as a priority, both qualitative and quantitative analyses are vital:

> It is a matter of some importance that we develop forms of analysis that can provide a dynamic relationship between 'situated activities of negotiated meanings' and the 'structural' relationships which the former pre-suppose. (p. 157)

All in all, then, the call for modes of inquiry transcending the dichotomies of theory-&-practice, basic-&-applied, has been sounded well beyond the territory of AL-as-SLA+ELT. The central *difference* between the kind of AL emerging within the work of Hymes and Bernstein and the approach to AL outlined by Widdowson and Brumfit in the late '70s/early '80s seems to be that in the generalist version, the applied linguist's job is to interpret the wider educational or social significance of intricate theories and findings from elsewhere, whereas in the Hymes and Bernstein enterprise, the relationship is reversed and, instead, the task is either to draw wider intellectual frameworks into the analysis of linguistic topics or to take on larger political, social or educational ideas and to try to work through what they mean in linguistic and discursive detail.[13] Admittedly, the success of this more specialist AL was something that, in 1972, Hymes didn't feel he could predict ([1972] 1977: 207): 'from the vantage point of the year 2000 AD[, w]hat are the chances ... [of seeing] the transformation of linguistics and adjacent social science disciplines to encompass what I have called "socially constituted linguistics"?' 'Quite uncertain', he concluded. In fact, deferring to the timetable that Hymes himself set out, we could say that retrospection on this second trajectory seems just as timely.

Applied linguistics in the 1990s

Nik Coupland's paper raises many of the issues sketched out above, and as a case study, it serves as a useful focus for wider discussion of what, if it's not just SLA+ELT, we now think that applied linguistics looks like. As final elements of this introduction, I would first like to make some brief and derivative suggestions myself, largely in line, I think, with Hymes and Bernstein above, Coupland below, and van Lier in other places, and then offer a few observations about applied linguistics as an institution in the UK.

Following the lead variously given in the 1970s and early '80s, the ideal, I take it, is an interdisciplinary area of inquiry in which fundamental research on language and communication can arise from and/or be integrated with dialogue outside the academy about a range of issues in which language figures prominently.

In the first instance, it is important to contradict a couple of inferences that one might legitimately draw from the way the arguments have been stated so far. First, arguing for the desirability, indeed the superiority, of AL as some kind of 'socially constituted, practical linguistics' isn't to deny any value to other kinds of linguistic and AL research (Hymes [1972] 1977: 203; Pateman 1987).[14] Secondly, even though the non-educational sources I have cited have been closely associated with sociolinguistics, a 'socially constituted, practical linguistics' wouldn't be confined to people researching traditionally sociolinguistic topics to do with, for example, language and social groups or language in institutions. As well as sociological concerns, Hymes' vision of an integrated field of research encompasses the psychological (where Vygotsky's work would presumably serve as a major source of inspiration) and 'the traditional and indispensible work oriented toward specific languages, language families and language areas' ([1972] 1977: 208).

With those clarifications in place, it seems to me that rather than becoming identified with any unified model of language use, as has sometimes been suggested,[15] applied linguistics will continue to be most productively defined as a relatively open space where a large variety of practical interest groups, research programmes and development projects can meet (cf. Strevens [1976] 1977: 37–40). The significant recent development, though, lies in the likelihood that there is now much more scope for genuinely reciprocal dialogue – dialogue that is neither just top-down, nor reliant on the applied linguist as mediator/go-between. Of course, as before, shared interest in substantive topics will remain a basic requirement for fruitful interaction between basic researchers, generalists and others, and as ever, a wide range of other contingencies will also come into play. The *difference* lies

1 in the fact that, contrary to the situation envisaged by Strevens (p. 40), people calling themselves applied linguists are certainly now no longer the only scholars interested and experienced in 'multi-based, interdisciplinary, language-related' work, and
2 in the emergence and/or consolidation of at least three general assumptions about the nature of research, action, knowledge and reality, which in some sense guarantee or underwrite the seriousness of these exchanges (cf. van Lier 1994b).

Some initial predisposition towards taking dialogue seriously is, in the first instance, encouraged by (i) the assumption that human reality is extensively reproduced and created anew in the socially and historically specific activities of ordinary life, rather than being the product of forces that actors neither control nor comprehend (Giddens 1984: xvi; Sapir [1931] 1949: 104; Halliday 1978; Bernstein 1975). With learning seen as an interactional process and reality viewed as a social construction, the understanding of meaning in interaction becomes a central objective, and the analysis of discourse becomes a potentially vital tool.

Of itself, of course, commitment to interpretive methodologies and discourse as key elements in the study of human processes need not lead researchers to anything more than rather limited interaction with professionals and non-academics – trying to understand your informants' activities, perspectives and priorities doesn't necessarily entail *their* finding out about your own (Bauman 1990: 126–7; Rampton 1992: 57). The notion that reality is socially constructed does entail, though, that (ii) 'theory making is itself a social practice in the "real world"' (Cameron 1994: 19; Hymes [1973] 1980), and recognition of this *is* likely to produce greater attentiveness to social processes both within and *beyond* the confines of research. Researchers can't help being socially located, with biographies and subjectivities that are brought to bear at every stage of the research process, influencing in some form or other the questions they ask and the way they try to find answers. And their social locatedness is not only vital as a matrix for the interpretive and dialogic capacities that are required for valid analysis of the particular realities that researchers seek to analyse.[16] It also itself needs to be the focus of careful reflection, both to ensure that the claims made in any given research project are properly qualified and to try to achieve some understanding and influence over its wider social ramifications.

Finally, (iii) consciousness of strict limits to research neutrality and a problematisation of the distinction between fact and value bring ethics to the foreground as a major concern (Bauman 1990: 201–3 and 1994; Hammersley 1992: 76–7; van Lier 1994b; Hymes [1972] 1977). Making choices and setting priorities becomes much more difficult if (a) problems are seen as only partly technical, if (b) researchers are no longer able to defer unthinkingly to an academy now recognised as only one historically contingent institution among many, and if (c) contact with a range of different discourse communities is now considered important. With this pluralisation of authority, values can no longer be taken for granted and instead, unless researchers opt for indifference, there may be much more pressure for decisions to be justified morally, again in dialogue.

Those, then, are some developments in the general intellectual climate which mean that there are now many others in addition to applied linguists willing to take part in 'multi-based, interdisciplinary' discussions about language. One of the consequences may be that generalist applied linguistics loses the kind of distinctiveness that Strevens claimed for it in the mid '70s. At the same time, there are opportunities for applied linguistics in the idiom of Hymes, Bernstein or Halliday: sufficiently outward-looking to connect up with the discussions elsewhere, but also specialised enough to make a distinctive contribution of its own.[17]

At least in England and Wales, some further encouragement for a socially constituted, practical linguistics seems likely to come from a second source: developments in linguistics education.[18]

In its generalist version, particularly in teacher education, the principal aim of an applied linguistic training is to produce people who are *intelligent readers* of research. Admittedly, there is usually an element of empirical work in the training, but there is only a limited amount that students can do in a one-year MA course; instead, the main goal is to produce people who can draw research knowledge into interaction with professional experience and who can bring it to bear on educational decision-making either alongside, or as a counterweight to, intuition, tradition, fashion or authority. In contrast, in 'socially constituted' applied linguistics, the goal is to produce people who are fairly adept at *devising and conducting systematic empirical analyses themselves*, and this inevitably takes longer. Indeed, in addition to quite a lot of worldliness, attempts to make responsible analytic sense of linguistic problems that are real-life rather than just discipline-internal requires descriptive competence in a range of semiotic levels, from the phonetic to the ethnographic.

Inspite of the purchase it offers on understanding and intervening in institutional life, all this puts something like an ability to do a good piece of interactional sociolinguistics well beyond the reach of students learning linguistics on an MA course. But with recent developments in education, this is likely to change.

In England and Wales, one of the fastest growing (pre-undergraduate) A-level courses is English Language (Freeborn 1992). This mainly relies on text-based and project-oriented pedagogies (e.g. Freeborn, French & Langford 1986), and it introduces techniques of linguistic description to large numbers of school and further education students,[19] whose enjoyment often seems to be related to the 'relevance' of language study and to the fact that it makes them think about everyday activities in new ways. The growing modularisation of BA degrees seems likely to continue this momentum. Far more students are likely to be studying linguistics alongside sociology, literature, education, business, etc. than doing it on its own, and the opportunity – indeed the pressure – to develop modules which resonate elsewhere in their degrees seems bound to increase – again, at this stage of their education, students are often more attracted by the wider connections that linguistics can make than by the focal problems generated inside particular research traditions. Admittedly, students of this kind may well need a year's MA study to get really focussed before they can make a serious research contribution to cross-disciplinary or practical problems, but they represent an invaluable base for building the kind of socially constituted, practical linguistics that Hymes envisaged – technically competent, familiar with interdisciplinarity, used to using real data to address felt problems (and in addition, increasing numbers of them are mature students).

If in the past in applied linguistics there has been a tendency to attribute special privileges to the generalist, casting him or her as either the central character, sage, or master of ceremonies, this now seems less relevant. Understood as an open field of interest in language, in which those inhabiting or passing through simply show a common commitment to the potential value of dialogue with people who are different, there is no knowing where, between whom, or on what the most productive discussions will emerge. The fullest and most creative interactions may indeed start up between language professionals on the one hand, and on the other, researchers with a relatively broad-based interest in language in particular institutions (educational, clinical, forensic etc.). But equally, there may be a lot of very socially productive talk with researchers who spend a lot of time specialising in particular approaches (for example, functional grammar, interactional sociolinguistics etc.). Nik Coupland has specialised in a particular research programme (speech accommodation theory), and his work warrants close attention from scholars doing basic research in the heartlands of sociolinguistics and the social psychology of language. But does this mean that it is only peripherally applied linguistic? At least according to the contributors to this edition of the *International Journal of Applied Linguistics*, the unanimous answer is 'no'.

The papers that follow

Nik Coupland's focal paper is a very honest, first-hand account of the concepts, methods and ground covered in the journey towards a position broadly in line with Hymes' socially constituted linguistics. His paper is invaluable both as the overview of developments in a particular research programme and as the case study of a larger shift over the last ten to fifteen years, both in sociolinguistics and in the social sciences more generally (where comparable changes can be seen in, for example, the study of ethnicity and gender).

The two papers immediately following Coupland's dwell extensively on the particular approach to language and ageing that he and his associates have taken. **Karin Aronsson** situates their work in a wider set of ideas about identity and interaction, and with social constructivism figuring prominently in a 'retuned' applied linguistics, her outline of epistemological developments is timely, as are her warnings about 'constructivist reductionism' and about 'discursive construction' as a sometimes facile term in 'somewhat anaemic modern rhetoric'.

While attesting, like Coupland, to the need for an 'ideological'/socio-culturally constituted applied linguistics rather than an 'autonomous' one, **Sinfree Makoni** takes a critical look at the extent to which concepts underpinning Coupland's work survive translation into research on language and ageing in South Africa. After that, he goes on to address some of the problems and possibilities involved in developing serious interdisciplinary, academic/professional dialogue about language and dementia.

Taking up some of the issues raised in the latter part of Makoni's paper, **Celia Roberts** suggests that usefulness in applied linguistics often amounts to little more than either 'home-spun wisdom' or 'bite-sized knowledge', 'bolted on' through a process of conceptual 'tooling down'. Raising questions about the scope for reconceptualising the relationship between academics and professionals, she instead looks towards a much more integrated approach to 'practical linguistic' research.

Monica Heller's paper also looks forward, and it provides a broad view of fundamental issues and assumptions comprising an agenda for research on 'language in the world'. Among other things, Heller suggests that the balance between autonomy and interdependence in linguistic systems should itself be a central question for research, and indeed this could be an important move in helping us beyond the declarations of ontological incompatibility and low-level academic warfare that the issue sometimes generates.

Christopher Brumfit's paper situates applied linguistics alongside a wide range of other sciences and disciplines, and its pitch is perhaps the most philosophical in this collection. Brumfit has played a leading role in the definition of applied linguistics, but he takes issue with the way I have constructed a 'Widdowson-Brumfit generalist' in the paragraphs above (in the process producing what I think is as dubious a reading of my position as he thinks mine is of his!).

Like Brumfit, **Leo van Lier** provides a map of how applied linguistics relates to other disciplines (including 'core' linguistics), but he also asks what conceptualisation of 'paradigm' best fits AL and elaborates his account with some institutional history.

Overall, then, this volume contains a very varied collection of reflections on applied linguistics, as well as its fair share of disagreements and misunderstandings. Even so, there is a significant measure of consensus on what applied linguistics looks like: as well as aiming to combine discovery with usefulness, there is a recurrent concern in these papers with participant meanings, with interdisciplinarity, with processes of social construction and with accountability to real-world evidence. At the same time, these are much more than a set of casual nostrums, and in different ways and with different emphases, all of the papers probe at complications and difficulties. It is also striking how many of the authors introduce quite strong personal voices.

How far do the authors in this collection feel that it is actually time to 'retune in applied linguistics'? Judging from their papers (and not from their biographies, which would raise all sorts of additional complexities), there are three kinds of response.

The first seems to be a matter of '*tuning to*' rather than '*retuning within*'. Here the papers appear to start from a strong base in fairly closely focused empirical research, and they then look across/outwards, pleased to find that people accustomed to calling themselves 'applied linguists' are keen to engage with them on their interests and objectives. This certainly characterises Coupland's paper, and maybe there are hints of a similar response in the papers by Aronsson, Makoni and Heller. The second response, illustrated in the papers by Brumfit and van Lier in this collection, is that applied linguistics has been playing 'good music' for quite a while – not easy listening, nor indeed trouble-free broadcasting, but varied, rewarding and absolutely open to interaction with and among more specialised styles and tastes. The third kind of response, like the second, professes quite long-standing participation in what's usually described as applied linguistics, but here the view is that certain adjustments would indeed now be welcome (Roberts and Rampton in this collection, and elsewhere – e.g. Brumfit 1995: 39; van Lier 1994a).

This range of responses is unsurprising, and insignificant when set against the points of agreement we have already referred to. But what does stand out in the context of a review of the state of play in AL – a review partly conceived as an update looking back to Hymes' programmatic ideas in the early '70s – is the level of enthusiasm that authors show for the challenges ahead, many of them as yet uncharted. It is difficult to say whether this forward orientation reflects the end of a phase of fragmentation and the resurgence of a spirit of cross-disciplinary interchange that somehow got submerged after the early to mid '60s (see van Lier's paper below), or whether it is the product of entirely local factors (like, for example, the constraints of space in this particular collection). But whatever, there seems to be a strong show of commitment to the broad trajectory in applied linguistics that these papers sketch out.

Is 'applied linguistics' really the best name for this project? The suggestion of dependence on 'pure' linguistics remains a misrepresentation, and the idea of 'applying' X (rather than simply doing 'useful' X) continues to be a problem even within a properly inclusive notion of linguistics (a notion where 'all activities that relate to the clarification of "language" ' are accepted as unmarked, non-hyphenated parts of the discipline (cf. Brumfit this volume, p. 90)). But maybe the most sensible perspective on this is van Lier's, who, in fact rather like the International Association for Applied Linguistics, conceptualises AL as a space superordinate to a range of more specific subdisciplines like sociolinguistics, educational linguistics, forensic linguistics and so forth. In this conception, our strongest academic identity investments lie at the lower level – in educational linguistics, socio-linguistics etc. – and this is also where we're most likely to harbour any ambitions of reshaping the terrain around us and reproducing others in our image. Freeing it up from many of our most insistent academic 'nesting instincts', this is a view that safeguards 'applied linguistics' as a relatively unregulated meeting place, locating it beyond the ground we're keenest to domesticate. This makes it quite easy to tolerate an awkward name like 'applied linguistics': as long as the discussions it accommodates are interesting and productive, no one need really worry.

Notes

1 The list of Scientific Commissions subsumed within AILA and the range of issues covered in both *InJAL* and the *Annual Review of Applied Linguistics* are both illustrative of this much wider conception.

2 Which is not to say that SLA and second language teaching aren't potentially the most relevant areas for the particular project that van Lier has in mind.

3 Of course, discussion about the relationship between linguistic scholarship and its uses dates back many centuries (cf. e.g. Robins 1979; Howatt 1984).

4 Widdowson [1981] 1984: 26–7) states:

> The relevant model of language for teachers of literature will take into account the cultural perspectives of literary criticism and aesthetics. The relevant model for students of physics doing a course in ESP will take into account the philosophy and methodology of science. The relevant models for learners in a particular cultural context will take into account the traditions, values, beliefs, and customary practices of that culture and the way language is used to express them. In all such cases, the starting point is the need and purpose that the model of language must provide for. You do not start with a model as given and then cast about for ways in which it might come in handy.

A good example of this approach, substantially predating the Widdowson-Brumfit discussion, is Leech 1969 (cf. pp. 1–7 in particular).

5 Brumfit (1985: 71–2) states:

> It is striking that the British contribution to scholarship, through influential hypothetico-deductive discussion and exciting speculation, in the field of second language acquisition and learning, has been considerable (we only have to think of the work of Corder, Widdowson, and Wilkins, for example), whereas the systematic empirical exploitation and the validated implementation of these ideas has been found most fully in the United States or in other European countries. This unfortunate divide results in British researchers being stereotyped as anti-data, and unwilling to become involved with basic empirical, experimental and descriptive work in this field. Yet the difficulty is far more one of funding than of principle. Most researchers in languages who enter academic life either start off with a strong literary bias ... or come to applied linguistic work via teaching. The latter group, by the time they have had enough teaching to understand the

nature of teaching and enough research training to understand the nature of research, are in their mid-to-late thirties, usually with family commitments. They are past the stage where they can be expected to attach themselves to someone else's research and live on a pittance, but they are uniquely equipped to contribute as researchers who genuinely understand the process of education. In most education or applied linguistics departments in the tertiary sector scholarship can be pursued in such time as is left over from the (higher than average) teaching duties. But systematic and serious empirical work cannot be pursued without time being bought. This is where the squeeze on university funding shows itself most rapidly.

6 On an applied linguistics relevant to language teaching, Brumfit (1984: 1–2) argues:

Research on teaching methodology entails three conditions:

1 generalisations and principles must be capable of being related directly to existing teaching conditions, including teachers as they actually are, institutions as they actually are, and resources as they actually are.

2 information, principles, metaphors, and … insights will be drawn from a whole range of different sources and integrated into some sort of coherent position which is directly translatable into classroom behaviour.

3 perceptions must reflect the position of the teacher in the classroom – that is to say that they must in the end refer to the process of intervening in the lives of others in order to assist desirable changes of behaviour.

The process of drawing upon research findings, theoretical constructs, and practical suggestions from a wide range of potentially relevant sciences inevitably results in major risks of error … Yet we cannot afford to leave all questions of how to synthesise research conclusions to teachers actually working in classrooms, for – more often than not – they lack expertise, training, and above all, time for such activity …

(See also Widdowson 1990 in Ellis 1994: 688.)

7 In their witty and stimulating introduction to Widdowson's *Festschrift*, Cook & Seidlhofer play with the idea of specialisation as a form of 'separatism', a fragmentation of applied linguistics into a set of indolent, inward-looking personality cults (1995: 1–2). But of course, in all of the research programmes mentioned above, a steady focus and a certain amount of specialisation are needed

— to build up and do justice to useful data-bases

— to investigate emerging patterns thoroughly, and to test and elaborate theories about them

— to keep sharp on technical analysis

— to stay in tune with relevant areas in the other disciplines, and

— to know who to talk to outside the academy and how to develop forms of communication that make the interaction really two-way.

8 Though there are in fact some notable exceptions to the way in which I characterise the SLA mainstream. See, for example, van Lier 1988, the work of Roberts & her colleagues (e.g. Roberts & Simonot 1987; Roberts, Davies &

Jupp 1992; Bremer, Roberts et al. 1996), and the growing school of
Vygotskyan SLA research (Frawley & Lantolf 1984; Lantolf & Appel 1994
[omitted from mention in Ellis 1994]). Also, for a declaration of the emergence
of alternative strands, see *TESOL Quarterly* 27.4 (for example, Lazaraton
1995; Davis 1995).

9　In sociolinguistics, the classic statement of this research-first-intervention-
after model is Labov 1982. For a critique, see Cameron et al. 1992: ch. 1 and
pp. 46–51.

10　Cf. Lazaraton 1995.

11　Hymes ([1977] 1980: 70) states:

> Whatever its label, [a study of language that is inseparable from a study
> of social life] is beginning to emerge into prominence, and it is the sort of
> study of language that is fundamental to education. From one standpoint,
> such a study of language may be 'applied' linguistics, especially if it is
> concerned with language use in schools. But 'applied' taken alone is a
> misnomer. Linguists do not now know enough about these phenomena
> for others to come to them to ask simply for application of knowledge
> already in hand. Research into these questions is not applied, but
> foundational and at the frontiers of linguistics. Its practical relevance is
> obvious, but it is no less concerned with issues of theory for that. The
> plain fact is that practical needs and theoretical challenges coincide here,
> as they do in so many places. And there are not enough who are taking
> them up.

The overlap with Widdowson's position in the early 1980s is clear, though so
too is Hymes' (much stronger) refusal to relinquish a claim on linguistics
itself.

12　Bernstein (1975: 156) claims:

> Whilst we are [warned] ... of the abstracted fictions created by observer's
> categories and arithmetic, [and informed] of the importance of close
> ethnographic study of situated activities, we are not told precisely what the
> new criteria are by means of which we can both create and judge the
> accounts of others. We are told and socialised into what to reject, but
> rarely told how to create.

13　Below, Coupland (1991: 14) cites Giddens:

> Modernity is a post-traditional order, in which the question, 'How shall I
> live?' has to be answered in day-to-day decisions about how to behave,
> what to wear and what to eat – and many other things – as well as
> interpreted within the temporal unfolding of self-identity.

He goes on to observe (this volume p. 35): 'There is an implicit appeal in texts
like these ... to linguists to generate the analyses of social interaction that
must be done to underpin their theoretical claims about the negotiation of
lifespan identity'.

14　In this context, it is probably first worth clarifying the nature of the challenge
to 'core'/'autonomous'/'mainstream' linguistics. The challenge from a socially
constituted practical linguistics is directed both towards (i) a lot of the specific
findings of autonomous linguistics (Hymes 1977: 197), and (ii) towards any
claims 'pure' linguists might make to *exclusive* insight into basic linguistic
and communicative phenomena (Hymes 1972b). The challenge isn't targetted

on the value of all autonomous linguistic research, or on its right to exist, a right that is nevertheless currently being contested in Britain where academic independence is under continuing threat from a government dedicated to putting commercial interest at the heart of all inquiry – political developments that applied linguists ought to help to resist (Brumfit 1991; Cameron et al. 1993: 144; BAAL 1995).

Secondly, and following on from this, it would be foolish to dismiss the research-first-application-after model represented in 'linguistics applied'. While this certainly has philosophical blindspots (see main text) and while there are strong arguments for preferring a more integrated relationship between intervention and analysis in principle, 'linguistics applied' may often be the best that can be managed in any given situation, and indeed, it has obviously often worked to the good (cf. Hymes 1977: 195–6, and Cameron et al. 1992, 1993 on 'advocate' vs 'empowering' research).

Thirdly, there is absolutely no cause to celebrate the difficulties currently facing applied linguists trying to bring research knowledge to bear on British teacher education. Education has been, after all, one of the foundational concerns of Hymesian sociolinguistics.

15 In 1981, Brumfit (p. 162) suggested that

[i]f applied linguistics is to be perceived as a fundamentally important discipline, this will only be when it produces ideas of sufficient generality to affect any language-using situation – when it performs the task of integrating all the various attitudes to language of researchers in other fields, and produces an account of language in use which is both convincing and readily comprehensible.

In fact, one could argue that at least as far as language education is concerned, a consensus model of language use has now emerged (cf. Carter 1990: 1–20). The problem with this idea of a consensus model is, though, that it privileges the wider social usability of a theory *above* its value as an instrument of discovery. Although a socially constituted linguistics is centrally dedicated to cultivating dialogue between researchers and people outside the academy, it seeks neither to deny their discursive differences, nor to place one in a position of permanent dominance. As well as being useful, socially constituted linguistics wants to carry on bringing 'news' back about language and communication (cf. Bernstein 1975: 146), and who knows which models of language – and indeed what kinds of intellectual conflict (Beretta & Crookes 1993) – are going to be most productive in that regard.

16 It is perhaps worth stressing that an emphasis on research as a part of reality, rather than as a vantage point detached from it, entails neither a rejection of scientific method nor a refusal to recognise ways in which it often differs from other forms of discourse. Accountability to logic and evidence; triangulation across theories, across data-sources and across methods (including quantitative ones); the search for counter-patterns, not just convergence; carefulness, scepticism and systematicity in general – all these remain important for the discovery, analysis and reporting of phenomena beyond our ordinary imagining, and meaning-oriented research retains a concern with issues of validity (cf. e.g. Hammersley 1992: ch. 4; Silverman 1992). But as van Lier notes (1994b: 333), rather than being 'a defense against the

vicissitudes of the social system within which the scientist has to work',
'methodological traditions are themselves part of the social system', and in
just the same way that they can sometimes contribute substantially to what
we admire in a society, they may also 'serve to force a false [and oppressive]
consensus', as has been argued in a number of recent discussions of the social
and historical embedding and effects of applied linguistics as a purportedly
neutral enterprise (Phillipson 1992; Pennycook 1994: ch. 4; also Scollon &
Scollon 1995: ch. 6; Hymes [1973] 1980: 55).

17 Admittedly, the massive explosion of interdisciplinary interest in discourse
has been the source of some unease, but it is worth making at least two points
in its broad defence.

In the first instance, there is some concern about the adequacy of
interdisciplinary attempts at actually analysing discourse. As is often pointed
out (e.g. Agar 1985; Fairclough 1992; Scollon & Scollon 1995: ch. 6), the
term 'discourse' is used in a number of different senses: both in grand theory,
referring to whole systems of thought and action, as well as in nose-to-data
accounts of the intricate details of everyday social interaction. The attempt to
see how these connect is obviously going to be difficult, and there are a
number of clear dangers: overgeneralising linguistic models, assuming
syntax-like standards of precision in the study of society, shuttling too fast up
into grand theory from theories of data, missing out mid-level theories and so
forth. But rather than reacting to reductionist models of discourse and society
by invoking the integrity and elegance of the linguist's models of discourse
(cf. e.g. Widdowson 1995), it is surely much more productive to respond with
a combination of richer data analyses and more subtle, detailed and
challenging theories. Levinson once referred to linguists as 'the snobs of social
science' (1988: 161) – it would be particularly ironic if, just at the moment
when the chances for interdisciplinarity really started to look good, applied
linguists retreated to the kinds of priority that had made them want to break
with linguistics in the first place.

The second worry seems to be that in trying to make links with other social
scientists, applied linguistics will abandon its traditional constituencies, give
up on ordinary people, and wander off to join a congregation camped
somewhere deep in the thickets of social theory. But the key point –
sometimes missed by advocates as well as by opponents – is that the general
social scientific interest in discourse is actually much more ontological than
theoretical. Rather than being a framework of concepts which generates
propositions to be examined empirically, it is more a set of basic assumptions
about social reality and social relations. As such, it is actually quite accessible
as a perspective; it is already making itself felt in the way social differences in
education are conceptualised; and it can be seen in discussions of both multi-
ethnic education in England and the teaching of English internationally.

As is well known, over the last 30 years, three very general perspectives
have been highly influential in attempts to account for inequalities in the
distribution of knowledge, influence and resources. The first perspective, the
deficit position, stresses the outgroup's inadequacies and the importance of
their being socialised into the ingroup's norms. The second, with *difference* as
its key word, emphasises the integrity and autonomy of the outgroup's

language and culture and the need for institutions to be hospitable to diversity. In the third, the focus shifts to larger structures of *domination*, and the need for institutions to combat the institutional processes and ideologies that reproduce the oppression of subordinate groups is stressed. There is obviously a lot of conflict between these interpretations of the basic character of inequality; different perspectives have gained ascendency at different times in different places; and they are fairly easily recognised as assimilation, multiculturalism and antiracism in British education, and as Quirk, Kachru and Phillipson in worldwide ELT.

More recently, a fourth very general perspective has emerged. This accepts the role that larger social, economic and political systems play in structuring majority-minority relations, but argues that their impact on everyday experience can't be easily predicted. Instead, the emphasis is on looking closely at how people make sense of inequality and difference in their local situations, and at how they interpret them in the context of a range of social relationships (gender, class, region, generation etc.). This perspective is wary of seeing culture *either* as an elite canon, *or* as a set of static ethnic essences *or* as a simple reflection of economic and political processes; it takes the view that the reality of people's circumstances is actively shaped by the ways in which they interpret and respond to them, and in line with this, it lays a good deal of emphasis on the cultural politics of imagery and representation. This fourth perspective can be seen in a book like Donald & Rattansi's *'Race' Culture and Difference*; it is central in Pennycook 1994; it tunes with much wider public discussion of 'post-modernity'; and to preserve the alliteration, it has been summarised as *'discourse'*.

At first glimpse, wide-spread assent to a view of 'reality as discourse' may seem alarming, conjuring a vision of hubristic discourse analysts claiming 'the Key to All Mythologies'. But it isn't necessary to look very far to see that without pushing it to deconstructive nihilism, a discourse perspective actually often encourages quite realistic modesty about research, emphasising the insecurity, limitations and context-sensitivity of its conclusions.

18 A number of other issues in the institutional organisation of different kinds of applied linguistics are addressed in Rampton 1995 (where what I refer to as an 'ideological' AL is broadly equivalent to the socially constituted practical linguistics discussed here).

19 In combination with their commitment to dissemination, the descriptive work of Crystal, Leech, Quirk and their associates has probably been the central plank in the development of a technical base for students interested in using linguistics to address practical and cross-disciplinary issues at both BA and A level.

References

Agar, M. (1985) Institutional discourse. *Text* 5.3: 147–68.

Barton, D. (1994) *Literacy: an introduction to the ecology of written language*. Oxford: Blackwell.

Bauman, Z. (1990) *Intimations of postmodernity*. London: Routledge.

—— (1994) *Alone again: ethics after certainty*. London: Demos.

Beretta, A. (1993) 'As God said, and I think, rightly ...'. Perspectives on theory construction in SLA: An introduction. *Applied Linguistics* 14.3: 221–4.

—— & Crookes, G. (1993) Cognitive and social determinants of discovery in SLA. *Applied Linguistics* 14.3: 250–75.

Bernstein, B. ([1972] 1975) The sociology of education: a brief account. In B. Bernstein, *Class, codes and control. Volume 3: Towards a theory of educational transmissions*. London: RKP. 146–62.

Bremer, K., Roberts, C., Vasseur, M.-T., Simonot, M. & Broeder, P. (1996) *Achieving understanding: discourse in intercultural encounters*. London: Longman.

British Association for Applied Linguistics (BAAL) (1995) Response to ESRC consultation on the future of social science funding. *BAAL Newsletter* 50: 12–14.

Brumfit, C. (1981) Being interdisciplinary – some problems facing applied linguistics. *Applied Linguistics* 1.2: 158–64.

—— (1984) *Communicative methodology in language teaching*. Cambridge University Press.

—— (1985) Some key problems. In C. Brumfit, H. Lunt & J. Trim, *Second language learning: Research problems and perspectives*. London: CILT.

—— (1991) Applied linguistics in higher education: riding the storm. *BAAL Newsletter* 38: 45–9.

—— (1995) Teacher professionalism and research. In Cook & Seidlhofer, *Principle and practice in applied linguistics*. Oxford University Press.

—— (1997) How applied linguistics is the same as any other science. *International Journal of Applied Linguistics* 7.1: 86–94.

Cameron, D. (1994). Putting our practice into theory. In D. Graddol & J. Swann, *Evaluating language*. Clevedon: Multilingual Matters/BAAL. 15–23.

——, Frazer, E., Harvey, P., Rampton, B. & Richardson, K. (1992) *Researching language: issues of power and method*. London: Routledge.

——, Frazer, E., Harvey, P., Rampton, B. & Richardson, K. (1993) Ethics, advocacy and empowerment: issues of method in researching language & Reply to comments. *Language and Communication* 13.2: 81–94 & 141–6.

Carter, R. (1990) Introduction. In R. Carter, *Knowledge about language and the curriculum: The LINC Reader*. London: Hodder & Stoughton. 1–20.

Cazden, C. (1986) Classroom discourse. In M. Merlin & C. Wittrock, *Handbook of research on teaching* (3rd edition). London: MacMillan. 432–63.

Christie, F. (1989) *Language education series*. Oxford University Press.

Cook, G. & Seidlhofer, B. (eds.) (1995) *Principle and practice in applied linguistics*. Oxford University Press.

Cook-Gumperz, J. & Gumperz, J. (1992) Changing views of language in education: The implications for literacy research. In R. Beach, J. Green, M. Kamil & T. Shanahan, *Multidisciplinary perspectives on literacy research*. Urbana: NCRE/NCTE. 151–79.

Corder, S. (1973) *Introducing applied linguistics*. Harmondsworth: Penguin.

Coupland, N. (1997) Language, ageing and ageism: a project for applied linguistics. *International Journal of Applied Linguistics* 7.1: 26–48.

——, Coupland, J., Giles, H. & Henwood, K. (1988) Accommodating the elderly: invoking and extending a paradigm. *Language in Society* 17.1: 1–42.

Davis, K. (1995) Qualitative theory and methods in applied linguistic research. *TESOL Quarterly* 29.3 427–53.

Donald, J. & Rattansi, A. (eds.) (1992) *'Race', culture and difference*. London: Sage.

Drew, P. & Heritage, J. (eds.) (1992) *Talk at work*. Cambridge University Press.

Ellis, R. (1985) *Understanding second language acquisition*. Oxford University Press.

—— (1994) *The study of second language acquisition*. Oxford University Press.

Erickson, F. & Shultz, J. (1982) *The counsellor as gatekeeper*. New York: Academic Press.

Fairclough, N. (1989) *Language and power*. London: Longman.

—— (1992) *Discourse and social change*. Oxford: Polity.

Freeborn, D. (1992). A levels in English language: a personal view. *BAAL Newsletter* 42: 20–5.

——, French, P. & Langford, D. (1986) *Varieties of English*, Basingstoke: MacMillan.

Frawley, W. & Lantolf, J. (1984) Speaking and self-order: a critique of orthodox L2 research. *Studies in Second Language Acquisition* 6.2: 143–59.

Giddens, A. (1984) *The constitution of society*. Oxford: Polity.

—— (1991) *Modernity and self-identity*. Oxford: Polity.

Gumperz, J. (1982a) *Discourse strategies*. Cambridge University Press.

—— (1982b) *Language and social identity*. Cambridge University Press.

Halliday, M. (1964). Syntax and the consumer. *Monograph Series of Language and Linguistics No 17*. Georgetown University Press. 11–18.

—— (1978) *Language as a social semiotic*. London: Edward Arnold.

—— (1985) *An introduction to functional grammar*. London: Edward Arnold.

——, McIntosh, A. & Strevens, P. (1964) *The linguistics sciences and language teaching*. London: Longman.

Hammersley, M. (1992) *What's wrong with ethnography?* London: Routledge.

Heath, S. (1983) *Ways with words*. Cambridge University Press.

Hewitt, R. (1986) *White talk, Black talk*. Cambridge University Press.

Howatt, A. (1984) *A history of English language teaching*. Oxford University Press.

Hymes, D. ([1972] 1977) The scope of sociolinguistics. In D. Hymes. *Foundations in sociolinguistics: an ethnographic approach*. London: Tavistock. 193–210.

—— (1972b) On communicative competence. In J. Pride & J. Holmes, *Sociolinguistics*. Harmondsworth: Penguin. 269–93.

—— ([1973] 1980) Speech and language: on the origins and foundations of inequality among speakers. In *Language in education: ethnolinguistics essays*. Washington: Centre for Applied Linguistics. 19–61.

—— ([1977] 1980) Qualitative/quantitative research methodologies in education: a linguistic perspective. In D. Hymes, *Language in education: ethnolinguistics essays*. Washington: Centre for Applied Linguistics. 62–87.

Kachru, B. (1985). The other side of English. In B. Kachru, *The other tongue*. Oxford: Pergamon. 1–12.

Klein, W. (1986) *Second language acquisition*. Cambridge University Press.

Kress, G. (1994) *Learning to write* (2nd edition). London: Routledge.

Labov, W. (1982) Objectivity and commitment in linguistic science: the case of the Black English trial in Ann Arbor. *Language in Society* 11: 165–201.

Lantolf, J., Appel, G. (1994). Theoretical framework: an introduction to Vygotskian approaches to second language research. In Lantolf & Appel, *Vygostkian approaches to second language research*. Norwood NJ: Ablex. 1–32.

Lazaraton, A. (1995) Qualitative research in applied linguistics: a progress report. *TESOL Quarterly* 29.3: 455–71.

Leech, G. (1969) *A linguistic guide to English poetry*. London: Longman.

Levinson, S. (1988) Putting linguistics on a proper footing: explorations in Goffman's concepts of participation. In P. Drew & A. Wootton, *Erving Goffman: exploring the interaction order*. Oxford: Polity Press. 161–227.

Lightbown, P. (1985) Great expectations: second-language acquisition research and classroom teaching. *Applied Linguistics* 6.2: 173–89.

Long, M. (1990) The least a second language acquisition theory needs to explain. *TESOL Quarterly* 24.4: 649–66.

—— (1993) Assessment strategies for SLA theories. *Applied Linguistics* 14.3: 225–50.

Pateman, T. (1987) Philosophy of linguistics. In J. Lyons, R. Coates, M. Deuchar & G. Gazdar, *New horizons in linguistics 2*. Harmondsworth: Penguin. 249–67.

Pennycook, A. (1994) *The cultural politics of English as an international language*. London: Longman.

Phillipson, R. (1992) *Linguistic imperialism*. Oxford University Press.

Quirk, R. (1990) Language varieties and standard language. *English Today* 21: 3–10.

Rampton, B. (1992) Scope for empowerment in sociolinguistics? In Cameron et al., *Researching language: issues of power and method*. London: Routledge. 29–64.

—— (1995) Politics and change in research in applied linguistics. *Applied Linguistics* 16.2: 233–56.

Roberts, C., Davies, E. & Jupp, T. (1992) *Language and discrimination*. London: Longman.

—— & Simonot, M. (1987) 'This is my life': How language acquisition is interactionally accomplished. In R. Ellis, *Second language acquisition in context*. Englewood Cliffs: Prentice Hall. 133–48.

Robins, R. (1979) *A short history of linguistics* (2nd edition). London: Longman.

Sapir, E. ([1931] 1949) Communication. In D. Mandelbaum, *Edward Sapir: Selected writings in language, culture and personality*. Berkeley: California University Press. 104–9.

Scollon, R. & Scollon, S. (1995) *Intercultural communication*. Oxford: Blackwell.

Silverman, D. (1992) *Interpreting qualitative data*. London: Sage.

Street, B. (1984) *Literacy in theory and practice*. Cambridge University Press.

Strevens, P. ([1976] 1977) On defining applied linguistics. In P. Strevens, *New Orientations in the Teaching of English*. Oxford University Press. 37–40.

van Lier, L. (1994a) Educational linguistics: field and project. Paper presented at Georgetown University Round Table 1994.

—— (1994b) Forks and hope: pursuing understanding in different ways. *Applied Linguistics* 15.3: 328–47.

Widdowson, H. G. ([1980] 1984) Applied linguistics: the pursuit of relevance. In H. G. Widdowson, *Explorations in Applied Linguistics 2*. Oxford University Press. 7–20.

—— ([1981] 1984). Models and fictions. In H. G. Widdowson, *Explorations in Applied Linguistics 2*. Oxford University Press. 21–7.

—— (1992) Innovation in teacher development. In H. Widdowson, *Annual review of Applied Linguistics, Volume 13: Issues in second language teaching and learning*. Cambridge University Press.

—— (1995) Review of N. Fairclough *Discourse and social change* 1992. *Applied Linguistics* 16.4: S10–16.

Text 30

Christopher Brumfit
University of Southampton

How applied linguistics is the same as any other science

This paper comments on Rampton's criticisms of a position characterised by him as 'Brumfit/Widdowson'. Applied linguistics is examined as a research project analogous to other 'disciplines' and is shown to share a range of characteristics with them. Boundaries and models are ways of imposing metaphorical order on experiental chaos and are provisional, being discarded when their usefulness is exhausted. The need for cross-disciplinary perspectives in language studies is imposed by the nature of an object of study instantiated in human behaviour or human mental processes. Applied linguistics distinctively models linguistic practices and is the meeting place for scholars concerned with understanding the linguistic elements of social, psychological, pedagogical, economic or any other activity or belief system. It is argued that applied linguistics shares a position intersecting with neighbouring sciences and with all other sciences, each of which demarcates its own space in contested and shared ground.

Introduction

Since much of Ben Rampton's paper 'Retuning in applied linguistics' consists of commentary on positions attributed to me, I hope that it will be appropriate for me to concentrate on responding to his argument. This is particularly necessary as it is based on a key misunderstanding of my position, for I do not at any point defend 'the generalist' as the key typical applied linguist. What I have asserted is that the *nature of language* requires cross-disciplinary perspectives – but that is because of the field of study, not because of a preference for particular types of researcher. At the same time, I believe that the position outlined in this paper is entirely compatible with that taken in Nik Coupland's paper – and indeed that Rampton's work (e.g. 1995) fits perfectly well into the framework that I propose.

In this paper I assume that applied linguistics – like linguistics, physics, history and other studies – is an attempt to explain certain phenomena; that it is a large-scale research project, which may spawn associated training, implications for policy and practice and professional institutions from its activity. But I see these last as derivative, because without knowledge and the ideological apparatuses that accumulate around it, the other practices cannot be described or accounted for (though of course the object of study – language, the physical world, human life or whatever – carries on whether or not it is being studied).

Metaphors and boundaries in science

Much of Rampton's paper is both relevant and exciting, and it is important that applied linguists are periodically self-conscious about their function, methods and public roles. But it is also important to recognise what applied linguists share with other scientists, particularly so that we do not claim too much for ourselves ('... there is virtually no human activity in which the applied linguist cannot play a role' Kaplan 1980: 63), nor too little by insisting on the unique particularity of our enterprise. We are in the business, I take it, of providing the best possible explanations of phenomena – in our case language practices. We do this because explanations are useful, both by problematising experience and enabling us to ask further questions and improve on current explanations, and in providing the bases for solutions to practical problems. By knowing why and how things appear to happen, we can address new phenomena with the benefit of prior experience, cut corners, avoid or anticipate difficulties, and generally act more expertly.

But this is of course to describe a process that never stops. Our explanations are only as good as the problems they solve, and when they fail to address new evidence, we have to rethink; they are not permanent knowledge, but the best available, and their relationship to experience is always metaphorical, in that they claim that if phenomena are explained like *this*, problem-solving will be helped better than if they are explained like *that*. Explanation, as the use of the word 'like' indicates, is a kind of analogy or metaphor.

Metaphorical too are the disciplines, subjects and fields within which we operate. If we pretend that isolating an object 'language' is helpful – how far can that take us towards making better explanations that we can use more fruitfully? If we pretend that the mechanisms causing language are biological, or cybernetic, or theological, how far do these metaphors take us? Does language 'develop', does it 'mature', is the mechanism started by a 'blind watchmaker', 'created by God', is it a 'pearl in an oyster', or was it 'crafted by guild-tradition'?

'Technical' versus 'generalist'?

Thus I find little to disagree with in Rampton's paper, or in Coupland's paper, insofar as they reflect the practices of investigation, interpretation and understanding. But in applied linguistics, as in analogous sciences like medicine, many different practices congregate. All practices share concerns to accumulate evidence and to interpret that evidence in the light of principles, assumptions, or beliefs – in other words, of more or less articulated theoretical positions. But the practices themselves, and the kinds of data they consider, are various, and the proponents of particular approaches regularly debate the status of alternative approaches: thus, in economics there are debates between quantitative and qualitative researchers; in psychology about the status of measurement – and so on (see e.g. Hudson 1972; Blaug 1980). In applied linguistics the data may be linguistic, as for formal linguists, but it may equally be accounts (by participants or other observers) of linguistic practices: descriptions by interpreters, therapists, teachers or teacher educators of their rationales for action constitute one kind of evidence for interpretation, just as accounts of less institutionalised practices do. Thus when Rampton remarks (p. 6) that 'immersion in particular data-bases doesn't appear to figure prominently … and … flexibility and breadth are the key intellectual values within this particular strand of applied linguistics', he is apparently limiting the data to language instances, rather than to the instantiation of language practices in the ideologies and belief-systems of practitioners – but these too are a kind of data, and interpretation of both is necessary.

The distinction between 'generalists' and 'specialists' seems unhelpful, for the level of detail required is a function of the phenomenon being interpreted, and investigation – at any level – requires a degree of specialisation (i.e. concentration on relevant previous work, technical skill and individual experience that is not too diffuse to generate useful understanding). But of course the specialisation needed for ideological or historical analysis is not the same as for syntactic or phonological analysis, so different specialisations come into play. It appears that these are being labelled 'generalist'. In this sense, Rampton seems to be demanding a return to the linguistic aspects of applied linguistics. While I agree about the need for a corpus of data, I would not privilege linguistic data over (for example) transcripts of interviews with practitioners, the published opinions about good practice of commentators, official pronouncements, or for that matter neurological patterns and eye movements. If applied linguists are interpreting language practices, all these and more may constitute their data.

At this point it should be clear that the conflation of Widdowson-Brumfit is inappropriate. Anyone reading the work of either of us over the past two decades will immediately see that Widdowson's work is much more overtly linguistic than mine is. His literary work (Widdowson 1992) depends substantially on detailed analysis of alternative versions of texts and the analysis of these readings; his work on discourse, on languages for specific purposes, or his recent critique of critical approaches (Widdowson 1995) depend on linguistic theory and linguistic analysis to a far greater extent than most of my own writings do. Whatever similarities there may sometimes be in our justifications of the applied linguistic enterprise, our practices are substantially divergent.

Some of these differences are deliberate. While I would not want to deny the value of any of Widdowson's work with text, I would not myself privilege linguistic form as much as he does. Literature exploits ideas and historical and cultural reference as semiotic systems as much as it uses language – which is why literature in translation contributes substantially to literary pleasure and practice. Recognising that many readers operate across linguistic traditions in responding to genres such as the novel or the epic leads to an unwillingness to use detailed linguistic analysis as too exclusive a technique in literary study. The short poem (where translation is more problematic) need not be seen as the prototype literary form.

Now, my intention here is neither to reject Widdowson's procedures nor to limit them to poetry. But I do want to show that the different practices are motivated by different views of the significant elements of literary experience. In other areas, for example where he writes on teaching discourse, I have a different view of the language teaching enterprise which affects my own research preferences in this area, but this difference does not prevent me welcoming all of his work (just as in the study of social practices I welcome all of Rampton's work) as a valuable and necessary contribution to understanding. Yet individuals' research agendas arise from perceived gaps in current practice, where investigation has neglected areas that our experience suggests are significant. This is why I have a different bias from Widdowson in language teaching: many researchers explore linguistic issues, but I did not experience language teaching as defined primarily by linguistic factors, so the other factors need investigation, if only to offset the dominance of linguistically orientated work.

Impulses for investigation by individual researchers no doubt vary greatly, but the nature of individual research procedures must reflect the nature of the problem being investigated. I have suggested above that some literature may be thought of as 'a philosophy put into images' (as Camus observed), and that language teaching may be more a social than a psycholinguistic phenomenon. I do not claim these as adequate or exclusive accounts, but they may be a helpful corrective to other claims; they ask us to consider a type of phenomenon as if it were like some other phenomenon, and as I said at the beginning of this paper, such intentions are essentially metaphorical. Similarly, the claims for autonomous linguistics of the Chomskyan movement depended partly on the value of an IT metaphor: what would human language look like if it could be generated by a computer programme? Is that metaphor more fruitful to pursue than semiological metaphors of the Saussurean tradition or anthropological metaphors from Boas or Malinowski? Metaphors act as hypotheses, to be rejected where they are felt to be no longer useful.

But so, too, are the boundaries of disciplines metaphorical: what if we treat this group of phenomena as a set with shared properties? Language study may be 'bound' up in semiotics or anthropology, and linguists may move across such boundaries as (for example) Kress and Halliday have, or they may remain more strictly within an autonomous linguistics, as Lyons has. But the usefulness for effective understanding of whatever delimitation is adopted remains paramount. If conceiving of 'language' as a reified and autonomous system enables us to understand it as a phenomenon (even though it is always instantiated in individual perceptions or acts, or in social practices), then the conception has value. Once such a conception is felt to have no value, other conceptualisations will become dominant – but because language, like culture, commerce, indeed science itself, is an abstract term, there will always be a tension between the idealised, autonomous version like linguistics (which is tidier and simpler to investigate) and the instantiated version experienced by all of us (which is fluid, contingent and inseparable from other modes of experience). The tendency towards idealisation enables us to 'understand' (that is, to simplify chaos in order to live in it more efficiently), but risks degenerating into a theology of glass bead games if it gets too out of touch with reality. The tendency toward contextualisation retains perceptual validity as much as it can (for *actual* experience cannot be understood in itself, it can only be experienced: apprehension is not the same as explanation), but is still part of a constant debate about how *much* reification, abstraction and idealisation is useful. 'Linguistics' has placed itself metaphorically towards the idealist end, 'applied linguistics' towards the contextualised; but both are in the business of explaining, of making metastatements and of problem-solving.

What is distinctive about applied linguistics?

> Thus both linguistics and applied linguistics combine empirical and theoretical activity, but linguistics reifies 'language'. What does applied linguistics reify? More than just language – 'language practices'.

I understand Rampton to be asking us to autonomise more, and to operate in the same sphere as linguistics, to engage with the same questions. In reacting to that demand, it is important not to be confused by the issue of names. Which group is engaged in 'proper' linguistics is a fruitless debate, only significant in the politics of funding, the designation of posts and the management of institutions. It is important in the sense that it affects career prospects and research opportunities, but it is not important in the development of understanding. All activities that relate to the clarification of 'language' can be part of linguistics. Our debate is about what *does* relate usefully to that clarification, and whether there are useful distinctions to be made between types of approaches.

One perspective (but only one of many) that linguistics researchers cannot offer, and applied linguists can usefully contribute, is research based on holistic apprehension of what it is to be a language-using practitioner. By this I mean immersion in the whole of practice and the use of that experience for the conceptualisation of the research process. Traditionally, linguistics research investigates language as a phenomenon; recently, applied linguistic research has investigated language as a practice. Clearly, such an approach favours people with histories similar to mine (coming to applied linguistics from experience as a practitioner), but I am not making a claim for privileging one life-experience over others. I am, however, making a claim that language is not an object that is *incidentally* embedded in practices, beliefs and human concepts, but that is an object that *consists of* that embedding – take away the embedding and only an unrealised potential is left. The holistic apprehension is the experience that has to be explained; the analytic idealisation is justified only as a means to that end.

Thus an investigation of a 'disembedded' phenomenon by its nature *has* to be in constant tension with simultaneous, and academically equal, investigation of the practices in which it operates – to prevent it from degenerating into unfruitful abstraction. And conversely, practices (whether social, psychological or others as yet unconceptualised) cannot be investigated 'pure' because the act of investigation itself requires idealisation, discipline boundaries, abstraction, generalisation, and a whole series of metaphorical activities which convert experience into (always partial and provisional) understanding. Without a view of 'language' and therefore of 'linguistics' to study it, we could not distinguish the 'language' of language teaching, of literacy, of friendship groups, of ethnicity, of nations, of literature, of negotiation, of economics, or any other field, from the psychological motivation, the sociological relationships, the historical structures, or any of the other factors which are universal in human social events. Any human event is simultaneously sociological, psychological, linguistic, and representative of an infinite range of possible disciplines, each of which will have an idealising pull, but each of which must be connected to reality by the unavoidable interdisciplinary nature of the study of instantiated, grounded, contextualised behaviour.

Thus the discussion of research on teaching methodology (Brumfit 1984: 1–2) that Rampton cites here in footnote 6 (p. 17–18) is an example of what must apply *mutatis mutandis* in any explanation of real-life experience *if understanding is not to depart from contact with normal practice*. Coupland (p. 33) indeed makes the same point. Such contact must rely on what is demanded by both myself and Coupland: the most rigorous possible analysis of serious questions needed in the experience of operating as a language user. But that experience is only available by immersion in the practice as a full participant: it is not available through researchers lending themselves to the practice in order to find research questions, or to observers, or external philosophers – but only to practitioners, or ex-practitioners, who recollect (in varying degrees of tranquillity) without losing contact with the conceptualisation as it appeared at the time, unmediated by a research agenda. (Note that such experience does require full participation, 'knowing what it is to be …' rather than 'knowing what it is like doing …' because the mind-set involved in being a therapist, a translator, an interpreter or a teacher is a complete experience of that social role, not the performance of identifiable tasks.)

Now, applied linguistics cannot only be this. It must also encompass close interaction with researchers who do not share this experience and who work on language problems from other disciplinary perspectives. But I believe the *context* of this interaction is something that can be uniquely offered by applied linguistics, and that a discipline that is solely the place of meeting of people who could equally well be psychologists, linguists, cultural theorists – or indeed teachers, therapists or translators – will fragment into separate groupings for each of those practical activities and each of those disciplines, and will fail to address the complexity of language. What holds AL together is the concern to theorise and analyse social roles and institutions which address language problems, and thus the problems which non-researchers, sometimes unwittingly, confront. If that leads (as it certainly will if it is done rigorously) to a modification and reconceptualisation of linguistics, it may equally have similar effects on sociology, pedagogical theory or any other associated discipline. Where I disagree with Rampton is not in the view of the extent to which we should influence (i.e. contribute to) linguistics, but in seeing the relationship I have just outlined between more and less autonomous disciplines as unusual or exceptional. All human-science disciplines, in practice, operate in that way; none is autonomous; none is central; all are metaphors for roles which we adopt, name and institutionalise insofar as we feel them to be useful – and none can be an island.

If we accept this view of AL, the arguments about social constitution become a separate issue. Any concern to redress linguistic inequalities demands some sense of universalities, for the very concept 'inequality' makes claims about an indivisible concept 'equality'. Bernstein's 'dedication to a problem' (1975: 160) becomes central to the conceptualisation of AL, and the contrast between Rampton's 'Widdowson/Brumfit' versus 'Hymes/Bernstein' disappears, because both are problem-centred. My point is not so much that his contrast is falsely made as that all intellectual endeavour has a tension between understanding from outside and from inside, and that there is no resolution to this, only a constant iteration between individuals who incline to one perspective and those inclining to the other, or a willingness to include in a single researcher's agenda orientations of both kinds at different times.

Rampton appears to want a degree of technical precision to apply to all activities. But technical precision is always bought at the expense of social contextualisation and the holistic experience through which we perceive our contexts; it always involves some degree of idealisation which then has to be interpreted. Thus the non-technical interpretation that Rampton appears uncertain about is always required, and indeed engaged in by both Rampton and Coupland (e.g. Rampton 1995: part V; Coupland this volume). In any discipline the processes of data collection, analysis and interpretation will be carried on sometimes by the same people, sometimes by different people – but it is the value of the collective enterprise that counts, not individual roles.

To argue that theory-making is a social practice, and that researchers and theorists should be honest about their roles, is scarcely an assault on past science. Once again, we are talking about a helpful metaphoric shift, which has been the stuff of scientific discussion from Dilthey (1976) in the 1890s through to postmodernism. The issue only becomes worrying if the claim is made that theory-making is *merely* a social practice, with an implication that it can make no claims to privileged usefulness, or that it has been asserted by someone that it is not a social practice. The latter position has not, as far as I am aware, been argued in British applied linguistics, though it lies behind transatlantic debates about the status of SLA in the past few years (see Block 1996). Rampton gets close to making the former claim, in his remark (p. 12) that 'researchers are no longer able to defer unthinkingly to an academy now recognised as only one historically contingent institution among many'. Here we have to be very careful. Outside tyrannies, *unthinking* deference to academies is rarely expected; but publishing a book or an article is a claim to have ideas worthy of consideration and is precisely the same kind of claim that any 'expert' may make. Is Rampton suggesting that there is no ground for giving anyone authority,* because if so he should never publish collections like this! This must be a bid for agreement, and ideas that achieve agreement bestow (at least temporary) authority on their proponents.

In sum, then, I am suggesting that applied linguistics is a research project that aims to understand language-related problems identified (not necessarily knowingly) in non-specialist language practices – by politicians, administrators, teachers, translators and others – because those give us a start in addressing language as human experience. But the exploration of these entails understanding linguistic beliefs and practices which are deliberately excluded from autonomous linguistics, but which are actually the only manifestations of the hypothetical construct 'language'. Such practices are never limited to language, but necessarily involve integration with elements that derive from psychology, cultural study and many other disciplines. A working definition of applied linguistics will then be:

> the theoretical and empirical investigation of real-world problems in which language is a central issue.

It will thus be in permanent tension with linguistics, psychology, anthropology, cultural theory and any other study (as they will be in tension with AL) – but out of this tension will arise criticism and problematising of the categories and practices of each discipline, and more developed explanations of linguistic (and other) phenomena. This is, however, the normal condition of any science, and we do not need to apologise for it.

Note

* Guest editor's footnote: No I'm not – see my footnote 16, p. 19–20.

References

Bernstein, B. (1975) *Class, codes and control. Vol. 3*. London: Routledge.

Blaug, M. (1980) *The methodology of economics*. Cambridge University Press.

Block, D. (1996) Not so fast: some thoughts on theory culling, relativism, accepted findings and the heart and soul of SLA. *Applied Linguistics* 17.1: 63–83.

Brumfit, C. J. (1984) *Communicative methodology in language teaching: the roles of fluency and accuracy*. Cambridge University Press.

Coupland, N. (1997) Language, ageing and ageism: a project for applied linguistics. *International Journal of Applied Linguistics* 7.1: 26–48.

Dilthey, W. (1976) *Selected writings*. Edited and translated from German by H. P. Rickman. Cambridge University Press.

Hudson, L. (1972) *The cult of the fact*. London: Jonathon Cape.

Kaplan, R. B. (ed.) (1980) *On the scope of applied linguistics*. Rowley: Mass.: Newbury House.

Rampton, B. (1995) Politics and change in research in applied linguistics. *Applied Linguistics* 16.2: 233–56.

—— (1997) Retuning in applied linguistics. *International Journal of Applied Linguistics* 7.1: 3–25.

Widdowson, H. G. (1992) *Practical stylistics: an approach to poetry*. Oxford University Press.

—— (1995) Discourse analysis: a critical view. *Language and Literature* 4.3: 157–72.

Text 31

H. G. Widdowson
University of London

Retuning, calling the tune, and paying the piper: a reaction to Rampton

Ben Rampton's recent paper which serves as an introduction to the thematic collection in *InJAL* 7.1 (Rampton 1997) is one we need to take serious note of, because it raises fundamental issues not only about applied linguistics but about the very nature of academic enquiry. And it does so in a particularly forthright and provocative way, which is designed, I take it, to stimulate debate. What I want to do in this short paper is to take issue with what he has to say, and so contribute to the debate from my point of view, and in a similarly forthright manner.

I should acknowledge right away that I found his paper not only provocative and hard to take, but also hard to follow, and I was frequently confused as to just what he was arguing for. The best I could manage was to pick out some points that I found especially tendentious and try to link them up as coherently as I could. It may well be that in what follows I have misconstrued his position. Apparently Brumfit has done the same. This may be as much a function of our own obtuseness as Rampton's obscurity. Whorfian forces may be at work here: our own position may prevent us from recognising (in both senses of the word) the existence of others. Which brings me to the first point.

Leaving aside the details of argumentation, what comes across clearly enough from Rampton's paper is that he advocates an applied linguistics which is at the same time practical ('a part of reality') and inter-disciplinary, in ways in which the Widdowson-Brumfit conception of it is not. One of the difficulties, perhaps the central difficulty, about interdisciplinary enquiry is that it is bound to involve the interpretation of one discourse in terms of another. You cannot understand what others say unless you in some degree appropriate it and accommodate it to your own view of the world. In this sense, accommodation theory applies as much to interdisciplinary enquiry as to other kinds of social behaviour. This being so, questions arise as to the motivation of the enquiry, and the validity of selective attention to theories developed in reference to other perspectives and principles. How far is it reasonable to interpret ideas on your own terms?

If one accepts the pragmatic inevitability of selective attention as a condition on all interpretation, then we have to recognise two kinds of partiality. An interpretation is partial in that it extracts what is convenient or relevant, that is to say it is incomplete; and it is partial in that this extraction reflects a particular ideological position, that is to say, it is not impartial. The problem then arises as to which partiality to prefer. This problem is all the more tricky since we may not recognise that there is a partiality to begin with. If you are a member of a particular community, sharing a set of cultural values, these values, as the critical linguists are fond of pointing out, become naturalised and their partiality thereby concealed. A community which is committed to a cause, and seeking to proselytize, will naturally promote its partiality in the name of truth.

This is just as evident in academic writing as in the popular press. I might point out a small but symptomatic instance in Rampton's own paper, which, naturally enough (following the principle of selective attention), I notice because it misrepresents something I said myself. Rampton quotes me as saying that I have 'recently argued for pedagogy rather than applied linguistics as a domain of enquiry' and have characterized applied linguistics as 'a patchwork of insights stitched together'. But I have said nothing of the kind. Reference to the actual text that is cited (incorrectly) makes it plain that I was attributing this view to others: '*Some argue that … What is needed, it is argued…*' (Widdowson 1992: 264 [sic]). Rampton is using my text on his terms, not mine, appropriating it to make his case, and so reading into it what he finds convenient. This might be seen as a trivial matter, and in a way it is, and I mention it partly, of course, because of personal pique. But, as I said, it is also symptomatic of a more general tendency to partiality. We find it *passim* in critical discourse analysis, for example, as I have indicated elsewhere (Widdowson 1995a, 1995b, forthcoming), and it is interesting to note that this area of enquiry is mentioned approvingly by Rampton as an example ('from where I stand') of 'a coherent interdisciplinary research programme'. From where I stand, this coherence is a function of

Rampton's partiality, for, as I have tried to demonstrate elsewhere, it is incoherence that characterises this particular research programme. And here I would indeed use the phrase 'a patchwork of insights stitched together'.

And the reason for its incoherence, I would argue, is precisely because of an uncritical borrowing of an assortment of linguistic and sociological notions. And the fact that this incoherence is not noticed, apparently, by its adherents, is precisely because they are communally committed to a common cause. That being so, the arguments do not need to be coherent so long as they are convincing. Now to say this is not at all to deny the validity of interdisciplinary enquiry in general. It is certainly not to invoke 'the integrity and elegance of the linguist's models of discourse', which Rampton interprets me as doing in yet another partial reading. But it is recognised that interdisciplinary enquiry is problematic, especially when it is motivated by a social cause. Its validity needs to be rigorously examined.

But who is to do the examining? And in reference to what principles? We return to what I see as the central issue here. If all discourses and the disciplines which practise them are partial representations, where can impartial principles come from? As I understand it (an important proviso), Rampton argues that applied linguistics should be *socially constituted* rather than (as has been the case in the past) *academically instituted*, that knowledge, in general, should not be the privileged preserve of scholars and researchers but should be democratised as common property. But it is one thing to say that academic enquiry should take *account* of other kinds of knowledge and accord it appropriate respect, but it is quite another to say that it should *defer* to them and incorporate them into its mode of enquiry. Different disciplines are areas of rational investigation, based on intellectual principles for the conduct of argument. They may draw on all kinds of data, but what these are evidence of is a matter of rational analysis. To conduct such argument and analysis is to accept the discipline of the discipline. Rampton's own paper is, of course, no exception: it is an intellectual work in a learned journal which argues a position in the traditional academic manner. And no matter how nonconformist his views, his manner of expressing them will call for a conformity (in some measure at least) to the norms of rational argument. This does not mean that rationality has absolute validity or is the only way of apprehending reality and leads to the only kind of knowledge possible. But if you are an academic, it is your way and your kind of knowledge. Of course you can say that it is simply a kind of privileged partiality given a special status by historical contingency. This may be so. But this is no reason to reject it. It may be that quite different modes of abstract thought are conceivable. But until they are conceived and formalised, there seems to be no alternative available. And one of the great advantages of academic enquiry is that it is reflexive: you can turn rational enquiry in upon itself to reveal its own limitations.

Rationality, I would argue, is the common factor of all disciplines and provides us with the basis for consensus as to what constitutes a valid process of enquiry and what does not. What you are rational *about* is a quite different matter, and disciplines continually change the scope of what they seek to account for, deal with different kinds of data, propose different models and set up different hypotheses. But clearly, if there are no commonly accepted criteria for what *counts* as a model or a hypothesis, disciplinary differences cannot be recognised at all. Rampton talks about a 'general intellectual climate' in which there is a 'pluralisation of authority', one in which 'researchers are no longer able to defer unthinkingly to an academy now recognised as only one historically contingent institution among many'. If research does not defer to the principles of academic enquiry, then what does it defer to? Principles of political expediency, perhaps, or commercial profit? There are plenty of precedents for such deference. And it is true that the term *research* is used to refer to all manner of activities designed to further the interests of political and commercial institutions. But the researchers that I presume Rampton has in mind are, like him, *academic* researchers who would wish to dissociate themselves from 'research' of this kind. Some of them may indeed defer unthinkingly to the academy, or particular schools within it, but most defer to it so as to think more effectively. And indeed, Rampton himself would appear to accept this when he talks about students needing 'a year's MA study to get really focussed before they can make a serious research contribution to cross-disciplinary or practical problems' – that is to say, it takes a year for them to learn how to defer to academic authority by being instructed in the particular intellectual processes which constitute 'serious research'.

Deference to such authority does not preclude 'contact with a range of different discourse communities', nor recognition and respect for their different values. On the contrary, it is only by such deference that we can identify and understand what these differences are. But then, it will be objected, we are describing these differences *in* our terms and so *on* our terms, not theirs. This, of course, is true. The description is partial, an intellectual version of reality, valid in its own terms, and limited like any other. The problem arises when academics think otherwise and claim a unique status for their version, denying the validity of others. And it is just this kind of thinking that, paradoxically enough, underlies Rampton's own paper, which, in typical academic idiom, argues for the greater validity of his own version of reality.

What he seems to be saying (though, given the indeterminacy of discourse, we cannot be sure) is that applied linguistics should be defined as linguistics *tout court*, but radically reconceived as a 'socially constituted, practical linguistics'. The expression 'socially constituted linguistics' comes from Hymes, but Hymes seems to mean by it the study of socially constituted *language*, what he refers to elsewhere as the 'ethnography of speaking'. But Rampton seems to use it to mean a *linguistics* that is socially constituted: that is to say, not just one whose concerns would be social but whose mode of enquiry should be constructed out of different discourses, including those of 'ordinary life'. No special privileges are accorded to the academy: '… an interdisciplinary enquiry in which fundamental research on language and communication can arise from and/or be integrated with dialogue outside the academy.'

Just how this constitution would come about, how such totally disparate (even incommensurable) discourses would be reconciled is not discussed (cf. Pennycook 1994). Such an enquiry, we are told, would provide both a comprehensive account of human language and the means for addressing 'felt problems', and in these respects could claim a validity which cannot be claimed by applied linguistics otherwise conceived. But which discourses will be drawn into this greater linguistics? Rampton gives an indication of what the academic ones would be: 'sociology, literature, education, business etc.' What does this *etc.* cover? Psychology? Genetics? Engineering? Economics? Medicine? Law? Theology? What are the criteria of inclusion?

And on whose terms, one also needs to ask, would such a linguistics be constituted? At times, Rampton seems to be suggesting that linguistics should be decentralised, so that rather than having any autonomy of its own, it attaches itself as a local appendage to other areas of enquiry: a kind of contingent linguistics. But at other times he talks of a linguistics which retains its independent identity as a discipline in its own right. Whether the new reconstituted linguistics is to be an appendage to other disciplines or an extension of linguistics itself as currently conceived, it will in both cases be a matter of making selective use of whatever concepts or principles are available in the other disciplines and appropriating them. They then lose their original validity within the discourses from which they have been derived, as they are integrated into the new one. So this newly formulated linguistics, whether appendage or extension, cannot be compounded of other disciplines but only be a partial fusion. This is perhaps as well, for who otherwise would be qualified to discourse about it? It is hard enough to achieve a degree of synthesis of two areas, and harder still for the hybrid to be recognised as valid by both sides.

Transferring ideas from one discourse into another and making them fit a different conceptual context will always be open to the charge of misrepresentation. Bernstein's account of restricted and elaborated codes has, for example, been criticised on linguistic grounds (Stubbs 1980, 1983) and Bernstein has himself suggested that much sociolinguistics, including some of Labov's work, is sociologically uninformed. Rampton, drawing on a Hymes distinction, says that whereas Labov's work is *socially realistic*, Bernstein's is *socially constituted*. But the essential difference seems to be in the disciplinary vantage points they take their bearings from. Labov is a linguist who makes expedient use of ideas from sociology, and Bernstein a sociologist who makes expedient use of ideas from linguistics. If it is the Bernstein enterprise which is to serve as the model for the new (applied) linguistics, then it would seem that its central feature is that its conceptual framework has to be that of some other discipline: linguistics becomes a contingent appendage. Sociology would apparently be preferred, since it looks, on the face of it, to be more socially constituted than any other, but in principle any other discipline would do, so long as it is not linguistics. If this is what Rampton is seriously proposing (even though, as I have indicated, it is contradicted elsewhere in his paper), what it amounts to is not just a retuning of (applied) linguistics. It is more like the complete rejection of its music and the disbandment of the orchestra.

The implication is that this newly (and socially) constituted field of enquiry will necessarily be more comprehensive and by its very constitution, closer to the social reality of 'ordinary life'. But, as I have tried to show, the comprehensiveness is likely to be an illusion, since however widely you seek to draw on different areas of knowledge, this is bound to be a matter of selective appropriation whereby you reduce them to your own terms in order to conform to disciplinary requirements. You have to integrate what you find into a coherent scheme so as to meet the usual academic standards of rationality. And as such, and as a very condition on coherence, this scheme will be a partial version of reality, of relative validity like any other.

It seems to me that it is reasonable (I use the term advisedly) to recognise that different discourses of knowledge are limited, and legitimate, in different ways. And (to note in passing) it is curious that those who are most strident in their espousal of cultural plurality are so intolerant of it in their own academic domain. But this does not mean that we cannot evaluate these different schemes of thought and establish preferences accordingly. One kind of evaluation I have mentioned already. In any discourse, we can examine the extent to which it is internally consistent with its own conventions. In the case of academic discourse, we can, by the same token, examine the extent to which it conforms to principles of rational enquiry: whether it is clear and coherent in argument, empirically well-founded, and so on. If it is not, no matter how well meaning it is, or how ideologically desirable, it is open to criticism on academic grounds.

There is another kind of evaluation, and this is quite different. It has to do with practical relevance, with utility rather than validity. A theory, scheme of thought, intellectual version of reality may be inconsistent, incoherent, illogical but extremely effective in promoting a belief or in prompting action, for good or evil. If it is sufficiently persuasive, indeed (as I indicated earlier) it does not need to be rational. There is a danger here, of course, and one that is all too evident in the current 'general intellectual climate': the very effectiveness of ideas makes it less likely that they will be subjected to critical appraisal.

These two kinds of evaluation are not always clearly distinguished. Indeed, the general 'climate' at the moment, intellectual and political, seems favourable to a belief that they *should* not be, that the measure of the validity of a theory *is* its usefulness (Labov 1988). This is a convenient belief for makers of educational policy, and entirely in keeping with the materialistic temper of the times. But then who is to decide what is useful, and useful for what? For on this criterion, extremely useful theories of ethnic superiority, for example, become validated. By the same token, Einstein's Special Theory of Relativity, originally useless, was invalid until put to extremely effective use in the manufacture of the atom bomb. But some have given even greater status to usefulness, arguing that not only is it a crucial criterion for the post hoc assessment of the value of theories, but it should be a feature of their actual design. On this account, you first find out what your problem is and then devise a theory expressly to solve it. If the problem is solved, you have a valid theory – a valid *theory*, mark you, not an effective technology. I have discussed this position elsewhere (Widdowson 1997), and it does not take much effort of the imagination to see what disastrous consequences might follow from it, though these seem to have eluded those who take this view. One consequence is that science, as such, disappears, taken over by technology; and all knowledge is reduced to know-how. Another is that those who have the authority to determine what is useful and what is not for their present and particular purposes dictate the course of academic enquiry and use its findings to further their own interests. They pay the piper and call the tune.

This position would not seem to be rationally tenable. And yet, it would appear to be precisely the position that Rampton takes in this paper. He talks of a 'socially constituted, practical linguistics'. This is not a linguistics that is 'socially realistic' or can be made socially relevant, it is socially *constituted*; not a linguistics which can be put to practical use, but one which is *designed to be practical*. But again the obvious objection to this is that practicality, as a design

308 Controversies in Applied Linguistics

principle, not only limits the scope of your enquiry but also determines its findings. Of course your enquiry may be *motivated* by a desire to be practical, just as it may be motivated by political belief, or personal ambition, or racial hatred, but when the motivation drives the research rather than the researcher, academic standards disappear, results get fixed, and we end up with fraud. And yet Rampton seems at times to be suggesting that motivation is a legitimate, even desirable, design feature of the linguistics he is proposing. As mentioned earlier, he makes reference to a number of what he calls 'coherent inter-disciplinary research programmes'. These, he says, 'combine (a) the empirical investigation of fundamental communciative processes with (b) a commitment to using research knowledge to improve communicative relationships in everyday life.'

It is not clear how one should read this, but it looks as if commitment is to be taken as a *condition* on the coherence of the programmes that are referred to. If so, then partiality is privileged: it is not seen as a necessary limitation to be guarded against, but as a positive advantage to be embraced and the very guarantee of the validity of what you are doing. This, we should note, is not the same as saying (as Hymes does) that such empirical investigation provides researchers with the means to achieve 'higher ethical objectives' in that it 'prepares [sociolinguists] to speak concretely to actual inequalities'. What Hymes is saying (as I understand it) is that this 'socially constituted' work develops an expertise which can *subsequently* serve your commitment to social causes. What Rampton seems to be saying is that for it to be practical, a socially constituted linguistics has to be a socially *committed* linguistics. Naturally, the commitment has to be to what are deemed to be good causes (Liberté, Egalité, Fraternité etc.), and the assumption is that we can all agree on what these are. But good causes are not always easy to identify, and the commitment could easily be to malevolent causes cunningly disguised. One would not wish to question the probity of those who at present advocate and practise this new approach to (applied) linguistics. But what if it were to fall into the wrong hands?

It seems to me that linguistics as the academic study of language, and thus subject to the rationality of intellectual enquiry which defines it as a discipline, cannot be socially constituted or practical in the sense that (I think) Rampton intends. It cannot incorporate within its own (meta)discourse of enquiry the (object) discourses it seeks to describe, quite simply because these do not conform to the required conventions of enquiry. Of course, you may choose to reject these conventions and even claim to be setting up an alternative order of rationality which renders them irrelevant. But this is not what Rampton advocates. On the contrary, he is insistent that this new kind of enquiry is subject to the same standards of intellectual rigour as the old. Thus, he says that 'an emphasis on research as part of reality, rather than as a vantage point detached from it' does not entail 'a rejection of scientific method'. But it does. For adherence to the scientific method ('Accountability to logic and evidence, triangulation across theories ... etc.') necessarily entails detachment and an abstract formulation of reality which is necessarily remote from the reality of everyday experience and (as he puts it himself) 'beyond our ordinary imaginings'. You really cannot have it both ways.

The notion of a 'socially constituted, practical linguistics' is appealing and persuasive, and that, in a way, is what is wrong with it. It sounds so good that it deflects critical examination. And, not infrequently, it furthers its cause by invoking the very academic authority which it claims to reject. To refer again to the example of critical discourse analysis: this is entirely based on the assumption that readers in the real world are incapable of apprehending the underlying significance of texts, so specialists schooled in linguistic analysis have to tell them what it is. There is not much evidence here of a 'socially constituted applied linguistics' entering into a dialogue or recognising any pluralism of authority or the legitimacy of other values.

You really cannot have it both ways. If you defer to the discourses of 'ordinary life' you cannot at the same time impose you own. If you want to work within an academic discourse, you cannot do so without accepting its conventions and recognising that they are different from others. You cannot argue for the separate identity of the discipline of linguistics and seek to make it a contingent appendage at the same time. You cannot meet the conditions of validity if they are over-ridden by considerations of practicality and commitment, commercial, political or whatever, no matter how well-meaning they may be. To say all this is no doubt to run the risk of being accused of intellectual snobbery. But it seems to me that unless we can conduct our enquiries by rigorous adherence to the rational principles which define our discourse, the discourse of academic discipline, then, with nothing distinctive to offer in the way of understanding and thus no justification for exercising influence, we have no reason to exist.

The kind of applied linguistics that I have been engaged in over the years, inadequate though it may be in many respects, is, in this one crucial respect, a disciplinary enquiry. It is a process of intellectual mediation whereby practical problems in which language is implicated are referred to theoretical ideas and, reciprocally, theoretical ideas are made relevant to the clarification of these problems (see Widdowson 1990). This process inevitably involves the consideration of different discourses, disciplinary and otherwise, and how they may be reconciled, and so has to wrestle with the difficult issues of partiality and practicality that I have discussed in this paper and which Rampton fails to address or even, it seems, to recognise. For him, to mediate in this way is simply to play the role of sage or master of ceremonies. He contrasts it with a vision of his kind of applied linguistics: a vision (not unlike that of Piers Plowman) of 'a field full of folk':

> Understood as an open field of interest in language, in which those inhabiting it or passing through simply show a common commitment to the potential value of dialogue with people who are different, there is no knowing where, between whom, or on what the most productive discussions will emerge. (Rampton 1997:14)

The view is of a vast party to which everybody is invited. If you happen to be passing, pop in for a chat, and who knows what might crop up in conversation. You need to bring no special knowledge or expertise – all you need is an interest in language and a commitment to talk to different people about it. There can be no recognition of authority of any kind, and so no deference can be paid to it (no academics, as such, will be present, and certainly no sages); and there will be no busy-body to initiate or guide the discussions or give direction to the dialogues (no master of ceremonies). There is no knowing what productive discussions will emerge. Very true, but unfortunately there would be no knowing either what would *count* as productive, or indeed what would constitute a dialogue or a discussion, let alone a productive one, since these presuppose agreed purposes and a common set of values and conventions whereby they are achieved. All that would emerge, I imagine, from a free-for-all of this kind would be cacophony and confusion.

It is hard to believe that Rampton is being serious. Apart from anything else, what he puts forward here flatly contradicts his insistence on methodological rigour elsewhere in his paper, and indeed the very academic idiom of the paper itself. At a superficial affective level, it is an appealing vision: anti-elitist, egalitarian, populist, pluralist, down-to-earth. And that is just the problem with it. The appeal is disarming. But when you look more closely at this proposal and get it into critical focus, it turns out to be incoherent. In other words, it does not measure up to the requirements of rational enquiry. There is room for differences of opinion about the scope and method of applied linguistics, for different visions and revisions; and there needs to be dialogue between people holding different views. But this can only happen on the terms, and in the terms, of agreed conventions for academic argument. Applied linguistics will not get retuned simply, and certainly not by simply invoking interest and commitment in the Micawber-like hope that something will eventually emerge.

References

Labov, W. (1988) The judicial testing of linguistic theory. In D. Tannen (ed.) *Linguistics in context: connecting observation and understanding.* [*Advances in discourse processes. Vol XXIX*]. Ablex. 181–2.

Pennycook, A. (1994) Incommensurable discourses. *Applied Linguistics* 15.2: 115–38.

Rampton, B. (1997) Retuning in applied linguistics. *International Journal of Applied Linguistics* 7.1: 3–25.

Stubbs, M. W. (1980) *Language and literacy.* London: Routledge & Kegan Paul.

—— (1983) *Discourse analysis: the sociolinguistic analysis of natural language.* Oxford: Basil Blackwell.

Widdowson, H. G. (1990) *Aspects of language teaching.* Oxford University Press.

—— (1992) Innovation in teacher development. *Annual Review of Applied Linguistics* 13: 260–75.

—— (1995a) Discourse analysis: a critical view. *Language and Literature* 4.3: 157–72.

—— (1995b) Review of Fairclough's *Discourse and social change. Applied Linguistics* 16.4: 510–16.

—— (1997) The use of grammar and the grammar of use. *Functions of Language.*

—— (forthcoming) The theory and practice of critical discourse analysis: a review article. *Applied Linguistics.*

Text 32

Ben Rampton
Thames Valley University

Problems with an orchestral view of applied linguistics: a reply to Widdowson

In this reply, I would like to take a critical look at Widdowson's position and then try to place our differences in a wider context. But before that, I would like to thank him for his impassioned response and apologise for the incorrect page referencing.

As I see it, Widdowson's argument is built up around a number of binary oppositions. My problem with this is that (a) he ignores the complicated connections and the difficult middle ground that lies between the poles he presents, and (b) that he consistently pins me like a straw demon to one pole, defending the other against phantasms that I find hard to recognise in what I said in *InJAL* 7.1.

The first opposition is between *partiality-as-inevitable-selectivity/incompleteness* and *partiality-as-ideological-bias* (p. 132). In fact, like nearly everybody else, I absolutely agree with Widdowson in condemning partiality-as-bias where this is a matter of ignoring relevant facts, of making up evidence, of deliberate misreporting, maybe even of ducking out from discrepant case analysis and the search for counterexamples. Beyond that, I can also think of research traditions where, to my mind, there hasn't been a clear enough distinction between fact and value (cf. the critical observations in Rampton, Harris & Leung 1997: 227). Even so, the distinction between these two kinds of partiality – between incompleteness and ideological bias – is very far from clear-cut, as social science's historic neglect of, e.g., women makes obvious. Research doesn't exist in a social and historical vacuum, and indeed even the most reputable forms of linguistics have had political motivations, characteristics and effects (cf. e.g. Bolinger 1975: Ch. 15; Robins 1979; LePage & Tabouret-Keller 1985: Chs. 5 & 6). In fact, the relationship between politics and research amounts to much more than the propaganda, expediency (p. 132), and even fraud (p. 137) that Widdowson tends to attribute to it, and without in any way claiming that their extrapolations are privileged and authoritative, it seems to me (a) entirely legitimate for academics to reflect and argue over social influence and the manner and extent to which what people do and don't say is affected by their social position, and (b) perfectly possible for them to conduct this debate in principled, honest, self-critical ways, alert to the difference between evidence and belief.

The second dichotomy is the one Widdowson draws between *science* and *everyday experience* (p. 137). For reasons I spell out below, I wouldn't want to generalise about all science, but this division is very far from absolute in the qualitative research tradition that I'm most familiar with, and it also contravenes the hermeneutic principles that I would actually associate with some of Widdowson's own work (Thompson 1985: 354–5; Widdowson 1984: 26–7, cited in Rampton 1997: fn. 4). In her classic account of bringing ethnographic methods to schoolrooms in the Piedmont Carolinas, Shirley Brice Heath comments:

> Teachers in the classes described here captured for schooling purposes their
> students' natural abilities and daily habits as participant observers, hypothesis

builders, and information synthesisers. These teachers saw nothing particularly mystical or forbidding about participant observation as practised by the ethnographer. In the words of several teachers: 'We do that every day, and so do our students.' What these teachers did with these everyday habits, however, was to help their students learn to see their daily action in new terms: as the recording of events, discovering patterns, and figuring out of options in making decisions. (Heath 1983: 339, also 272, 354)

At the same time (and contrary to one of Widdowson's more extravagantly partial readings of my position (pp. 133 and 137), neither Heath nor I would deny certain crucial differences between academic and everyday thinking: among other things, academics (are supposed to) have more time and space for thinking, their analysis should be more systematic, accountable and disciplined by a 'higher level of routine scepticism' (Hammersley 1992: 138), and their emerging insights can reach well beyond common sense. But these are differences of degree rather than kind.

The polarities *science* vs. *technology*, and *validity* vs. *utility* constitute the third area of difficulty (p. 136). Widdowson certainly isn't alone in worrying about practical potential outweighing validity in the evaluation of research (cf. e.g. Lather 1986; Hammersley 1992: Part II), but I am surprised (a) that he gives (internal) validity such clear priority, and (b) that he formulates this as a choice between alternatives, rather than seeing these as sometimes complementary, sometimes conflicting considerations that any piece of applied linguistic research needs to reckon with. I certainly wouldn't expect all linguistic research to be practice-, policy- or market-oriented (Rampton 1992: 1; Rampton, Harris & Leung 1997: 11 & fn. 14; Cameron et al. 1993: 144),[1] but practical relevance does seem to me a legitimate issue in applied linguistic research. Ideally, AL research should be governed by the recognition that 'relevance without rigour is no better than rigour without relevance' (Guba 1981, cited in Lather 1986: 65), though it is also necessary to live with the recognition that in, e.g., an applied linguistics relevant for language teaching, '[t]he process of drawing upon research findings, theoretical constructs, and practical suggestions from a wide range of potentially relevant sciences inevitably results in major risks of error' (Brumfit 1984: 1–2). In fact, rather than treating practical and commercial considerations as likely sources of contamination, I would prefer to try to work out the relationship between different kinds of inquiry, as we tried in drawing up the BAAL *Recommendations on Good Practice in Applied Linguistics*:

> Consultancy, evaluation, action research, and traditional research are all potentially valuable. Indeed, it would be easy to argue that this diversity in forms of inquiry is an important factor contributing to the vitality of applied linguistics as a whole. However, this diversity can become a problem if different kinds of research are confused with one another. Government, commerce and other bodies often seek the assistance of academic research because of the authority generated by its traditional independence. It would be wrong if this were claimed for work in which a disproportionate amount of the final shaping rested either with sponsors or with informants. Because of the risk of this confusion, it is essential to be absolutely clear about the conditions governing the production of a piece of work. (BAAL 1994: §5.2; see also §5.1 on some key differences, and Rampton 1995)

The polarisation of *sociology* and *linguistics* (p. 135) represents a fourth problematic area in Widdowson's text. Firstly, the boundary between disciplines seems much less clear to me – under what disciplinary heading should one put conversation analysis, for example (or speech accommodation theory, or the ethnography of communication). Secondly, rather than suggesting that 'linguistics *should* be decentralised' (p. 134, my emphasis), it seems to me that linguistics, sociology and lots of other disciplines already *are* decentralised. Programmes of research in both applied linguistics (cf. the list of AILA's Scientific Commissions) and 'core' linguistics (phonology, syntax, semantics) are heterogeneous and often highly sophisticated. This makes it very difficult indeed (a) to keep abreast of all current research (I often struggle to get beyond anything but introductions), and then (b) to assess the significance of cutting-edge developments within particular programmes. In this context, I would guess that only the most exceptional scholars could provide the kind of commanding (and centralised) overview that Widdowson seeks, and I'm afraid I don't feel apologetic about failing to provide a blueprint for how 'such totally disparate (even incommensurable) discourses would be reconciled' (p. 134). The strategies for achieving productive cross-disciplinary and cross-sector dialogue are likely to vary from encounter to encounter, and in the first instance (and for probably quite a long way after that) it will be the participants in these encounters who themselves decide on both 'the criteria of inclusion' (p. 134) and on whether or not their discussions are valuable. All this will only sound like cacophony if you conceptualise AL as some kind of orchestra and try to listen to everyone at once.

To try to place this dispute in a wider context, it may be helpful first of all to quote Ulf Hannerz on an anthropological tendency to think of culture in terms of coherence, in terms of 'the sort of integration one finds in a Bach fugue, in Catholic dogma, or in the general theory of relativity' (Geertz 1957: 34):

> This conception of coherence ... largely disregards the fact that (complex) cultures ... are characterised rather more by their internal diversity than by any overarching uniformity. What can we mean by coherence, in the case of cultures where perspectives diverge and then clash, where people may seek advantage by being different, where groups of people are forever pushing further and further away from the taken for granted in their search for new understandings, where the gains of expertise are suspected to be at the expense of common sense, and where in a division of knowledge specialists prefer to speak to other specialists? ... Cultures change in ways which some regret and which please others – sometimes, in ways which seem to be to nobody's liking ... It is most unlikely that, in the end, there will be a stylistic unity of a kind that offers intellectual and aesthetic delight. (Hannerz 1992: 163, 167)

Though there are obvious differences of scope, Hannerz's view of 'complex' culture approximates my own view of applied linguistics. More importantly, however, Hannerz goes on to provide an account of intellectual life which helps situate my argument with Widdowson within a rather more general tension in Western societies.

In a discussion of the ways in which a spirit of inquiry has been institutionalised, Hannerz draws on Gouldner's (Widdowson-sounding) distinction between the 'intelligentsia' and 'intellectuals'. The 'intelligentsia' are in some way technicians, turning knowledge into disciplines and typically concentrating on solving puzzles within a paradigm. Committed to one line of inquiry and pressing on with it, they roll back the frontiers of the unknown, often 'with little apparent concern for the no-man's-lands of meaning which may line their paths, or for keeping the lines of communication open to the rear' (ibid.: 139, 167). In contrast, if the intelligentsia are hedgehogs, 'intellectuals' are foxes. They are less bound by paradigms, and

> [t]hey stand in opposition to the normalisation of cognitive work, and often transgress the boundaries of conventionally defined fields of knowledge. Credentialling intellectuals is more difficult ... The cultural management of concerns of the intellectuals ... above all involve issues of coherence and incoherence; they often investigate, and fill in, the internal spaces of a culture rather than its frontiers. It is the business of intellectuals to carry on traffic between different levels and fields of meaning; to translate between abstract and concrete, to make the implicit explicit ... to seize on inconsistency, and to establish channels between different modes of giving meanings external shape. Not least are intellectuals concerned with the center-periphery relationships intrinsic to culture itself; that is to say, with the critique of developing and passing facts of life in terms of durable core values. (ibid.: 139, 140)

In the first instance, this distinction seems to me to capture one very influential view of the relationship between applied and non-applied linguistics: non-applied linguistics as an activity for the intelligentsia, and applied linguistics for the intellectuals. Within this, Widdowson has himself played a formative role as AL intellectual, and some (though not all) elements of Hannerz's characterisation can be seen in his text here (e.g. the concern with coherence/incoherence, and with academic rationality as a core value). It seems to me, however, that the ground around us is now shifting, and that like the other sharp polarities, the distinction between intellectuals and intelligentsia is becoming blurred. As I have tried to argue above, there are unworkable oversimplifications in Widdowson's attempt to establish a reign of coherence by declaring boundaries around the linguistic academy, separating it off from politics, commerce, technology, other disciplines and everyday understanding. More than that, for some of the reasons I suggested in *InJAL* 7.1 and as a number of its contributors attest, quite a lot of scholars working in what might previously have been construed as hedgehog traditions are now becoming very interested indeed in the terrain behind and beside them. The central tasks that Hannerz uses to differentiate intelligentsia and intellectuals – advancing knowledge and making connections – will obviously both continue to be vital, but it seems to me that as long as we adjust our conceptual tools to the complexity of the cultures we inhabit, and as long as we reconcile ourselves to usually seeing shorter distances, we're now at a moment in applied linguistics when we can engage in both of Hannerz's activities, both as individuals and as a loosely linked, mixed and mobile area of academic, professional and lay interest in language issues. Nothing Widdowson says persuades me to the contrary.

Note

1 I have no hesitation in admitting that my own preference is for a Hymesian, socially constituted, practical linguistics, and have no inhibitions about arguing its merits (aren't academics supposed to argue?). But (contrary to Widdowson's interpretation), this is very different from trying or being able to insist that all linguistics should be reconfigured as along the lines I prefer (and anyway, who'd take any notice if I did!).

References

British Association for Applied Linguistics (BAAL) (1994) *Recommendations on good practice in applied linguistics*. Clevedon: BAAL/Multilingual Matters.

Brumfit, C. (1984) *Communicative methodology in language teaching*. Cambridge University Press.

Bolinger, D. (1975) *Aspects of language* [2nd edition]. New York: Harcourt Brace Jovanovich.

Cameron, D., Frazer, E., Harvey, P., Rampton, B. & Richardson, K. (1993) Reply to comments. *Language and Communication* 13.2: 141–5.

Geertz, C. (1957) Ritual and social change: a Javanese example. *American Anthropologist* 59: 32–54.

Gouldner, A. (1979) *The future of intellectuals and the rise of the new class*. London: Macmillan.

Guba, E. (1981) Criteria for assessing the trustworthiness of naturalistic inquiries. *Educational Communications and Technology* 29: 75–81.

Hammersley, M. (1992) *What's wrong with ethnography?* London: Routledge.

Hannerz, U. (1992) *Cultural complexity: studies in the social organisation of meaning*. New York: Columbia University Press.

Heath, S. B. (1983) *Ways with words*. Cambridge University Press.

Lather, P. (1986) Issues of validity in openly ideological research: between a rock and a soft place. *Interchange* 17.4: 63–84.

LePage, R. & Tabouret-Keller, A. (1985) *Acts of identity*. Cambridge University Press.

Rampton, B. (1992) Editorial. *BAAL Newsletter* 42: 1–2.

—— (1995) Politics and change in research in applied linguistics. *Applied Linguistics* 16.2: 233–56.

——, **Harris, R. & Leung, C.** (1997) Multilingualism in England. *Annual Review of Applied Linguistics* 17: 224–41.

Robins, R. H. (1979) *A short history of linguistics* [2nd edition]. London: Longman.

Thompson, J. B. (1985) Hermeneutics. In A. Kuper & J. Kuper (eds.) *The social science encyclopedia*. London: Routledge. 354–5.

Widdowson, H. (1984) *Explorations in applied linguistics 2*. Oxford University Press.

—— (1998) Retuning, calling the tune, and paying the piper: a reaction to Rampton. *International Journal of Applied Linguistics* 8.1: 131–40.

Text 33

H. G. Widdowson

Further clarifications
Positions and oppositions: hedgehogs and foxes

Ben Rampton's reply seems to me to illustrate very well the problem of partiality that I referred to. I welcome his intention to take a critical look at my position. The problem is that this involves a reformulation of my position in his terms so as to make it more amenable to his criticism. Of course we are all disposed to read our own discourse into somebody's else's text. The main point I was trying to make was that since there will always be this tendency to tendentiousness, we need to be on our guard against it and to correct it, as far as possible, by appealing to the standards of rational coherence which define academic enquiry. Such an appeal cannot resolve differences of opinion, but it ought, at least, to make it clear what these differences are: it cannot provide criteria for preferring one partial position rather than another, but it can help us to identify the grounds of the partiality. With this in mind, let me, again, try to make clear what I was saying in my paper, and what I was not.

Let me begin with what would seem to be a fairly straightforward matter of fact. In response to my complaint about misrepresentation, Rampton apologises, graciously, for making an incorrect page reference. But this was not what I was complaining about. What I objected to was that he attributed to me an opinion that I was reporting as held by others and which I was pointedly dissociating myself from. Getting a page reference wrong is a trivial matter; reading the page partially and misrepresenting what the author actually said is not. So in effect Rampton is misrepresenting me twice over, and this is, of course, galling. But the important point is that whatever it is that motivates this double misrepresentation, it is not something we should indulge in but seek to counter.

Rampton reads my argument as 'built up around a number of binary oppositions' and that it ignores the 'complicated connections and the difficult middle ground that lies between the poles'. I do not understand how my argument could have been read in that way.

The first opposition he identifies is between two kinds of partiality. But I am not setting these up in opposition. I am not saying that you *either* have one *or* the other. Quite contrary, what I am saying is that you cannot have one *without* the other, that an incomplete account is bound to be a function of a particular point of view, and so conditioned by ideological perspective. I am saying that this is a major difficulty in interdisciplinary discourse, and that this is not always recognised. And that, I would argue (quite rationally, it seems to me) is precisely why it is worth drawing attention to the distinction. Rampton's misunderstanding of my position seems to me to reveal a fundamental difference between us about the nature of academic discourse. For I would take the view that such discourse must deal in conceptual distinctions, but there is no implication that such abstractions directly correspond with experienced actuality. They are devices for understanding reality, not for replicating it. Which brings us to the second opposition.

This is what Rampton refers to as a dichotomy I draw between science and everyday experience. The point I am making here is that the discourse of scientific enquiry is defined by certain rational principles applied to the data of everyday experience. These are not fixed, of course, and are subject to continual revision. Indeed, our present debate can be seen as part of the dynamic process of evaluating what the principles of linguistic enquiry should be, how far perspectives other than those so far privileged can be accommodated. But whatever principles are adduced, they must be distinct from the primary data of everyday experience, or otherwise there would be no way of accounting for such data. There would be no disciplinary discourse at all. The essential distinction is between object language and metalanguage, between actual experience and the abstractions that are set up to (partially) account for them. And this applies as much to qualitative research as any other: somebody decides on the quality by reference to some set of principles. Rampton himself would presumably not confuse a research thesis with a collection of data from everyday experience. The difference is not one of degree, but of *kind*.

On now to validity and utility. The point I was trying to make here is that these represent two kinds of evaluative criteria, and that if the tension between them is to be reconciled, we need to recognise that there is a tension in the first place. I suggested that it is a mistake to equate the two – that you can have useful theories which are invalid, and valid theories which are useless. There may be reasons for promoting ideas which are politically or socially useful, in disregard of their validity as established by the academy. There may be reasons, too, for making the academy more accountable to criteria of usefulness. But then these reasons need to be made explicit in terms of the relationship between these evaluative criteria. And it is surely this relationship that is referred to in the BAAL recommendations that Rampton quotes, when mention is made of a problem arising when 'different kinds of research are confused with each other'. And the difference, again, is indeed one of kind and not of degree.

Finally, the 'polarisation' of sociology and linguistics. I am not saying that the boundary between these disciplines is clear. What I am saying is that it is unstable and indeterminate, and this is because there are claims to common ground. These claims are based on different ideas of what the common ground is, and these ideas derive from the central point of reference of the established disciplines. Of course, claims can be reconciled, as in other border disputes, and even interdisciplinary provinces with relative autonomy set up. But although the centres shift, they are always there: points of reference in the principles which define the disciplinary discourses. Rampton says that linguistics and sociology and 'lots of other disciplines' are decentralised. In my view, if they were, they would not be disciplines but simply areas of ad hoc description. A field of enquiry has to be staked out in some way, in reference to some principles of demarcation. It is not just a place where people dig at random.

Having reduced my argument to these oppositions, Rampton is able to dismiss it as a series of 'unworkable oversimplifications', which constitute 'an attempt to establish a reign of coherence by declaring boundaries around the linguistic academy'. I have to say that, even allowing for the effects of partiality, I find it depressing that Rampton should misrepresent my position so completely. And it is even more depressing to think that this is because of unintentional misunderstanding, for then it is hard to see how rational discussion can be carried out at all.

As to the wider context, it is of interest to note that Rampton readily accepts, and indeed cites as authoritative, oppositions/polarisations/dichotomies when they are convenient for his own position, thus again providing illustration of the problem of partiality that I have been talking about. The distinction between intelligentsia and intellectuals is an interesting one, but it does not, as Rampton seems to think, contradict my argument. The difference between the two, as I understand it from Rampton's account, is that the intelligentsia are essentially conformist and work within established paradigms, the intellectuals essentially non-conformists who destabilise them by making explicit covert contradictions and connections. But you can only destabilise something that you acknowledge to exist, and non-conformity necessarily presupposes a discoursal or cultural norm. Intellectuals are as much in the system as the intelligentsia: they are concerned with centre-periphery relationships, and these, as Hannerz says, are 'intrinsic to culture itself'. What they do is not just anarchic and random: they 'make connections' in the rational mode accepted by convention in order to advance knowledge and so change the cultural norm. The fact that cultures, including disciplinary cultures, are diverse and dynamic does not mean that they have no commonalities which define them as cultures. These commonalities will shift, but without them, there is no way of recognising cultural diversity and dynamism at all.

So I would agree with Rampton that both activities that Hannerz associates with intelligentsia and intellectuals need to be pursued in conjunction. Indeed I would argue that both are required academic roles, both intrinsic to academic culture itself, with no necessary conflict between them. You cannot advance knowledge without making connections not currently sanctioned by the norm, but equally you cannot make relevant connections without recognising what the norm is that *makes* them relevant. What Hannerz refers to as different kinds of people I would see as complementary roles, both crucial to the disciplines of academic enquiry.

In this respect, they are not at all like the hedgehog and the fox, and here we can indeed 'place this dispute in a wider context'. The reference here is, I assume, to the distinction that the late Isaiah Berlin explores in his essay on Tolstoy and his view of history entitled 'The Hedgehog and the Fox'. Berlin takes as his text a fragment from a Greek poem: 'The fox knows many things, but the hedgehog knows one big thing.' These words, Berlin acknowledges, can be interpreted in various ways, but he uses them to distinguish what he sees as two fundamentally different kinds of 'intellectual and artistic personality'. It is worth quoting his distinction in full:

> For there exists a great chasm between those, on the one side, who relate everything to a single central vision, one system less or more coherent or articulate, in terms of which they understand, think and feel – a single, universal, organising principle in terms of which alone all that they are and say has significance – and, on the other side, those who pursue many ends, often unrelated and even contradictory, connected, if at all, only in some de facto way, for some psychological or physiological cause, related by no moral or aesthetic principle; these last lead lives, perform acts, and entertain ideas that are centrifugal rather than centripetal, their thought is scattered or diffused, moving on many levels, seizing upon the essence of a vast variety of experiences and objects for what they are in themselves, without consciously or unconsciously seeking to fit them into, or exclude them from, any one

unchanging, all-embracing, sometimes self-contradictory and incomplete, at times fanatical, unitary inner vision. (Berlin 1957: 7–8)

The first group are the hedgehogs and the second are the foxes. Dante is a hedgehog, says Berlin, as are Plato, Dostoevsky and Proust. Shakespeare, Aristotle, Pushkin and Moliere, on the other hand, are foxes.

Now it is obvious that Berlin's distinction is not the same as Hannerz's as reported by Rampton. Intellectuals cannot be equated with foxes. Intellectuals, according to Hannerz, make connections, they 'fill in the internal spaces of a culture', 'seize on inconsistency' and so on: in other words, they seek to integrate what appears to be disparate. In this they are hedgehoglike, for the point about foxes is that they do not make connections at all, but are content with inconsistency and contradiction. Nor are the intelligentsia like hedgehogs, for there is no implication in Berlin that the hedgehogs' adherence to a 'single, universal, organising principle' makes them conservative custodians of some established set of norms. There is no suggestion that Dante and Dostoevsky are bound by a paradigm and are therefore more conformist, less creative than Shakespeare and Pushkin. Furthermore, and perhaps most significantly for our present argument, Berlin's distinction is between two intrinsically contrasting modes of thought: the fox can make no contribution to the hedgehog's scheme of things. The two kinds of apprehension of reality cannot be reconciled: there is a chasm between them. They constitute incommensurable discourses. And Berlin illustrates this by referring to a speech Dostoevsky made about Pushkin which, he says:

> perversely represents Pushkin – an arch-fox, the greatest in the nineteenth century – as a being similar to Dostoevsky who is nothing if not a hedgehog; and thereby transforms, indeed distorts, Pushkin into a dedicated prophet, a bearer of a single, universal message which was indeed the centre of Dostevsky's own universe, but extremely remote from the many varied provinces of Pushkin's protean genius. (Berlin 1957: 9)

What Berlin is pointing out here, it seems to me, is just the kind of partiality of interpretation that I have referred to earlier: the tendency to recast another's discourse in terms of our own. But Berlin's distinction, and its lack of correspondence with that which Hannerz makes, raises another issue, it seems to me, which really does place our current dispute into a wider context. Berlin says of his distinction that it marks 'one of the deepest differences which divide writers and thinkers, and it may be, human beings in general.' Now of course we may question this, and indeed we may reject the whole hedgehog/fox thesis as fanciful. But if we accept what Berlin says, then we might argue that academic enquiry constitutes a privileged socialisation of one mode of thought over the other. The universal and unitary disposition of the hedgehog can indeed be readily institutionalised into conventional frameworks of centripetal knowledge as disciplines, whereas the unprincipled, scattered and diffuse ideas of the fox cannot, since they fly off centrifugally in all directions. But what if we now decide that it is time to give the fox its due and to privilege its mode of thought instead? This would radically alter the whole nature of academic enquiry. Validity would be accorded to imaginative vision, flashes of inspirational thought, the radial, centrifugal scatter of insightful ideas not required to be related in any systematic way to any more general scheme of things. Academic enquiry conceived in such foxlike terms would take on an appealing impressionistic character, more like artistic expression than rational analysis, and aimed at further awareness rather than explanation. The distinctiveness of academic discourse as conventionally conceived would disappear into an intertextual blend with anecdote and verbal art.

'Things fall apart, the centre cannot hold.' It may be that this is the way things are going in this post-modernist era, with its fundamental distrust of rationality or of anything which smacks of authority or established convention. If this is so, what we see in Rampton's position is the shape of things to come: not just a new orchestration but a different kind of music, and one I am not attuned to. In this case, my arguments (composed in an outdated idiom) are simply the relics of a bygone age, and at best only of historical interest.

Reference

Berlin, Isaiah (1957) *The hedgehog and the fox*. Mentor Books.

Further reading

Readers looking for a quick overview may be best served by consulting the entries on Applied Linguistics in one of the big linguistics encyclopedias, such as Asher (1994) or Bright (1992):

Asher (1994): The entry 'Applied Linguistics' by David Wilkins covers 1. The Scope of Applied Linguistics; 2. Applied Linguistics in Language Learning and Teaching (with subsections on topics such as the origins of applied linguistics, applied linguistic theory and research, the role and methods of the applied linguist, and the relation of applied linguistics to other disciplines); 3. Second Language Acquisition and Learning; 4. Second Language Skills; 5. Language Variety; 6. Bilingualism; 7. Research Methods; 8. Applied Linguistics and Language Pedagogy; 9. The Limits of Applied Linguistics; and 10. Conclusions.

Bright (1992): The entry 'Applied Linguistics' comprises four articles: 'An Overview' (by Robert Kaplan and Henry Widdowson) covering 1. Scope, 2. Main areas (speech therapy, communicative interactions, language planning and language policy, language in education, language teaching and learning), and 3. Goals; 'History of the Field' (by Peter Strevens); 'Language Planning' (by Michael Clyne) covering 1. Issues, 2. Domains, 3. Agents of planning, 4. Piecemeal or coordinated policies 5. The discipline; and 'Minorities and Applied Linguistics' (by Alison D'Anglejan).

There are several reference books devoted uniquely to applied linguistics itself, and it is of interest to compare how the field is differently divided up and topicalized in each case. For example, Johnson and Johnson (1998) and Richards, Platt, and Platt (1992) – where the close link and overlap between applied linguistics and language teaching is expressed in the title: *Longman Dictionary of Language Teaching and Applied Linguistics*.

A number of introductions to applied linguistics have recently appeared, and these too reveal interesting differences in the way the field is conceived, both in terms of scope of coverage and approach to enquiry. These include Davies (1999) and Pennycook (2001):

Davies (1999) (with the chapters 1. History and 'definitions'; 2. Doing being applied linguists: the importance of experience; 3. Language and language practices; 4. Applied linguistics and language learning/teaching; 5. Applied linguistics and language use; 6. The professionalising of applied linguistics; and 7. Applied linguistics: no 'bookish rhetoric'.)

Pennycook (2001) (with the chapters 1. Introducing critical applied linguistics; 2. The politics of knowledge; 3. The politics of language; 4. The politics of text; 5. The politics of pedagogy; 6. The politics of difference; and 7. Applied linguistics with an attitude.) As will be clear from the title and chapter headings, this book will be particularly useful for readers wanting to relate this current section to Section 3 on critical discourse analysis.

The most concise general introduction is to be found in Cook (2003).

There are also introductions which consist of articles by different authors, each providing a conceptual survey of their own particular area of expertise. These include Grabe and Kaplan (1991) and Kaplan (2002).

There are a number of periodicals exclusively dedicated to (what they define as) applied linguistics, notably (but not only) the following:

Annual Review of Applied Linguistics (Cambridge University Press): As the title indicates, this comes out once a year, with thematic issues covering a range of topics. Recent ones include technology of language, multilingualism, foundations of second language teaching, discourse and dialogue. Each issue comprises overviews of selected topics, an annotated bibliography and ample references. Probably of particular relevance for the concerns of this section is the fact that every fifth issue offers a broad survey of the field of Applied Linguistics.

Applied Linguistics (Oxford University Press) is published in cooperation with AILA (The International Association of Applied Linguistics), AAAL (the American Association of Applied Linguistics) and BAAL (the British Association of Applied Linguistics) – and thus, not surprisingly, has been sometimes faced with allegations of Anglo-centrism. Founded in 1980, this is the best-known AL journal. Its 'mission statement' is quoted in the introduction to the present section.

International Journal of Applied Linguistics (InJAL) (Blackwell Publishers) also publishes in English, but it seems fair to say that English-speaking applied linguists are rather less prominently represented. Having said that, this is of course also the journal in which the above controversy was published: Rampton, B. (1997) (guest editor) *Special Issue: Retuning Applied Linguistics. International Journal of Applied Linguistics* 7/1. (See p. 273. This issue also includes further contributions by Nik Coupland, Karin Aronsson, Sinfree Makoni, Celia Roberts, Monica Heller, and Leo van Lier.)

This journal has also published a continuation of the controversy presented here: Rajagopalan (1999) – Brumfit (1999b) – Widdowson (1999).

According to its inside cover, 'InJAL seeks to cover all areas of applied linguistics represented by the various commissions of AILA (L'Association internationale de linguistique appliquée). The journal also encourages the development of new fields of applied language study.'

The *International Review of Applied Linguistics in Language Teaching* (IRAL) (Mouton de Gruyter), as its title suggests, focuses its attention on language acquisition and language teaching. Until 2002 it accepted articles in French and German as well as in English, but from that year publication was in English only.

AILA also publishes its own periodical, the *AILA Review*. In the context of the present Section, *AILA Review* No. 12 (1997) might be of particular interest; entitled *Applied Linguistics Across Disciplines*, it gives, as the editors say in their introduction, 'prominence to reflections of the place and constitution of applied linguistics today'. One of the contributions is Brumfit (1999a).

References

Asher, R. (editor in chief) 1994. *The Encyclopedia of Language and Linguistics.* 10 vols. Oxford: Pergamon.

Bright, W. (editor in chief) 1992. *International Encyclopedia of Linguistics.* 4 vols. Oxford: Oxford University Press.

Brumfit, C. 1995. 'Educational linguistics, applied linguistics and the study of language practices' in G. Blue and R. Mitchell (eds.). *Language and Education.* Clevedon: BAAL in association with Multilingual Matters.

Brumfit, C. 1999a. 'Theoretical practice: applied linguistics as pure and practical science' in Mauranen and Sajavaara.

Brumfit, C. 1999b. Response to Rajagopalan. *International Journal of Applied Linguistics* 9/1: 120–2.

Cook, G. 2003. *Applied Linguistics* in the series 'Oxford Introductions to Language Study'. Oxford: Oxford University Press.

Davies, A. 1999. *An Introduction to Applied Linguistics. From Practice to Theory.* Edinburgh: Edinburgh University Press.

Ellis, R. 1994. *The Study of Second Language Acquisition.* Oxford: Oxford University Press.

Grabe, W. and R. Kaplan (eds.). 1991. *Introduction to Applied Linguistics.* London: Addison-Wesley.

Johnson, K. and H. Johnson (eds.). 1998. *Encyclopedic Dictionary of Applied Linguistics.* Oxford: Blackwell.

Kaplan, R. (ed.). 1980. *On the Scope of Applied Linguistics.* Newbury House.

Kaplan, R. (ed.). 2002. *The Oxford Handbook of Applied Linguistics.* Oxford: Oxford University Press.

Krashen, S. 1980. 'Towards a redefinition of applied linguistics' in Kaplan.

Mauranen, A. and K. Sajavaara (eds.). 1997. *Applied Linguistics across Disciplines* (*AILA Review* 12): AILA.

Meara, P. 1989. 'Matrix models of vocabulary acquisition' in P. Nation and R. Carter (eds.). *Vocabulary Acquisition*. (*AILA Review* 6): AILA.

Meara, P. 2000. 'Applied linguistics' in M. Byram (ed.). *Routledge Encyclopedia of Language Teaching and Learning*. London: Routledge.

Pennycook, A. 2001. *Critical Applied Linguistics: A Critical Introduction*. Mahwah, New Jersey and London: Lawrence Erlbaum Associates.

Rajagopalan, K. 1999. 'Tuning up amidst the din of discordant notes: on a recent bout of identity crisis in applied linguistics'. *International Journal of Applied Linguistics* 9/1: 99–119.

Rampton, B. 1995. 'Politics and change in research in applied linguistics'. *Applied Linguistics* 16/2: 233–56.

Rampton, B. (guest editor) 1997. *Special Issue: Retuning Applied Linguistics*. *International Journal of Applied Linguistics* 7/1.

Richards, J., J. Platt, and H. Platt. 1992. *Longman Dictionary of Language Teaching and Applied Linguistics*. 2nd edition. London and New York: Longman.

Sampson, G. 1980. *Schools of Linguistics. Competition and Evolution*. London: Hutchinson.

Widdowson, H. G. 1996. *Linguistics* in the series 'Oxford Introductions to Language Study'. Oxford: Oxford University Press.

Widdowson, H. G. 1999. 'Positions and perspectives: a partial response'. *International Journal of Applied Linguistics* 9/1: 123–6.

Widdowson, H. G. 2000. 'On the limitations of linguistics applied'. *Applied Linguistics* 21/1: 3–25.

Websites:

AILA Website: http://www.aila.soton.ac.uk/scientific01.htm (accessed 25 July 2002)

Applied Linguistics Website: http://www3.oup.co.uk/applij/instauth (accessed 6 September 2002)

Working with controversies: Study questions

The set of study questions (or points for reflection and discussion) below can be considered in reference to any of the papers in this collection. They are primarily meant to prompt readers to engage critically with the texts and to encourage them to think about their own reactions to the points raised, and to the way the points are raised. They can be used for self-study and as preparation for (class) discussion and the writing of assignments.

Some of these study questions focus attention on particular points in the arguments presented, others on the manner in which they are argued. How different readers make use of them will obviously be a matter for them to decide, and they will find some more relevant to particular controversies than others. The fact that they can all, in principle, be asked about each component of this book (including my contextualizing comments which introduce each section) ensures that they cannot selectively favour some views over others.

A Content of the argument

1 In your view, what are the key statements of each paper? (You may want to select several.)

2 If you had to provide five key words for characterizing the paper for, say, a library catalogue, which ones would you choose?

3 What are the main 'allegations' that the authors level at each other?

4 What are the points of contact between the individual papers, in the sense that the different sides of one aspect or problem get discussed from different perspectives?

5 What are the key incompatibilities between the opposing sides?

6 How are issues taken up selectively in responses, with others being avoided, and how are new issues introduced?

7 What is your favourite quotation from this paper?

8 Which headings (probably quite different from the actual ones!) might the 'opponents' give to each other's pieces?

9 In cases where there is more than one response to a paper, what are the similarities and differences in the responses? (For instance, do they disagree with the same points in the 'stimulus paper'? And to the same degree?)

10 Where does the author 'come from'? i.e., which tradition of enquiry does s/he follow, which theoretical framework does s/he work in, and which disciplinary perspective does s/he take? And how can you tell?

11 Are there any complaints of unfairness, and if so, how justified do you think they are?

B Organization of the argument

12 Do the titles of the papers capture what the papers are about?

13 What is the relationship between the abstract (if applicable) and the main body of the text? In your view, does the abstract give you a good idea as to what to expect? Did it when you first read the paper?

14 For a response, a varied repertoire of strategies is available to authors, ranging roughly between concession and counter-attack, with other possibilities such as clarification, adding information, or apology, ranging somewhere in between. Which options does the response in question draw on, and in which proportion? You may find it helpful to go through the paper(s) and to find a label for each paragraph.

15 What is the relative proportion of information-giving and opinion-giving? How much text is devoted to offering information, and how much to presenting opinions?

16 What is cited as evidence in support of a certain claim or statement?

17 How much do different authors use references to and quotations from other authors' publications to support their arguments?

18 Which arguments put forward by the 'opponent' are accepted and which rejected, and how is this done?

19 In articles which are very critical in tone, what (if any) are the positive points that are conceded to the 'opponent'? Which function do they serve?

20 Are there any instances in responses where something is imputed to an author that she or he did not actually say?

21 Have you caught the author(s) doing what they themselves say shouldn't be done? (for example, arguing against generalization and then generalizing themselves)

22 What is put in footnotes/endnotes, and why do you think this is?

23 Academic discourse is usually thought of as 'objective' and 'logical'. Do you think this is the case here?

C Expression and style

24 How would you characterize the tone of the controversy, and how does it compare with those of the other controversies in this volume?

25 Do you prefer the style of one author to that of the other? Can you specify why?

26 Which lexical choices are made, for example, of reporting verbs ('X claims that …'), pronouns ('we all know …' vs 'those who …'), terms of reference ('Professor X', first name, surname), evaluating items such as adjectives ('valid', 'polemical'), and adverbs ('clearly, …')?

27 How is hedging effected, i.e. do authors employ expressions such as 'one might say that …', 'this tends to happen …', 'it is often claimed that …', 'X seems to think …', or 'perhaps', 'possibly', in order to avoid committing themselves completely to a point of view? Which purposes does this hedging serve in each case?

28 Are there certain words employed (deployed even) for the specific connotations they carry? What effect do they have? For instance, are there any 'buzzwords' used that you suspect are there for their positive connotations rather than for presenting an actual argument?

29 Are there emotive terms used? If so, where and how?

30 Are there any technical terms used whose meanings are not (made) quite clear, or which are used differently from the way you have always understood them?

31 How are pronouns used to involve the reader? ('we', 'let us', 'I')

32 Are there instances of irony? If so, what functions does the irony serve?

33 Are there cases where authors manage to imply something without spelling out explicitly what it is they are saying?

34 How is 'reporting what was said' done?

35 Are there passages which you would call 'polemical', and if so, what makes you think they are?

36 Is it always clear to you what point the author is making, or are there cases where even a re-reading of a passage does not bring clarity?

37 How and for what purposes are direct quotations/quotation marks used?

38 What is the range of sources that different authors refer to? (For instance, do British and American authors refer to each other in equal measure? How many non-English-language sources are referred to? What other areas – apart from those clearly relevant to applied linguistics – are drawn on?)

D Reader reaction

39 To what extent does the paper relate to your own experience of the field in question?

40 How do you feel as the reader of this paper, i.e. what is your gut reaction to the way it is written?

41 Having read an original paper and a response, is the response what you expected?

42 Where do you stand in this dispute? If you had to decide to support either one or the other side, which one would you go for and why?

43 Do aspects get discussed in these papers which you have not thought of before, and which therefore genuinely shed new light on the matter for you? In other words, what have you learnt from reading these contrasting views?

44 Are there passages where you feel you lack the necessary background knowledge to appreciate the point that is being made?

45 Are there issues that arise in a paper that you expected to be taken up in the response, which, however, do not get dealt with? If so, how would you deal with them?

46 Are there individual points and arguments you would be prepared to concede in a paper that you generally disagree with?

47 If you were a reviewer, for example, a member of the editorial board of the journal that this paper appeared in, what suggestions (if any) for revision would you make to the author(s) before you would be happy to see this paper in print?

48 Which of the books and papers cited by the authors has the article made you want to read?

49 If you were asked to group all the scholars involved in the various different controversies according to some criteria you could choose, which criteria would you go for and how would you group the authors?

50 From what you know about the journal the paper in question appeared in, do you think it is the appropriate one for publishing this paper? If not, which journal do you think it would have fitted in better?

Author index

Bold page numbers indicate an author's own text that is reproduced in the book. Italic numbers indicate a response to that text. Other references are in plain numbers. Names beginning 'Mac' and 'Mc' are interfiled (as though all spelt 'Mac').

Subject index

Entries are arranged in letter-by-letter filing order, in which spaces between words are ignored: 'socially constituted linguistics' is therefore filed after 'social justice' and before 'social practice'.

Titles of publications, and foreign words, are shown in italic type.

cultural bomb 24, 29
cultural capital 243

data, SLA 183, 184, 215, 224–7, 234
data-driven learning 78
data modelling 99–100, 109
'death of the author' 260
deep patterning 110n2
defamiliarization 127, 130
deficit linguistics 20, 22, 27, 29, 290n17
Denmark, English as 'mother tongue' 37
description
    vs. explanation 215
    vs. interpretation 157
    vs. prescription 78, 80–1, 106–7
dialectical relationship 125
dialogues, literary/drama 100–1
dictionaries, corpus-referenced 78
difference 30, 290n17
Diffusion of English paradigm 60, 69
disciplines
    discipline-specific reductions 172
    see also interdisciplinary enquiry
disclaimer of homogeneity 23
discourse
    in SLA research 173–98
    vs. sentence and text 132, 134–8, 146
discourse analysis 125–68, 264, 270, 275,
    290n17, 303
discourse model 189
discourse sociolinguistics 164
discursive construction 284
disparity 150
divergence 169
diversity of language 59, 279
dominance 67, 228n10
domination 149, 291n17
    see also linguistic imperialism
drama dialogues 100–1

East African English 12, 16
Ecology of Language paradigm 60, 69
economic imperialism 54, 67
Economy Principle 217
education
    language in 56–7
    sociology of 279–80
educational codification 28
educational language policies 56, 57
educational realities 23
effect 138–9, 141, 147, 158

EFL (English as a Foreign Language)
    distinctions from ESL 22
    real and authentic English 87
    training 29, 273
elaborated codes 306
ellipsis 92, 99–100
ELT (English Language Teaching)
    ELT business 55, 57
    linguistic imperialism 7, 33–50
ELT Journal 6
embedding 299
    embedded repair 192n10
'empowering' research vs. 'advocate'
    research 289n14
English
    British English 8, 12, 13, 16
    global spread 7–75
    hegemony 7, 33–50, 166
    international language 9, 11, 73, 89, 107
    lingua franca 7, 73, 84, 184, 192n18,
        193n22, 263
    native speaker (real) 16, 78, 82–7,
        90–120
    native (Standard) 8, 9–19, 72
    spoken 90–104
    World Standard Spoken 69
    varieties 9–33
        indigenized 7, 263, 266
    world Englishes 24, 25–6, 265
    see also EFL; ELT; ESL
English Only movement 39, 52, 57, 64
errors 169–70, 201, 265
ESL (English as a Second Language)
    course 240–1
    distinctions from EFL 22
Esperanto 59
ESSE (European Society for the Study of
    English) 50, 63
ethical issues and objectives 55–6, 278–9
ethnographic study
    classroom 203, 311–12
    communication 313
    critical discourse analysis 129–30
    learners 201
    SLA 175
    socialization, education and literacy 275
    speaking 305
ethnomethodological perspective 280
ethnopolitics 12, 16
Eurobarometer 58
European Bureau for Lesser Used Languages
    58

variation 9–19, 72–3
    socially realistic linguistics 278
    within a variety 22
variationist approach 27
varieties of English 9–33
    indigenized 7, 263, 266
Verstehen 276
vocabularies, spoken and written English 86

Wales, languages 65
Welsh 68
West Africa, English 21
    see also Nigeria

word frequencies 81
'worldliness' 7
World Bank 57
world Englishes 24, 25–6, 265
World Englishes 6
World Standard Spoken English 69
writers, role in language policy 25–6

Yorkshire English 13

Zone of Proximal Development 203